First published in Great Britain 2017 by Egmont UK Limited.
This edition published in 2020 by Dean, an imprint of Egmont UK Limited,
2 Minster Court, 10th Floor, London EC3R 7BB

Written by Craig Jelley
Additional material by Stephanie Milton, Marsh Davies and Owen Jones
Designed by Joe Bolder and John Stuckey
Illustrations by Ryan Marsh, John Stuckey and James Bale
Cover designed by John Stuckey
Cover illustration by Ryan Marsh
Production by Louis Harvey and Laura Grundy
Special thanks to Lydia Winters, Owen Jones, Junkboy,
Martin Johansson, Marsh Davies and Jesper Öqvist.

ISBN 978 0 6035 7928 8

71019/001

Printed in China

ONLINE SAFETY FOR YOUNGER FANS

Spending time online is great fun! Here are a few simple rules to help younger
fans stay safe and keep the internet a great place to spend time:

- Never give out your real name – don't use it as your username.
- Never give out any of your personal details.
- Never tell anybody which school you go to or how old you are.
- Never tell anybody your password except a parent or a guardian.
- Be aware that you must be 13 or over to create an account on many sites. Always check the
site policy and ask a parent or guardian for permission before registering.
- Always tell a parent or guardian if something is worrying you.

Stay safe online. Any website addresses listed in this book are correct at the time of going
to print. However, Egmont is not responsible for content hosted by third parties. Please be
aware that online content can be subject to change and websites can contain content that is
unsuitable for children. We advise that all children are supervised when using the internet.

Egmont takes its responsibility to the planet and its inhabitants very seriously.
We aim to use papers from well-managed forests run by responsible suppliers.

GUIDE TO:

CREATIVE

CONTENTS

INTRODUCTION

Welcome to the official Guide to Creative! Almost everything you do in Minecraft involves some kind of creativity, and though true creativity is hard to teach, we're hoping this guide will inspire you to build some brilliant, beautiful things.

We've split the guide into three parts. The first section will help you plan your build. Without good preparation, even the most modest of creations can go awry. You'll learn how to use the very shape of the land to your advantage.

Next, we move on to the components you use to create your builds. Creative mode gives you access to unlimited materials but exactly which ones you use will affect the look and feel of your constructions. Hopefully, we'll stop you from getting overwhelmed by all the choices!

The third part of the guide is more concerned with the details. A few finishing touches can help your creations shine. Learn how to decorate your build and design your own personal motif, as well as how to light your designs for maximum drama.

Let your imagination run wild. Get creative!

OWEN JONES
THE MOJANG TEAM

MOJANG STUFF

Look out for these boxes throughout the book to discover super-exclusive info from the developers at Mojang.

1

PLANNING

This section introduces the simple concepts of planning your build, whether it's deciding on the best location, putting together a simple framework for your creation, or selecting textures and a colour scheme.

BEFORE YOU BEGIN

There are a few things to consider before you join the ranks of Minecraft's master builders. Follow these tips to ensure you start your creative masterpiece in the right way and set yourself up for success.

THE ADVANTAGES OF CREATIVE MODE

If you set up your world in Creative mode you'll be able to make incredible builds quickly and easily. Here's a summary of the key features that make this mode so useful to builders.

1 Hostile mobs are passive in Creative mode, so you don't have to fend them off whilst building.

2 Your hunger and health won't deplete as you work, so you don't have to worry about monitoring your food and health bars.

3 You can fly! Double press the jump button to start flight, then you're free to ascend and descend as needed, making building and decorating tall buildings much easier.

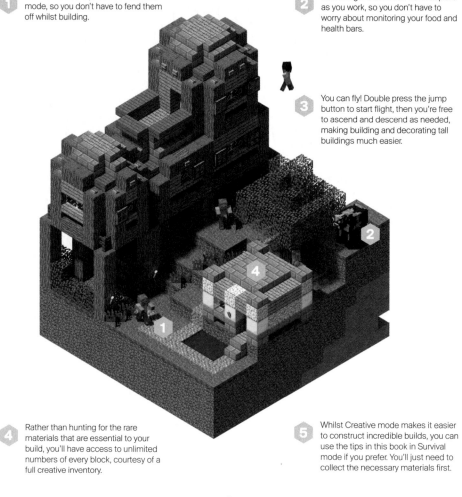

4 Rather than hunting for the rare materials that are essential to your build, you'll have access to unlimited numbers of every block, courtesy of a full creative inventory.

5 Whilst Creative mode makes it easier to construct incredible builds, you can use the tips in this book in Survival mode if you prefer. You'll just need to collect the necessary materials first.

BEGINNER'S BUILD TIPS

Attempting grand feats of architecture can be difficult at first, especially if you're used to constructing buildings to function well rather than to look nice. Following these tips will make your creative builds all the more impressive.

FIND INSPIRATION

Research the theme you want to incorporate into your build. Whether it's a busy rail station, a dwarven fortress or a medieval cathedral, you can draw from examples in books, films, TV and the internet.

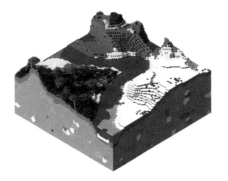

BIOMES

Some biomes are easier to build in than others. If you choose a plains biome, you'll hardly need to do anything to the terrain before you can begin, but if you want to build in a roofed forest you'll need to clear a lot of vegetation first. Consider how much time you have before choosing a biome.

LOCATION, LOCATION, LOCATION

A moon base will look odd by a flowing river, as will a skyscraper peeking out the top of a jungle canopy. Spend some time scouting the right location before you begin.

THINK OUTSIDE THE BOX

Oak wood stairs in the roof? Trapdoors for windows? The blocks in Minecraft are incredibly versatile, and have a number of unintended uses that can really enhance the look of your build.

DEPTH AND DETAIL

Full blocks are perfect for defining your build's shape, but a lot of them are lacking in detail. You can use partial blocks like slabs and stairs to create depth in walls and floors.

USING THE LAND

Where you choose to build is just as important as the build itself, so you should make sure that your ingenious idea has a setting that cleverly complements it. You can either search for the perfect location, or you can build it yourself.

BIOMES

Each biome and sub-biome in Minecraft has characteristics that lend themselves to certain types of build. Consider each biome in terms of the unique combination of these characteristics, then choose the one that is best suited to your build.

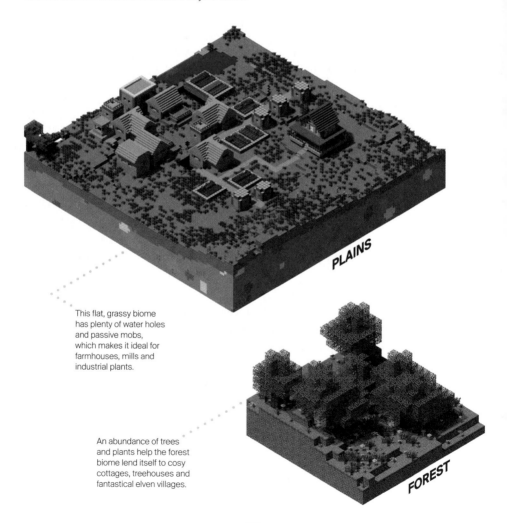

PLAINS

This flat, grassy biome has plenty of water holes and passive mobs, which makes it ideal for farmhouses, mills and industrial plants.

FOREST

An abundance of trees and plants help the forest biome lend itself to cosy cottages, treehouses and fantastical elven villages.

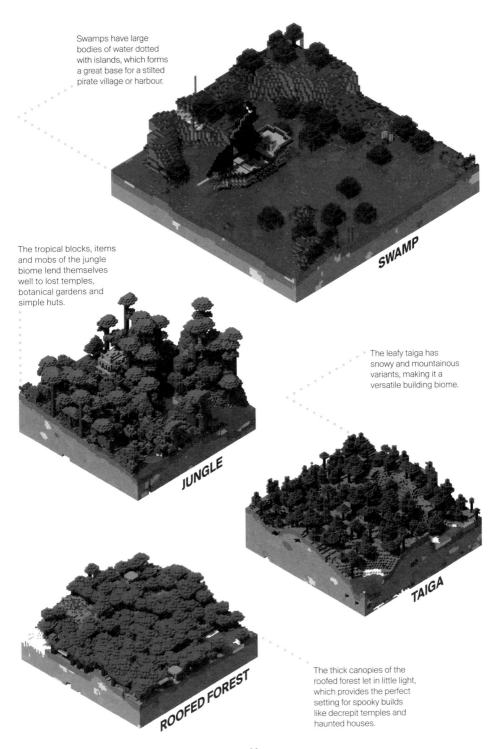

Swamps have large bodies of water dotted with islands, which forms a great base for a stilted pirate village or harbour.

SWAMP

The tropical blocks, items and mobs of the jungle biome lend themselves well to lost temples, botanical gardens and simple huts.

JUNGLE

The leafy taiga has snowy and mountainous variants, making it a versatile building biome.

TAIGA

The thick canopies of the roofed forest let in little light, which provides the perfect setting for spooky builds like decrepit temples and haunted houses.

ROOFED FOREST

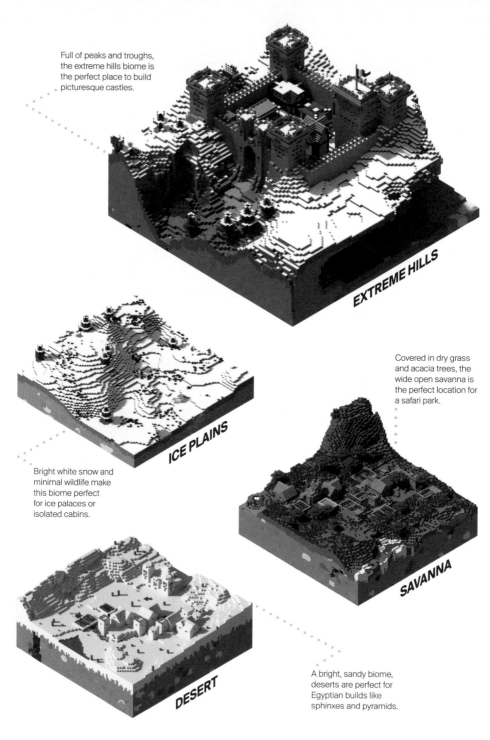

Full of peaks and troughs, the extreme hills biome is the perfect place to build picturesque castles.

EXTREME HILLS

ICE PLAINS

Covered in dry grass and acacia trees, the wide open savanna is the perfect location for a safari park.

Bright white snow and minimal wildlife make this biome perfect for ice palaces or isolated cabins.

SAVANNA

DESERT

A bright, sandy biome, deserts are perfect for Egyptian builds like sphinxes and pyramids.

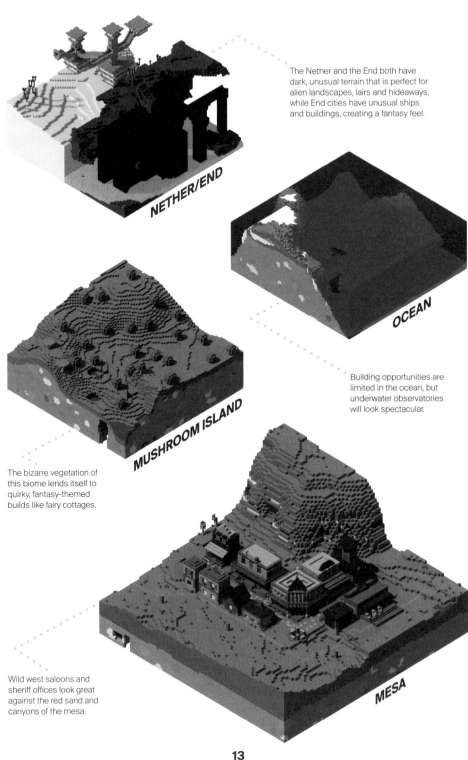

The Nether and the End both have dark, unusual terrain that is perfect for alien landscapes, lairs and hideaways, while End cities have unusual ships and buildings, creating a fantasy feel.

NETHER/END

OCEAN

Building opportunities are limited in the ocean, but underwater observatories will look spectacular.

MUSHROOM ISLAND

The bizarre vegetation of this biome lends itself to quirky, fantasy-themed builds like fairy cottages.

MESA

Wild west saloons and sheriff offices look great against the red sand and canyons of the mesa.

NATURAL FEATURES

From simple rivers to more complex structures like villages, the Minecraft landscape is a source of many natural features. These features can be integrated into your builds, either as they are or with a little customisation. Work with the landscape to create something truly impressive.

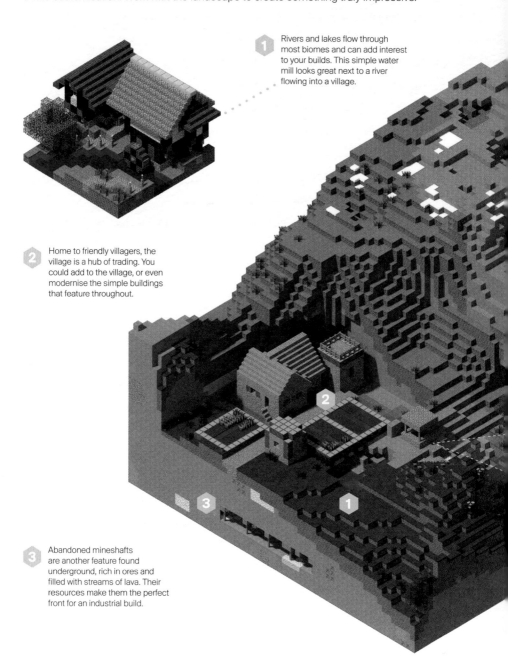

Rivers and lakes flow through most biomes and can add interest to your builds. This simple water mill looks great next to a river flowing into a village.

Home to friendly villagers, the village is a hub of trading. You could add to the village, or even modernise the simple buildings that feature throughout.

Abandoned mineshafts are another feature found underground, rich in ores and filled with streams of lava. Their resources make them the perfect front for an industrial build.

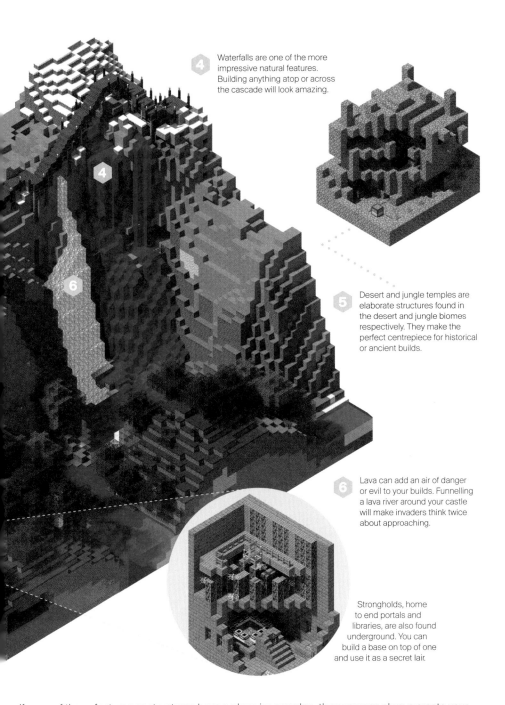

4 Waterfalls are one of the more impressive natural features. Building anything atop or across the cascade will look amazing.

5 Desert and jungle temples are elaborate structures found in the desert and jungle biomes respectively. They make the perfect centrepiece for historical or ancient builds.

6 Lava can add an air of danger or evil to your builds. Funnelling a lava river around your castle will make invaders think twice about approaching.

Strongholds, home to end portals and libraries, are also found underground. You can build a base on top of one and use it as a secret lair.

If none of these features or structures have a place in your plan, then you can always create your own terrain for your builds. If you have enough time you could make anything from a giant quartz moon crater to a snowy stone city, or a colourful candyland.

AESTHETICS

The blocks you choose for your structure will define the look and character of your build. From the colour schemes and block textures of your build's base to the unique finishing touches, every detail is important.

COLOURS

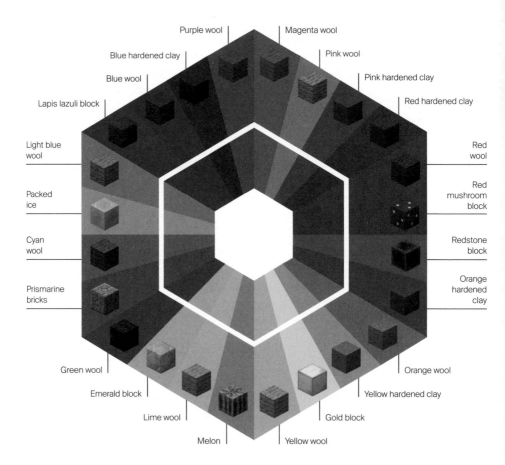

COLOUR WHEEL
The colour wheel is a handy tool for choosing a colour scheme for your build. The wheel covers the whole spectrum of colours, which change in subtle gradients. The colours interact in different ways with the colours around them to create a variety of colour schemes, which can be used to accent a building's exterior, or decorate its interior rooms.

ANALOGUE COLOURS

An analogue colour scheme is the simplest. This requires that you choose two or three blocks adjacent to each other on the colour wheel. For instance, you could make a colour scheme using gold, yellow wool and yellow hardened clay blocks.

COMPLEMENTARY COLOURS

Complementary colour schemes are made by choosing blocks directly opposite on the colour wheel. These colours will contrast dramatically, but still look good together.

TRIADIC COLOURS

A triadic colour scheme is slightly more complicated. Choose three blocks equally spaced out on the colour wheel to create this scheme and give your build greater variety and interest.

MONOCHROMATIC SCALE

The monochromatic scale uses a spectrum of shades between black and white. Black is classed as the absence of colour, while white is the combination of all colours. Black and white contrast with each other, but can also be used to balance a build that involves lots of colourful blocks.

ADDING DEPTH

One way to fine-tune the outside of your build is to add depth. This is easy to do and results in more points of interest rather than endless flat surfaces. The best blocks for creating depth are partial blocks like stairs and slabs since they are a different shape and size to regular blocks.

Stairs and slabs can also be used to replace regular blocks in walls.

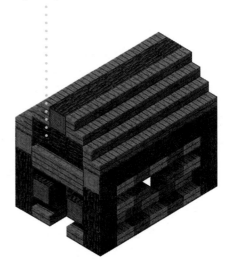

Stairs and slabs can be placed on the side of flat walls to create decorative features.

Another way to create depth is to make your walls two or more blocks thick. This allows you to create patterns by removing some of the outer blocks.

You could also combine these ideas and use partial blocks in a double thickness wall.

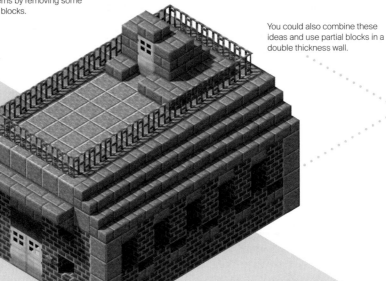

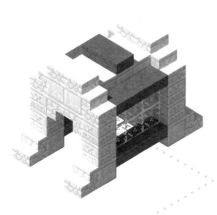

Glass panes sit in the middle of wall blocks, unlike glass blocks, which sit flush with the outer edge.

Glass can also be set into a small extension to make bay-style windows.

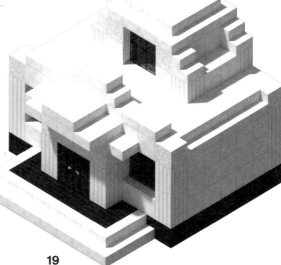

You can use partial blocks to create window sills and awnings over windows.

Did you add any overhangs to your build? Use upside-down stairs to create support brackets for them.

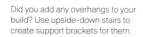

Doors, slabs and stairs can be used to make doorsteps and decorative areas above door frames.

AESTHETIC THEMES

Some blocks inherently lend themselves to certain themes. This can be down to the colour of the block, or the texture of it. By combining carefully-selected base blocks you can create endless themed builds. Take inspiration from these examples and create some of your own ideas.

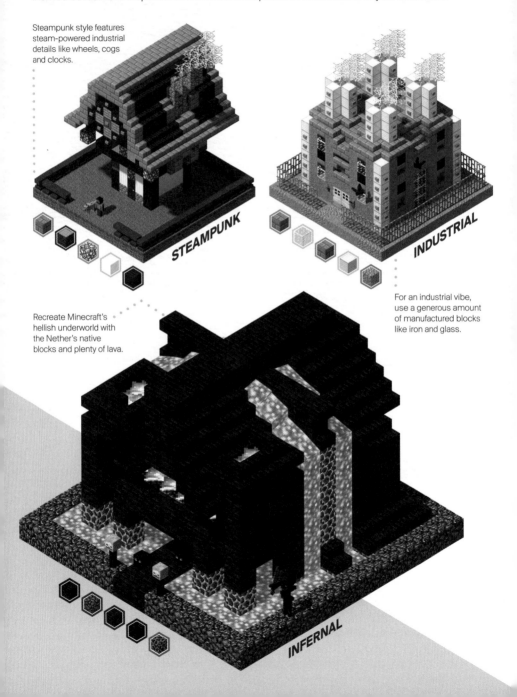

Steampunk style features steam-powered industrial details like wheels, cogs and clocks.

STEAMPUNK

INDUSTRIAL

For an industrial vibe, use a generous amount of manufactured blocks like iron and glass.

Recreate Minecraft's hellish underworld with the Nether's native blocks and plenty of lava.

INFERNAL

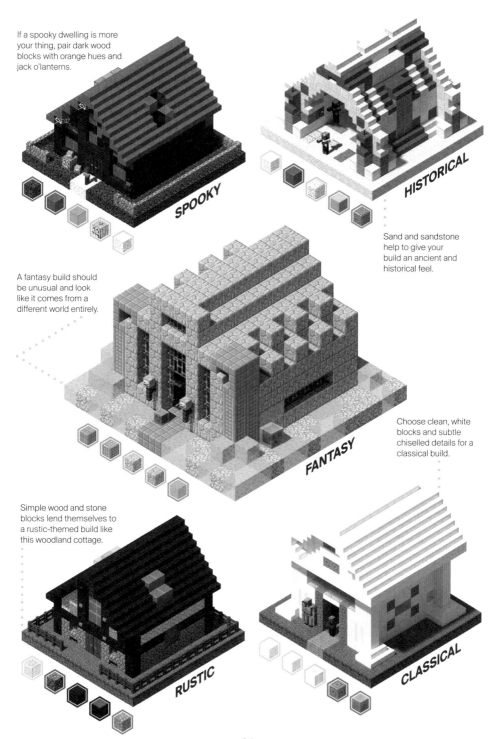

If a spooky dwelling is more your thing, pair dark wood blocks with orange hues and jack o'lanterns.

SPOOKY

HISTORICAL

Sand and sandstone help to give your build an ancient and historical feel.

A fantasy build should be unusual and look like it comes from a different world entirely.

FANTASY

Choose clean, white blocks and subtle chiselled details for a classical build.

Simple wood and stone blocks lend themselves to a rustic-themed build like this woodland cottage.

RUSTIC

CLASSICAL

BLOCK HACKS

There are hundreds of blocks available for use in your constructions. Many of them have a clear purpose, but, with a little imagination, you can also use them in unexpected ways. Check out these clever block hacks for the exterior of your builds.

1. Stairs are perfect for building roofs as they look like staggered tiling. They're available in a variety of woods and stones and can be worked into many different build styles.

2. Cobblestone walls make excellent boundary markers for the perimeter of a build, but they can also be used as supports for raised structures like lookouts and balconies.

3. Usually used to keep mobs and animals at bay, fences can also save you from falls by lining stairs, balconies and roofs.

MOJANG STUFF

Interior designers might take advantage of one of Jeb's favourite block hacks. Take a fence pole then place a leaf block on top for a quaint indoor shrub.

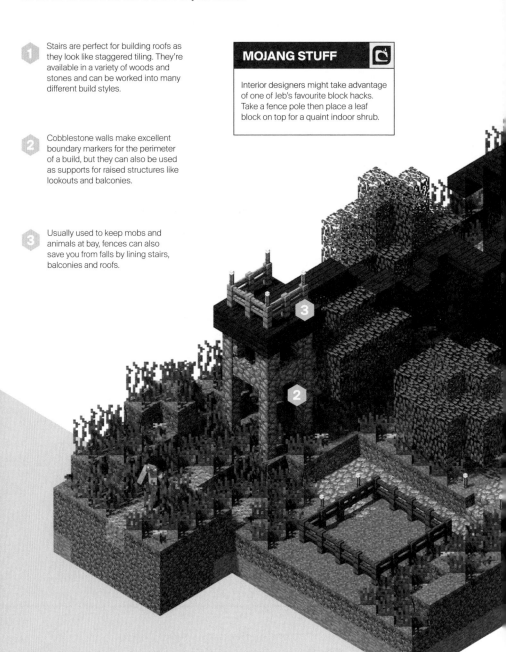

Cobwebs seem like a relatively useless item, but can be used around chimneys and fires to give the impression of billowing smoke.

Trapdoors can be used to create rustic windows. An advantage of using these over glass panes is that they can be opened and closed.

Place a torch on an outside wall, then an item frame over the top of it, and finally a stone slab to give the effect of a medieval wall-mounted torch.

STRUCTURE

It's important to get the structure of your constructions right so that the rest of the build will go according to plan. Once you have an idea, the next step is to plan it out and begin to lay the foundations.

SHAPES

The shape of your build affects everything from the foundations to the roof. For many builders simplicity is key, but more complicated shapes, which are harder to get right, can make for a truly impressive build. Take inspiration from these simple shapes to get you started.

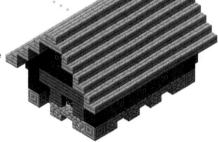

QUADRILATERALS
Squares and rectangles are the easiest shapes to make. Use them as a base for simple, four-sided rooms, and to create flat walls. They are perfect for simple builds.

TRIANGLES
Most often incorporated into roofs, triangles can also be used as a base if you're happy to have diagonal walls. Be aware that this could make it awkward to decorate inside, or to join to other builds.

CIRCLES
Flying in the face of Minecraft's blocky nature, circles are often integrated into more impressive builds. The tricky part is knowing how to successfully make curves – consult the outlines below for guidance.

| 5 x 5 | 7 x 7 | 9 x 9 | 11 x 11 | 11 x 11 |

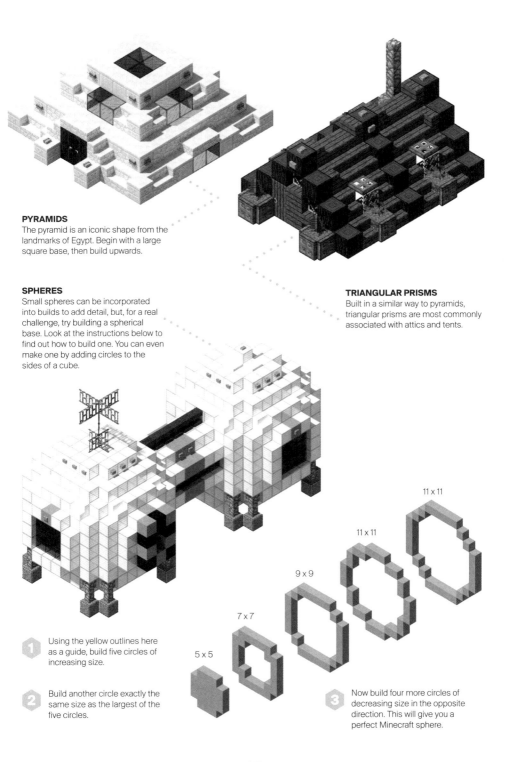

PYRAMIDS
The pyramid is an iconic shape from the landmarks of Egypt. Begin with a large square base, then build upwards.

SPHERES
Small spheres can be incorporated into builds to add detail, but, for a real challenge, try building a spherical base. Look at the instructions below to find out how to build one. You can even make one by adding circles to the sides of a cube.

TRIANGULAR PRISMS
Built in a similar way to pyramids, triangular prisms are most commonly associated with attics and tents.

11 x 11

11 x 11

9 x 9

7 x 7

5 x 5

1 Using the yellow outlines here as a guide, build five circles of increasing size.

2 Build another circle exactly the same size as the largest of the five circles.

3 Now build four more circles of decreasing size in the opposite direction. This will give you a perfect Minecraft sphere.

BUILD FRAMEWORK

Once you've chosen a shape for your build you can create the framework. Starting from the ground and working upwards, follow these steps to create the outer framework and add internal levels. We've chosen a simple rectangular build to outline the process.

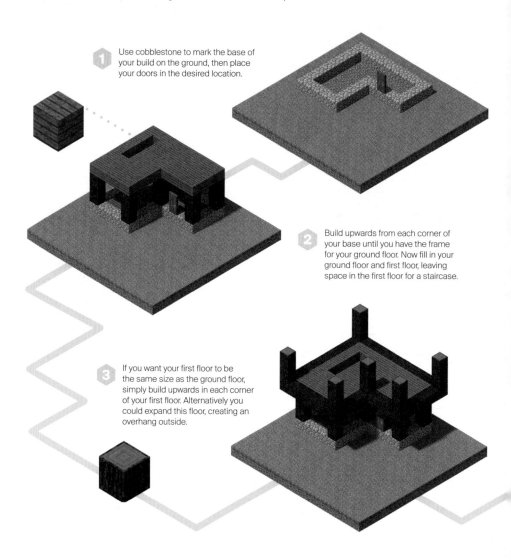

1 Use cobblestone to mark the base of your build on the ground, then place your doors in the desired location.

2 Build upwards from each corner of your base until you have the frame for your ground floor. Now fill in your ground floor and first floor, leaving space in the first floor for a staircase.

3 If you want your first floor to be the same size as the ground floor, simply build upwards in each corner of your first floor. Alternatively you could expand this floor, creating an overhang outside.

BUILDING BLOCKS

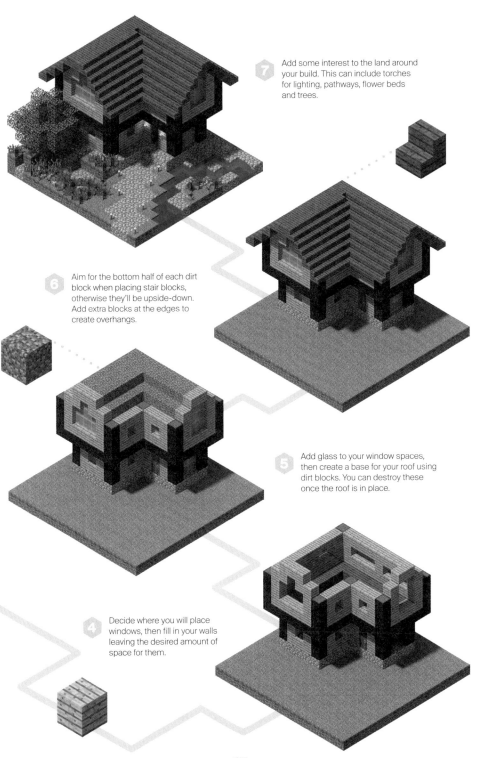

7 Add some interest to the land around your build. This can include torches for lighting, pathways, flower beds and trees.

6 Aim for the bottom half of each dirt block when placing stair blocks, otherwise they'll be upside-down. Add extra blocks at the edges to create overhangs.

5 Add glass to your window spaces, then create a base for your roof using dirt blocks. You can destroy these once the roof is in place.

4 Decide where you will place windows, then fill in your walls leaving the desired amount of space for them.

ARCHITECTURAL STRUCTURES

Once the basic framework of your build is complete, you can adapt it with a variety of decorative and functional structures. Take inspiration from real-life architecture and add some finishing touches and iconic features to finish off the exterior of your build.

ARCH

A decorative adornment for buildings, arches are often used to frame doors and windows. They can also be a supporting structure, forming a walkway underneath part of a building.

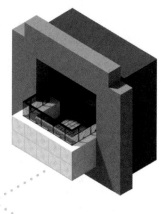

BALCONY

A small outdoor platform that extends out from the wall, a balcony is accessed via a door from the building, and enclosed by walls or rails.

BAY WINDOW

A bay window is a type of window that extends out of the wall, forming a bay within a room and providing extra space, with a view of the area outside.

MOJANG STUFF

Though it's not too much of a problem in Creative mode, use an item enchanted with silk touch in Survival if you're working with glass. It's a lot easier to correct your mistakes!

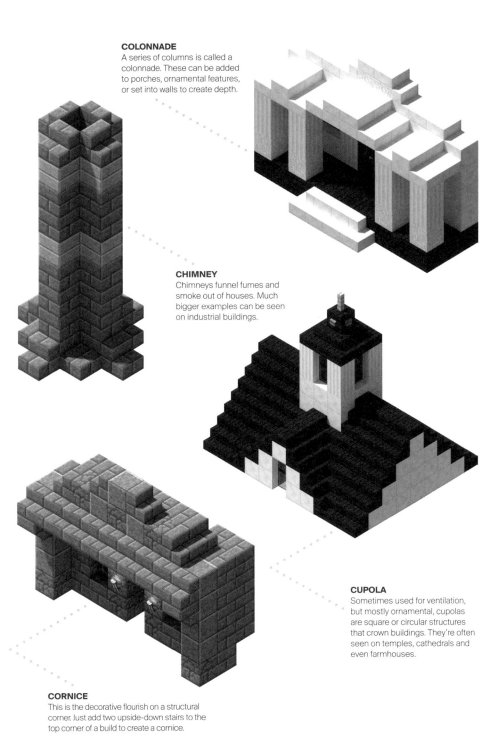

COLONNADE
A series of columns is called a colonnade. These can be added to porches, ornamental features, or set into walls to create depth.

CHIMNEY
Chimneys funnel fumes and smoke out of houses. Much bigger examples can be seen on industrial buildings.

CUPOLA
Sometimes used for ventilation, but mostly ornamental, cupolas are square or circular structures that crown buildings. They're often seen on temples, cathedrals and even farmhouses.

CORNICE
This is the decorative flourish on a structural corner. Just add two upside-down stairs to the top corner of a build to create a cornice.

FLYING BUTTRESS

An arched structure used in huge builds, flying buttresses provide additional support to walls and roofs and make for striking decorative features. Flying buttresses are often seen on the exterior of cathedrals.

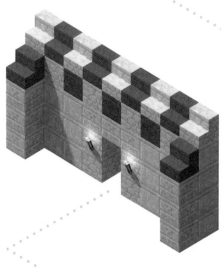

GABLE

A gable is the triangular area of wall between two roof pitches. Adding windows to a gable will provide light for an attic space in the roof.

FRIEZE

This is a row of decorative bricks or blocks that breaks up a plain wall. They are often seen in ancient and classical structures.

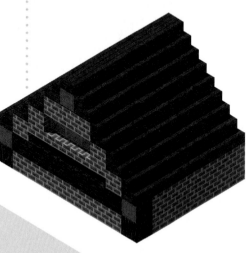

PORTICO

Also known as a simple porch, this is a permanent structure attached to a building, with a roof and solid supports.

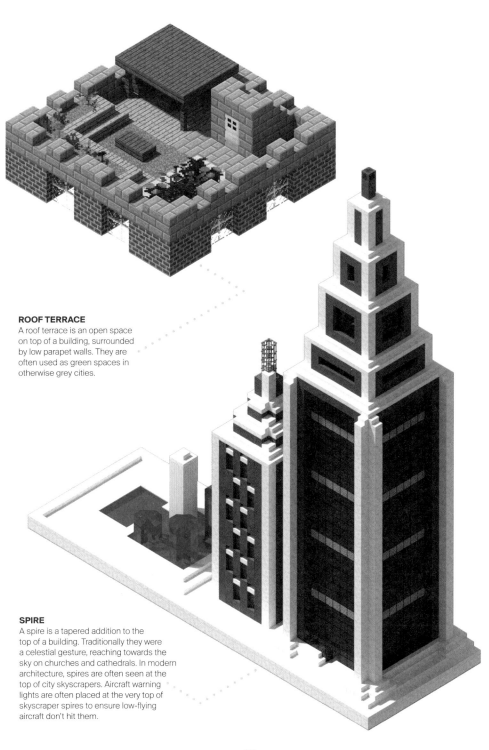

ROOF TERRACE
A roof terrace is an open space on top of a building, surrounded by low parapet walls. They are often used as green spaces in otherwise grey cities.

SPIRE
A spire is a tapered addition to the top of a building. Traditionally they were a celestial gesture, reaching towards the sky on churches and cathedrals. In modern architecture, spires are often seen at the top of city skyscrapers. Aircraft warning lights are often placed at the very top of skyscraper spires to ensure low-flying aircraft don't hit them.

LINKING BUILDS

Now you've got the exterior of your build completed, you can consider how it interacts with other buildings. Having lots of separate builds will leave a lot of negative space (unused space) between them. Here are some ways to turn that negative space into something cool, and combine your buildings in effective and attractive ways.

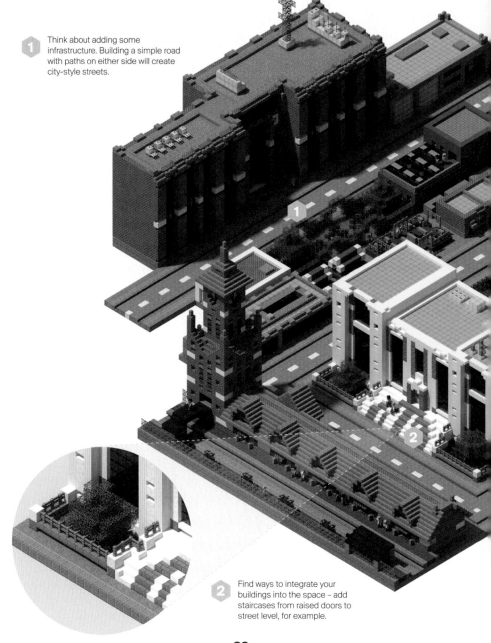

1 Think about adding some infrastructure. Building a simple road with paths on either side will create city-style streets.

2 Find ways to integrate your buildings into the space – add staircases from raised doors to street level, for example.

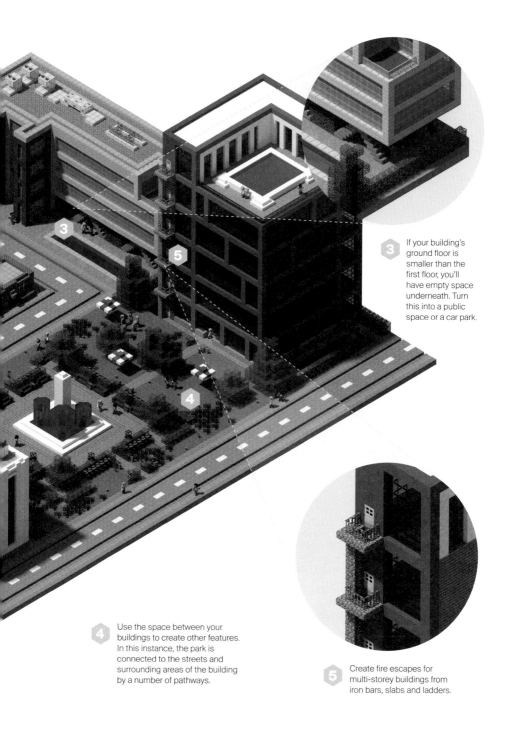

3 If your building's ground floor is smaller than the first floor, you'll have empty space underneath. Turn this into a public space or a car park.

4 Use the space between your buildings to create other features. In this instance, the park is connected to the streets and surrounding areas of the building by a number of pathways.

5 Create fire escapes for multi-storey buildings from iron bars, slabs and ladders.

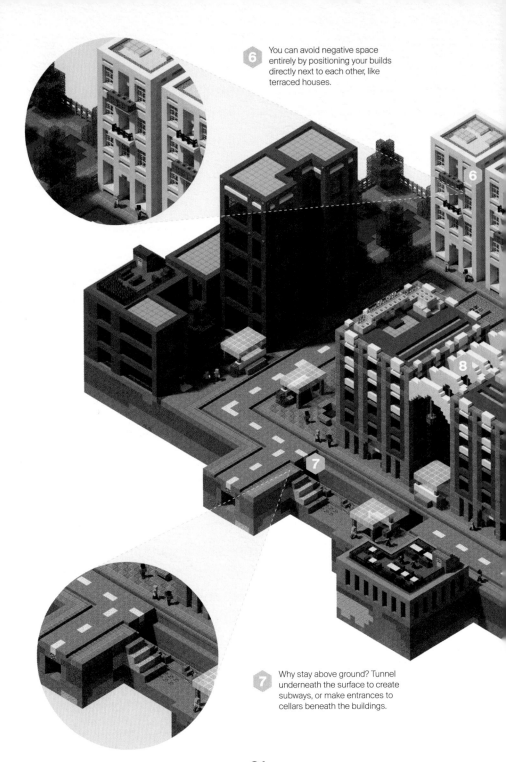

You can avoid negative space entirely by positioning your builds directly next to each other, like terraced houses.

6

8

7

Why stay above ground? Tunnel underneath the surface to create subways, or make entrances to cellars beneath the buildings.

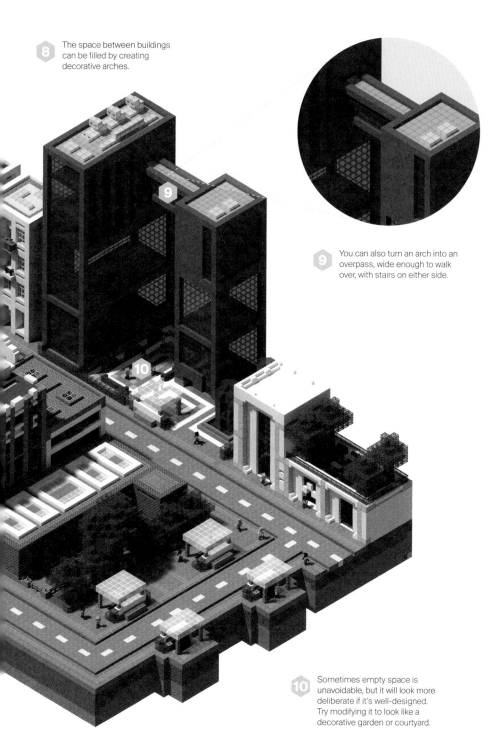

8 The space between buildings can be filled by creating decorative arches.

9 You can also turn an arch into an overpass, wide enough to walk over, with stairs on either side.

10 Sometimes empty space is unavoidable, but it will look more deliberate if it's well-designed. Try modifying it to look like a decorative garden or courtyard.

2

DECORATION

Now you've created the frame of your builds you can add character with some carefully selected decoration. This section contains ideas for decorating floors and walls, clever designs for interior decor, and inspiration to help you make the most of external spaces.

FUNCTIONAL DECOR

There are dozens of blocks in Minecraft that perform useful functions, but they can also double as decorative items too. Let's take a look at these versatile blocks in more detail and learn how to weave them into your creation.

LIGHTING

Light can come from various sources in the Minecraft world: naturally from the sun and moon, from light-emitting blocks, or when activated as a part of a redstone circuit. Some light sources may be quite unexpected.

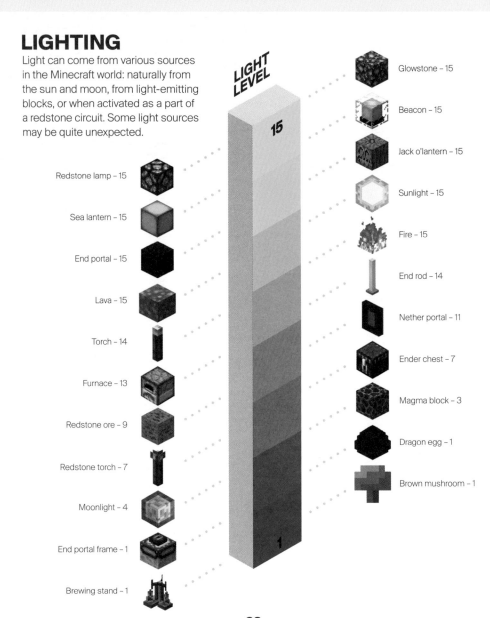

LIGHT LEVEL

15

1

Redstone lamp – 15

Sea lantern – 15

End portal – 15

Lava – 15

Torch – 14

Furnace – 13

Redstone ore – 9

Redstone torch – 7

Moonlight – 4

End portal frame – 1

Brewing stand – 1

Glowstone – 15

Beacon – 15

Jack o'lantern – 15

Sunlight – 15

Fire – 15

End rod – 14

Nether portal – 11

Ender chest – 7

Magma block – 3

Dragon egg – 1

Brown mushroom – 1

LIGHT FIXTURES AND FEATURES

Now you know which blocks emit light, here are some clever ideas to harness them and make unique features to illuminate your constructions.

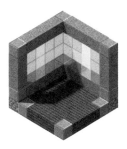

COLOURFUL WINDOW
Take advantage of natural light by creating stained glass windows. See pages 42-43 for more info.

CHANDELIER
Simple End rods can be turned into fancy chandeliers by attaching them to fences.

COSY FIREPLACE
Make a fireplace by combining netherrack with cobblestone and iron bars.

FRAMED LIGHTING
Add torches and slabs to item frames to create unusual interior lighting.

BEACON
Exterior beacons can be created from netherrack, brick stairs and fences.

INSET LIGHTING
Light-emitting blocks can feature in walls and floors for unobtrusive lighting.

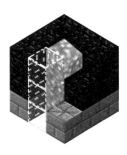

LAVA LAMPLIGHT
Utilise lava as a light feature by pouring it into wall cavities covered with glass.

LAMP POST
Fire-topped netherrack can be housed in wooden trapdoors to let light out.

ARTY LIGHT INSTALLATION
Combine stained glass and glowstone to create colourful and arty light features.

UTILITY BLOCKS

Minecraft has many utility blocks - blocks that perform valuable functions. Many of these fit obviously into certain styles of builds. The following themed builds showcase some of these blocks and how they might be used for decoration.

RUSTIC WORKSHOP

The raw, unpolished finish of the furnace and anvil blends well with the basic wooden textures of the crafting table and chest, in addition to the room itself, which is constructed from wood and stone.

CHEST
Useful for item and tool storage, the chest is a necessity.

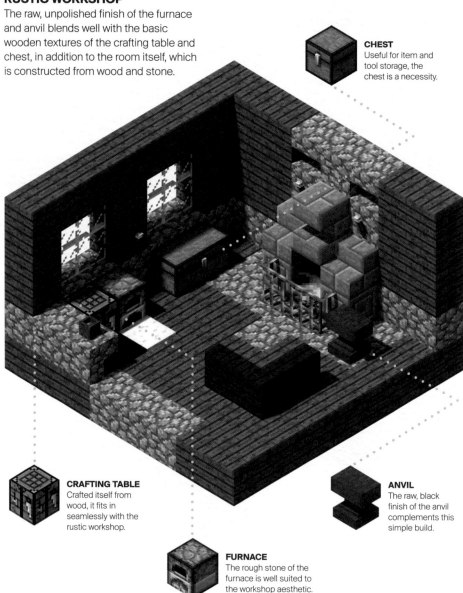

CRAFTING TABLE
Crafted itself from wood, it fits in seamlessly with the rustic workshop.

ANVIL
The raw, black finish of the anvil complements this simple build.

FURNACE
The rough stone of the furnace is well suited to the workshop aesthetic.

MYSTIC LAIR

Bookshelves, ender chests and enchantment tables lend their mystical aesthetic to builds like clandestine hideouts or underground lairs.

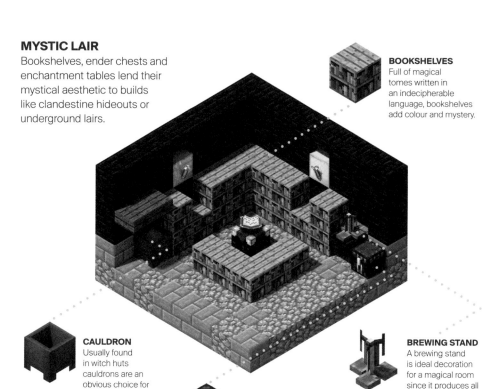

BOOKSHELVES
Full of magical tomes written in an indecipherable language, bookshelves add colour and mystery.

CAULDRON
Usually found in witch huts cauldrons are an obvious choice for any mystical build.

ENDER CHEST
A form of storage forged in the ethereal End, the ender chest is at home in a mystical lair.

BREWING STAND
A brewing stand is ideal decoration for a magical room since it produces all manner of powerful potions.

MODERN DEN

More modern blocks such as the jukebox, armour stands and beds fit perfectly in a minimalist, modern den.

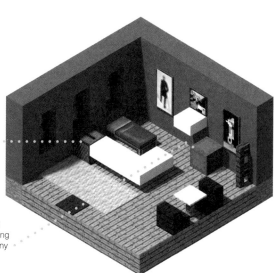

JUKEBOX
A fun Minecraft device, no modern build would be complete without a jukebox to play music.

SHULKER BOX
Shulker boxes can be altered with dye, making them easy to fit into any modern room.

AESTHETIC DECOR

As well as incorporating useful function blocks, you'll want to create something bespoke for your build so that it stands out. This section covers decorative features that you can combine to make your builds unique.

WINDOWS

Windows can make great decorative features on your build. Here are just a few ways to make eye-catching window features from a variety of glass blocks.

SHAPED WINDOWS
Windows don't have to be rectangular - glass can be placed in shapes within the wall. Use the guide to shapes on page 24 if you need to refresh your memory.

ORNATE WINDOWS
Glass can be combined into intricate patterns or elaborate designs, like those found on castles, temples and other extravagant buildings.

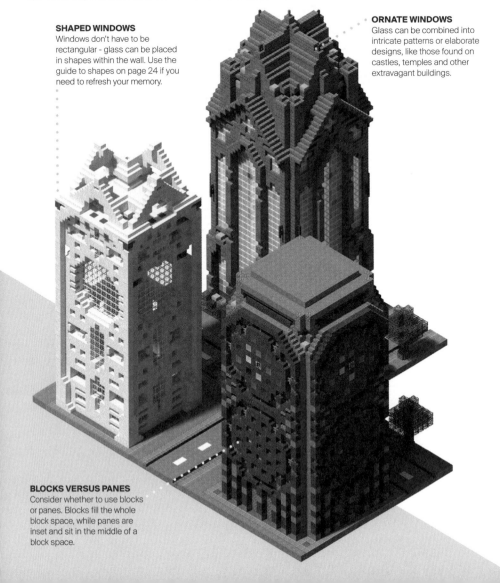

BLOCKS VERSUS PANES
Consider whether to use blocks or panes. Blocks fill the whole block space, while panes are inset and sit in the middle of a block space.

GLASS BUILDINGS
For a striking, modern effect, why not use glass for the majority of the build's exterior? This will make rooms brighter and feel more spacious.

PICTORAL WINDOWS
Stained glass can even be used to make colourful pictures, from simple flowers to more complicated pixel art.

COLOURED GLASS
You can use stained glass panes and blocks to add some colour to plain walls, or to complement a colour scheme.

WALLS AND FLOORS

There are many ways to customise the walls and floors of your builds and add a little artistic flair. Let's take a look at some of the blocks you can use and how they are best suited to different rooms and areas.

AREA RUGS
These can be made from carpet and placed over wooden floorboards. They work well in open spaces like living rooms.

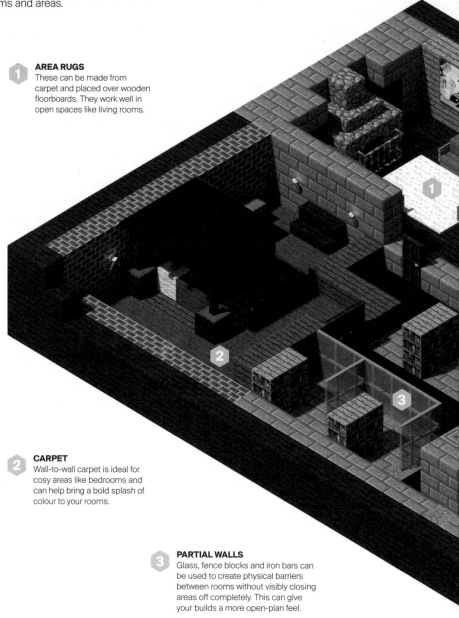

CARPET
Wall-to-wall carpet is ideal for cosy areas like bedrooms and can help bring a bold splash of colour to your rooms.

PARTIAL WALLS
Glass, fence blocks and iron bars can be used to create physical barriers between rooms without visibly closing areas off completely. This can give your builds a more open-plan feel.

CHECKERBOARD TILES
A classic checkerboard tile effect will look good anywhere but is particularly well-suited to kitchens and hallways.

TIP

Make your walls two blocks-thick – one wall will be your exterior design, while the other will be the interior pattern that you choose.

FEATURE WALLS
The blocks you construct your buildings with will dictate what your interior walls are made of and will often be exposed brick or stone. You can add another layer on top of your walls to create a colourful feature wall.

MOSAIC TILES
Hardened clay can be used to create mosaic tiles suited to hallways, foyers and formal areas.

PAINTINGS AND ITEM FRAMES

Some functional blocks are decorative by design. Paintings provide an artistic splash of colour for your interiors – the smallest covers just a single block, while the largest will span a 4 x 4-block area. Item frames allow you to display meaningful items on your walls.

PAINTINGS
There are 26 available paintings. The smallest are 1 x 1 block, and the largest are an impressive 4 x 4 blocks. Keep placing and destroying them until you get the one you want.

TIP

Paintings can be used to conceal entrances to secret rooms if they are placed over a 1 x 2 block gap.

PAINTING PLACEMENT

Painting placement is random and also depends on the available space. You won't know which painting you're getting until you place it on a vertical surface, when a random painting will appear.

ITEM FRAMES

Item frames can be placed on plinths or walls to display everything from your favourite armour and weapons to maps or spawn eggs. They make great features for museums or galleries.

TIP

Once they've been placed in a frame, items can be rotated. Try rotating an arrow to make a stylish signpost.

BANNERS

Minecraft's most customisable block is the banner. Using dyes and a few other items, you can create patterned banners to use as wallpapers, signs and decorations for any build. Here are the basic patterns. You can use whichever dye you like.

HALVES

Bold blocks of colour form a good base for an asymmetric banner.

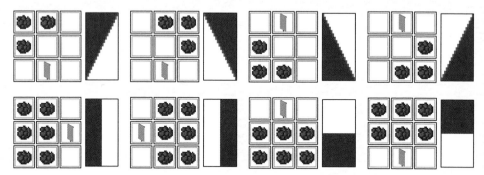

STRIPES

Swashes of colour will cut through a more dominant base.

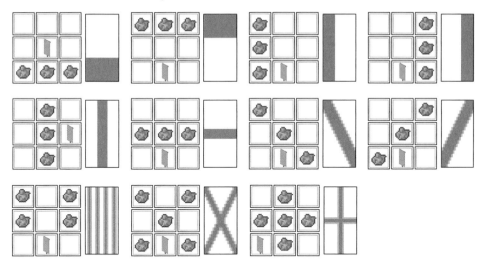

BORDERS AND BACKGROUNDS

Simple patterns can frame a creation, or form a detailed background.

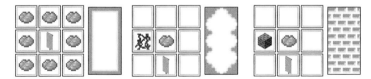

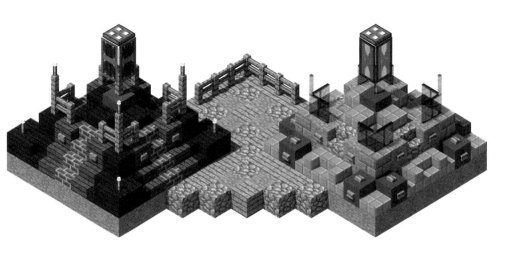

GRADIENTS

Subtle, gradual changes in colour cover the whole banner.

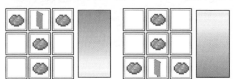

SHAPES

Small shapes can be combined and scattered across simple backgrounds.

ICONS

Interesting pictures are best placed as a top layer on a banner.

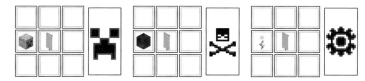

LAYERING

You can place up to 6 different patterns on a banner to create unique combinations like the ones here. If you make a mistake then you can remove the last pattern you placed by using the banner on a cauldron to wash it off.

DISPLAYING

As well as using banners to decorate the interior of builds, you can create structures specifically designed to show them off. They can be placed on full or partial blocks and displayed on your build's exterior.

FURNITURE HACKS

The interior of your building is taking shape nicely, but it is still a little bare. Several blocks can be used in imaginative ways to create pieces of furniture. Let's take a look at some of the most common block hacks and what can be created with them.

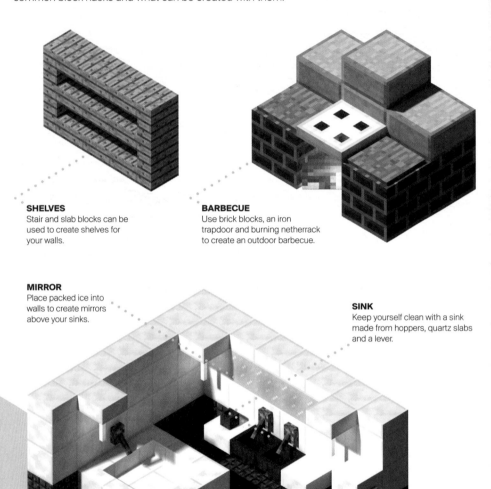

SHELVES
Stair and slab blocks can be used to create shelves for your walls.

BARBECUE
Use brick blocks, an iron trapdoor and burning netherrack to create an outdoor barbecue.

MIRROR
Place packed ice into walls to create mirrors above your sinks.

SINK
Keep yourself clean with a sink made from hoppers, quartz slabs and a lever.

BATH
Create a luxurious bathtub with quartz stairs, dark prismarine blocks and levers for taps.

TOILET
Create a toilet – a bathroom essential – with a quartz slab, quartz block, pressure plate and button.

COMPUTER
Place a painting on the back of a stair block and a pressure plate in front to make a computer.

GRAND PIANO
For musical entertainment, create a grand piano from wood plank slabs, fences and rails.

GRANDFATHER CLOCK
With this timepiece, made from trapdoors and a clock inside an item frame, you'll never be late.

CHAIR
Living spaces need lots of seating, so create these armchairs out of stairs and signs.

SOFA
Turn stair blocks into long settees and create arms at each end using sign blocks.

FIREPLACE
Make your build cosy in the cold with a fireplace. Light netherrack inside a cobblestone chimney.

DJ DECKS
Mix pressure plates, note blocks and a lever-activated redstone lamp to create a sound system.

SMALL TABLE
For a single-space table, place a redstone torch under pistons that are facing upwards.

FAMILY TABLE
Place carpet on top of torches or fences to create longer tables to seat more guests.

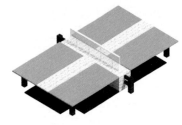

PING-PONG TABLE
Create your own ping-pong table with carpet, glass panes, wool and fences.

TELEVISION
Cover a 4 x 2 set of black wool with a painting to create a television, then add jukeboxes either side as speakers.

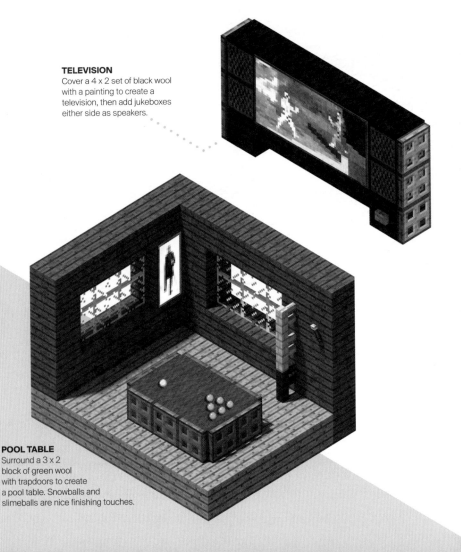

POOL TABLE
Surround a 3 x 2 block of green wool with trapdoors to create a pool table. Snowballs and slimeballs are nice finishing touches.

BUNK BEDS
Place beds on top of slabs jutting out of the wall to create bunk beds, perfect for dorms and bedrooms.

WINDOW BOXES
You can make attractive window boxes using dirt placed against a wall, trapdoors and flowers.

FRIDGE
For cleverly storing food, use an iron block, iron door, dispenser and button to make a fridge.

STOVE
What kitchen is complete without an oven? Place a trapdoor on top of a furnace to make a hob.

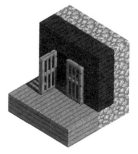

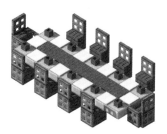

FOUR-POSTER BED
If a regular bed isn't fancy enough, use wood blocks, fences and trapdoors to create a four-poster.

WARDROBE
Use a small alcove to create a wardrobe – add armour stands and place wooden doors at the front.

FORMAL DINING TABLE
Make a formal dining table with gold weighted pressure plates, red carpet and flower pots.

OUTDOOR SPACES

The area around your build deserves as much attention as the build itself. The next few pages showcase some inspired ways to make the most of your outdoor space so that your build flows seamlessly into its environment.

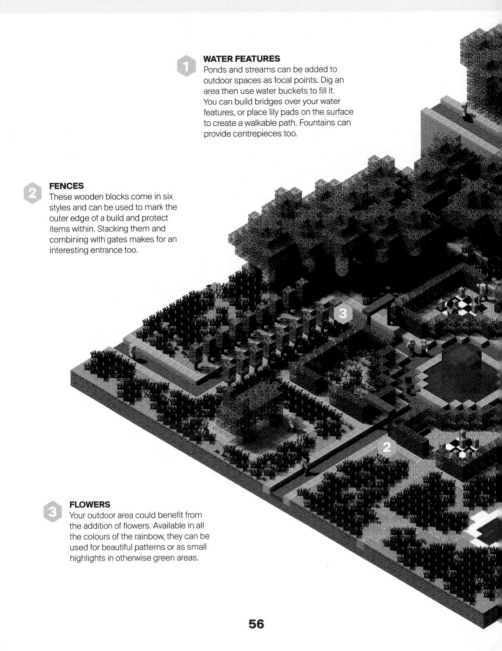

1 WATER FEATURES
Ponds and streams can be added to outdoor spaces as focal points. Dig an area then use water buckets to fill it. You can build bridges over your water features, or place lily pads on the surface to create a walkable path. Fountains can provide centrepieces too.

2 FENCES
These wooden blocks come in six styles and can be used to mark the outer edge of a build and protect items within. Stacking them and combining with gates makes for an interesting entrance too.

3 FLOWERS
Your outdoor area could benefit from the addition of flowers. Available in all the colours of the rainbow, they can be used for beautiful patterns or as small highlights in otherwise green areas.

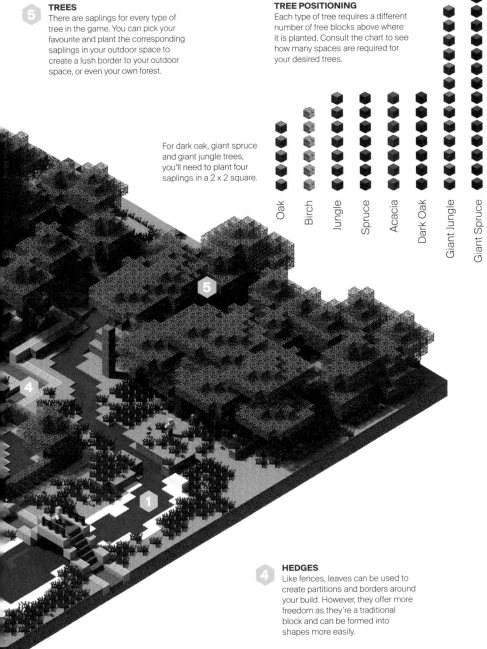

TREES

There are saplings for every type of tree in the game. You can pick your favourite and plant the corresponding saplings in your outdoor space to create a lush border to your outdoor space, or even your own forest.

TREE POSITIONING

Each type of tree requires a different number of free blocks above where it is planted. Consult the chart to see how many spaces are required for your desired trees.

For dark oak, giant spruce and giant jungle trees, you'll need to plant four saplings in a 2 x 2 square.

Oak   Birch   Jungle   Spruce   Acacia   Dark Oak   Giant Jungle   Giant Spruce

HEDGES

Like fences, leaves can be used to create partitions and borders around your build. However, they offer more freedom as they're a traditional block and can be formed into shapes more easily.

DESIGN YOUR OWN TREES

It can take a while for saplings to grow, but you can skip the wait and design your own trees. Wood and leaves obviously work well and can be combined in new ways, but you can also experiment with more unusual designs and different blocks.

SPHERICAL TREE
Put your sphere-making skills to good use and create neat, spherical trees for a stylish garden.

SPOOKY TREE
Create a spooky, bare tree from wood blocks and hanging jack o'lanterns. The more crooked you can make the trunk and branches, the better.

BONSAI TREE
After something a little more ornamental? Create a pretty, full-size bonsai tree with carefully crafted branches and foliage.

CANDYFLOSS TREE
For a fantasy build, use colourful blocks instead of wood and leaves. This candyfloss tree is perfect for a fantasy candyland.

ADDITIONAL STRUCTURES

Now that you have the basics of your outdoor area in place you can add some more complex structures to help personalise the space and bring it to life.

BRIDGES
Bridges are the easiest way to cross the rivers, lakes and streams of your outdoor space. These can range from simple wooden footpaths to elaborately sculpted crossings.

MEETING POINTS
Outdoor areas are often dotted with meeting points and social venues. You can make your outdoor area into a public space with additions like bandstands and open terraces.

ARCHES
Basic pathways can be upgraded with the addition of some decorative arches. These can serve as gateways to different areas, or just brighten up an otherwise dull walk.

COMMUNAL SPACE
Outdoor spaces are the perfect location for communities to come together and create. Whether it's a public garden or a communal greenhouse, locals can add to and benefit from these additions.

MAZES
Leafy hedges can be used to fill and transform space into intricate mazes. Mark out the route to the end point on the floor first, then create walkways and dead ends all around it.

BUILDING

Now you've learnt how to plan and decorate builds, this section shows you how to incorporate your new-found skills into cohesive structures. You'll see builds that cross different themes, styles, functions and locations to inspire more of your own ideas.

REMOTE OUTPOST

This secluded outpost incorporates a natural theme combining wood, diorite and cobblestone. Slabs and stairs add depth to the exterior features, while the simple interior is split between two floors across two complementary structures.

TIP

Create a billowing flag by using wool blocks. Place them at different depths to make it look like it's blowing in the wind.

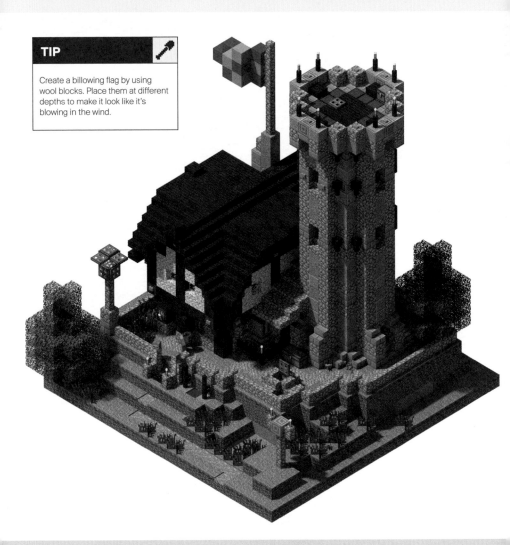

RUSTIC THEME

COMPLEMENTARY

SCHEMATICS

These plans show the sentry outpost from various perspectives. The turret base begins as part of the main building, sharing the ground floor, and cuts through the roof. There is no first floor within the turret, but there is an accessible rooftop.

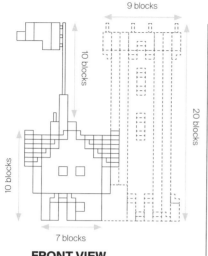

FRONT VIEW

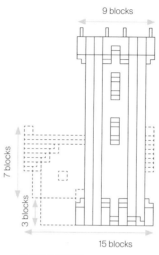

SIDE VIEW

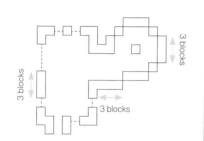

GROUND FLOOR

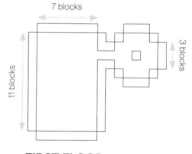

FIRST FLOOR

EXTREME HILLS

IDEAL LANDSCAPE

A remote sentry outpost is most useful when positioned at a good vantage point, but in an obscured spot. The best location to place this build is on a high mountain, surrounded by tall trees. Clear a flat piece of land in an extreme hills biome before laying the foundations.

REMOTE OUTPOST EXTERIOR

1 Create a colourful flag. This could be a pattern you like, or colours that signify your alliance with a group.

2 The exterior lighting is a makeshift beacon, used for signalling other outposts or villages in the area. The trapdoor encasement can be opened and closed to modify visibility.

3 The land space of the outpost is enclosed in a simple cobblestone wall and filled with flowers, small trees and lighting.

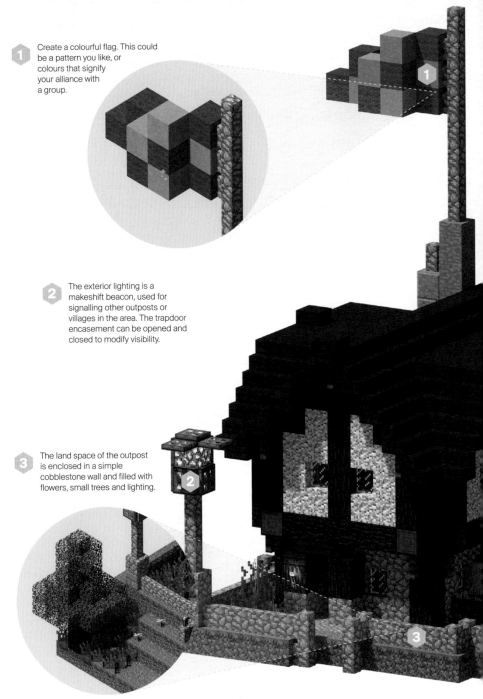

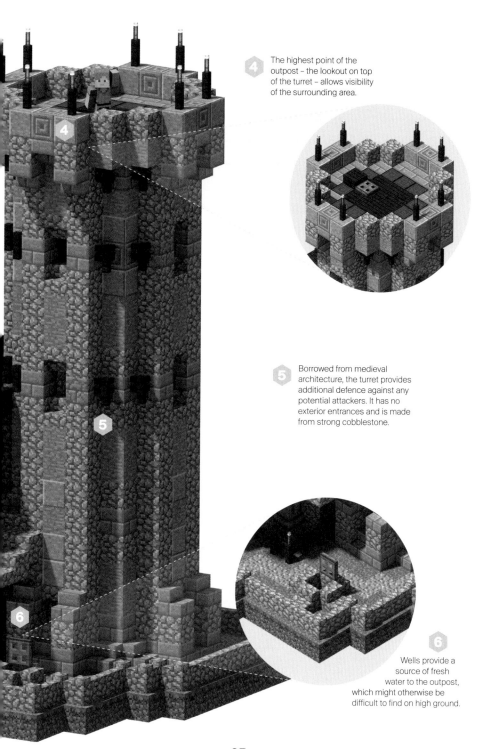

The highest point of the outpost – the lookout on top of the turret – allows visibility of the surrounding area.

Borrowed from medieval architecture, the turret provides additional defence against any potential attackers. It has no exterior entrances and is made from strong cobblestone.

Wells provide a source of fresh water to the outpost, which might otherwise be difficult to find on high ground.

REMOTE OUTPOST INTERIOR

1 The interior comforts are basic – a solitary chair and table, a single bed and chests for storage of foraged resources.

2 The interior lighting consists of a few torches placed on the walls. This makes the outpost less visible at night and requires fewer resources.

3 The open stone fireplace is the only source of warmth in the outpost, placed directly underneath the chimney so smoke can escape.

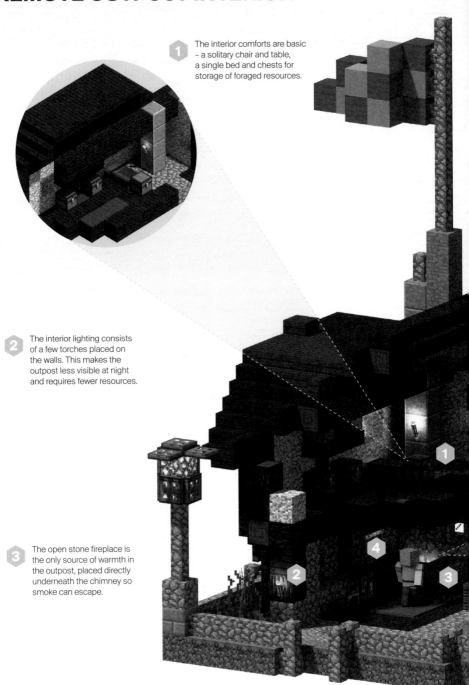

Inside the turret there is a spiral staircase and ladder leading to a trapdoor, which separates the interior from the rooftop lookout.

The remote outpost has many workstations, used to craft resources into useful tools, food and weapons to help survive the wilderness.

LIGHTING SYSTEM

You'll need a lighting system to illuminate your creations. Lights can be activated manually by a switch, or set to come on automatically. This example shows how to incorporate a lighting system into a simple house with two rooms.

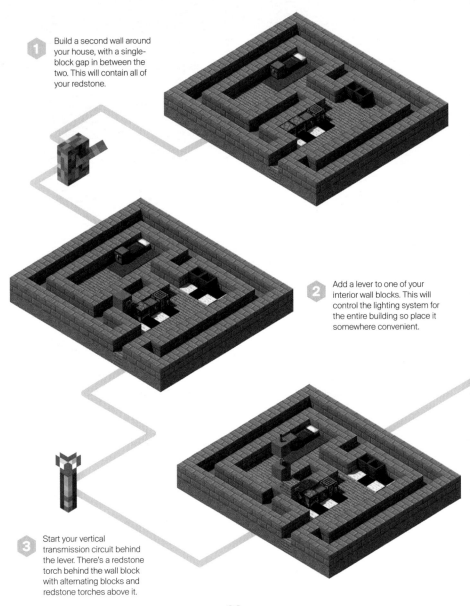

1 Build a second wall around your house, with a single-block gap in between the two. This will contain all of your redstone.

2 Add a lever to one of your interior wall blocks. This will control the lighting system for the entire building so place it somewhere convenient.

3 Start your vertical transmission circuit behind the lever. There's a redstone torch behind the wall block with alternating blocks and redstone torches above it.

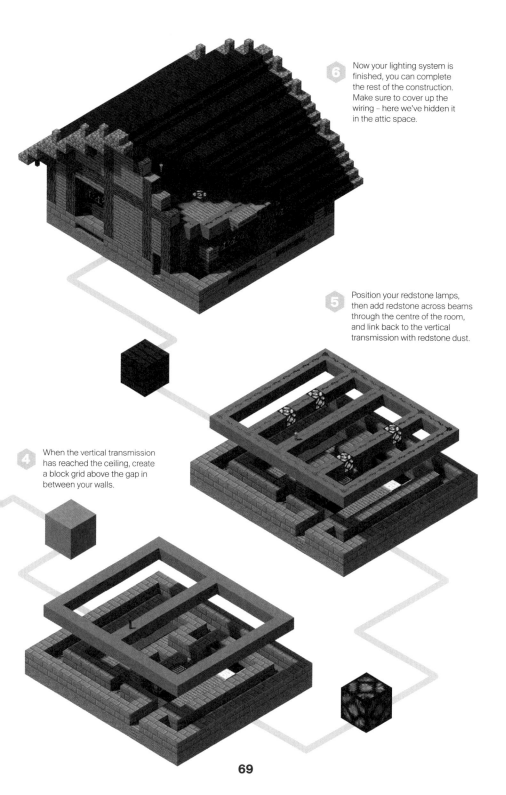

6 Now your lighting system is finished, you can complete the rest of the construction. Make sure to cover up the wiring – here we've hidden it in the attic space.

5 Position your redstone lamps, then add redstone across beams through the centre of the room, and link back to the vertical transmission with redstone dust.

4 When the vertical transmission has reached the ceiling, create a block grid above the gap in between your walls.

LIGHTING SYSTEM VARIATIONS

Larger builds may benefit from having several independent circuits so the lighting can be customised for each room or area. Let's take a look at some internal lighting ideas as well as options for the exterior of your builds.

FLOOR LIGHTING
Floor lighting is a stylish alternative to wall or ceiling lights and works well in bathrooms and kitchens. It's powered by redstone hidden underneath the floor blocks.

SECURITY LIGHTING
In external areas your lighting can be connected to a tripwire or to pressure plates. The system will be activated when mobs or enemy players trespass on your land, providing effective security lighting.

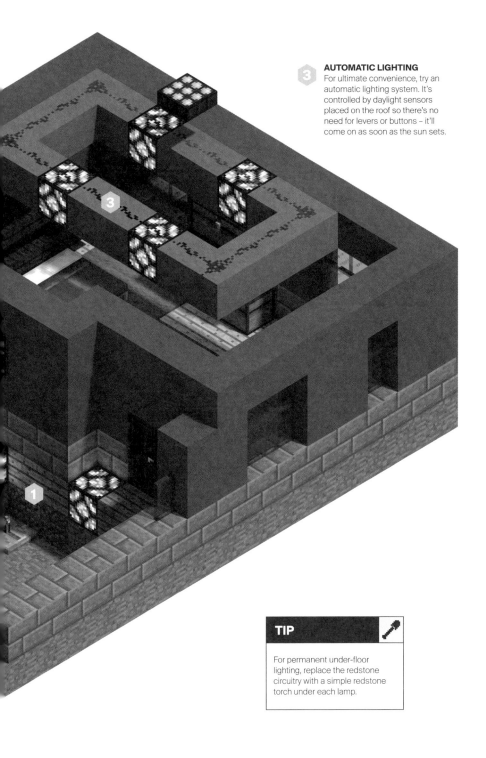

AUTOMATIC LIGHTING

For ultimate convenience, try an automatic lighting system. It's controlled by daylight sensors placed on the roof so there's no need for levers or buttons – it'll come on as soon as the sun sets.

TIP

For permanent under-floor lighting, replace the redstone circuitry with a simple redstone torch under each lamp.

EXOTIC VILLA

An archetype of Mediterranean architecture, this stylish villa incorporates classical features in a luxury residence. The minimalist colour scheme is complemented with splashes of colour inside, and contrasted by an extravagant outdoor space.

CLASSICAL THEME

MONOCHROMATIC ANALOGUE

SCHEMATICS

The simplistic cuboid shape of the villa is embellished with various features that add depth and interest to the build, from colonnades and arches to cornices and gables. The interior has an intermediate level, called a mezzanine, between the ground and first floors.

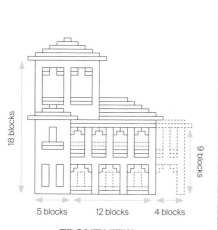

FRONT VIEW

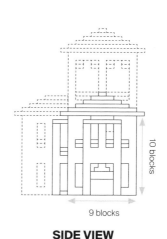

SIDE VIEW

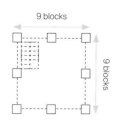

GROUND FLOOR

FIRST FLOOR

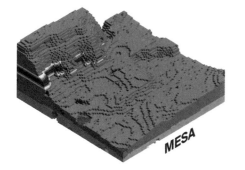

MESA

IDEAL LANDSCAPE

The Mediterranean is usually very hot, so the scorched red sand and hardened clay of the mesa biome provides the perfect staging for the villa. It's equally suitable at the top of one of the mesa's many peaks or situated in a wide open plateau.

EXOTIC VILLA EXTERIOR

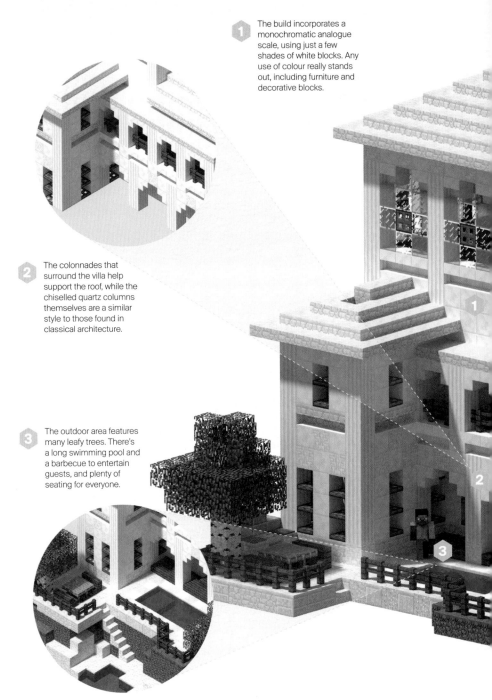

1 The build incorporates a monochromatic analogue scale, using just a few shades of white blocks. Any use of colour really stands out, including furniture and decorative blocks.

2 The colonnades that surround the villa help support the roof, while the chiselled quartz columns themselves are a similar style to those found in classical architecture.

3 The outdoor area features many leafy trees. There's a long swimming pool and a barbecue to entertain guests, and plenty of seating for everyone.

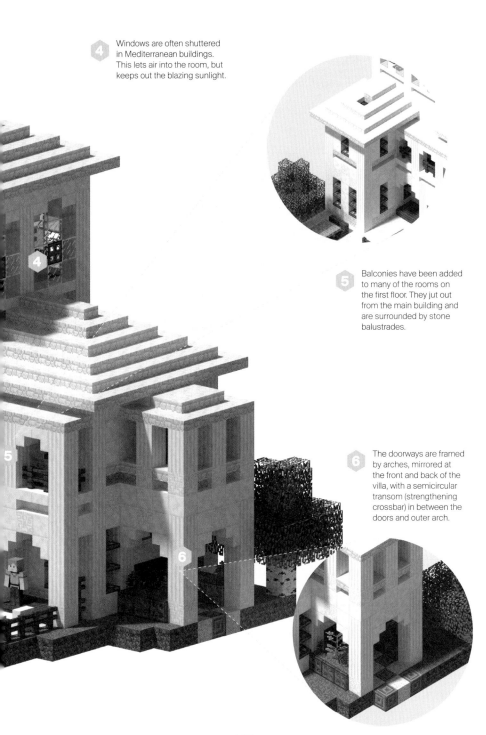

4 Windows are often shuttered in Mediterranean buildings. This lets air into the room, but keeps out the blazing sunlight.

5 Balconies have been added to many of the rooms on the first floor. They jut out from the main building and are surrounded by stone balustrades.

6 The doorways are framed by arches, mirrored at the front and back of the villa, with a semicircular transom (strengthening crossbar) in between the doors and outer arch.

EXOTIC VILLA INTERIOR

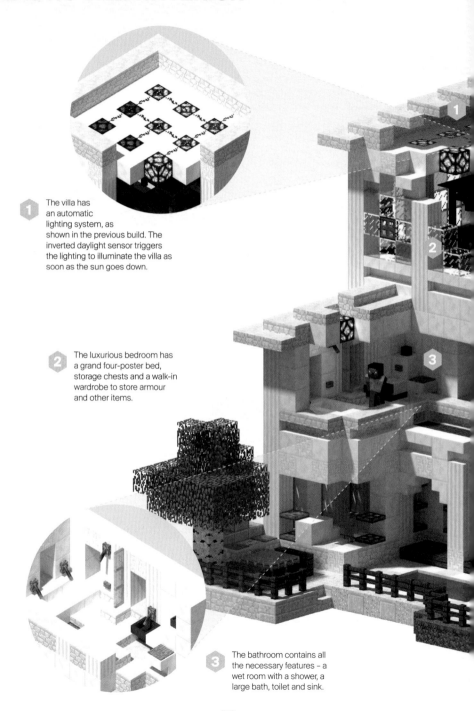

1 The villa has an automatic lighting system, as shown in the previous build. The inverted daylight sensor triggers the lighting to illuminate the villa as soon as the sun goes down.

2 The luxurious bedroom has a grand four-poster bed, storage chests and a walk-in wardrobe to store armour and other items.

3 The bathroom contains all the necessary features – a wet room with a shower, a large bath, toilet and sink.

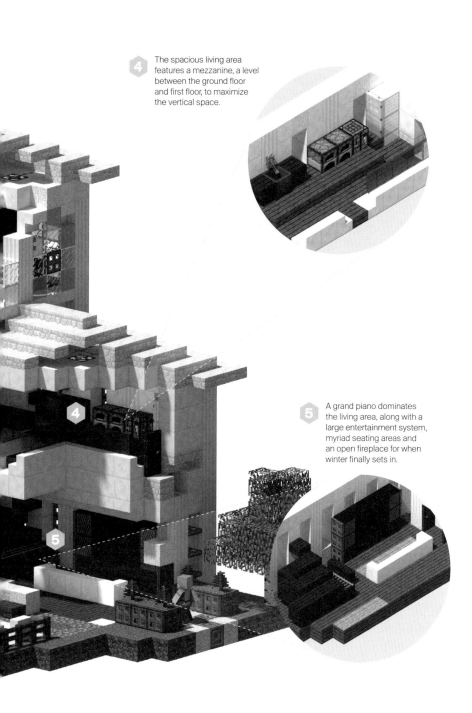

4 The spacious living area features a mezzanine, a level between the ground floor and first floor, to maximize the vertical space.

5 A grand piano dominates the living area, along with a large entertainment system, myriad seating areas and an open fireplace for when winter finally sets in.

VERTICAL TRANSPORT SYSTEM

The distance between sea level and bedrock is 62 blocks, and it can be difficult to transport goods from the bottom of the world to the top, and vice versa. This clever vertical transport system will automate the process for you.

1 The entire transport system will be built within a 5 x 5 vertical shaft. Create a 5 x 5 base at your chosen underground location.

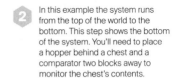

2 In this example the system runs from the top of the world to the bottom. This step shows the bottom of the system. You'll need to place a hopper behind a chest and a comparator two blocks away to monitor the chest's contents.

3 Now add your redstone circuitry. Add the extra clay blocks first, then the redstone and the redstone torch as shown.

4 Place a powered rail on top of the hopper. When a minecart with a full chest reaches the hopper it will release its contents. Once the chest is empty the cart is sent back up the track.

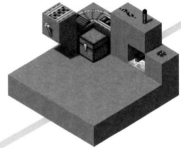

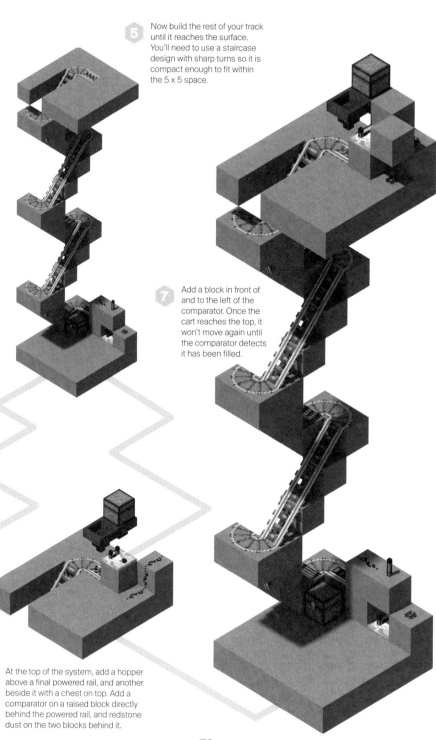

5 Now build the rest of your track until it reaches the surface. You'll need to use a staircase design with sharp turns so it is compact enough to fit within the 5 x 5 space.

7 Add a block in front of and to the left of the comparator. Once the cart reaches the top, it won't move again until the comparator detects it has been filled.

6 At the top of the system, add a hopper above a final powered rail, and another beside it with a chest on top. Add a comparator on a raised block directly behind the powered rail, and redstone dust on the two blocks behind it.

TRANSPORT SYSTEM ALTERNATIVES

There are many ways to customise and expand on a vertical transport system. Take inspiration from the alternatives on this page.

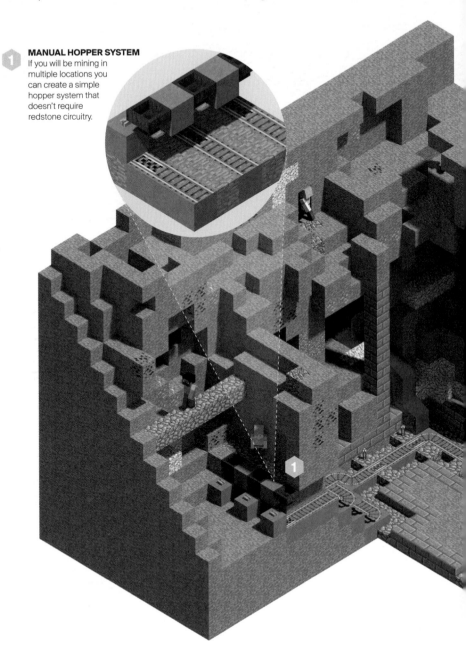

MANUAL HOPPER SYSTEM
If you will be mining in multiple locations you can create a simple hopper system that doesn't require redstone circuitry.

TERMINAL
One way to disguise your
redstone circuitry is to build a
terminal at ground level.

UNDERGROUND SYSTEM
You can build an entire
underground system to link
different mining areas. If you
want to switch your track
at junctions simply place a
lever or button as shown.

OCEAN OBSERVATORY

This ocean observatory is a glass megastructure based around a modified dome, with an entrance above sea level. Built from sturdy iron with glass for easy observation, its underwater location is something of an industrial accomplishment.

INDUSTRIAL THEME

COMPLEMENTARY

SCHEMATICS

The majority of the observatory is situated underwater, but the central shaft ascends to the surface, where it is linked to a departure platform for boats. The space within the dome is small, so there are no individual rooms, rather everything is situated in an open-plan environment.

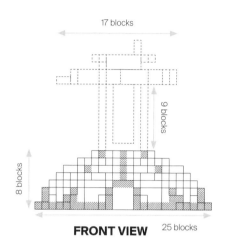

17 blocks

9 blocks

8 blocks

FRONT VIEW 25 blocks

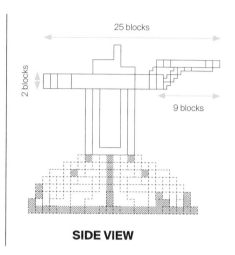

25 blocks

2 blocks

9 blocks

SIDE VIEW

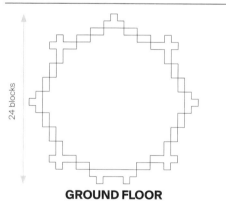

24 blocks

GROUND FLOOR

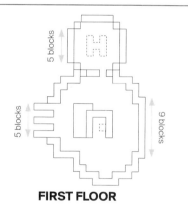

5 blocks

5 blocks

9 blocks

FIRST FLOOR

OCEAN

IDEAL LANDSCAPE

The isolated depths of the ocean biome offer a prime location for the ocean observatory, although lake and river beds would also suffice. It's best to situate the observatory towards the edge of the ocean biome so that land and resources are also accessible.

OCEAN OBSERVATORY EXTERIOR

1 The central shaft is wide enough to incorporate a transport system. The redstone circuitry can be housed within the dome, or in an annex attached to the dome.

2 The dome is the top half of a sphere, made from layered concentric circles, with a single cylindrical entrance through the top.

3 Glass blocks have been used rather than glass panes, as they are easier to construct shapes with.

The port at the top of the shaft aids travel between the observatory and land. It has lots of space for loading and unloading goods.

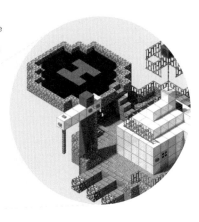

A huge structure such as this would require support, particularly deep underwater where pressure is greater. Flying buttresses added to the outside and columns inside provide this support.

The observatory is anchored underwater by iron foundations, which encircle the base of the dome, both inside and out.

OCEAN OBSERVATORY INTERIOR

1 Space is at a premium for the inhabitants of the observatory, so bunks are stacked to provide sufficient sleeping quarters.

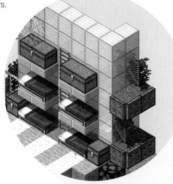

2 Everyone working in the observatory has access to a research station, consisting of a desktop computer and testing area.

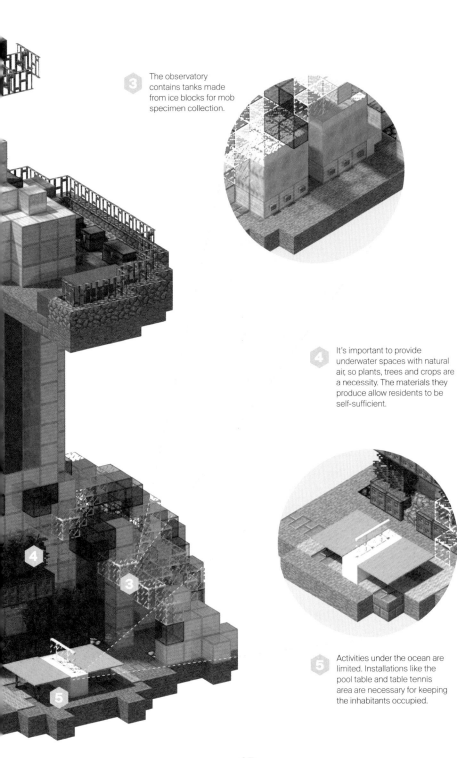

The observatory contains tanks made from ice blocks for mob specimen collection.

It's important to provide underwater spaces with natural air, so plants, trees and crops are a necessity. The materials they produce allow residents to be self-sufficient.

Activities under the ocean are limited. Installations like the pool table and table tennis area are necessary for keeping the inhabitants occupied.

STEAMPUNK AIRSHIP

Combining Victorian-era technology with sci-fi machinery, this steampunk airship may seem like an abnormality in terms of architecture, but the shapes, features and decoration share more similarities with regular builds than you would expect.

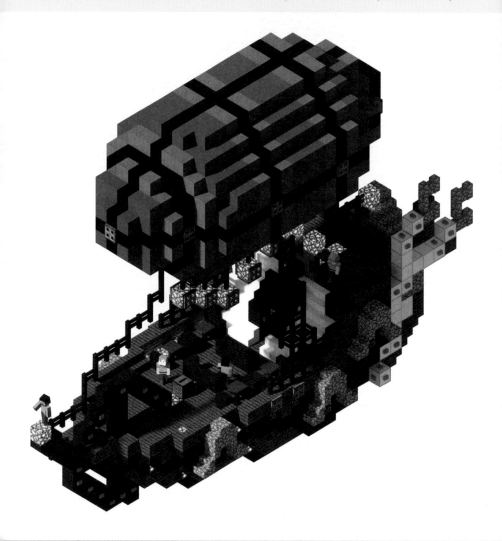

STEAMPUNK THEME

TRIADIC

SCHEMATICS

The airship's balloon is an ovoid, or 3D oval. This is constructed in a similar way to a sphere, but the widest circle of the sphere is duplicated many times to elongate the shape. The deck is an irregular shape, but is similar to an upside-down triangular prism.

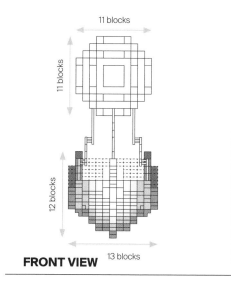

FRONT VIEW

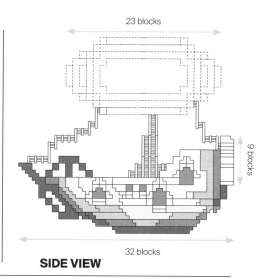

SIDE VIEW

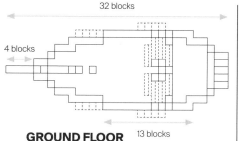

GROUND FLOOR

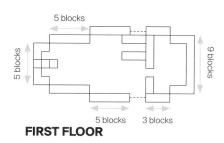

FIRST FLOOR

END CITY

IDEAL LANDSCAPE

The airship doesn't require any land, but you'll need to create foundations to begin building in the sky. It can be constructed in any biome, but a more fantastical landscape like the End city, with its unusual colours, crooked towers and floating pirate ships, suits the science fiction nature of this build.

STEAMPUNK AIRSHIP EXTERIOR

1 Gold is often used in steampunk-style constructs, so glowstone lends itself well to this build. Attach blocks to wooden fence posts hanging above the deck.

2 Cogs and clockwork mechanisms are characteristic of steampunk style. Solid blocks are used to create these on the hull, adding depth through decoration.

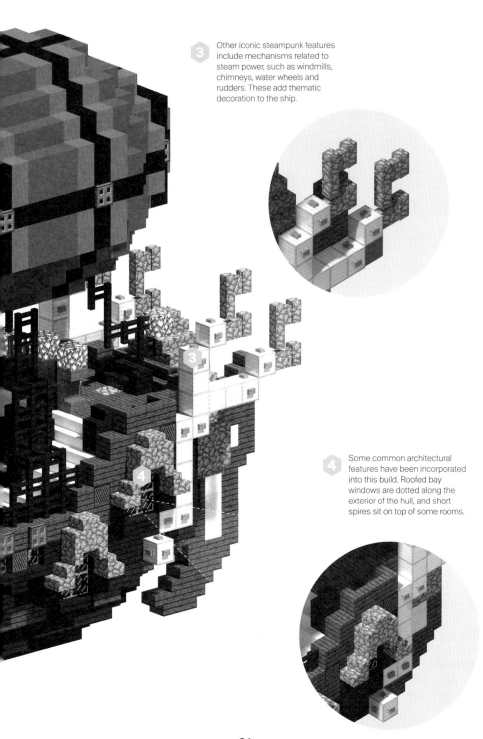

3 Other iconic steampunk features include mechanisms related to steam power, such as windmills, chimneys, water wheels and rudders. These add thematic decoration to the ship.

4 Some common architectural features have been incorporated into this build. Roofed bay windows are dotted along the exterior of the hull, and short spires sit on top of some rooms.

STEAMPUNK AIRSHIP INTERIOR

1 Additional detail like levers, framed maps, banners and a grandfather clock complete the interior decoration and fit into the mechanistic style.

2 The galley contains everything required to feed the crew: ovens, fridges and plenty of seating for everyone.

3 An industrial-style floor made from sideways pistons makes a suitable steampunk grounding inside the hull of the ship.

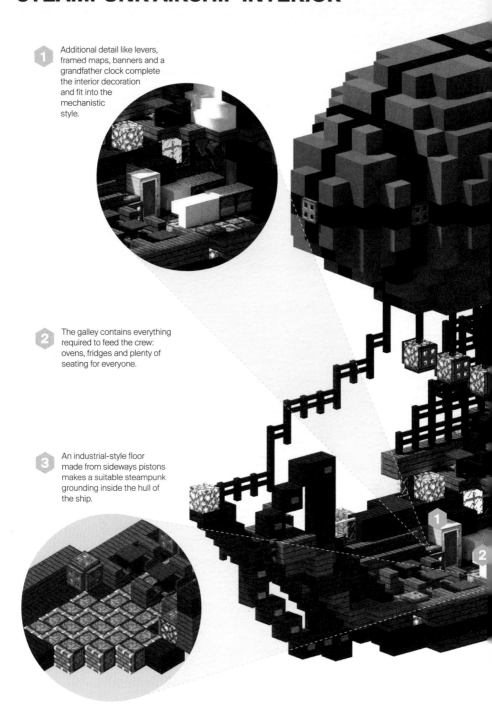

4 The ship travels around collecting loot and trading, so there needs to be plenty of storage space. More functional decoration like shulker boxes and chests serve this purpose.

5 The engine room of the airship is filled with functional furnaces to make the steam that powers the airship.

FINAL WORDS

C ongratulations! You've reached the end of our Guide to Creative! We hope
you've been inspired to make something amazing.

One of the best things about Creative mode is that there's no right or wrong
way to play. You set your own goals. Never feel disheartened when you see
someone else's unbelievably epic creation. Remember that lots of the epic
builds you might find on the internet have been worked on for months on end
and constructed by large teams of experienced builders.

Having access to limitless resources can be intimidating too, but using most
of the blocks on offer won't necessarily make your creations shine. It's more
important to follow through on a vision, whether it's a monumental skyscraper
that dominates the skyline or a modest forest home.

Enough reading! Get building!

OWEN JONES
THE MOJANG TEAM

First published in Great Britain 2019 by Egmont UK Limited.
This edition published in 2020 by Dean, an imprint of Egmont UK Limited,
2 Minster Court, 10th Floor, London EC3R 7BB

Written by Stephanie Milton
Designed by Design Button Ltd.
Illustrations by Ryan Marsh
Cover designed by John Stuckey
Cover illustration by BSmart
Production by Louis Harvey and Laura Grundy
Special thanks to Alex Wiltshire, Jennifer Hammervald, Filip Thoms,
Amanda Ström and Isabella Balk.

ISBN 978 0 6035 7928 8

71019/001

Printed in China

ONLINE SAFETY FOR YOUNGER FANS

Spending time online is great fun! Here are a few simple rules to help younger fans stay safe and
keep the internet a great place to spend time:

-Never give out your real name – don't use it as your username.
-Never give out any of your personal details.
-Never tell anybody which school you go to or how old you are.
-Never tell anybody your password except a parent or a guardian.
-Be aware that you must be 13 or over to create an account on many sites. Always check the site
policy and ask a parent or guardian for permission before registering.
-Always tell a parent or guardian if something is worrying you.

Stay safe online. Any website addresses listed in this book are correct at the time of going
to print. However, Egmont is not responsible for content hosted by third parties. Please be
aware that online content can be subject to change and websites can contain content that is
unsuitable for children. We advise that all children are supervised when using the internet.

Egmont takes its responsibility to the planet and its inhabitants very seriously. We aim to use
papers from well-managed forests run by responsible suppliers.

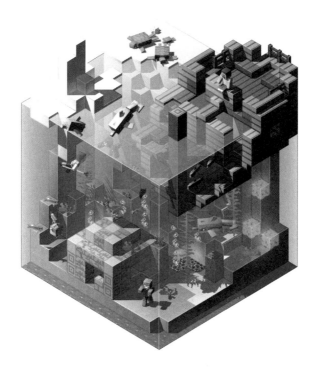

GUIDE TO:
OCEAN SURVIVAL

CONTENTS

1. STRUCTURES AND LOOT

2. OCEAN MOBS

3. SURVIVAL TIPS

INTRODUCTION

Welcome to the official Guide to Ocean Survival! Thanks so much for picking up this super guide to all the beautiful and terrible things you'll encounter in the Overworld's seas!

I guess you want to become an aquatic expert, ready to discover the most precious treasures under the waves, identify every weird and wonderful mob and construct amazing underwater builds. Well, you've made a great start!

You probably already know that it can get dangerous down there. You'll need to prepare yourself with special enchantments, potions and items to help you hold your breath and see in the dark. Perhaps you also know about some of the fearsome mobs that lurk in forgotten ruins on the ocean floor? All you need to face them and tell the tale is right here. There are lots of great ideas for show-stopping undersea bases, too. After all, to make the very best of your time in the depths, you need a great place to kick back and relax.

So come on in, it's time to take a deep dive!

ALEX WILTSHIRE
THE MOJANG TEAM

THE OCEAN BIOMES

Once you start to explore, you'll soon realise that not all areas of ocean are the same. In fact, there are several different ocean biomes and each has unique features. Before you dive in, let's take a look at the differences between each ocean biome, so you'll know how to recognise them.

FROZEN OCEAN

You'll know you've strayed into an area of frozen ocean pretty quickly – the water is a dark purple colour and the surface is covered in ice. You'll also see icebergs, which are made from blue ice, packed ice and snow. Any underwater ruins you find will be made of stone.

There are frequent holes in the ice, so watch your step when exploring.

Be very careful – the ice acts like solid ground, allowing dangerous mobs to spawn on top of it at night-time.

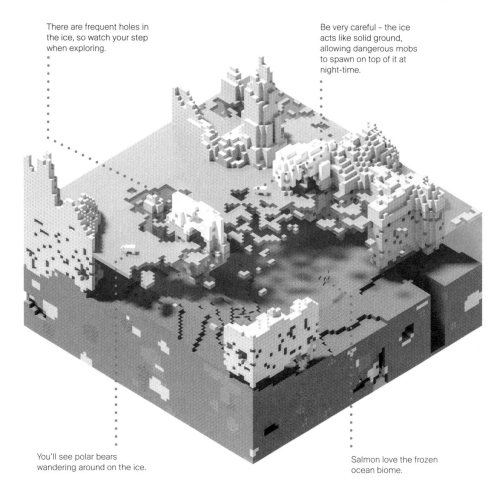

You'll see polar bears wandering around on the ice.

Salmon love the frozen ocean biome.

COLD OCEAN

Cold oceans have dark blue water at the surface and the ocean bed is mostly made of gravel.
Any underwater ruins will be made of stone blocks and you'll see some seagrass and kelp.

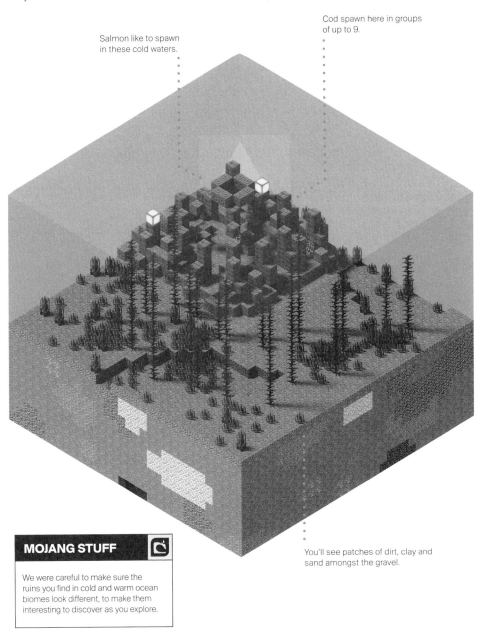

Salmon like to spawn
in these cold waters.

Cod spawn here in groups
of up to 9.

You'll see patches of dirt, clay and
sand amongst the gravel.

MOJANG STUFF

We were careful to make sure the
ruins you find in cold and warm ocean
biomes look different, to make them
interesting to discover as you explore.

LUKEWARM OCEAN

Light-blue surface water is the first sign that you're in a lukewarm area of ocean. The ocean bed is made of sand, and kelp and seagrass thrive here. Any underwater ruins you find will be made of sandy blocks rather than stone.

The seabed is composed of dirt, clay and gravel amongst the sand.

Tropical fish like to spawn in these warmer waters.

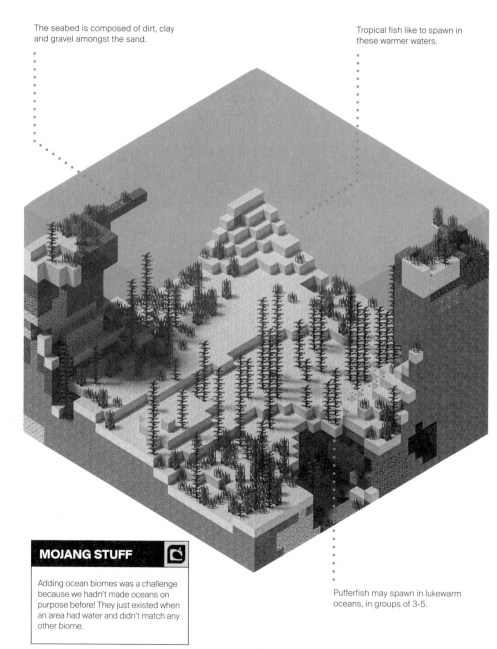

Pufferfish may spawn in lukewarm oceans, in groups of 3-5.

WARM OCEAN

The water at the surface of warm areas of ocean is an inviting, light green colour and the ocean floor is sandy. There's plenty of seagrass, but no kelp. Like lukewarm areas, the underwater ruins here will be made of sandy blocks.

Tropical fish love warm ocean biomes so you'll see plenty of them here.

Warm oceans are the only biome in which you'll find coral reefs.

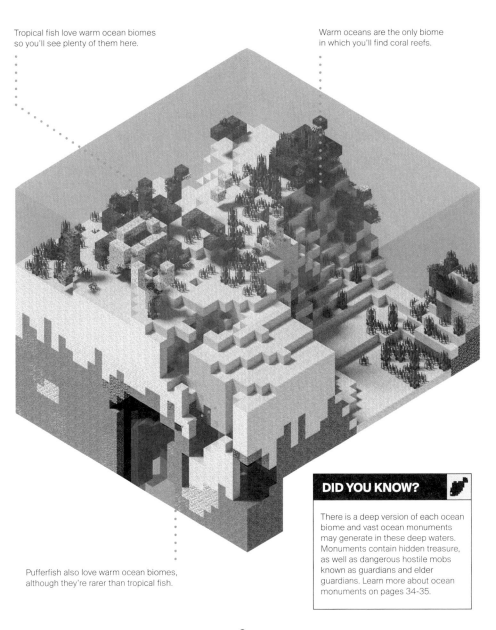

Pufferfish also love warm ocean biomes, although they're rarer than tropical fish.

DID YOU KNOW?

There is a deep version of each ocean biome and vast ocean monuments may generate in these deep waters. Monuments contain hidden treasure, as well as dangerous hostile mobs known as guardians and elder guardians. Learn more about ocean monuments on pages 34-35.

BEFORE YOU DIVE IN

Now you know how to recognise the different types of ocean, you're almost ready to begin your first aquatic adventure! But before you dive in, you need to make sure you're ready for what awaits. There are several special items that are essential to your survival, including potions and enchanted equipment.

FOOD

You'll need to take some good quality food with you on your underwater escapade so you can replenish your health and hunger bars. In general, meat is better than fruits and vegetables, as it restores more hunger points, and cooked meat is more nourishing than raw meat. Steak is always a good options as each piece restores 8 hunger points. Cooked pork chops will restore 8 hunger points apiece, too. Cake is another good idea – each cake has 7 slices and each slice restores 2 hunger points.

WOOD

Wood is an essential crafting ingredient and you'll want to have a few stacks in your inventory at all times so you can craft replacement tools and weapons when necessary. In an emergency, you can mine wood from any shipwrecks you come across – they're almost entirely constructed from wood and wood planks.

POTION OF WATER BREATHING

When drunk, each bottle of this handy potion allows you to breathe underwater for 3 minutes rather than the usual 15 seconds. Just brew a pufferfish with awkward potion. For the extended version, which lasts 8 minutes, brew potion of water breathing with redstone.

AWKWARD POTION RECIPE

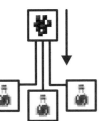

WATER BREATHING RECIPE

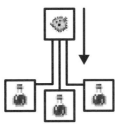

WATER BREATHING (EXTENDED) RECIPE

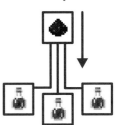

POTION OF NIGHT VISION

It's murky down in the ocean depths, so you'll need potion of night vision to bring everything back to maximum light level. Brew awkward potion with a golden carrot to make night vision – each bottle lasts 3 minutes. You can extend this to 8 minutes by brewing potion of night vision with redstone.

NIGHT VISION RECIPE

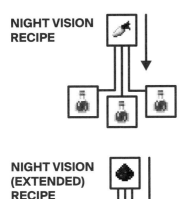

NIGHT VISION (EXTENDED) RECIPE

POTION OF REGENERATION

This potion will restore your health by around 2 health points every 2.4 seconds. Each potion lasts for 45 seconds. Brew awkward potion with a ghast tear to make it. For the extended version, which lasts for 1 minute 30 seconds, brew potion of regeneration with redstone.

REGENERATION RECIPE

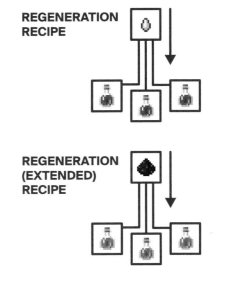

REGENERATION (EXTENDED) RECIPE

RESPIRATION HELMET

Enchant your helmet with respiration on an enchantment table and each level will increase your underwater breathing time by 15 seconds.

DEPTH STRIDER BOOTS

This is a good enchantment for your boots because your movement is slower when you're underwater. Each level of the enchantment reduces the amount water slows you down by a third – so by level 3 (the maximum level) you'll be able to swim as quickly as you can walk on land.

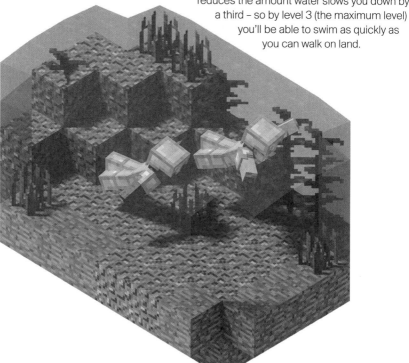

TURTLE SHELL

Have you spotted any turtles during your land-based adventures? When they're not swimming in the ocean, these passive mobs can often be seen in groups on warm, sandy beaches. When they become adults, baby turtles drop an item called a scute. Collect 5 scutes and you'll be able to craft a turtle shell – a helmet that provides the wearer with the water breathing effect.

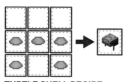

TURTLE SHELL RECIPE

FROST WALKER BOOTS

It's worth keeping a pair of frost walker boots in your inventory if you're serious about exploring large areas of ocean. That way, if you want to travel across a large expanse of ocean quickly, you can simply run across the surface and your boots will create frosted blocks of ice under your feet as you travel. Just bear in mind that if you stop moving, the ice will gradually melt.

LOOTING SWORD

Enchant your sword with looting and hostile underwater mobs will drop more items when defeated. They'll also be more likely to drop uncommon and rare items, as well as any equipment they may be holding or wearing. An iron sword is good, but a diamond sword is better if you have enough materials.

EFFICIENCY PICKAXE

The efficiency enchantment will allow you to mine blocks more quickly than usual. It's very useful when you're mining underwater and can be applied to your shovel and axe as well as your pickaxe. Make sure you're using the correct tool for the block you're mining, otherwise the effect won't work – use a pickaxe for stone or a shovel for gravel.

1

STRUCTURES AND LOOT

There are all sorts of mysterious structures waiting to be explored in the ocean. Although they may be crawling with dangerous mobs, they also contain valuable items and rare treasures. In this section we'll explore these structures and find out where to search for loot.

FISHING

There are many rare treasures to be found in the ocean, and some of them can be retrieved from the relative safety of a boat. Let's take a look at how fishing works and discover what you might reel in on a very good day.

1 Craft a fishing rod. You'll just need sticks and string.

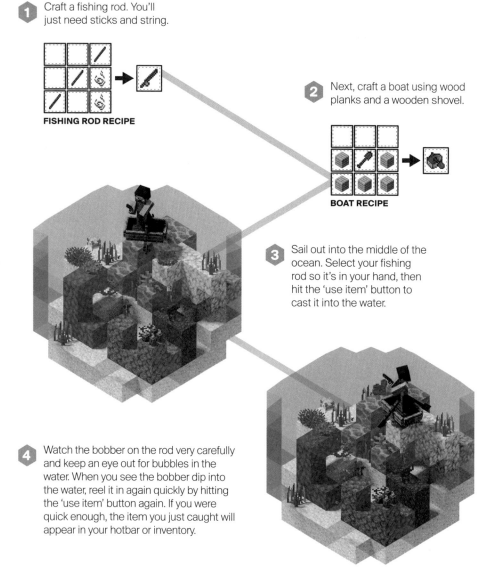

FISHING ROD RECIPE

2 Next, craft a boat using wood planks and a wooden shovel.

BOAT RECIPE

3 Sail out into the middle of the ocean. Select your fishing rod so it's in your hand, then hit the 'use item' button to cast it into the water.

4 Watch the bobber on the rod very carefully and keep an eye out for bubbles in the water. When you see the bobber dip into the water, reel it in again quickly by hitting the 'use item' button again. If you were quick enough, the item you just caught will appear in your hotbar or inventory.

WHAT YOU CAN CATCH

There's more than just fish in these waters! You might also reel in junk or treasure items while fishing. Here's a complete list of all the possible items you might find on the end of your rod.

Raw cod	Raw salmon	Tropical fish	Pufferfish	Bow
Enchanted book	Fishing rod	Name tag	Nautilus shell	Saddle
Lily pad	Bamboo	Bowl	Leather	Leather boots
Rotten flesh	Stick	String	Water bottle	Bone
Ink sac	Tripwire hook			

TIP

To increase the chance of reeling in treasure items and reduce the chance of reeling in junk items, enchant your fishing rod with luck of the sea using your enchantment table.

THE OCEAN FLOOR

The ocean floor is home to a variety of blocks and plant life. In many ways it's similar to the land above sea level – different blocks and plants appear in different areas and it's worth taking some time to explore.

1 SAND AND GRAVEL
These two blocks cover large areas of ocean floor – gravel covers the floor in cold areas of ocean and sand covers the floor in warm areas of ocean.

2 CAVES
The ocean floor is very similar to the terrain above sea level – it's hilly and you'll find lots of caves to explore. Be careful – some lead to caves that aren't flooded by water, so you'll bump into lots of dangerous mobs like zombies and creepers.

3 SEAGRASS
Seagrass grows in all types of ocean except for frozen ocean. If you want it to drop as an item you'll need to mine it with shears. You can use seagrass to breed turtles.

4 KELP
Kelp grows in all areas of ocean except for warm ocean. It can be mined with any tool or by hand. Smelt kelp in a furnace to make dried kelp – this food item restores 1 hunger point. Craft 9 dried kelp into a block of dried kelp, which can be used for decoration.

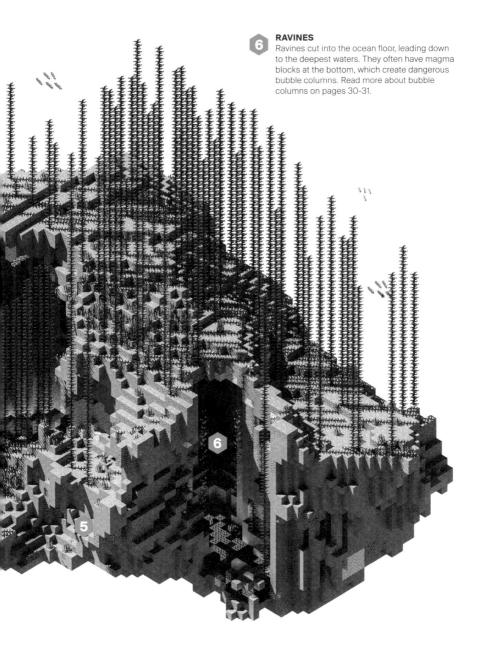

STONE AND ORES

All varieties of stone can be found on the ocean floor and inside caves and ravines. Valuable ore blocks like coal, iron and gold can be seen running through the stone in rich veins.

RAVINES

Ravines cut into the ocean floor, leading down to the deepest waters. They often have magma blocks at the bottom, which create dangerous bubble columns. Read more about bubble columns on pages 30-31.

SHIPWRECKS

You're likely to see several shipwrecks on your underwater adventures – they appear in all areas of the ocean. They're worth checking out whenever you see one – you can find some valuable items inside, and you can turn them into underwater bases, too, so you have somewhere to take shelter.

UPRIGHT

Shipwrecks look a bit like pirate ships.

They're often missing their bow, stern and mast, but occasionally you'll find a ship in one piece.

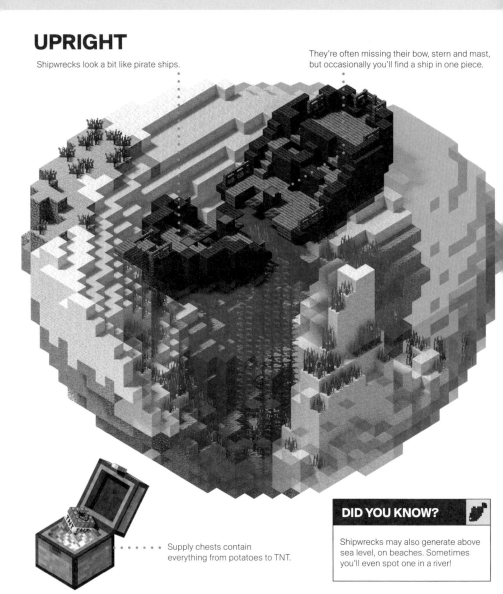

Supply chests contain everything from potatoes to TNT.

DID YOU KNOW?

Shipwrecks may also generate above sea level, on beaches. Sometimes you'll even spot one in a river!

SIDEWAYS

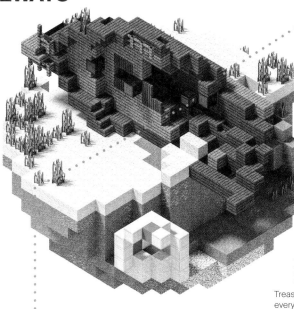

Shipwrecks are mainly built out of wood blocks – you'll find wood, wood planks, fences, stairs, trapdoors and doors.

Treasure chests contain everything from iron ingots to diamonds.

Map chests contain a buried treasure map, which will lead you to buried treasure chests. Find out more about those on pages 26-27!

UPSIDE-DOWN

You'll find 1-3 chests hidden inside each shipwreck – these could be supply chests, map chests or treasure chests.

UNDERWATER RUINS

Mysterious underwater ruins are a common sight on the ocean floor. Nobody knows the story behind these structures – perhaps they were once villages that fell victim to rising sea levels ... There are several types of ruin to explore – let's discover what you'll find in each.

COLD UNDERWATER RUINS

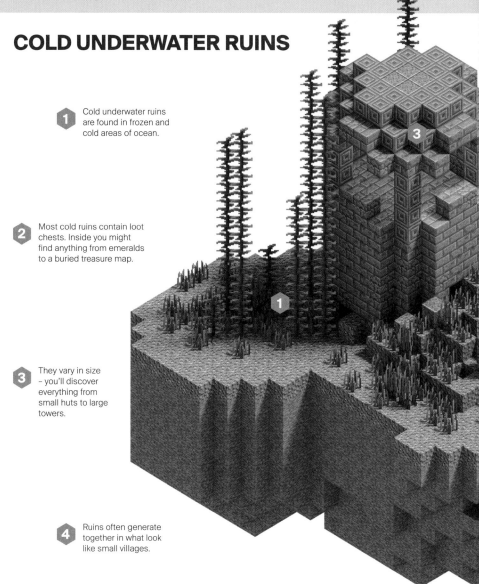

1 Cold underwater ruins are found in frozen and cold areas of ocean.

2 Most cold ruins contain loot chests. Inside you might find anything from emeralds to a buried treasure map.

3 They vary in size – you'll discover everything from small huts to large towers.

4 Ruins often generate together in what look like small villages.

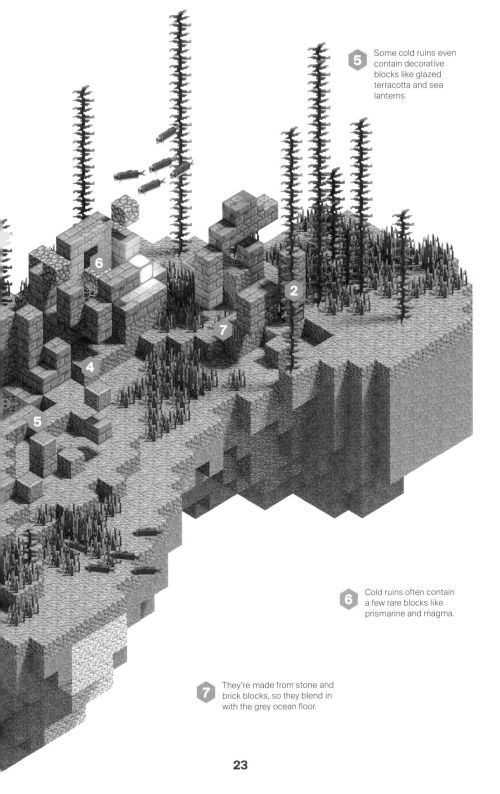

5 Some cold ruins even contain decorative blocks like glazed terracotta and sea lanterns.

6 Cold ruins often contain a few rare blocks like prismarine and magma.

7 They're made from stone and brick blocks, so they blend in with the grey ocean floor.

WARM UNDERWATER RUINS

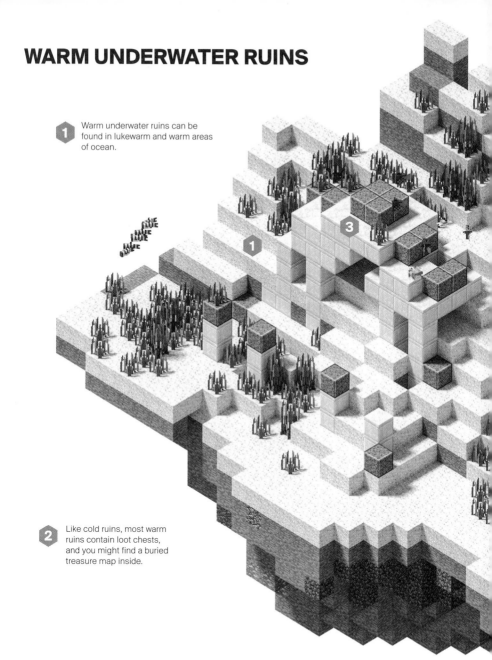

1 Warm underwater ruins can be found in lukewarm and warm areas of ocean.

2 Like cold ruins, most warm ruins contain loot chests, and you might find a buried treasure map inside.

3 Warm ruins often have blocks like polished granite and polished diorite.

4 They're made from sand and sandstone blocks, so they blend in with the sandy ocean floor.

TIP

You can turn ruins into emergency underwater bases so you have somewhere safe to retreat to if things get difficult.

5 You'll often see damaged arches in between the ruins.

DID YOU KNOW?

Occasionally, underwater ruins will appear on land, where the ocean meets the shore.

BURIED TREASURE

Once you've found a buried treasure map in a shipwreck or a ruin, you can set off on a quest to locate a buried treasure chest. Follow these steps and you'll soon find yourself the proud owner of some very valuable treasure.

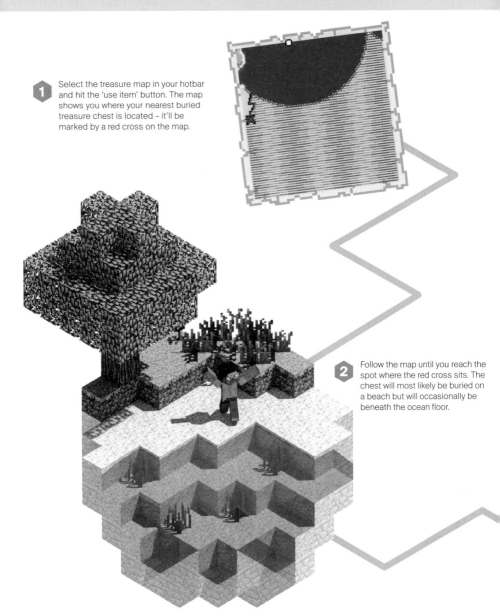

1 Select the treasure map in your hotbar and hit the 'use item' button. The map shows you where your nearest buried treasure chest is located – it'll be marked by a red cross on the map.

2 Follow the map until you reach the spot where the red cross sits. The chest will most likely be buried on a beach but will occasionally be beneath the ocean floor.

Buried treasure chests will also contain several other items of loot like emeralds, diamonds and prismarine crystals. Be sure to grab these, too!

 These chests are the only place you'll find the heart of the sea, a very rare item. Each chest contains one of these, and you'll need it to craft a conduit – a valuable block that will help you survive underwater. Learn more about conduits on pages 56-59.

 Dig around the spot marked on the map until you find the chest. It's usually hidden by blocks like sand or gravel.

ICEBERGS

As you would expect, icebergs are only found in areas of frozen ocean. They're made from several different blocks of ice, and snow has usually settled on top of them, too. Here are some interesting facts about icebergs.

1 Icebergs are made from a combination of packed ice, ice and blue ice.

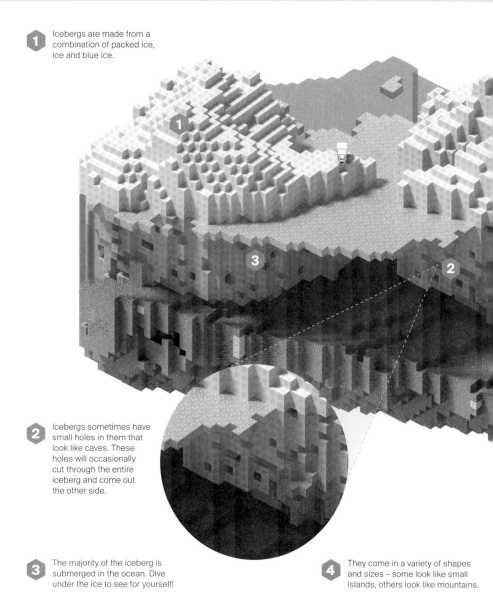

2 Icebergs sometimes have small holes in them that look like caves. These holes will occasionally cut through the entire iceberg and come out the other side.

3 The majority of the iceberg is submerged in the ocean. Dive under the ice to see for yourself!

4 They come in a variety of shapes and sizes – some look like small islands, others look like mountains.

Icebergs are the only place that blue ice occurs naturally. This type of ice is even more slippery than regular ice or packed ice, and it won't melt if it's positioned next to a light source.

5 You can hollow out an iceberg and turn it into a base if you need to hide from dangerous mobs.

6 Dangerous mobs walk around on icebergs and the ice surrounding them.

BUBBLE COLUMNS

If you see a stream of bubbles emerging from a ravine, be very careful! They may look innocent, but they can be deadly, as they can push and pull players in different directions. Here's everything you need to know about bubble columns.

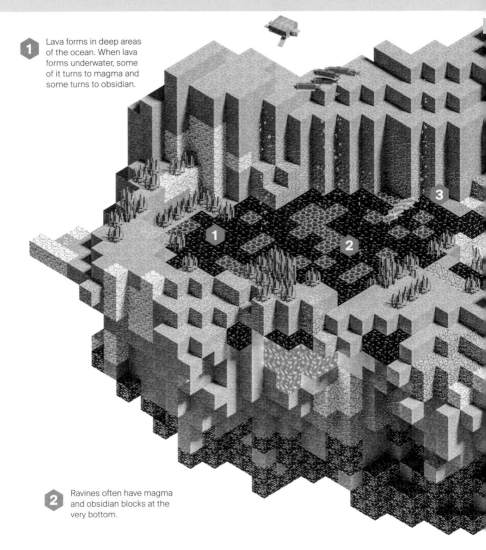

1 Lava forms in deep areas of the ocean. When lava forms underwater, some of it turns to magma and some turns to obsidian.

2 Ravines often have magma and obsidian blocks at the very bottom.

3 Magma blocks create bubbles when they're in water. These bubbles travel downwards and they're known as whirlpool bubble columns.

4 Whirlpool bubble columns can drag players down to the bottom of the ravine, where they can take damage from the magma and drown.

5 If you travel over a whirlpool bubble column in a boat, your boat will begin to shake and then sink.

6 If you're careful, you can also enter bubble columns to replenish your air supply.

CORAL REEFS

As you're exploring warm oceans, you're likely to come across a colourful coral reef. This vast structure is teeming with life and it's the only place you'll find coral. Let's explore a coral reef in more detail.

1 CORAL BLOCKS
You'll see clusters of colourful coral blocks all over the reef. There are five types: tube (blue), brain (pink), bubble (purple), fire (red) and horn (yellow). Coral blocks make great decoration for your builds, but one of the blocks surrounding each block of coral must be water or they will turn into dead coral.

3 MINING CORAL
You must mine coral blocks and coral fans with a pickaxe enchanted with silk touch if you want to collect them – if you mine them with a regular pickaxe they'll drop dead coral instead. Coral blocks can be used as decoration in your builds, but one of the blocks surrounding each block of coral must be water or they will turn into dead coral.

CORAL FANS

On top of coral blocks you'll see another type of coral – coral fans. These come in the same five variants as coral blocks. Like the block version, coral can be used as a decoration in your builds, but if it isn't placed in water it will turn to dead coral within a matter of seconds.

TIP

If you find yourself being attacked by drowned mobs, you can hollow out one of the larger coral outcrops and make a colourful emergency base.

DEAD CORAL

You'll also see some grey coral blocks and coral fans amongst all the colour – this is dead coral.

SEA PICKLES

Sea pickles are tiny, light-emitting animals. They like to live on top of coral and on the seabed in warm oceans. They can be mined by hand or with any tool. You can place sea pickles on top of solid blocks, but they'll only emit light when underwater.

33

OCEAN MONUMENTS

Ocean monuments are the largest structures in the ocean, which is why you'll only find them in the deepest waters. They're very dangerous, but worth exploring as they contain some valuable loot.

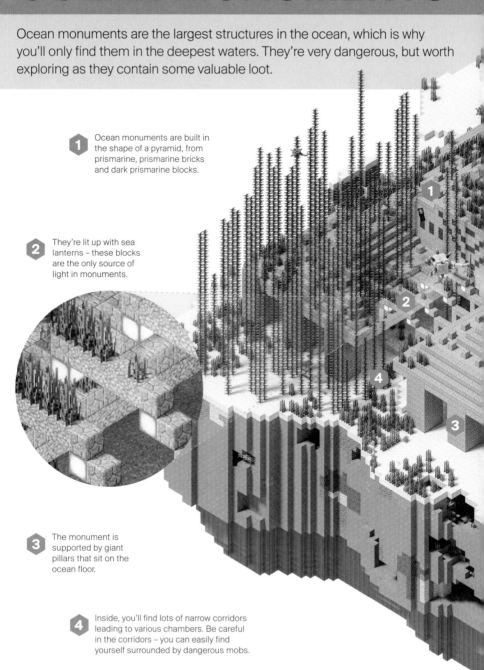

1 Ocean monuments are built in the shape of a pyramid, from prismarine, prismarine bricks and dark prismarine blocks.

2 They're lit up with sea lanterns – these blocks are the only source of light in monuments.

3 The monument is supported by giant pillars that sit on the ocean floor.

4 Inside, you'll find lots of narrow corridors leading to various chambers. Be careful in the corridors – you can easily find yourself surrounded by dangerous mobs.

5 The most important chamber for explorers is the treasure chamber. Inside, encased in dark prismarine, you'll find 8 solid gold blocks.

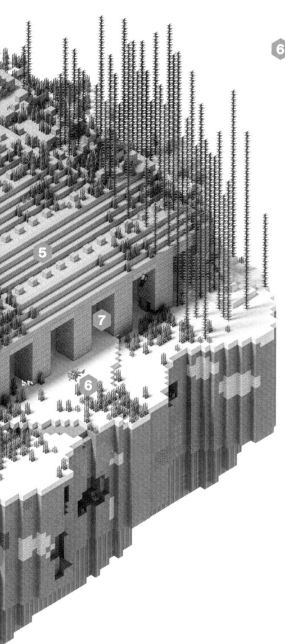

6 Guardians and elder guardians patrol the monument and protect its treasure. Find out more about how to handle these dangerous mobs on pages 48-51.

7 Some rooms are filled with wet sponge. This handy block absorbs water when dry. Ocean monuments are the only place it generates naturally, although elder guardians will drop 1 wet sponge or 1 sponge when defeated by a player.

TIP

Struggling to find an ocean monument? Cartographer villagers may have just the thing to help you out – trade with one and see if they offer you an ocean explorer map, and it will lead you right to the monument.

2

OCEAN MOBS

As we've seen, Minecraft's oceans are full of life – some of it is friendly and some of it is extremely dangerous. In this section we'll take a closer look at the creatures you'll meet beneath the water so you can recognise friend from foe.

FISH

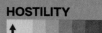
Wherever you go in the ocean, you're sure to see plenty of fish. These passive mobs come in several different varieties and they each behave in different ways. Let's find out where you'll find each one and what they drop.

HOSTILITY

Indicates the hostility level of a mob – yellow is passive, orange is neutral and red is hostile.

1 COD

You'll find cod in normal, lukewarm and cold areas of ocean. They like to swim in groups of up to 9. They drop 1 raw cod when defeated, which restores 2 food points, and 5 food points if cooked.

2 SALMON

Salmon spawn in cold and frozen oceans, and will also spawn in rivers. There are 3 sizes – small, regular and large. They swim around in groups of 3-5. Salmon are also capable of swimming up waterfalls. They drop 1 raw salmon when defeated, which restores 2 food points, and 6 food points if cooked.

3 PUFFERFISH

Pufferfish prefer lukewarm and warm oceans and can often be found hiding in coral reefs. Pufferfish can be defensive and will puff up when near hostile mobs. If you approach a pufferfish when it's puffed up, it will inflict 7 seconds of poison, and if you touch it, you'll take more damage. Like salmon, they can also swim up waterfalls. They drop 1 pufferfish when defeated – it's not a good idea to eat pufferfish as they inflict hunger, poison and nausea. They will, however, come in handy for brewing a potion of water breathing.

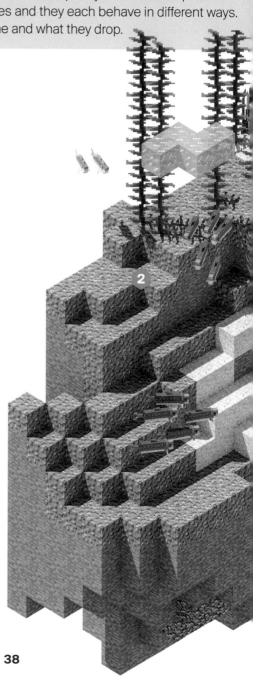

TROPICAL FISH

Tropical fish only spawn in lukewarm and warm oceans. There are 22 common varieties, but there are 2 possible shapes, 15 colours, 6 patterns and 15 pattern colour options, giving a total of 2700 possible combinations! They will drop 1 tropical fish when defeated, which restores 1 food point.

FISH BUCKETS

This handy item allows you to transport fish from one place to another, which means you can make your very own aquarium! If you use a water bucket or an empty bucket on a fish, the fish will be scooped up into the bucket, turning it into a fish bucket. To place the fish back into the world, just hit the 'use item' button.

SQUID

HEALTH POINTS	10	
ATTACK STRENGTH	0	
ITEMS DROPPED		

1-3   1-3

SPAWN LOCATION
In any area of ocean.

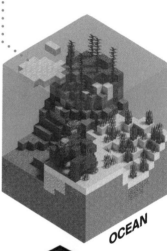

OCEAN

MOJANG STUFF

During Beta, squids didn't despawn when you moved away from them, so players kept them as pets! We had to change that, though, because at the time they could only swim downwards and they'd collect in writhing masses on the seabed that wouldn't go away ...

BEHAVIOUR

These passive creatures spawn in the ocean in groups of up to 4. They propel themselves through the water using their tentacles. They have a large mouth full of teeth on their underside – this can sometimes alarm explorers, but squid are harmless and will never use their teeth to hurt you. They can't survive out of water and will suffocate if beached.

USEFUL DROPS

As well as experience points, squid drop 1-3 ink sacs when defeated, which can be used to dye things black. Try crafting a bed or glass with an ink sac to see the result.

SPECIAL SKILLS

Squid can produce a cloud of black ink as a defence mechanism when attacked. This obscures their attacker's vision, allowing them to escape. They will swim away from a player or a guardian if attacked.

TURTLES

HEALTH POINTS	30
ATTACK STRENGTH	0
ITEMS DROPPED	

0-2   1   1-3

SPAWN LOCATION

On warm beaches.

BEACH

MOJANG STUFF

The idea for the turtle originally came from Reddit user billyK_, who mounted a two-year campaign for them as a replacement for boats, and suggested their shells could be used as helmets.

TIP

Undead mobs like zombies, drowned and skeletons will try to stamp on turtle eggs and will attack baby turtles, too. Wild ocelots and wild wolves will also attack baby turtles. Keep an eye out for these mobs and make sure you fend them off before they do any damage.

BEHAVIOUR

Turtles spawn in small groups. They are strong swimmers and can often be seen exploring the ocean, but move much more slowly on land. They are passive and will retreat if attacked by a player or other mob.

USEFUL DROPS

Turtles may drop up to 2 pieces of seagrass when defeated, but nobody wants to see such a sad event. Baby turtles drop a scute when they grow up, and this can be used to craft a turtle shell. See page 12 for a reminder of the recipe.

SPECIAL SKILLS

Feed 2 turtles seagrass and they will breed. One of the turtles will then return to its home beach (the beach where it spawned), find a sand block and lay 1-4 turtle eggs. These take a while to hatch so you'll need to keep an eye on them over a period of a few days and nights. They go through two stages of cracking before finally hatching to reveal a baby turtle.

DOLPHINS

HEALTH POINTS	10
ATTACK STRENGTH	2-4
ITEMS DROPPED	

0-1

SPAWN LOCATION

Dolphins spawn in all areas of ocean except for frozen ocean.

OCEAN

MOJANG STUFF

There are lots of scary and dangerous things in the ocean and the dolphin was our way of making it a bit friendlier. But they were pretty annoying while we developed them. They kept accidentally destroying our boats when they jumped out of the water!

BEHAVIOUR

Dolphins are intelligent and friendly. They swim around in large groups and can often be seen jumping in and out of the water. They will avoid guardians and elder guardians. They need air every so often but can't survive for long out of the water. If they find themselves on land they will try to find a body of water.

USEFUL DROPS

In the unfortunate event of a dolphin's demise, they may drop 1 raw cod. It's something to be avoided, so make sure you do everything you can to keep the dolphins happy!

SPECIAL SKILLS

Dolphins have been known to chase after player in boats. They can also give a speed boost to players who swim near them. If you drop an item in the ocean, dolphins will come over to investigate – they'll knock the item around and chase after it. If you attack a dolphin, the entire group will become hostile towards the attacker. If you feed dolphins raw cod or raw salmon, they will begin to trust you, which means they'll interact with you more. Once you've fed them, they'll lead you to the nearest loot chest in an underwater ruin or shipwreck to say thank you.

DROWNED

HEALTH POINTS	20
ATTACK STRENGTH	2-9
HOW TO DEFEAT	
ITEMS DROPPED	

0-2   0-1   0-1   5

MOJANG STUFF

We made sure that the drowned really don't like being far from water. If, during the day, they're prevented from being able to get back to water, they become passive. Once they get soggy again they'll return to fighting form.

SPAWN LOCATION

In all areas of ocean except for warm ocean as well as rivers and swamps.

OCEAN

BEHAVIOUR

Drowned mobs spawn in water at light levels of 7 or lower. They also spawn in rivers and swamps. Like zombies, they will attack you with their hands. They will come up onto dry land at night, where they will stamp on turtle eggs and attack baby turtles as well as players. They will also chase after villagers and iron golems.

SPECIAL SKILLS

Drowned may spawn with a trident – a powerful weapon that can be thrown at enemies. They may also spawn with a fishing rod, or with a nautilus shell, which is needed to craft a conduit. More about conduits on pages 56-59.

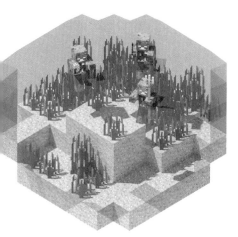

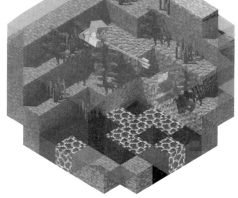

USEFUL DROPS

Drowned may drop their trident if they're holding one. Find more about this weapon on pages 54-55. They may also drop a gold ingot.

HOW TO DEFEAT

Hit the drowned with a diamond sword. You can also use its own weapon against it and attack it with a trident, or use a bow.

DID YOU KNOW?

Drowned are a variant of zombies. If a zombie is submerged in water for 30 seconds it will turn into a drowned. You'll know this is happening if the submerged zombie starts to shake.

GUARDIANS

HEALTH POINTS	30
ATTACK STRENGTH	4-9
HOW TO DEFEAT	
ITEMS DROPPED	0-2 0-2 0-1 0-1 0-1 0-1

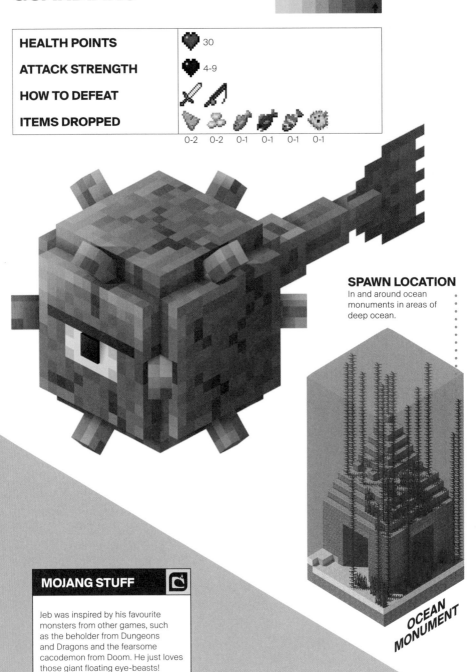

SPAWN LOCATION
In and around ocean monuments in areas of deep ocean.

OCEAN MONUMENT

MOJANG STUFF

Jeb was inspired by his favourite monsters from other games, such as the beholder from Dungeons and Dragons and the fearsome cacodemon from Doom. He just loves those giant floating eye-beasts!

BEHAVIOUR

Guardians are found swimming around ocean monuments – their job is to protect the treasure inside the monuments. They attack players and squid on sight, shooting a laser that deals 4-9 points of damage, depending on the level of difficulty your game is set to. This laser has a range of up to 15 blocks. Guardians can also attack with their spikes, which can deal 2 points of damage.

USEFUL DROPS

Guardians may drop prismarine shards or prismarine crystals, which can be crafted into blocks of prismarine and sea lanterns. They may also drop raw fish, although this is rare.

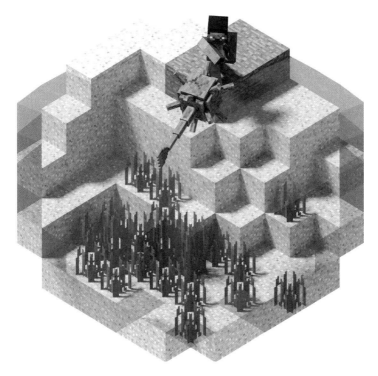

HOW TO DEFEAT

Hit the guardian repeatedly with a diamond sword or stand on land and use a fishing rod to pull it out of the water, then hit it with your diamond sword.

SPECIAL SKILLS

Guardians can live out of water, although they won't be happy about it – they'll squeak angrily at any nearby players and flop around, trying to find water.

ELDER GUARDIANS

HEALTH POINTS	80
ATTACK STRENGTH	2-12
HOW TO DEFEAT	
ITEMS DROPPED	0-2 0-2 0-1 0-1 0-1 0-1 1

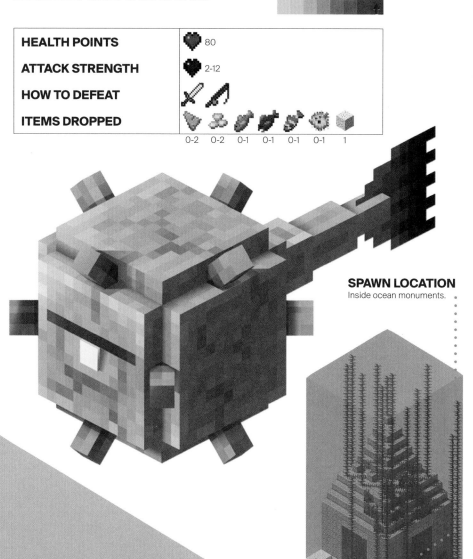

SPAWN LOCATION
Inside ocean monuments.

OCEAN MONUMENT

MOJANG STUFF

The elder guardian's mining fatigue effect was Jeb's solution to prevent players from simply mining their way through the ocean monument to get to its precious loot!

BEHAVIOUR

You'll find three elder guardians inside each ocean monument – one in the top room and one in each of the two wings. They are also there to guard the monument's treasure. They attack players on sight with the same laser attack as guardians.

SPECIAL SKILLS

Elder guardians can inflict mining fatigue III on players who dare to venture into the monument. You'll know this is happening to you if a ghostly version of the elder guardian begins to circle you. The effect lasts for 5 minutes – any blocks you mine will break more slowly and your attack speed is reduced. Like guardians, elder guardians won't suffocate on dry land.

USEFUL DROPS

Elder guardians will drop 1 sponge block when defeated. Sponge blocks absorb water so they can be used to clear water from your underwater base.

HOW TO DEFEAT

Hit the elder guardian with your diamond sword or stand on land and use a fishing rod to pull it out of the water, then hit it with your diamond sword.

3

SURVIVAL TIPS

Now that we've explored the ocean's structures and mobs, it's clear that the ocean is a very dangerous place. But fear not! This section is full of survival tips, from how to enchant a trident and craft a conduit to building an underwater farm.

TRIDENTS

Tridents can't be crafted – you'll only be able to get your hands on one if a drowned mob drops it when defeated. This rare and powerful weapon can be used in hand-to-hand combat, or from a distance to take out your foes. Let's find out how it works – it's going to make your life much easier.

MELEE ATTACK

Melee means hand-to-hand, or close-quarters combat. If you hit the 'use item' button while holding a trident, you will deal 2 points more damage than if you were holding a diamond sword.

RANGED ATTACK

Hold down the 'use item' button for a few seconds to charge your trident and aim it at the mob or player you want to attack. When you release the button, the trident will be launched towards your target. If it makes contact with a mob or player, it will bounce off them and fall to the ground nearby. If it hits a block it will become embedded in that block.

ENCHANTING YOUR TRIDENT

You can enchant a trident on an enchantment table to give it several useful effects. Let's take a look at each effect and how it can help you.

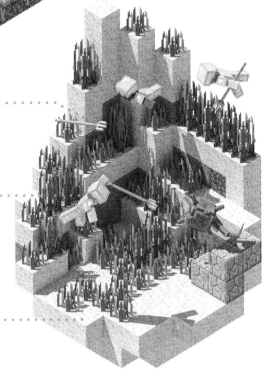

CHANNELING
This only works during thunderstorms. It summons a lightning bolt when a mob is hit by a thrown trident, so the mob is set on fire.

RIPTIDE
It will drag you in the direction the trident is thrown. If you hit a mob or another player, they will be dealt damage. You can use this enchantment to travel to out-of-reach spots.

MENDING
This allows you to repair your trident using your experience points. Hold the trident in your hand, and any experience points you collect will repair the item – 2 durability points are repaired per experience point.

LOYALTY
The loyalty enchantment makes your trident come back to you after you've thrown it. This is very handy – you don't want to lose such a valuable weapon!

IMPALING
Impaling will add 2.5 extra damage points to each hit for aquatic mobs – that's dolphins, fish, squid, turtles, elder guardians and guardians. It won't work on drowned mobs as they're classed as undead.

UNBREAKING
This effect increases your trident's durability so it will last longer – like other tools and weapons, a trident will eventually break.

CONDUITS

Wouldn't it be brilliant if there was a way to breathe, see and mine quickly whilst underwater, without having to rely on enchantments and potions? That's where the conduit comes in – this clever block acts like a beacon and provides you with these abilities when you're within range.

 To craft a conduit you'll need 8 nautilus shells and 1 heart of the sea. Nautilus shells are sometimes dropped by drowned mobs and can be caught when fishing. You can find a heart of the sea in every buried treasure chest.

2 Choose a spot for your conduit. When surrounded by an activation frame, it will provide its effect to any players who are within a spherical range of 32-96 blocks, so you might want to place it next to an underwater base.

3 Place your conduit in the centre of a 3 x 3 cube of water. Try building a few blocks up from the ocean floor in your chosen spot, placing the conduit on top of these blocks, then removing them so the conduit is floating in position.

DID YOU KNOW?

Conduits also give off light – they provide a light level of 15, which is the maximum possible and the equivalent of full daylight.

TIP

Once you have enough materials you can build several conduits and position them across the ocean floor so you'll benefit from the conduit status effect wherever you go.

6 As an added bonus, if you build all 3 rings, the conduit will attack any hostile mobs that come within 8 blocks of it, dealing 4 points of damage every 2 seconds.

5 You'll know you built your activation frame correctly when the conduit block expands to reveal its heart of the sea core and begins to move. You'll also hear what sounds like a heartbeat. You'll be able to breathe underwater, see clearly and mine quickly while you're within range.

4 Surround this 3 x 3 cube of water with up to 3 square rings, each 5 x 5 blocks, centred around the conduit. The rings must be made from prismarine, dark prismarine, prismarine bricks or sea lanterns, so you'll need to visit an ocean monument before you can build the frame. 1 square ring is enough to activate the conduit, but 3 will maximise the conduit's power.

57

CONDUIT STRUCTURES

Conduits will soon become essential to your underwater adventures. So, why not build something a little more permanent for them to sit in? Here are some fun conduit structure ideas for you to try.

THE TREASURE CHEST

The heart of the sea is one of the ocean's most valuable treasures, so why not place your conduit inside a treasure chest? This one's built from wood planks as a nod to the many shipwrecks on the ocean floor. The insides are lined with prismarine and some solid blocks of gold, diamond and emerald.

Cover parts of the chest in seagrass to make it feel overgrown.

THE TREE

Trees don't grow under the ocean, so this structure will really add some drama. It's built from various prismarine blocks and looks like a new, aquatic variety of tree. The blocks are placed strategically so that they activate the conduit without forming solid rings.

Dark prismarine has been used to build the trunk, while regular prismarine looks great for the leaves.

THE TOWER

For this design, simply build your conduit activation structure on top of a decorative pillar. This pillar is made from a combination of prismarine blocks and quartz, with some mossy stone bricks for variety.

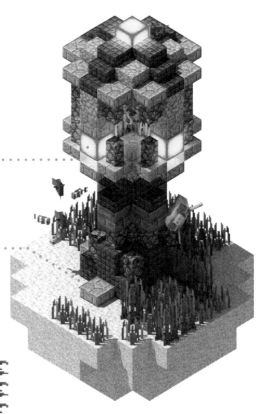

Sea lanterns are a fitting light source for this tower.

Slab blocks and wall blocks help add smaller details.

THE THRONE

Set your conduit in pride of place on top of this giant prismarine throne. Prismarine stair blocks are useful for creating smaller details for the back and sides of the throne, as well as steps at the front leading up to the conduit.

DID YOU KNOW?

It's possible to activate a conduit without using the exact activation frame design on pages 56-57. As long as there are 16 blocks around the 3 x 3 cube of water, the conduit will still be activated.

CORAL HOUSE

Now that you're an experienced underwater explorer, why not make yourself a more permanent base of operations on the ocean floor? This colourful coral house build is the perfect underwater starter home, and it's dry inside! Follow these steps to build your own coral house.

YOU WILL NEED:

SCHEMATICS

These plans show the coral house from various perspectives so you can see how it's constructed. It's built from various sand, prismarine and coral blocks. Inside there are two floors, with plenty of space for all your underwater supplies.

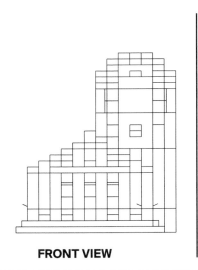

FRONT VIEW

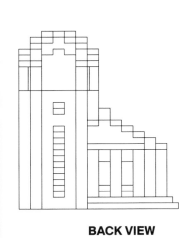

BACK VIEW

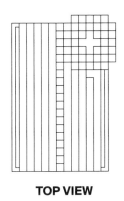

TOP VIEW

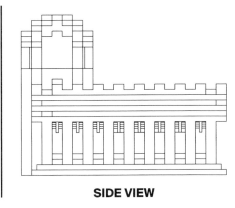

SIDE VIEW

IDEAL LOCATION

This house is particularly well suited to an area of warm ocean. A coral garden has been designed around the outside of the house, but it would also sit well next to a naturally-occuring coral reef.

WARM OCEAN

CORAL HOUSE EXTERIOR

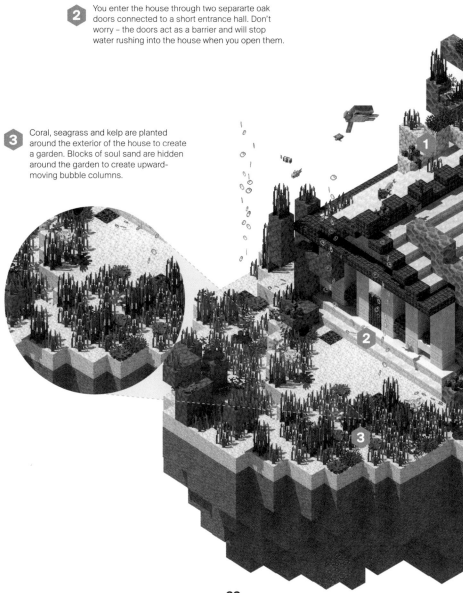

1 The combination of blocks used to build this house help it blend into the seabed and coral reefs.

2 You enter the house through two separarte oak doors connected to a short entrance hall. Don't worry – the doors act as a barrier and will stop water rushing into the house when you open them.

3 Coral, seagrass and kelp are planted around the exterior of the house to create a garden. Blocks of soul sand are hidden around the garden to create upward-moving bubble columns.

4 The windows provide a clear view of the surrounding area. They're made from glass blocks and positioned at various heights across the build.

5 Coral fans placed on slab blocks make colourful window boxes. We've used a combination of prismarine slabs and quartz slabs.

6 Sea lanterns are the perfect light source for this house. They've been placed underneath the overhanging eaves of the roof to light up the exterior of the house.

CORAL HOUSE INTERIOR

1 This house has a large ground floor, which is divided into different areas. There's also a tower that is accessible via a ladder.

2 Sea lanterns are the perfect lighting for the interior, too. Some are built into the ceiling, others into the walls and floor.

3 Use sponge blocks to absorb the water inside the house so you don't have to worry about breathing. Keep placing them until all the water has been absorbed.

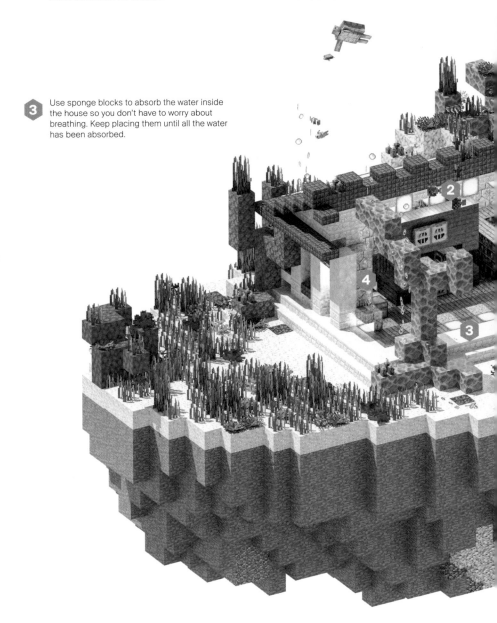

4 Set up a crafting area in an easily-accessible part of your house. You'll need a crafting table, a furnace and a chest for supplies, so you can put everything you collect on your underwater adventures to good use.

5 The floor is lined with sponge blocks. This works well with the ocean theme and acts as a flood prevention feature – if water is accidentally let into your house, some of it will be absorbed by the sponge.

6 Make sure you have everything you need to enchant your trident or quickly brew potions of water breathing and night vision. Set up an enchantment table, bookshelves, a brewing stand, a cauldron and a chest full of supplies like lapis lazuli, blaze powder and potion ingredients.

UNDERWATER FARM

Most food sources and plants are only found back on dry land, so it's worth taking the time to build yourself an underwater farm. That way, if you run out of wood or have a sudden craving for cookies you'll be able to remedy the situation without returning to the surface.

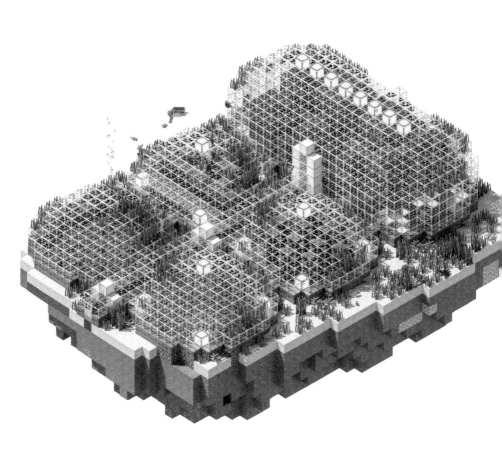

YOU WILL NEED:

SCHEMATICS

These plans show the underwater farm from various perspectives so you can see how it's built. It's enclosed in a large glass structure that looks a bit like a greenhouse, and divided into several sections for different crops.

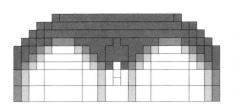

FRONT VIEW

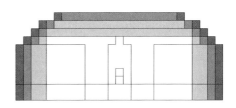

BACK VIEW

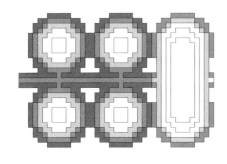

TOP VIEW

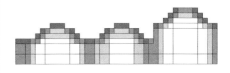

SIDE VIEW

IDEAL LOCATION

You'll need a fair bit of space to accommodate this farm, so find a clear area of ocean floor near your house or base. You could even join the farm onto the side of your house so you can access it safely whenever you like.

OCEAN

UNDERWATER FARM STRUCTURE

1 Enclose your farm in a glass structure so you can keep an eye on it from outside. This design looks like several dome-shaped greenhouses from the outside, but they're joined together by a long walkway down the middle.

2 Connecting your crop farm to your underwater base ensures you can always access it safely. You could build a tunnel linking the two structures or build the farm directly to the side of your base so you can visit your farm whenever you like.

3 Make sure you can access all areas of your farm without having to trample over seeds by constructing pathways between each section.

This farm consists of several 9 x 9 areas, each containing a different plant or crop. Turn the page for a reminder of the growing conditions each plant or crop requires in order to thrive.

 Most plants and crops need light to grow, so make sure every area of your farm is lit with sea lanterns or torches. Mushrooms are an exception – there's more info about mushrooms on page 70.

PLANTS AND CROPS

1 You can grow wheat, carrots, potatoes and beetroot in the usual way. Place dirt blocks and till them using a hoe, then plant wheat seeds, carrots, potatoes and beetroot seeds. Make sure each plant is at most 4 blocks away from water – the block in the centre of each field is a water block covered with a trapdoor.

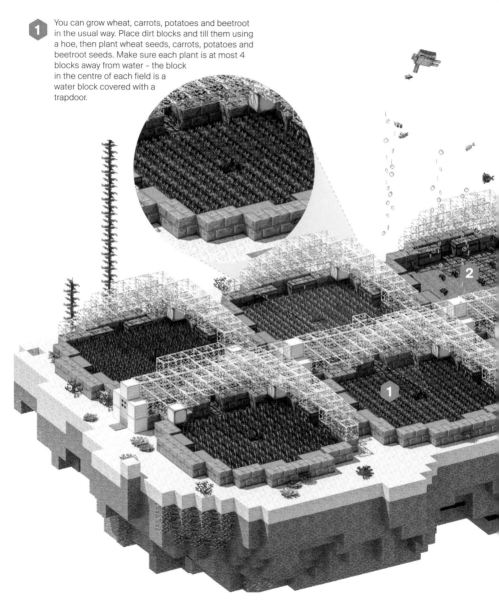

2 Mushrooms usually prefer the dark, but plant them on podzol or mycelium blocks and they'll grow at any light level. You can find mycelium in mushroom field biomes and podzol in giant tree taiga biomes. Mycelium can only be mined with a tool enchanted with silk touch, otherwise it will just drop dirt.

3 You'll need melons if you want to craft glistering melon so that you can brew potion of healing. Melon seeds can be planted in tilled dirt and will need to be within 4 blocks of water. You'll also need to leave 1 empty block of dirt next to each plant for the melon to grow into.

4 Plant oak saplings in dirt to provide you with a renewable source of wood. Saplings will need at least 4 empty blocks above them. Try spacing them 4 blocks apart so they have plenty of space to grow. Oak saplings are better than other types of sapling because the leaves may drop apples when broken.

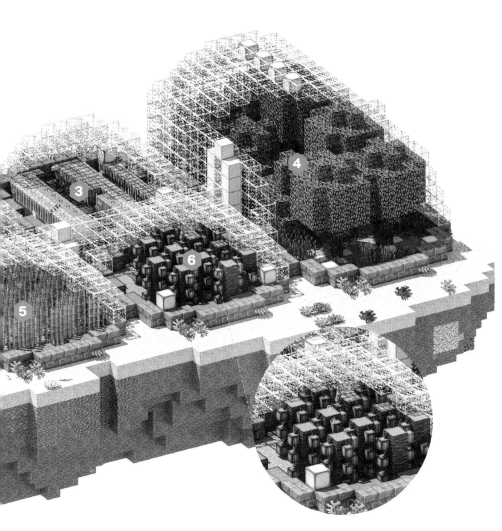

5 You'll need sugar to make fermented spider eye, which in turn is needed to brew various potions. Plant sugar canes on dirt, podzol or sand right next to water.

6 You don't need an entire jungle tree to grow cocoa beans – a few blocks of jungle wood will be enough. Place cocoa beans on the side of jungle wood and a new cocoa pod will form. Remember to wait until the pod is an orange-brown colour before you harvest it, or it won't drop anything. You can then craft cocoa beans with wheat to make cookies. Yum!

OCEAN OBSERVATORY

Now that you have plenty of experience building underwater, why not go one step further and construct an entire ocean observatory? This expansive structure allows you to study ocean life from complete safety.

YOU WILL NEED:

SCHEMATICS

These plans show the ocean observatory from various perspectives so you can see how it's constructed. The entrance is above sea level but the observatory sits just above the ocean floor.

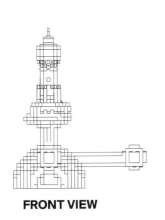

FRONT VIEW

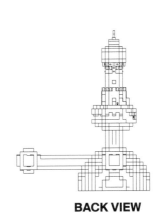

BACK VIEW

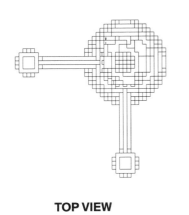

TOP VIEW

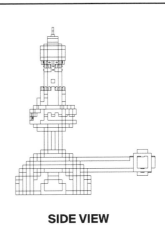

SIDE VIEW

OCEAN

IDEAL LOCATION

This observatory can be built anywhere, but the ideal location would be at the boundary between two or more different areas of ocean. That way, you can study the widest possible variety of ocean life without having to leave the observatory.

OCEAN OBSERVATORY EXTERIOR

1 The entrance to the observatory is above sea level, on an island that can be reached by boat. The entrance also doubles as a lighthouse with a giant glowstone lamp at the top, so it's easy to spot at night.

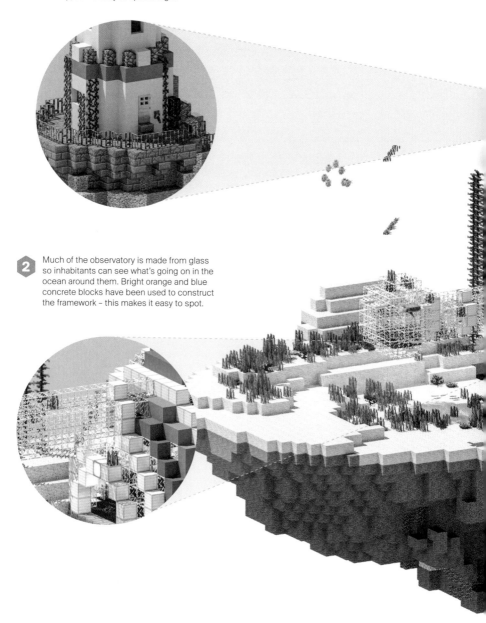

2 Much of the observatory is made from glass so inhabitants can see what's going on in the ocean around them. Bright orange and blue concrete blocks have been used to construct the framework – this makes it easy to spot.

3 A large concrete dome lies at the centre of the observatory. It has two floors – the bottom floor is open so you can swim out into the ocean.

4 Several glass tunnels lead from the central dome to smaller stations. These stations have been built in particularly interesting areas of ocean – above a ravine which produces bubble columns, for example, and next to some underwater ruins.

OCEAN OBSERVATORY INTERIOR

1 A crafting area has been set up on the top floor of the central dome. Inhabitants can craft, brew and enchant all the supplies they need to go on ocean expeditions.

2 Near the crafting area is a kitchen where explorers can cook any fish they've collected. There are also stores of other food items here like steak, pork chops and cake.

3 The bottom floor of the central dome has no base and is open to the ocean. It looks a bit like a swimming pool from above, but swim downwards and you'll find yourself in open ocean. Ladders are positioned every few blocks around the pool to help divers climb in and out. Be careful – drowned mobs might be able to climb up these ladders, so keep an eye out for unwanted guests.

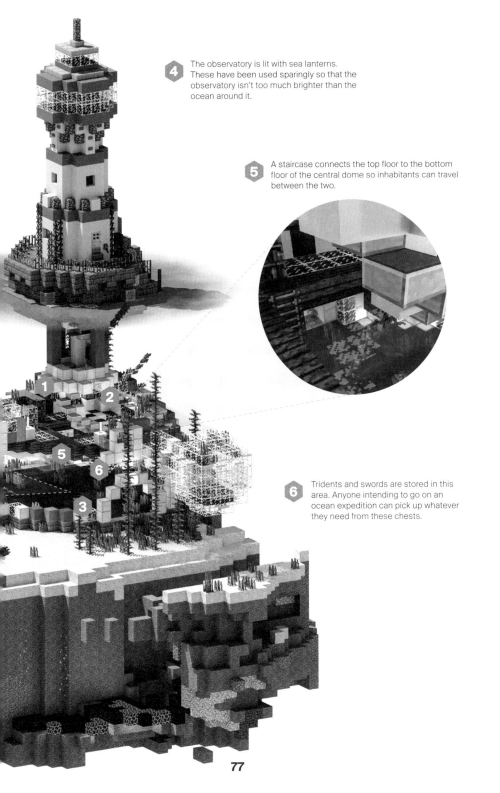

4 The observatory is lit with sea lanterns. These have been used sparingly so that the observatory isn't too much brighter than the ocean around it.

5 A staircase connects the top floor to the bottom floor of the central dome so inhabitants can travel between the two.

6 Tridents and swords are stored in this area. Anyone intending to go on an ocean expedition can pick up whatever they need from these chests.

FINAL WORDS

Well then, now you're looking ready to jump in! You must be feeling pretty excited about getting to practise everything you've learned. Take care down there, and we wish you the very best of luck in finding every fabulous treasure the ocean can offer. Thanks for playing!

ALEX WILTSHIRE
THE MOJANG TEAM

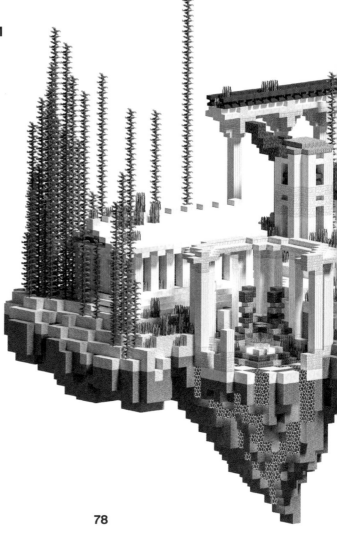

79

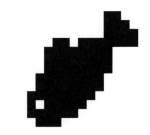

First published in Great Britain 2018 by Egmont UK Limited.
This edition published in 2020 by Dean, an imprint of Egmont UK Limited,
2 Minster Court, 10th Floor, London EC3R 7BB

Written by Alex Wiltshire
Edited by Stephanie Milton
Designed by Joe Bolder & Ant Duke
Illustrations by Sam Ross
Cover designed by John Stuckey
Cover illustration by BSmart
Production by Louis Harvey and Laura Grundy
Special thanks to Owen Jones, Martin Johansson and Marsh Davies.

ISBN 978 0 6035 7928 8

71019/001

Printed in China

ONLINE SAFETY FOR YOUNGER FANS

Spending time online is great fun! Here are a few simple rules to help younger fans stay safe and
keep the internet a great place to spend time:

- Never give out your real name – don't use it as your username.
- Never give out any of your personal details.
- Never tell anybody which school you go to or how old you are.
- Never tell anybody your password except a parent or a guardian.
- Be aware that you must be 13 or over to create an account on many sites. Always check the
site policy and ask a parent or guardian for permission before registering.
- Always tell a parent or guardian if something is worrying you.

Stay safe online. Any website addresses listed in this book are correct at the time of going
to print. However, Egmont is not responsible for content hosted by third parties. Please be
aware that online content can be subject to change and websites can contain content that is
unsuitable for children. We advise that all children are supervised when using the internet.

Egmont takes its responsibility to the planet and its inhabitants very seriously.
We aim to use papers from well-managed forests run by responsible suppliers.

GUITE TO:

FARMING

CONTENTS

INTRODUCTION

Welcome to the official Guide to Farming! There are many ways to play Minecraft, but one of the most satisfying is journeying through Survival mode to the End. Along the way you'll need many items and blocks, and creating them quickly and efficiently is what farming is all about.

Figuring out systems to do the work for you is fun, and they're fulfilling to watch in action. This guide shows you what you can produce, why you'd want to produce it, and how. It starts with growing crops and moves on to livestock, and then turns to farming hostile mobs, finally finishing with generating blocks.

As farming at its purest is about making the resources you need to survive and venture onwards, the focus here is on farms that are practical, using few rare resources while being safe and straightforward to build and use. They're meant to be about making your Minecraft life easier, after all. But that doesn't mean you can't be a little creative and silly with them, too.

Let your inventive side loose, and enjoy!

OWEN JONES
THE MOJANG TEAM

WHAT IS FARMING?

In Survival mode you'll often find yourself needing special items, blocks and food in order to stay alive and to access new abilities and places. But you don't always have to go out on dangerous expeditions to find them. With a little ingenuity, you can make all the useful items you need, right at home.

CROPS

Learn ways of cultivating delicious crops, from simple field layouts to amazing automatic farming systems. And for when you've harvested your crops, find out what to make with them.

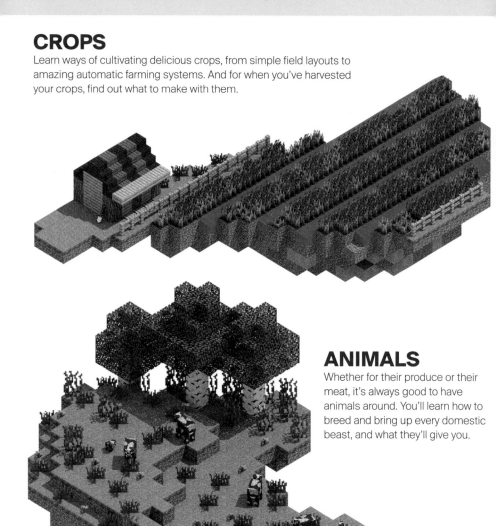

ANIMALS

Whether for their produce or their meat, it's always good to have animals around. You'll learn how to breed and bring up every domestic beast, and what they'll give you.

HOSTILE MOBS

Hostile mobs drop precious treasures and can even grant you experience when you kill them. Farming them takes great care and isn't for the faint of heart, but will reap you big rewards.

BLOCKS

If you're a builder or landscaper with a mind to creating something huge, you can produce many of the materials you need to construct your vision instead of having to find them in the wild.

FARMING BASICS

To make the most of farming, it's very useful to have knowledge of some of the common tools, items, concepts and processes that it involves. Let's take a quick look at some key elements.

HOPPERS AND CHESTS

Many farming systems use hoppers to automatically collect produce and send them to a chest. They suck in any item that touches their top. To connect hoppers, first place the chest in which you want the produce to end up, then, while crouching, place a hopper on either its sides or above. Connect more hoppers as required, always while crouching. Remember that things can only go across or down through hoppers, never up.

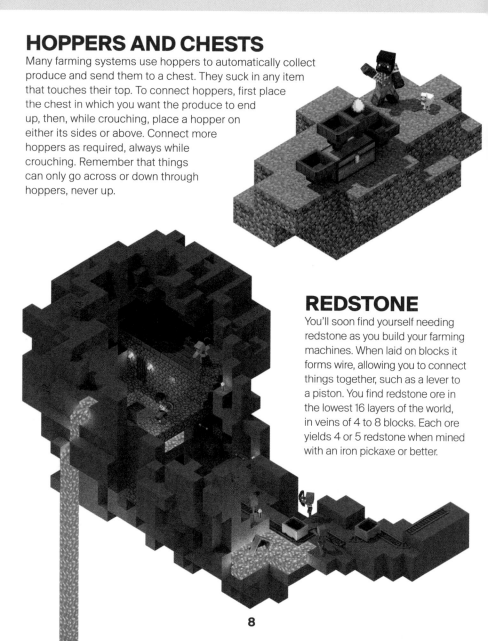

REDSTONE

You'll soon find yourself needing redstone as you build your farming machines. When laid on blocks it forms wire, allowing you to connect things together, such as a lever to a piston. You find redstone ore in the lowest 16 layers of the world, in veins of 4 to 8 blocks. Each ore yields 4 or 5 redstone when mined with an iron pickaxe or better.

LIGHT

Many crops will only grow if there is enough light, and many mobs only appear in the dark. There are 16 levels of light. The brightest is 15, which is the Overworld's surface on a sunny day. The darkest is 0, when you can't see anything. A torch creates 14 light, but with each block's distance from a source of light, its brightness drops by one. So the block right next to a torch has a light value of 13, and the one next to that is 12. Consider light levels if crops are not growing or if mobs are not spawning.

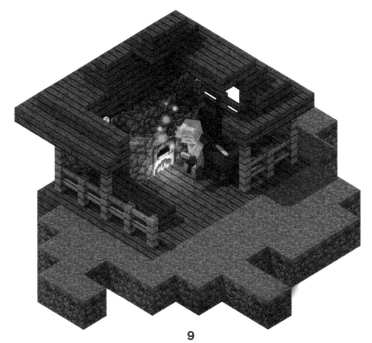

EXPERIENCE

Whenever you perform certain actions, such as defeating hostile mobs, mining ores and smelting, you earn experience. You can spend it on enchanting tools, weapons and armour with enchantment tables and anvils. Many enchantments make farming quicker, easier and more effective!

1

FARMING CROPS

In this section you'll learn what plants you can grow and how they'll feed you, how to bring in bumper harvests by planting perfect fields, and also how to construct amazing farming machines that will do all the hard work for you.

PRINCIPLES OF CROP FARMING

Growing your own food will save you hours of hunting for it, or having to go hungry. Here's what you need to know to get started, and what tools and space will help you establish your fields and grow your crops successfully.

1 For most crops, fields should start as flat land with a surface layer of dirt blocks. Consider building them near a source of water for easy access.

IRON BUCKET RECIPE

2 Most crops need water to grow at their full rate, so ensure you plant within 4 blocks of water. Without water nearby they'll still slowly grow, but any unused farmland will quickly revert to dirt. Dig channels and place water in them with a bucket.

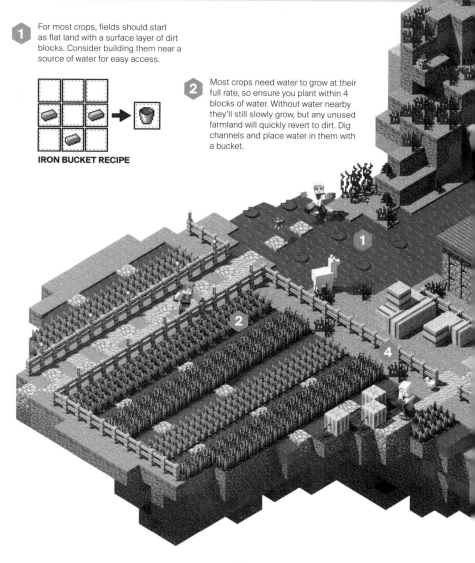

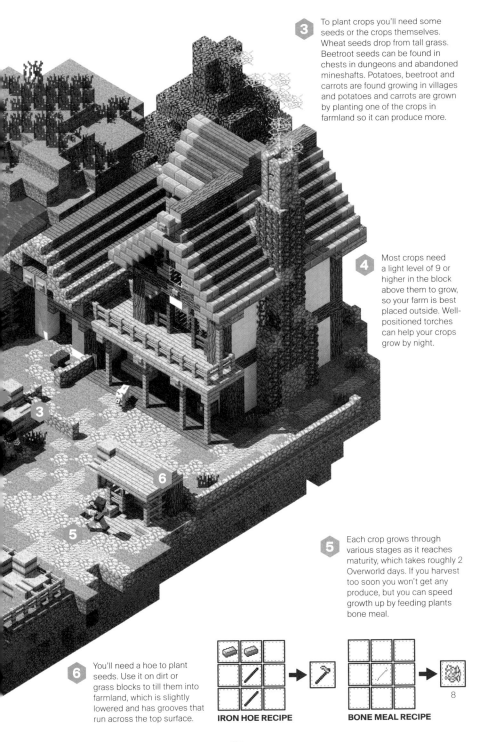

3 To plant crops you'll need some seeds or the crops themselves. Wheat seeds drop from tall grass. Beetroot seeds can be found in chests in dungeons and abandoned mineshafts. Potatoes, beetroot and carrots are found growing in villages and potatoes and carrots are grown by planting one of the crops in farmland so it can produce more.

4 Most crops need a light level of 9 or higher in the block above them to grow, so your farm is best placed outside. Well-positioned torches can help your crops grow by night.

5 Each crop grows through various stages as it reaches maturity, which takes roughly 2 Overworld days. If you harvest too soon you won't get any produce, but you can speed growth up by feeding plants bone meal.

6 You'll need a hoe to plant seeds. Use it on dirt or grass blocks to till them into farmland, which is slightly lowered and has grooves that run across the top surface.

IRON HOE RECIPE

BONE MEAL RECIPE

8

WHEAT, CARROTS, POTATOES & BEETROOT

Wheat, carrots, potatoes and beetroot grow in similar ways, so they can be farmed together using the same farming methods. Let's take a look at how these crops behave, and how to grow them in the most efficient way.

WHEAT

One of the first crops you'll farm, wheat makes delicious baked products and can be used to breed cows, sheep, mooshrooms and tame horses (see pages 36-40).

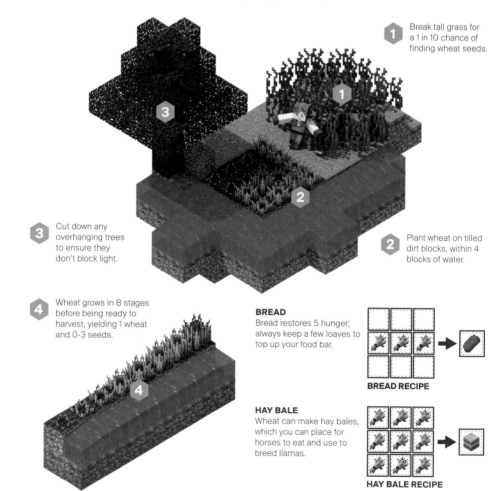

1 Break tall grass for a 1 in 10 chance of finding wheat seeds.

3 Cut down any overhanging trees to ensure they don't block light.

2 Plant wheat on tilled dirt blocks, within 4 blocks of water.

4 Wheat grows in 8 stages before being ready to harvest, yielding 1 wheat and 0-3 seeds.

BREAD
Bread restores 5 hunger; always keep a few loaves to top up your food bar.

BREAD RECIPE

HAY BALE
Wheat can make hay bales, which you can place for horses to eat and use to breed llamas.

HAY BALE RECIPE

CARROTS

You can use carrots to breed rabbits and pigs, or you can eat them yourself. Carrots are a useful food to farm, but they can be tricky to get hold of.

 Find carrots in village fields and chests, and as rare drops from zombies.

 Plant carrots within 4 blocks of water so they grow at full speed.

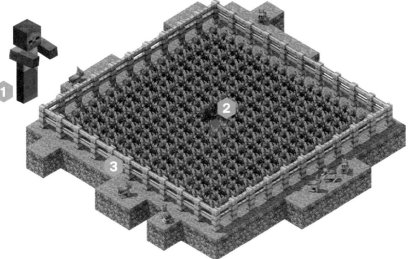

 Build a fence around your field to keep hungry rabbits from eating your crops.

 Harvest 1-4 carrots from each plant when you can see them poking out of the ground.

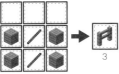

WOOD FENCE RECIPE

GOLDEN CARROT
The wondrous golden carrot tames and breeds horses and donkeys, and is also the most filling food in all of Minecraft.

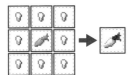

GOLDEN CARROT RECIPE

CARROT ON A STICK
To gain control over a pig you're riding with a saddle, craft a carrot on a stick!

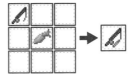

CARROT ON A STICK RECIPE

POTATO

This root vegetable is a good source of easy food because it doesn't need to be crafted with anything else to produce a nutritious meal.

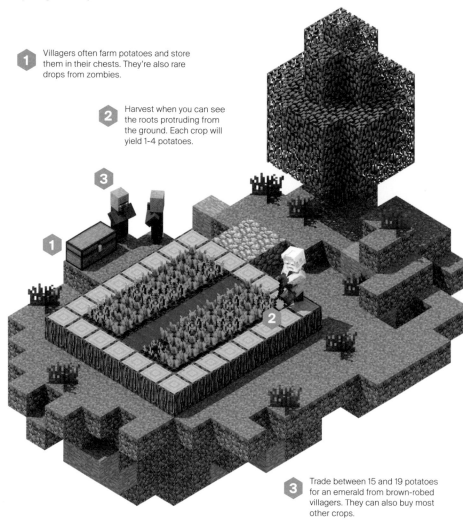

1 Villagers often farm potatoes and store them in their chests. They're also rare drops from zombies.

2 Harvest when you can see the roots protruding from the ground. Each crop will yield 1-4 potatoes.

3 Trade between 15 and 19 potatoes for an emerald from brown-robed villagers. They can also buy most other crops.

BAKED POTATO
Bake a potato in your furnace to produce a meal that restores 5 hunger.

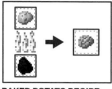

BAKED POTATO RECIPE

TIP

Watch out! Very rarely, poisonous potatoes drop as you harvest. You can recognise them by their green tinge. Eating one might poison you.

BEETROOT

Beetroot has several handy uses. You can give it to pigs to encourage them to breed, cook it to make soup, or use it to make red dye.

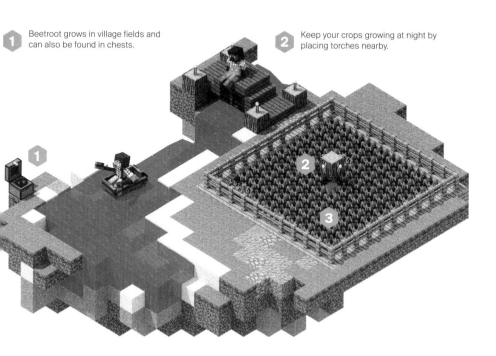

1 Beetroot grows in village fields and can also be found in chests.

2 Keep your crops growing at night by placing torches nearby.

3 Plant beetroot seeds to grow them. Harvest from plants or find them in chests outside villages.

4 Each plant yields 1 beetroot and 0-3 beetroot seeds.

BONE MEAL
Bone meal can be used on most crops to speed up their growth. It's expensive for big fields but great for helping to gather plenty of crops to sow in the first stages of establishing your fields. Bones are dropped by skeletons and often found in chests. See page 50-51 for how to farm them.

BEETROOT SOUP
Crafting beetroot with a bowl will give you beetroot soup which restores 6 hunger.

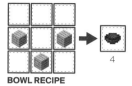

4

BOWL RECIPE

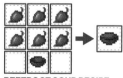

BEETROOT SOUP RECIPE

GROWTH MECHANICS

To farm wheat, carrots, potatoes and beetroot efficiently you need to understand how they grow, which means learning a little about how Minecraft works.

 Things happen during each tick. Pistons move, your hunger bar decreases, plants grow. The game chooses three random blocks in every nearby 'chunk', a 16 x 16-block area, 256 blocks high, and checks to see if it's possible for something to happen to them.

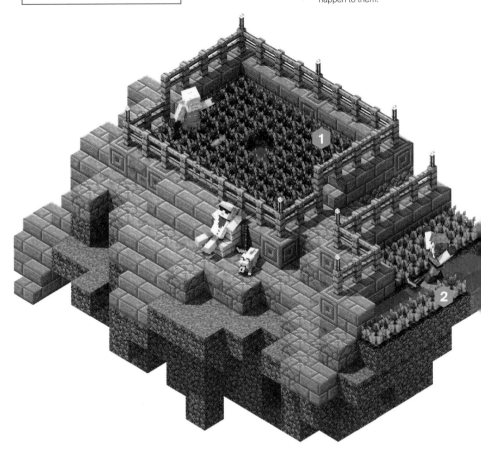

 If the selected block is your carrot plant, there's a chance it will grow to its next stage of development if the light in the block above is to be 9 or more. This is more likely to happen if it's within 4 blocks of water, and if the blocks around it are hydrated farmland. But if the 8 blocks around the plant have the same plant growing in them, it becomes half as likely to grow, unless they are in a row.

GETTING YOUR FIELD STARTED

Using these rules, we can make an efficient field. It grows crops quickly and is useful when you're building up your supplies of seeds for new crops early in the game.

Plant your crops in rows.

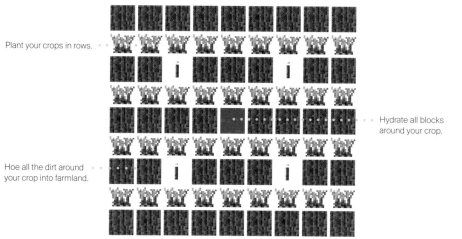

Hydrate all blocks around your crop.

Hoe all the dirt around your crop into farmland.

LATER GAME FIELD

Once you have lots of seeds and a choice of crops, fill in the gaps to use the space efficiently. This layout grows slightly slower but you'll get more out of your farm in the long term.

Suspend blocks above the field with torches on each face so they don't take up space in the field.

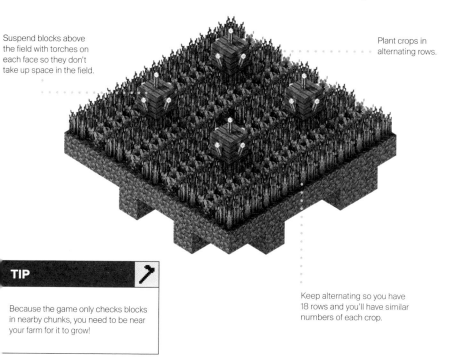

Plant crops in alternating rows.

TIP

Because the game only checks blocks in nearby chunks, you need to be near your farm for it to grow!

Keep alternating so you have 18 rows and you'll have similar numbers of each crop.

EFFICIENT FIELD DESIGN

This semi-automatic stacked wheat, carrot, potato and beetroot farm gets the most out of the available space and makes quick work of harvesting. If you need more fields, you can add as many levels as you like.

 Plant crops in alternating rows for speedy growth (see previous page).

 Place water below the glass at the edge of each field to irrigate the land.

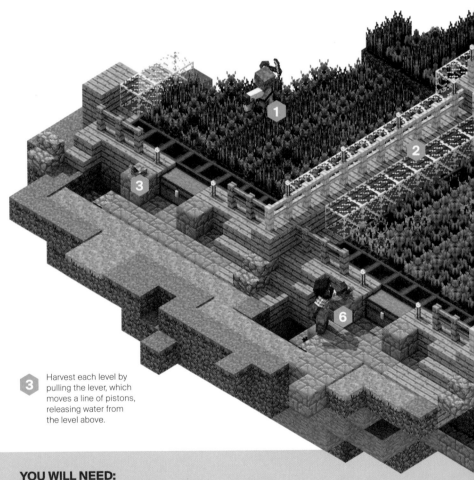

Harvest each level by pulling the lever, which moves a line of pistons, releasing water from the level above.

YOU WILL NEED:

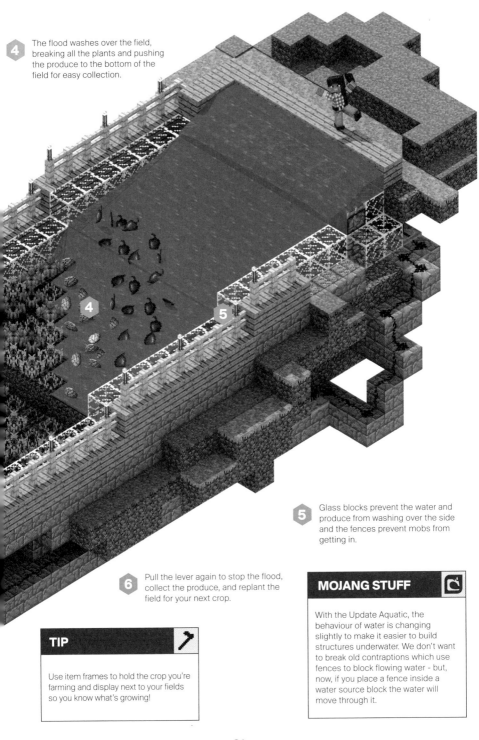

4 The flood washes over the field, breaking all the plants and pushing the produce to the bottom of the field for easy collection.

5 Glass blocks prevent the water and produce from washing over the side and the fences prevent mobs from getting in.

6 Pull the lever again to stop the flood, collect the produce, and replant the field for your next crop.

MOJANG STUFF

With the Update Aquatic, the behaviour of water is changing slightly to make it easier to build structures underwater. We don't want to break old contraptions which use fences to block flowing water - but, now, if you place a fence inside a water source block the water will move through it.

FULLY AUTOMATIC FARM

Wheat, carrots, beetroot and potatoes need to be replanted after each harvest, so it's difficult to completely automate your farms. One way it can work is with farmer villagers, who plant and harvest fields. But it takes a lot of preparation to get it going.

BUILD YOUR COLLECTION SYSTEM

With its pockets full, your villager will leave produce on the field as it harvests. A minecart with a hopper inside it running below the field will gather them and deposit them in a chest.

1 Design a rail layout that exactly matches the shape and size of the field you'll build above it.

2 Powered rails keep the minecart moving. Place one every 10 blocks or so along the track and power them from below with levers.

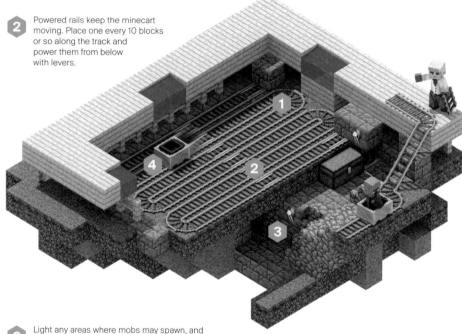

3 Light any areas where mobs may spawn, and enclose the track with a fence to prevent spiders from getting inside and stopping the minecart.

4 Craft a minecart with a hopper inside it; as it runs up and down the track it collects items on the block above at a rate of 20 a second and deposits them in a chest at the end.

YOU WILL NEED:

HIRE A VILLAGER

Finding the right kind of villager and getting it to work for you can be difficult.

Brown-robed farmer villagers will tend crops, planting and harvesting when they're mature. Your field needs to be at least 32 blocks from the edge of any village so the villager doesn't try to return home. A way of moving a villager is pushing them into a minecart in their village and building a track to your field.

To tend crops, villagers need to carry seeds. To prevent them from picking up harvested produce, you need to fill their 8 inventory slots. Collect 8 stacks (64 items) of wheat and beetroot seeds, carrots and potatoes and drop them by your villager so it picks them up.

PREPARE YOUR FIELD

This is where the magic happens! Get the villager in place and wait for it to get working. Remember to return to your field to give your villager more seeds.

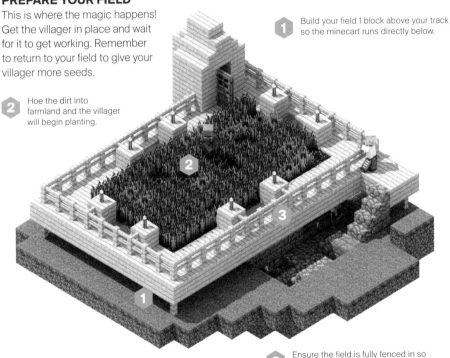

1 Build your field 1 block above your track so the minecart runs directly below.

2 Hoe the dirt into farmland and the villager will begin planting.

3 Ensure the field is fully fenced in so the villager cannot escape and mobs cannot get inside.

YOU WILL NEED:

MELONS AND PUMPKINS

These vine-based fruit-bearing plants grow in very similar ways. Both grow fruit that provides good food, but pumpkins can also be crafted into snow golems and can even be worn in place of a helmet.

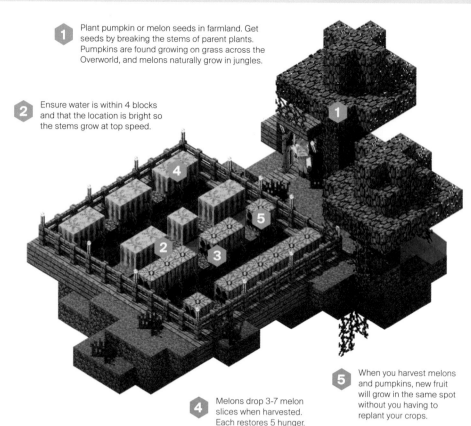

1 Plant pumpkin or melon seeds in farmland. Get seeds by breaking the stems of parent plants. Pumpkins are found growing on grass across the Overworld, and melons naturally grow in jungles.

2 Ensure water is within 4 blocks and that the location is bright so the stems grow at top speed.

3 Leave at least 1 empty block of dirt next to each plant for the fruit to grow into. The more empty dirt around the stem, the sooner you'll see fruit.

4 Melons drop 3-7 melon slices when harvested. Each restores 5 hunger.

5 When you harvest melons and pumpkins, new fruit will grow in the same spot without you having to replant your crops.

GOLEM GETTER
Build friendly golems with your pumpkins.

IRON GOLEM TEMPLATE

SNOW GOLEM TEMPLATE

24

EFFICIENT PLANTING

This layout gives a high chance of each of the dirt blocks being filled with a melon or pumpkin, while keeping the blocks with stalks hydrated.

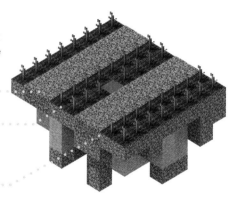

Ensure your farm is fully lit.

You can repeat this pattern to make big fields, but make sure there are always two rows of dirt together, and two rows of stalks.

Harvest crops with an axe, taking care not to hit the stalks.

AUTOMATIC MELON AND PUMPKIN FARM

This automatic farm doesn't grow produce fast, but is compact and can be left to itself to run.

When the melon or pumpkin block grows, it completes a redstone circuit and pushes a piston.

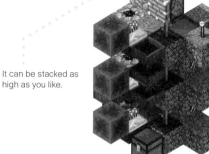

It can be stacked as high as you like.

Remember to place water next to your pumpkin.

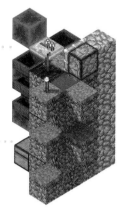

A torch will help speed up growth at night.

The piston breaks the melon/pumpkin block and the produce is collected by 3 hoppers on each level.

Connect hoppers in a backwards S shape like this, to a chest at the bottom.

YOU WILL NEED:

SUGAR CANES

These tall plants will allow you to craft paper, from which you can make books and maps. They'll also allow you to craft sugar, enabling you to create sweet delicacies like pumpkin pie, brew potions and heal horses if fed directly to them.

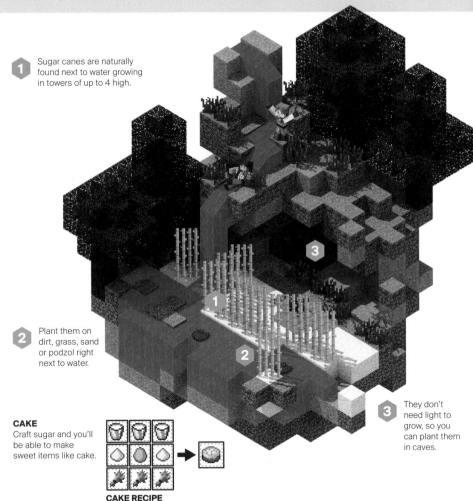

1 Sugar canes are naturally found next to water growing in towers of up to 4 high.

2 Plant them on dirt, grass, sand or podzol right next to water.

3 They don't need light to grow, so you can plant them in caves.

CAKE
Craft sugar and you'll be able to make sweet items like cake.

CAKE RECIPE

PAPER
3 sugar canes make paper which you'll need to create maps, books and fireworks.

PAPER RECIPE

TIP	⚒

Sugar canes grow up from their base, so if you harvest from the second block upwards, you won't have to replant.

AUTOMATIC SUGAR CANES FARM

This simple machine uses the observer block to harvest sugar canes into a chest.

 Water flows from source blocks and along the planted row of sugar canes so they grow.

 An observer block detects when the left-most sugar canes grow 3 blocks high.

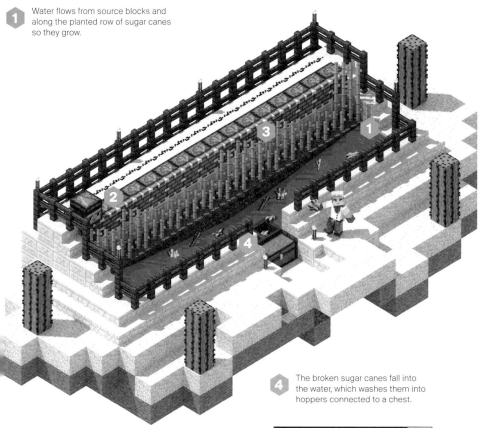

 The broken sugar canes fall into the water, which washes them into hoppers connected to a chest.

 Pistons then push the full second row of sugar canes into the water, leaving a row to begin growing again.

MOJANG STUFF

Originally, sugar canes were just reeds, the only purpose being to create paper for books. We rebranded them as sugar canes to increase their number of (delicious) uses!

YOU WILL NEED:

MUSHROOMS

Not all crops need light in order to thrive. Some, like the mushroom, prefer the darkness. This fungus makes nourishing soup and stew, and is also an important ingredient for many useful potions.

1 Look for red and brown mushrooms in any dark place, including under trees and in caves.

2 Plant small mushrooms on dirt that isn't exposed to the sky and has a light level of under 12, or on podzol or mycelium, where they will even grow outside in the day.

3 Mushrooms will spread if there are fewer than 5 in a 9 x 9 area.

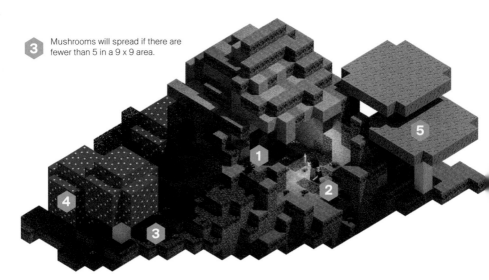

4 Huge mushrooms naturally grow in forests, swamps and on mushroom islands. Breaking their blocks will give you 0-2 small mushrooms.

5 Create huge mushrooms by using bone meal on a small mushroom. Ensure it has lots of space above and around it to grow into.

FERMENTED SPIDER EYE

Mushrooms are needed to craft fermented spider eye, which forms the base for a range of harming potions, including slowness and weakness, and invisibility. Fermented spider eye can be crafted from a mushroom, sugar and a spider eye.

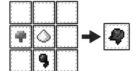

FERMENTED SPIDER EYE RECIPE

MUSHROOM STEW

Mushroom stew is a simple and very nutritious meal crafted from a brown mushroom, a red mushroom and a bowl.

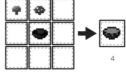

MUSHROOM STEW RECIPE

MUSHROOM FARM

The tricky thing about mushrooms is that mobs tend to spawn where they're growing. However, with clever lighting you can keep the level low enough for growing, but high enough to prevent spawning.

1 The light level at floor level is never higher than 12 so mushrooms will grow.

2 Mushrooms spread in a very random fashion, and so it's difficult to design a space- and work-efficient farm.

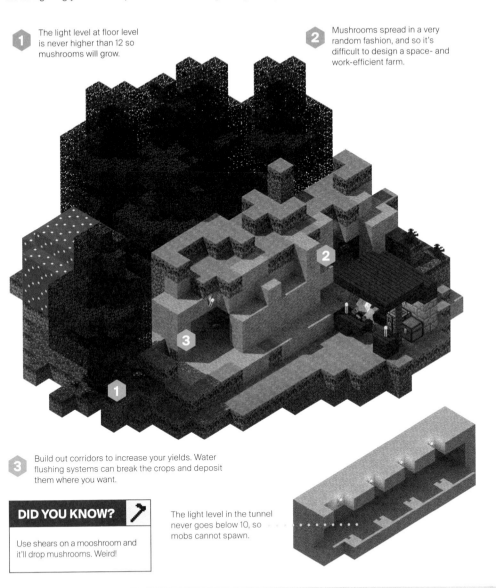

3 Build out corridors to increase your yields. Water flushing systems can break the crops and deposit them where you want.

DID YOU KNOW?

Use shears on a mooshroom and it'll drop mushrooms. Weird!

The light level in the tunnel never goes below 10, so mobs cannot spawn.

YOU WILL NEED:

COCOA

Deep in the jungle you'll find cocoa pods growing on jungle tree trunks. They drop cocoa beans when mined, which produce chocolate and can be used to make lots of brown items and blocks, from fireworks to concrete.

1 Find cocoa growing on jungle trees; break to get cocoa beans.

2 Plant beans on jungle wood, which begin small and green and grow larger and browner as they mature. They don't need light to grow.

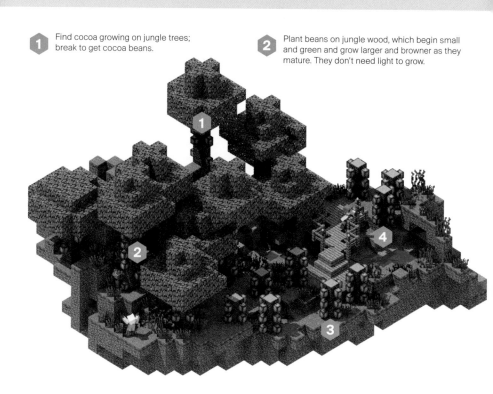

3 When creating wooden towers to grow cocoa, leave a block of space adjacent to each face for the cocoa pod to grow into.

4 Harvesting when unripe drops 1 cocoa bean; the third and final growth stage drops 2-3 cocoa beans.

COOKIES
Cookies restore 2 hunger, but don't feed them to parrots! They'll instantly die. You'll need wheat and cocoa beans to craft.

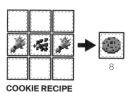

8

COOKIE RECIPE

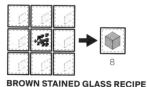

8

BROWN STAINED GLASS RECIPE

TIP

You can craft cocoa beans with glass, wool and many other coloured items to make them brown.

EFFICIENT PLANTING

Cocoa beans will only grow on jungle wood, but it's quite simple to farm them in an efficient layout that packs lots in.

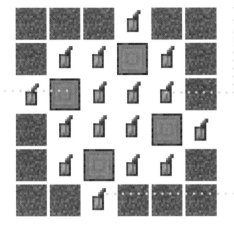

This pattern uses space very efficiently because each tree and its cocoa fits into each other.

Build each wooden 'pole' 3 blocks high so you can reach the top cocoa pods from the ground for easy harvesting.

It's a quick and easy farm to build, but crops are slow to harvest.

COCOA WATER WALL

This structure uses water from a reservoir of water above to wash the mature beans down for easy harvesting.

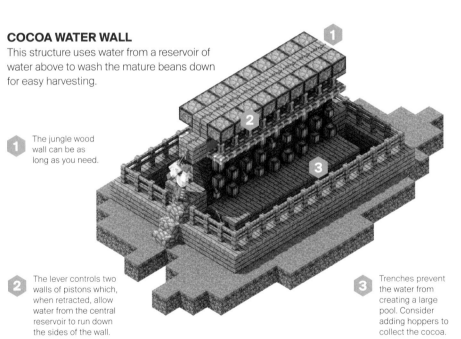

1 The jungle wood wall can be as long as you need.

2 The lever controls two walls of pistons which, when retracted, allow water from the central reservoir to run down the sides of the wall.

3 Trenches prevent the water from creating a large pool. Consider adding hoppers to collect the cocoa.

YOU WILL NEED:

2

ANIMAL FARMING

We turn now to the art of farming passive mobs, which are the source of many useful items and food, as well as experience points. We'll look at how to breed and keep livestock, and how to gather their produce.

PRINCIPLES OF ANIMAL FARMING

Many passive mobs supply food and other useful items. Once you have a herd (or flock, pack, or parcel) you can produce lots of items. Breeding can take time and requires knowledge and access to each mob's favourite foods, so it's a good idea to make a crop farm first.

FENCING

You'll need to keep your livestock from wandering, especially if they're hunted by predators, such as chicken-loving ocelots. Fences are ideal because no mob can jump over them but you can see through them and easily get inside by placing gates.

LEADING

Most mobs will follow you if you're holding the food that is required to breed them. This comes in handy when you want to guide them into your paddocks.

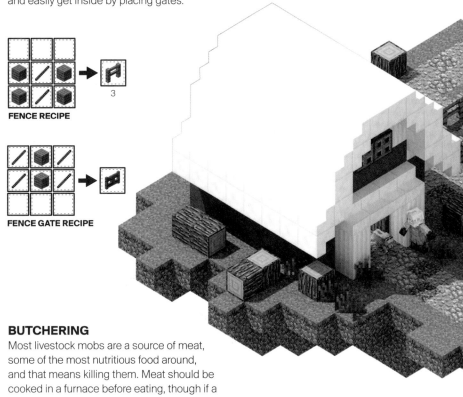

FENCE RECIPE

FENCE GATE RECIPE

BUTCHERING

Most livestock mobs are a source of meat, some of the most nutritious food around, and that means killing them. Meat should be cooked in a furnace before eating, though if a mob is killed by fire it will drop cooked meat.

SPACE

If there are too many mobs in a space enclosed by a fence they'll begin to pop through it, and if enclosed by solid blocks they'll start to suffocate and die.

BREEDING

Most adult mobs produce offspring when a pair is fed a specific item of food, awarding 1-7 XP. Their children take around 20 minutes to reach adulthood, but if fed their species' breeding food, their growing time is cut by 10%. It usually takes five minutes before parents can breed again.

PASSIVE MOBS

Passive mobs can be seen wandering across the Overworld, often in grassy areas. Let's take a look at their behaviour, what each mob drops, and the best way to go about collecting those drops.

CHICKEN

Spawning in grassy areas, adult chickens lay 1 egg every 5 to 10 minutes, which can be crafted into pumpkin pies and cake. Cooked chicken restores 6 hunger. Ocelots will hunt chickens.

BREEDING

Feed a pair of chickens with seeds, melon seeds, pumpkin seeds or beetroot seeds, or you can quickly grow a big flock by throwing eggs. 1 in 8 will successfully spawn a chick, and 1 in 32 of those will hatch into 4 chicks, which grow faster if fed seeds.

EGG FACTORY

This machine makes it much simpler to gather eggs from a large flock of chickens. It uses water to wash the eggs to one place.

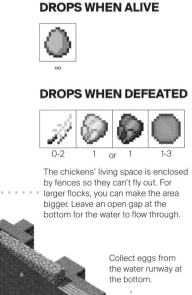

DROPS WHEN ALIVE

∞

DROPS WHEN DEFEATED

0-2	1	or 1	1-3

Use a water bucket to place water source blocks at the top of the structure.

Find as many eggs as you can and throw them inside. 1 in 8 will hatch.

The chickens' living space is enclosed by fences so they can't fly out. For larger flocks, you can make the area bigger. Leave an open gap at the bottom for the water to flow through.

Collect eggs from the water runway at the bottom.

PUMPKIN PIE RECIPE

YOU WILL NEED:

COW

Cows spawn in herds of between 4 and 8 in grassy areas. They are important as a source of leather for crafting armour and books. Use a bucket on a cow and it will be filled with milk.

BREEDING

Give wheat to 2 adult cows standing near to each other to encourage them to breed.

DROPS WHEN ALIVE

∞

DROPS WHEN DEFEATED

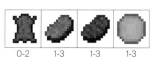

| 0-2 | 1-3 | 1-3 | 1-3 |

> **TIP** >
>
> Fence a cow into a 1 x 2 block area near your home so you can easily milk it!

MOOSHROOM

Found only in the mushroom island biome, mooshrooms behave like cows, but use a bowl on one and it will be filled with mushroom stew. Shear one and it will drop 5 mushrooms and turn into a cow.

BREEDING

Mooshrooms can only be bred with their own kind, not cows. Use wheat on a pair.

DROPS WHEN ALIVE

| ∞ | ∞ | ∞ |

DROPS WHEN DEFEATED

| 0-2 | 1-3 | 1-3 | 1-3 |

PIG

Found in grassy areas in rough groups of 4, pigs are a great source of nutritious food. Their porkchops restore 8 hunger.

BREEDING

Feeding carrots, potatoes or beetroot to a pair of pigs will create a piglet.

DROPS WHEN DEFEATED

| 1-3 | or | 1-3 | 1-3 |

RABBIT

Rabbits live in grasslands, deserts and ice plains in groups of an adult and two babies. Their meat restores 5 hunger. Their hide can only be crafted into leather, but 1 in 10 will drop a rabbit's foot, which, when brewed with awkward potion will give you potion of leaping.

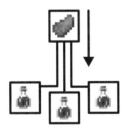

POTION OF LEAPING BREWING RECIPE

DROPS WHEN DEFEATED

| 0-1 | 0-1 | or | 0-1 | 0-1 | 1-3 |

BREEDING

Feed a carrot or a dandelion to adult rabbits. The baby rabbit's fur will match that of one of its parents, or there's a 5% chance it will match the biome you're in. To maximise the chance of breeding rabbits with specific fur, ensure both parents have it.

SHEEP

Sheep spawn on grass. Their mutton fills 6 hunger, but they're most useful as a source of wool. Most are white, but there's a 5% chance one will spawn as light grey, dark grey or black, and there's a 1 in 600 chance it will be pink. You can also dye them. Shear a sheep to gather 1-3 wool of its colour; it will need to eat tall grass or a grass block before its wool will regrow.

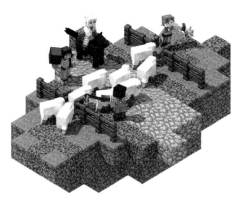

BREEDING

Feed wheat to a pair of sheep. If their wool colour is compatible, their lamb will be a mix of both, so red and yellow parents will have an orange lamb. Otherwise, the lamb will be one of its parents' colours.

DROPS WHEN DEFEATED

1	1-2	or 1-2	1-3

DROPS WHEN ALIVE

∞

TIP

Sheep are hunted by wild wolves, so keep them protected behind fences.

SHEARING STATION

This structure makes shearing easy, collecting the wool in a chest.

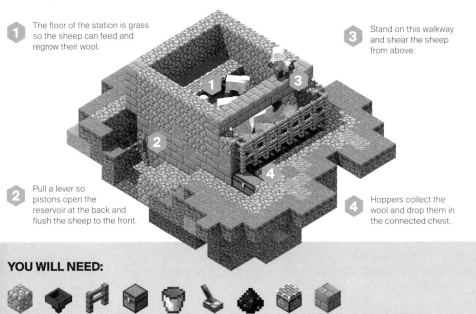

1. The floor of the station is grass so the sheep can feed and regrow their wool.

2. Pull a lever so pistons open the reservoir at the back and flush the sheep to the front.

3. Stand on this walkway and shear the sheep from above.

4. Hoppers collect the wool and drop them in the connected chest.

YOU WILL NEED:

TAMEABLE MOBS

These mobs are a little more complicated than passive mobs – they'll need to be tamed before you can breed them or use them for any other purpose. Let's take a look at where they're found and how to earn their trust.

HORSE

Horses and donkeys roam savannas and plains. Once tamed by attempting to ride them until they stop trying to throw you off, they can perform several useful functions for farmers. Once given a saddle you can control them while riding, and donkeys and mules (which are not found in the wild and can only be bred) are smaller and stockier and can be given a chest so they'll carry goods.

BREEDING

Once tamed, horses can be bred with golden apples and carrots. Their foal's species depends on its parents, so two horses will have a horse, and a horse and donkey will birth a mule. The foal will need to be tamed. Speed up its growth with (from least to most effective): sugar, wheat, apple, golden carrot, hay bale, or golden apple.

DROPS WHEN DEFEATED

0-2   1-3

CAT

Cats are tamed from ocelots, which are found in jungles. They deter creepers from coming close, so can help protect your farm from explosions. Taming is a delicate process: hold raw salmon or raw fish nearby an ocelot and wait as it approaches. It will be frightened away by any sudden movement. Cats follow their owner but can be commanded to sit to stay in place.

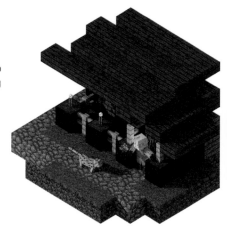

BREEDING

Feed raw salmon or raw fish to a pair of cats and they will produce a kitten, which will have the colouring of one of its parents.

DROPS WHEN DEFEATED

1-3

LLAMA

Llamas are native to savannas. Once tamed, they can be ridden, but can't be controlled. Once equipped with a chest they're a great pack animal. A llama will carry 3, 6, 9, 12, or 15 slots, depending on its strength rating. Use a lead on a llama and all nearby llamas will form into a caravan.

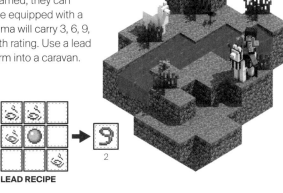

TIP

Give your strongest llama a distinctive carpet to wear so you can easily identify it.

LEAD RECIPE

Leads can be crafted from a slimeball and string.

BREEDING

Use hay bales on two tamed adults. The baby llama's strength will be influenced by its strongest parent's strength, so to get a strong pack, always breed with your strongest llama to raise your chances of having strong babies. Hay bales can be crafted from wheat.

DROPS WHEN DEFEATED

0-2   1-3

. . . .

WOLF

Wild wolves live in taiga biomes in packs of 4. Neutral to players, they can be tamed so that they will faithfully follow you, attacking skeletons and any other mobs that attack you. To tame, feed a wolf bones until a collar appears and its eyes change to look friendlier.

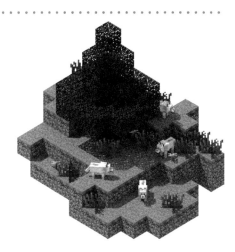

BREEDING

Feed a pair of tame wolves any kind of meat other than fish, such as raw beef, and they will produce a baby wolf.

DID YOU KNOW?

You can tell how healthy your wolf is by how high it holds its tail. Heal it by feeding it meat.

DROPS WHEN DEFEATED

1-3

3

HOSTILE MOB FARMING

Many hostile mobs drop wonderfully useful items that will aid you on your journeys, as well as experience points. But hunting these foes can be arduous as well as dangerous. In this section we'll look at how to farm hostile mobs safely.

PRINCIPLES OF HOSTILE MOB FARMING

Hostile mobs are the source of valuable and sometimes vital items that will aid you in your quest to defeat the ender dragon. Learning how to farm them often means embarking on complex constructions, but they're worth the work.

KILLING

Hostile mobs only drop certain items if they're killed by a player (or their wolf), so many farms collect live mobs for you to kill them manually. But there's a limit to the number of hostile mobs that can be around. To maximise the output of your farms, you'll need to kill them quickly to keep fresh mob spawns flowing.

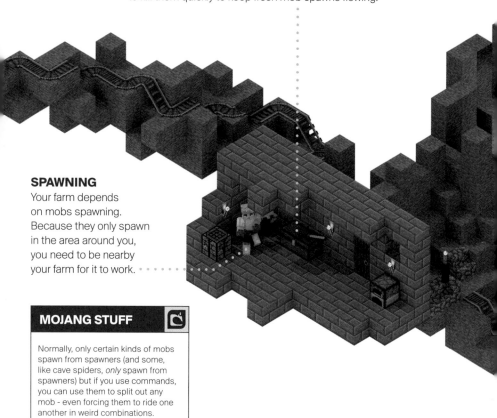

SPAWNING

Your farm depends on mobs spawning. Because they only spawn in the area around you, you need to be nearby your farm for it to work.

MOJANG STUFF

Normally, only certain kinds of mobs spawn from spawners (and some, like cave spiders, *only* spawn from spawners) but if you use commands, you can use them to split out any mob - even forcing them to ride one another in weird combinations.

LIGHT

To get mobs spawning quickly where you want them to be, you need to stop them from spawning elsewhere. Ensure there are no dark places in hidden caverns within range and light up open ground or cover with slabs to prevent them from appearing outside your farm.

THE NETHER

Some hostile mobs only spawn in the Nether, so to farm them you'll need to set up a base so you can live there. However, many Overworld farming techniques, such as those that use water, won't work there.

SPAWNERS

Spawners found in dungeons, abandoned mineshafts, mansions, strongholds and fortresses are an excellent way of generating hostile mobs. If you find one, consider not destroying it so you can use it.

45

SPAWNING

Hostile mobs spawn according to a set of rules, and understanding these rules can help you build clever farms. Let's take a look at the factors that will affect the spawn rate of hostile mobs.

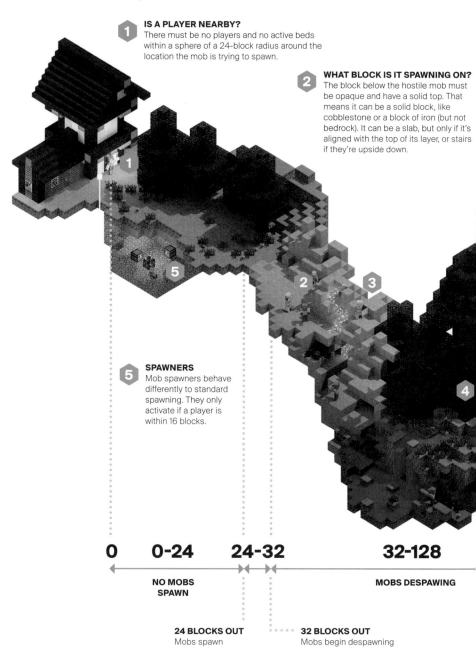

1 IS A PLAYER NEARBY?
There must be no players and no active beds within a sphere of a 24-block radius around the location the mob is trying to spawn.

2 WHAT BLOCK IS IT SPAWNING ON?
The block below the hostile mob must be opaque and have a solid top. That means it can be a solid block, like cobblestone or a block of iron (but not bedrock). It can be a slab, but only if it's aligned with the top of its layer, or stairs if they're upside down.

5 SPAWNERS
Mob spawners behave differently to standard spawning. They only activate if a player is within 16 blocks.

0	0-24	24-32	32-128
	NO MOBS SPAWN		**MOBS DESPAWING**

24 BLOCKS OUT
Mobs spawn

32 BLOCKS OUT
Mobs begin despawning

IS THERE ENOUGH FREE SPACE?
Each hostile mob needs a certain amount of clear space around the spawning point. Most require a 2-block high space, but spiders need 1 vertical block and 3 lateral blocks, and endermen need 3 vertical blocks. These blocks must be free of liquids, rails and solid blocks.

IS IT DARK ENOUGH?
Most mobs only spawn in blocks below light level 8, but some, like blazes, can spawn in brighter conditions. The darker the block is, the more likely the spawn will succeed. Direct sunlight makes it a lot more likely the spawn will fail.

DESPAWNING
Mobs also despawn - which means that they disappear from the world - according to a set of rules.

1. For mobs that haven't been within 32 blocks of a player for over 30 seconds, every second there is a one in 40 chance it will despawn.

2. If players are more than 128 blocks from a mob in any direction, it will despawn immediately.

3. If the hostile mob is named with a name tag, or if it has picked up any items dropped by a player, it will not despawn.

MOJANG STUFF

If you use a nametag on a mob it becomes persistent and will never despawn. This can be handy: if you find a zombie villager, you can name them, lock them up, and venture off far and wide in search of the cure.

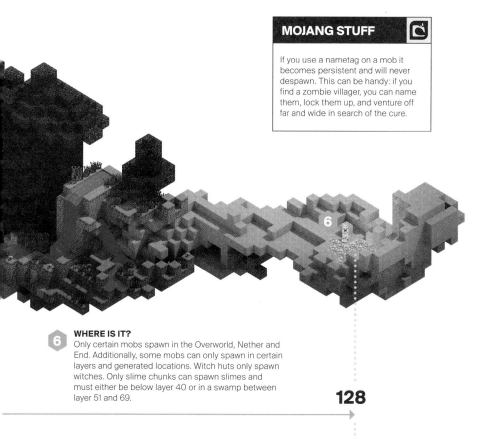

WHERE IS IT?
Only certain mobs spawn in the Overworld, Nether and End. Additionally, some mobs can only spawn in certain layers and generated locations. Witch huts only spawn witches. Only slime chunks can spawn slimes and must either be below layer 40 or in a swamp between layer 51 and 69.

128

128 BLOCKS OUT
All mobs despawn immediately

EQUIPMENT

Farming hostile mobs can be difficult and dangerous, but you can make your work easier and more profitable by investing in some special equipment and items.

DIAMOND SWORD

Because a lot of mob farms require you to do the killing, you need a strong and durable sword to make quick work of it. That means diamond.

Diamond ore is rare, and is only found in small seams from levels 5 to 20 in the Overworld, so you will need to dig deep beneath the surface. It's most common between levels 12-16.

Mining with TNT can find diamond quickly. Once you have your simple mob farm set up (see page 52-53) you'll start quickly collecting gunpowder from creepers. Place a TNT block every 5 blocks around level 14, detonate, then examine the holes for seams of diamond ore. Watch out for lava floods!

ENCHANTMENTS

Improve your equipment for better drops and quicker killing with enchantments. Place up to 15 bookshelves around your enchantment table to increase its power. Offered enchantments depend on your level; the list is reset every time you enchant something. Pay for each enchantment with XP and lapis lazuli. Or use an anvil to apply enchanted books to your equipment and combine enchanted items.

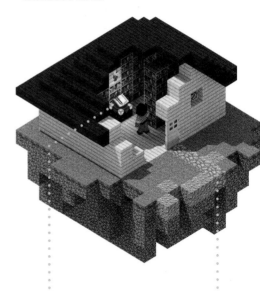

Enchantment tables can be crafted from obsidian, diamond and a book.

Anvils can be crafted from iron ingots and solid blocks of iron.

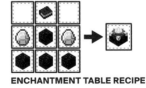

ENCHANTMENT TABLE RECIPE

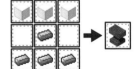

ANVIL RECIPE

LOOTING

To get the most drops from mobs and to raise the chances of their rare drops appearing, enchant your sword with looting. You'll get one extra drop for each level of enchantment, up to level III.

SILK TOUCH

This allows you to pick up some items which are normally destroyed when their block is broken, e.g. cobwebs (useful for the blaze farm on pages 62-65) and ice (see pages 74-75).

UNBREAKING

Unbreaking raises the durability of your equipment, up to level III. It's best used on your enchanted diamond sword.

SHARPNESS

Sharpness increases the damage of your melee (hand-to-hand) attacks, with a level V sharpness doing 1.5 hearts of extra damage. Level V is only reached with use of an anvil.

SMITE

Smite raises the damage you do to undead mobs, like zombies and skeletons, with level V smite doing 6.5 hearts of extra damage. It's excellent for killing wither skeletons.

POTIONS

Become more powerful or deal damage to groups of mobs by quaffing potions made at a brewing stand. You'll need many items to get the potions you want, including glass bottles, water, Nether wart, fermented spider eyes and gunpowder.

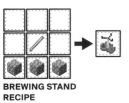

BREWING STAND RECIPE

A brewing stand can be crafted from cobblestone and a blaze rod.

POTION OF STRENGTH
Increases melee damage by 1.5 hearts for either 3 or 8 minutes.

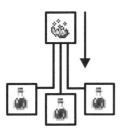

SPLASH POTION OF HARMING
Throw to do instant damage to groups of mobs, though it heals undead mobs. I: 3 hearts; II: 6 hearts.

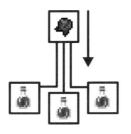

SPLASH POTION OF HEALING
Throw to do instant damage to groups of undead mobs.

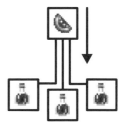

OVERWORLD MOBS

The Overworld is home to a variety of hostile mobs. They all pose unique threats and drop different valuable items. Let's take a look at each mob and learn how they can be farmed so you can collect as many of their drops as possible.

SKELETON

SPAWNS
In the Overworld on blocks under light level 8, and in Nether fortresses. In snowy biomes, most skeletons will be strays, which have a 50% chance of dropping an arrow tipped with slowness.

DROPS WHEN DEFEATED

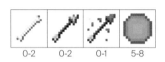

| 0-2 | 0-2 | 0-1 | 5-8 |

Arrows are useful, but all farmers treasure the bone meal that is crafted from skeleton bones. This wonder substance makes most crops grow faster.

ZOMBIE

SPAWNS
In the Overworld in groups of 4 on blocks under light level 8, or in groups of up to 20 near large villages at midnight. 1 in 20 zombies is a baby, which is smaller, faster and gives more XP.

DROPS WHEN DEFEATED

| 0-2 | 0-1 | 0-1 | 0-1 | 5-12 |

Rotten flesh will poison you if you eat it, but it has two other uses: it heals and tames wolves, and villagers can trade it for emeralds. Potatoes, carrots and iron ingots are rare drops. They also drop any armour or weapons they are holding.

SIMPLE MOB FARM

This farm collects items from zombies, skeletons, creepers, witches and spiders, using gravity to do the dirty work. It requires a lot of blocks, but is so simple it can be built very early in your journey.

TIP

To collect XP as well as items, reduce the fall height to 22 blocks and mobs will survive and most will die in a single punch.

1 Mobs spawn in the upper chamber. Open trapdoors trick them into thinking they can walk on them.

2 Light the top of the structure and the area at the bottom as well so hostile mobs can't spawn, maximising spawns inside the chamber and minimising danger.

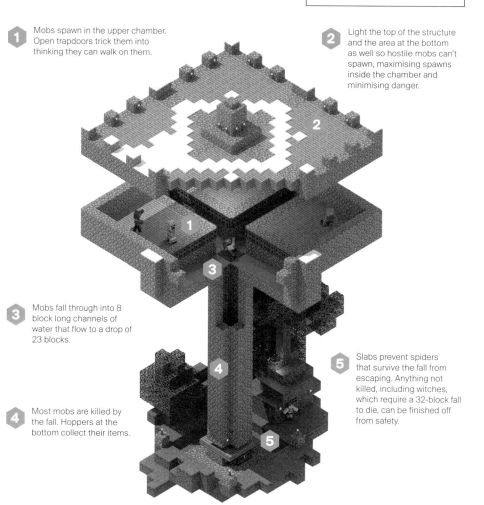

3 Mobs fall through into 8 block long channels of water that flow to a drop of 23 blocks.

5 Slabs prevent spiders that survive the fall from escaping. Anything not killed, including witches, which require a 32-block fall to die, can be finished off from safety.

4 Most mobs are killed by the fall. Hoppers at the bottom collect their items.

YOU WILL NEED:

SPIDER

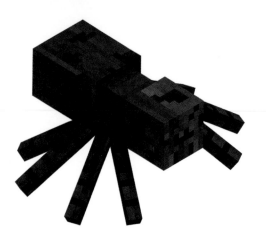

SLIME

SPAWNS

In the Overworld on blocks under light level 8 in spaces of one block and higher, or from spawners. The common spider's smaller and poisonous relative, the cave spider, only spawns from spawners in abandoned mineshafts.

DROPS WHEN DEFEATED

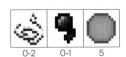

| 0-2 | 0-1 | 5 |

String is handy for crafting bows, fishing rods and leads, and can be placed as a block to create tripwires. Spider eyes are poisonous if eaten but are crucial for brewing various potions, including poison, slowness, invisibility, harming and weakness. Note that spiders only drop eyes when killed by a player, not if killed by fall damage.

SPAWNS

Slimes spawn in random areas in the Overworld at level 40 and below at any light level, and in swamps at normal ground level at light level of under 8. Slimes come in three sizes; larger slimes split into smaller ones when they're defeated. Only the smallest slimes drop slimeballs when defeated.

DROPS WHEN DEFEATED

| 0-2 | 1-4 |

Slimeballs are handy items, used to craft leads, sticky pistons and magma cream (needed to brew potions of fire resistance), as well as the bouncy slime block.

DID YOU KNOW?

Spiders' ability to climb walls means they often survive drop trap farms.

DID YOU KNOW?

If a charged creeper, a creeper super-powered by a lightning bolt, kills a zombie, skeleton or creeper, it will drop its head as an item!

CACTUS SLIME TRAP

If you can find a place where slimes spawn, this trap will use their stupidity to gather lots of slimeballs. It will also work for magma cubes in the Nether.

1 Find an area in a swamp or below level 40 where slimes spawn. If underground, you'll need to carefully mine out an area and note where slimes are appearing from.

2 Create a square chamber measuring around 30 blocks across. Light it well to prevent other mobs from spawning.

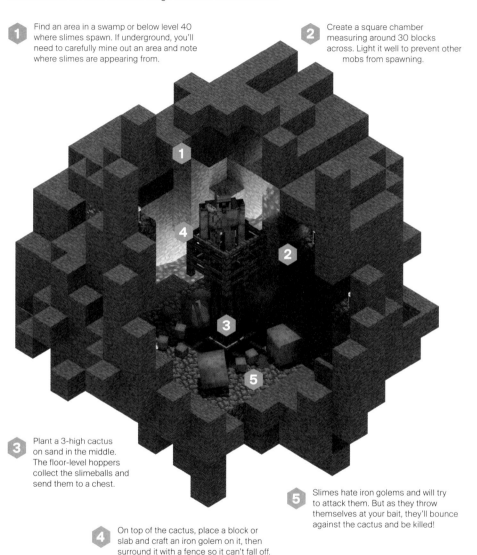

3 Plant a 3-high cactus on sand in the middle. The floor-level hoppers collect the slimeballs and send them to a chest.

5 Slimes hate iron golems and will try to attack them. But as they throw themselves at your bait, they'll bounce against the cactus and be killed!

4 On top of the cactus, place a block or slab and craft an iron golem on it, then surround it with a fence so it can't fall off.

YOU WILL NEED:

CREEPER

WITCH

SPAWNS

Anywhere in the Overworld on blocks of under light level 8.

SPAWNS

Anywhere in the Overworld on blocks of under light level 8, and in witch huts.

DROPS WHEN DEFEATED

0-2	0-1	5

Gunpowder is a handy item that's needed to craft many volatile items and blocks: TNT, fireworks and fire charges. It's also needed to brew splash potions. If a creeper is killed by a skeleton's arrow, it will drop a random music disc to play in a jukebox.

DROPS WHEN DEFEATED

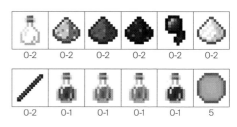

0-2	0-2	0-2	0-2	0-2	0-2
0-2	0-1	0-1	0-1	0-1	5

Witches will drop a maximum of 6 items when defeated, and if they're killed while using a potion, they'll drop that, too. Their drops are useful, but the most useful is glowstone dust, which is only naturally found in the Nether. It brews potions and crafts glowstone, fireworks and the spectral arrow, which reveals its targets from behind walls.

TNT
Gunpowder is a key ingredient in everyone's favourite explosive block – the other is sand.

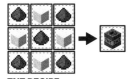

TNT RECIPE

DID YOU KNOW?

Minecraft's music, which you can play from discs that creepers drop, is by the artist C418.

WITCH FARM

This farm uses a special property of witch huts: only witches will spawn inside their 7 × 9 × 5-block area. They can take some searching but they can produce large numbers of useful items.

 Light as much of the surrounding area, above and below ground, as you possibly can, or flood it to prevent other hostile mobs from being able to spawn in the area.

Witch huts are found in swamps. Despatch its resident witch and build a box that encloses the whole hut.

 Destroy the hut from within and put 2 floors with at least 2 blocks above them inside your new box. Witches will spawn on these 2 floors.

 Dig a 32-block drop next to the open end of the water trench so witches are washed along it and down the hole, where they will die at the bottom. Place hoppers connected to a chest at the bottom to collect the items.

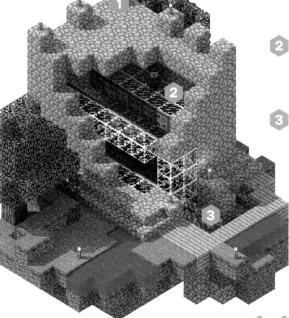

Place a 2-block wide line of open trapdoors along the same position on both floors so witches will fall from upper levels.

Dig a 3-block high trench under the lower spawning floor, ensure it is 8 blocks long and set up flowing water from one end.

YOU WILL NEED:

ENDERMAN

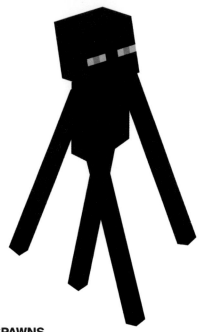

THE BOAT TECHNIQUE

Enderman farming in the Overworld is not easy. Their ability to teleport and their hatred of water means many mob farming techniques won't work. But this hunting method is somewhat safe

1 Pick an area of open ground where you can see a long way. Arrange about 15 boats in a circle around you.

2 Light a radius of around 20 blocks around the boats to help avoid attracting the attention of other hostile mobs.

SPAWNS

In the Overworld, Nether and End, on blocks with a light level of under 8. In the Overworld they are rare, appearing in groups of between 1 and 4, and in the Nether they're very rare.

3 Wait for nightfall and look for endermen. Note that they will not spawn in rain. Look directly at their eyes to anger them. When they come towards you to attack they will get caught in the boat, making it easier to hit them.

4 Endermen will teleport from the boat when you attack them, and they can attack you while they sit, so take care and a good suit of armour is advised.

DROPS WHEN DEFEATED

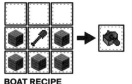

0-1   5

When thrown, ender pearls will teleport players, and are also used to craft the eye of ender, an item which helps locate End portals in strongholds. Eyes of ender sometimes break when used. You'll need up to 12 to insert into the End portal in order to activate it.

BOAT
Boats are cheap and easy to make, requiring just wood planks and a wooden shovel.

BOAT RECIPE

YOU WILL NEED:

ENDERMITE TRAP

Another technique uses the fact endermen hate endermites, but a warning: setting it up consumes the very ender pearls you're collecting.

1 Prepare a name tag for the endermite with an anvil. The name tag will prevent it from despawning.

2 At ground level, build a 3-block high tower, place a rail on top, and place a minecart on it. The endermite is going to sit in this minecart.

3 Place a ring of trapdoors around the base of the tower and dig a 43-block deep trench down from them. The drop will kill the endermen.

4 Place a block above the minecart and build a 2-block deep 1 x 1 bowl above it. Stand on the edge and throw ender pearls towards the opposite edge. You'll teleport to the other side, losing a little health. Repeat, healing as necessary. It will take an average of 20 throws until the endermite appears in the bowl.

5 Wait in a safe place nearby for endermen to spawn, attempt to attack the endermite, and fall to their deaths.

6 Quickly name tag the endermite and then destroy the block below so it falls into the minecart, and destroy all the other blocks you placed around your tower so it's all tidy.

YOU WILL NEED:

NETHER MOBS

Every mob you'll meet in the Nether is highly dangerous, but they drop rare and valuable items, many of which are essential for brewing potions. Let's take a look at each mob and how it can be farmed so you can collect drops.

MAGMA CUBE

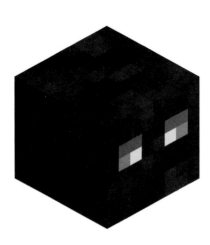

ZOMBIE PIGMAN

SPAWNS

In one of three different sizes, at any light level, anywhere in the Nether. They're more commonly found around Nether fortresses.

SPAWNS

Common in the Nether, zombie pigmen spawn in groups of 4, on any solid blocks, at any light level. They can also rarely spawn on Nether portals in the Overworld.

DROPS WHEN DEFEATED

0-1	1-4

Magma cream is needed to brew potions of fire resistance, which make the Nether a lot easier to explore.

DROPS WHEN DEFEATED

0-1	0-1	0-1	1	5-12

Zombie pigmen are a good source of gold; 9 nuggets craft into a gold ingot, or craft golden carrots, which tame horses and brew into potions of night vision, and glistering melons, which brew potions of healing. They also have a chance of dropping their gold swords, which can be smelted into a gold nugget.

ZOMBIE PIGMAN GOLD RUNS

This technique requires a little effort, but it's reliable and very easy to set up, and you can therefore start using it as soon as you arrive in the Nether. For a more advanced farm, see pages 66-67.

 Find an area of Nether that has a good deal of flat space and easily connects to one or more nearby areas.

For a more advanced farm, see pages 66-67.

TIP

Make sure you have food and healing items in case you get hit, and watch for ghasts.

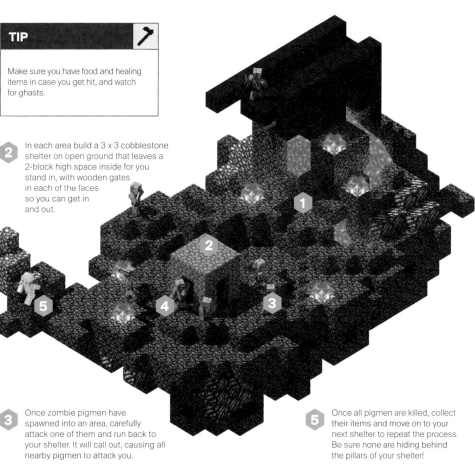

2 In each area build a 3 x 3 cobblestone shelter on open ground that leaves a 2-block high space inside for you stand in, with wooden gates in each of the faces so you can get in and out.

3 Once zombie pigmen have spawned into an area, carefully attack one of them and run back to your shelter. It will call out, causing all nearby pigmen to attack you.

5 Once all pigmen are killed, collect their items and move on to your next shelter to repeat the process. Be sure none are hiding behind the pillars of your shelter!

4 Ensure the gate is closed behind you and stand in the precise middle so the pigmen can't reach you, and attack them with your sword.

YOU WILL NEED:

WITHER SKELETON

SPAWNS

In groups of up to 5 in Nether fortresses at a light level of under 8.

DROPS WHEN DEFEATED

0-1	0-2	0-1	5

Wither skeletons' real value is their skull. It only has a 2.5% chance of dropping, but it helps summon the fearsome wither. From the wither you get Nether stars, which are necessary to create beacons.

Wither skeletons spawn in specific locations in and around Nether fortresses. A good place for a farm is on an open intersection, because it grants a large, flat area. The very best locations are on fortresses standing over lava, because lava prevents mobs spawning nearby.

SIMPLE WITHER SKELETON FARM

Building in the Nether is dangerous and difficult, but this simple farm helps to make collecting wither skeleton skulls safer.

1 Wither skeletons will spawn 9 blocks from the middle of the intersection, including into its corners, so build a square 20-block wide platform centred on the intersection.

2 Destroy nearby areas of fortress and cover as much exposed ground around it as you can with slabs or glass to prevent mobs spawning elsewhere.

YOU WILL NEED:

Wither skeletons also spawn below the top of the platform. To maximise your farm's output, build a second floor underneath with a 3-block high gap. Wither skeletons only spawn in the dark, so do not light the area with torches.

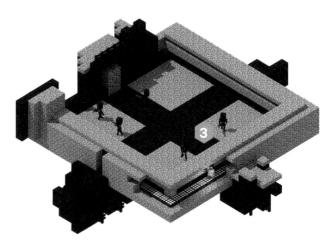

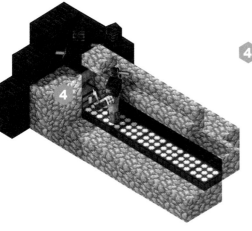

 Build a corridor around the edge of the spawning space, using daylight sensors for the floor and stairs to make the wall looking into the space. The daylight sensors allow you to stand at a height at which only tall wither skeletons can see you, but they can't hit you.

Now lure wither skeletons to the end of the corridor, where they will climb the steps so you can kill them. Their items are automatically collected by the hoppers. If too many other types of mobs spawn, move away for a while and wait for them to despawn before returning.

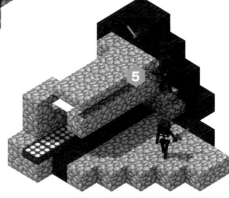

DAYLIGHT SENSOR
Since you're in the Nether, it's easy to find Nether quartz, which you'll need to craft a daylight sensor.

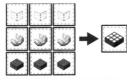

DAYLIGHT SENSOR RECIPE

TIP >

A good block to use in Nether constructions is cobblestone, because it withstands ghast fireballs. See page 72 for more info.

BLAZE

BLAZE SPAWNER FARM

This farm is built around a blaze spawner you can find in Nether fortresses. It takes a lot of dangerous building, but it generates blaze rods at a fantastic rate. It also generates a great deal of experience points very quickly.

 Find a blaze spawner in a Nether fortress. They're often on the open top of towers. The best locations are enclosed so ghasts can't attack while you're hard at work.

SPAWNS

From spawners in Nether fortresses at a light level of under 12.

DROPS WHEN DEFEATED

0-1   10

Blaze rods craft brewing stands, opening up a world of potions to you. They're also crucial for making blaze powder, which is needed to craft eyes of ender. It also crafts fire charges and magma cream, which drops directly from magma cubes.

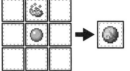

MAGMA CREAM
Brew magma cream with awkward potions to make potions of fire resistance.

MAGMA CREAM RECIPE

MOJANG STUFF

The blaze went through a few iterations before we settled on the design. Our early attempts lacked a sense of personality - then we added eyes and it suddenly felt a lot more alive. From then on, it was decided that all mobs need eyes!

YOU WILL NEED:

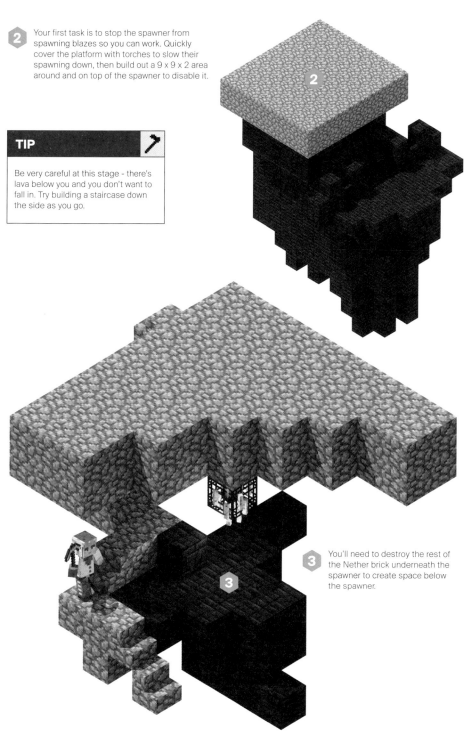

Your first task is to stop the spawner from spawning blazes so you can work. Quickly cover the platform with torches to slow their spawning down, then build out a 9 x 9 x 2 area around and on top of the spawner to disable it.

TIP

Be very careful at this stage - there's lava below you and you don't want to fall in. Try building a staircase down the side as you go.

You'll need to destroy the rest of the Nether brick underneath the spawner to create space below the spawner.

4 Build around the spawner to create
a room with an internal space of 9
x 9 x 12 blocks. There should be 2
blocks between the spawner and
the centre of the ceiling.

5 Cut a 3-block channel along the
centre of the floor and create the
corridors below that the blazes
will sink down into, and from
where you'll kill them.

TIP

You can collect cobwebs in the
Overworld in strongholds, abandoned
mineshafts and igloo basements with
shears enchanted with silk touch.
If you don't have cobwebs, you can
build a slightly less efficient version
of the farm by leaving the cobweb
blocks empty and change the stairs
for solid blocks.

HOW DOES IT WORK?

The height of the room allows you to be within range
of the spawner while maximising the space in which
blazes can spawn. Mobs can't see through iron
bars so the blazes won't be able to see you, and the
cobwebs stop them from drifting out.

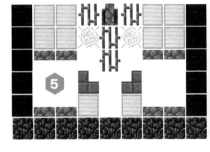

Destroy the blocks that are disabling the spawner and quickly go into the two side walkways below, because blazes will immediately spawn. As they float down, kill them with your sword. Watch for rods that sometimes fall into the central walkway.

GHAST

SPAWNS

In the Nether on solid blocks at any light level, but they are rare, spawning 20 times less frequently than other mobs.

DROPS WHEN DEFEATED

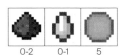

0-2	0-1	5

Ghast tears can be brewed with an awkward potion to create potions of regeneration. When crafted with glass and an eye of ender, they also craft the End crystal, which, when placed on the top of the pillars in the End, will respawn the ender dragon.

GHAST FARM

Ghasts are hard to farm effectively because they are so rare and float in the air. This farm ensures they spawn safely inside and nowhere else. It's a lot of work to build, but will also gain you gold and XP from zombie pigmen.

1 The biggest challenge is finding a good site. The ghast's rarity means it's vital that they spawn in your farm and not outside it. Find a large lava lake and cover all other ground up to a distance of around 100 blocks around the farm with slabs.

2 Build a large 4-block high cage with open windows high above the lava. You can make multiple floors. At ceiling level place slabs every 5 blocks to prevent ghasts from escaping.

3 Place iron bars across the windows to prevent ghasts from escaping and also from seeing you. Place slabs along the bottom to prevent ghasts from pushing pigmen to the edge.

4 On upper floors, create steps so pigmen from upper floors can jump down 3 blocks to the lower one.

5 Place trapdoors in front of the middle window, and create a 24-block drop trap for zombie pigmen below, with hoppers to collect their gold.

6 Build a cobblestone bridge that leads to the trapdoors and a shelter at the end, around 25 blocks away from the farm, where you can wait for ghasts to spawn.

YOU WILL NEED:

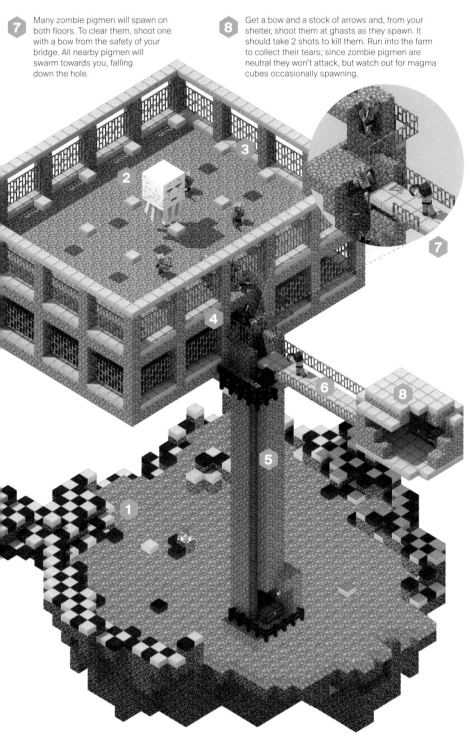

7 Many zombie pigmen will spawn on both floors. To clear them, shoot one with a bow from the safety of your bridge. All nearby pigmen will swarm towards you, falling down the hole.

8 Get a bow and a stock of arrows and, from your shelter, shoot them at ghasts as they spawn. It should take 2 shots to kill them. Run into the farm to collect their tears; since zombie pigmen are neutral they won't attack, but watch out for magma cubes occasionally spawning.

BLOCK FARMING

Some Minecraft constructions require thousands of blocks. Here we'll learn how to create large quantities fast so you don't have to hunt them down in your world. Whether you need cobblestone or cactus, wood or Nether wart, these farms will allow you to build big projects more quickly.

PRINCIPLES OF BLOCK FARMING

We can use the way in which some blocks reproduce to make big stocks of useful items. Some grow very similarly to the crops we explored earlier (see pages 12-13), though their produce isn't edible.

LOCATION

Blocks like ice and snow only form in specific biomes, so you may need to set out on expeditions to find them. Consider using Nether portals to make travelling between your main base and your special farms easier.

ENCHANTMENT

Many block farms are limited by how fast you can mine. Gold pickaxes are the fastest, but they wear out very quickly. Consider investing in enchantments like efficiency, fortune and unbreaking.

TOOLS

Some blocks only drop their item when destroyed with a specific tool. Obsidian needs a diamond pickaxe, vines can only be collected with shears, and ice requires a tool enchanted with silk touch.

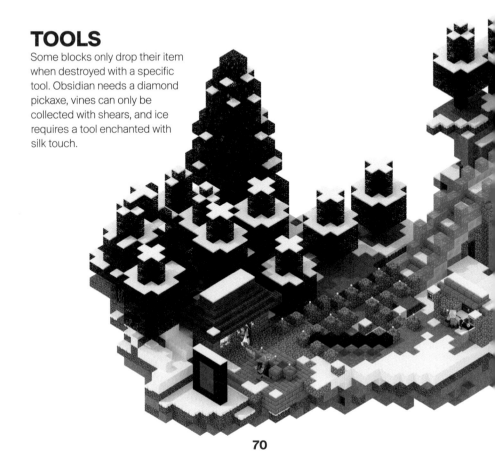

SITE

If you're building a big project, it might be a good idea to position a farm making the items you're using to build, like cobblestone, nearby. Or, if it's in the Nether, close to a portal so you can bring resources in quickly.

BLOCKS

From wood to obsidian, these blocks are frequently used in building, and are easy to farm if you know how. Let's take a look at what they can be used for and how to farm them efficiently.

COBBLESTONE

Cobblestone is the commonest building material, due to its strength and how easy it is to find. It's particularly effective in the Nether, because it can withstand ghast and blaze fireballs. But mining it from the ground is time-consuming and sometimes dangerous.

COBBLESTONE GENERATOR

You can mine cobblestone at speed, without even moving, using lava's ability to create cobblestone when it flows into water.

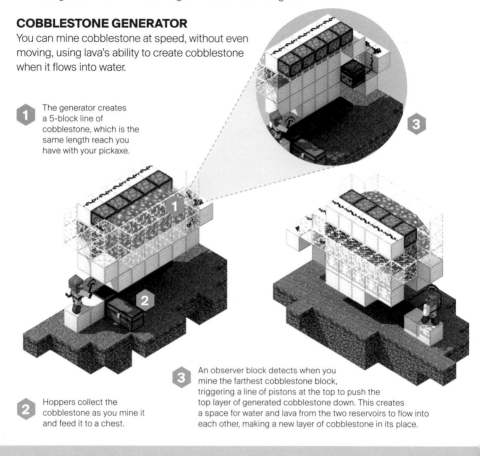

1 The generator creates a 5-block line of cobblestone, which is the same length reach you have with your pickaxe.

2 Hoppers collect the cobblestone as you mine it and feed it to a chest.

3 An observer block detects when you mine the farthest cobblestone block, triggering a line of pistons at the top to push the top layer of generated cobblestone down. This creates a space for water and lava from the two reservoirs to flow into each other, making a new layer of cobblestone in its place.

YOU WILL NEED:

OBSIDIAN

One of the strongest blocks, obsidian can't be destroyed by creepers or TNT blasts, so it can protect important constructions. It also builds the Nether portal. But it's relatively rare, and can only be mined with a diamond pickaxe.

SIMPLE OBSIDIAN GENERATOR

Obsidian is produced when flowing water moves into a lava source block, replacing that lava source block. Making it means collecting lava into lots of buckets. But this simple machine makes the final steps easier.

1 Craft buckets and gather lava into them. You'll get 1 obsidian block for each bucket of lava. Place the lava buckets into the dispenser, which carries a maximum of 9.

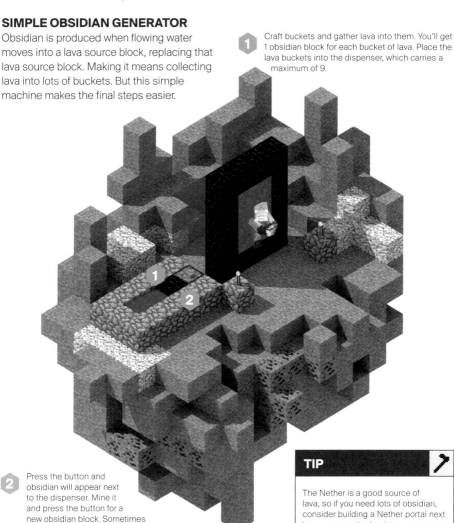

2 Press the button and obsidian will appear next to the dispenser. Mine it and press the button for a new obsidian block. Sometimes an empty bucket will be dispensed; just collect it and press the button again until lava is dispensed.

TIP

The Nether is a good source of lava, so if you need lots of obsidian, consider building a Nether portal next to your generator to give you an easy source of lava.

YOU WILL NEED:

SNOW

Snow falls in cold biomes, settling on the tops of blocks. When destroyed with a shovel, it drops snowballs. Snowballs can be thrown, causing no more than knockback on most mobs, but do 1.5 hearts of damage to blazes. They can also be crafted into a block of snow.

SNOWBALL FARM

Snow golems instantly generate snow on the ground they're touching, as long as they're in a cold biome. This snow can then be used to make snowballs.

1 The hoppers are connected to each other. Drop an item into one of them and they will put out a pulsing signal.

2 Make your snow golem here by placing 2 blocks of snow on top of one another, and a pumpkin on top.

3 Stand on the pressure plate to activate the piston.

4 This piston pushes the snow off the golem's base into snowballs. Don't worry, it doesn't harm the golem.

MOJANG STUFF

Ice is super useful for building high-speed transport systems thanks to a bug - sorry, *feature* - in the calculation of ground friction. Enclose an icy runway in a 2-block high tunnel, and you can sprint-jump along it at a searing 16 blocks a second!

YOU WILL NEED:

YOU WILL NEED:

ICE

Ice forms on water directly under the sky in biomes where snow settles. When laid as a long track it can make water, mobs and players move faster, and if under soul sand, it will enhance its slowing effect. Pickaxes break ice the fastest, but ice only drops when the tool is enchanted with silk touch (see page 50-51).

ICE FARM

After harvesting the ice, the water flows back into the pool so it freezes again. The pool can be as big as you like.

 Freezing transforms water blocks into ice.

 The water source blocks are directly under cover, which prevents ice forming on them, so they automatically refill the pool after harvest.

NETHER WART

Naturally found in Nether fortresses, Nether wart grows anywhere at any light level on soul sand. It's needed to brew awkward potion, which is the base for many key potions, including fire resistance, healing, night vision, strength and many more.

NETHER WART FARM

You have to replant Nether wart manually after harvesting, so this farm just harvests it automatically for you. You can extend by adding lower tiers.

 Plant from the central pathway. You should be able to reach the far blocks without having to walk on the soul sand.

 Pull the lever to release water that breaks the Nether wart when mature.

 The water flows to the hoppers very slowly because it's over soul sand!

YOU WILL NEED:

WOOD

Wood is an excellent building material and fuel, and also crafts many vital items, so a stock of trees is essential if no forest is nearby. Planted in dirt or podzol with a light level of 8 or more, saplings will grow into trees in around 1 Minecraft day, depending on the species. They grow anywhere, including caves, the Nether and the End, provided they have at least 4 blocks clear above them.

ACACIA

Acacia is only found in savannas. It has a good yield, but it's a tricky shape for harvesting.

BIRCH

Birch grows quickly, leaves grow higher for easy harvesting, but wood yield is low.

DARK OAK

Dark oak is the fastest growing wood, drops apples and a thick trunk means lots of wood, but requires 4 saplings to plant.

JUNGLE

Jungle trees are huge, which means lots of wood, but they also need plenty of space to grow.

OAK

Oak is common and drops apples and lots of saplings, but their many leaves can slow harvesting.

SPRUCE

Spruce is common but tall, making reaching their tops difficult. Saplings must be placed 2 blocks apart.

EFFICIENT LAYOUT

This layout uses 61 saplings of any type except spruce, 23 torches and 117 blocks. If lit well, as shown here, saplings will grow right next to each other. The yield isn't as high as trees growing far apart, but they're easy to harvest.

YOU WILL NEED:

VINES

Found in jungles and swamps, vines can only be gathered with shears. They craft moss stone and mossy stone bricks, and when placed against solid blocks they can be climbed. They will also break falls.

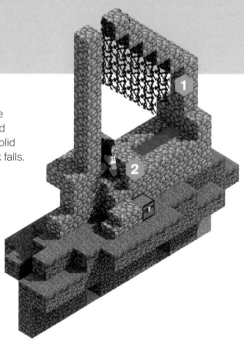

SIMPLE VINE FARM

Build this design as long as you like to maximise its output.

1 The vines grow down from the top of the structure.

2 Shear the vines as they grow downwards from the marked position, from where you won't accidentally destroy the seeding vines at the top of each row.

CACTUS

This prickly block grows in sand in deserts and mesas in a similar fashion to sugar canes, except it doesn't require water. It damages any mob or player which touches it, so it can be a useful form of defence.

CACTUS FARM

This farm can be enlarged as much as you like, upwards or across. It uses the fact that when a cactus grows into a space next to another block the new cactus block instantly breaks.

1 This farm uses fence posts, which also help prevent the broken cactus items from falling on to live ones and being destroyed.

2 The water below then washes them into hoppers connected to a chest.

YOU WILL NEED:

FINAL WORDS

Well done! You're now a master farmer. You can sit back and enjoy the fruits of your labour, with almost everything you could ever need at your fingertips. With all those riches, you can go out into the world, exploring even further and building ever bigger. Your only limit is your imagination. Thanks for playing!

OWEN JONES
THE MOJANG TEAM

First published as *Minecraft Guide to Exploration* in Great Britain 2017 by Egmont UK Limited.
This edition first published in 2020 by Dean, an imprint Egmont UK Limited,
2 Minster Court, 10th Floor, London EC3R 7BB

Written by Stephanie Milton
Designed by Richie Hull, Paul Lang and John Stuckey
Illustrations by Ryan Marsh
Cover designed by Richie Hull
Cover illustration by Ninni Landin
Production by Louis Harvey and Laura Grundy
Special thanks to Alex Wiltshire, Jennifer Hammervald,
Filip Thoms and Amanda Ström.

ISBN 978 0 6035 7928 8

71019/001

Printed in China

ONLINE SAFETY FOR YOUNGER FANS

Spending time online is great fun! Here are a few simple rules to help younger fans stay safe and
keep the internet a great place to spend time:

- Never give out your real name – don't use it as your username.
- Never give out any of your personal details.
- Never tell anybody which school you go to or how old you are.
- Never tell anybody your password except a parent or a guardian.
- Be aware that you must be 13 or over to create an account on many sites.
Always check the site policy and ask a parent or guardian for permission before registering.
- Always tell a parent or guardian if something is worrying you.

Stay safe online. Any website addresses listed in this book are correct at the time of going
to print. However, Egmont is not responsible for content hosted by third parties. Please be
aware that online content can be subject to change and websites can contain content that is
unsuitable for children. We advise that all children are supervised when using the internet.

Egmont takes its responsibility to the planet and its inhabitants very seriously.
We aim to use papers from well-managed forests run by responsible suppliers.

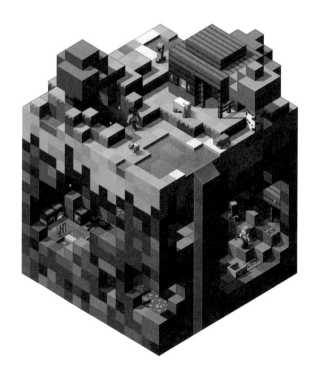

GUIDE TO:

SURVIVAL

CONTENTS

1. THE MINECRAFT LANDSCAPE

2. MOBS

3. SURVIVAL

INTRODUCTION

Welcome to the official Guide to Survival! There's something very special about starting a new game of Minecraft's Survival mode. A fresh, never-before-explored Overworld lies all around, and it's up to you to build the life you want to lead within it.

You know it'll take work. A lot of knowledge. Maybe a little luck, too. You'll go on adventures, and come across amazing sights and priceless treasures. It won't be long until you'll feel that the world is yours. But a little extra know-how is always helpful! We've packed this guide with hints and tips gathered from years of experience. You'll learn about the different biomes waiting to be discovered and what you might find in each one, the mobs you'll encounter on your journey, and some of the vital items you'll need to survive and thrive.

Happy Minecrafting!

ALEX WILTSHIRE
THE MOJANG TEAM

THE TECHNICAL STUFF

Before you start your first game there are some decisions to make about how you'd like to play. This page will help you decide whether you'd like to venture out alone or as part of a group, and which game mode is right for you.

WHICH DEVICE?

You can play Minecraft on lots of different devices. Bedrock Edition is the version of the game you play on Windows 10, Xbox One, Nintendo Switch, mobile devices, Gear VR and Fire TV. People across all these devices can play together. You can also play Minecraft on PC or Mac (Java Edition), on PlayStation, Xbox 360, Wii U and Nintendo 3DS. This book covers Bedrock Edition.

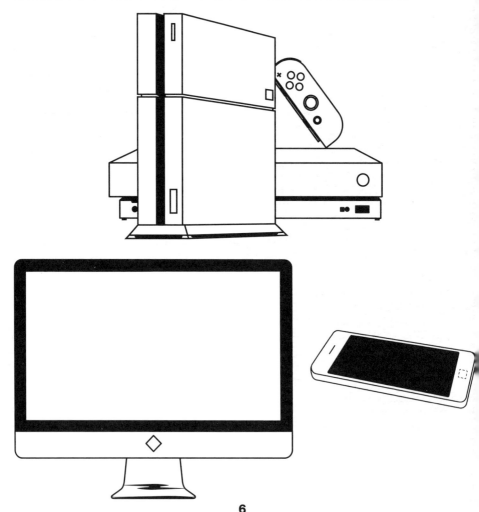

SINGLE PLAYER OR MULTIPLAYER?

Once you've chosen a device, you can decide what kind of adventure you want to have, whether that's alone or with friends.

Single player is the original, default mode for Minecraft. This mode is for you if you prefer to take on the challenges of Minecraft alone rather than in a team.

Choose multiplayer if you want to share your adventure with friends on the same network. One person will need to set up a LAN (local area network) game for the others to join.

GAME MODE

Finally, there are several different game modes to choose from, offering various degrees of difficulty.

SURVIVAL
Choose Survival mode and you'll have loads of fun fighting hostile monsters and collecting materials to help you stay alive. You'll need to eat, and you'll gain experience and levels as you play.

CREATIVE
In Creative mode you're free from hostile mobs, you can fly around and destroy blocks instantly. You'll also have a full inventory of materials with which to build amazing structures.

HARDCORE
If you choose Hardcore mode, the difficulty will be locked on hard and you'll only get one life. If you die it really will be game over – your world will be deleted and you'll have to start again.

PEACEFUL
You can also choose a peaceful option in Survival mode. You'll still collect materials and craft in order to survive, but without the hostile mobs. And your health will regenerate, too.

THIS IS YOU

Now you've decided how you want to play, you can open Minecraft. But before you hit 'play' and start your first game, you'll need to choose the character that you'll be playing as.

CHOOSING YOUR CHARACTER

Click on the clothes hanger icon towards the bottom of the screen. There are 2 skins (character designs) for you to choose from: Steve and Alex. Select the character you'd like to play as, then press 'confirm'. Now you're ready to play!

STEVE  **ALEX**

HEADS-UP DISPLAY

As you play, some important information about your character will be displayed on screen. This information is called your heads-up display (or HUD). Let's take a look at what everything means.

CROSSHAIRS
This little cross helps you to aim at blocks you want to mine, or at monsters you want to hit. It shows the exact point where you will use the tool or item you have in your hand.

HEALTH BAR
Your health bar shows how much life you have left. It's made up of 10 hearts – each heart is worth 2 health points, so you have a total of 20 health points. You lose health points if you don't eat, and if you take damage (e.g. when a monster attacks you). Always keep your health bar as full as you can.

HUNGER BAR
Your hunger bar is very important, too – it affects your health bar. It's made up of 10 drumsticks. You have a total of 20 hunger points, so each drumstick is worth 2 hunger points. You need to keep it topped up or you will start to lose health points.

EXPERIENCE
This bar shows you how much experience you've earned so far. You can earn experience points by mining, smelting ores and defeating mobs. Green balls called experience orbs will appear and you will automatically collect them if you're standing close enough. Experience adds up to levels.

HOTBAR
These 9 slots are great for storing the items you use most often. There's also a single slot to the left of the hotbar called the off-hand slot. If the hotbar slot you currently have selected is empty and you hit the 'use item' button, you will use the item in your off-hand slot.

INVENTORY

When you play in Survival, Hardcore or Peaceful mode you'll collect lots of useful blocks and items, which you'll need to store and manage in your inventory. You can open your inventory at any time while you're playing. Let's take a look at the inventory in more detail.

ARMOUR SLOTS
See page 89 for instructions on how to craft and equip armour.

CRAFTING GRID
Drag materials into the crafting grid to craft simple items such as wood planks and torches.

OUTPUT SQUARE
Your newly crafted item will appear in your output square ready to put in your inventory.

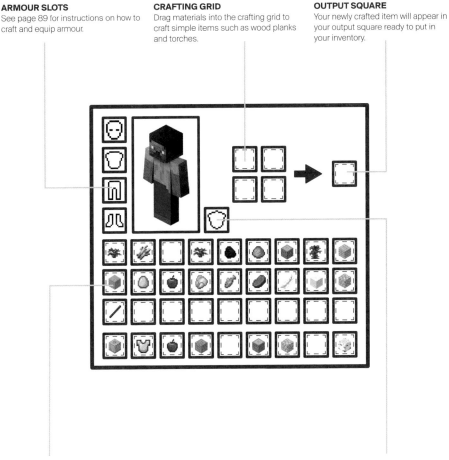

ITEM SLOTS
There are 27 item slots available. Many blocks and items can be stacked together, up to a maximum of 64. Some items, like eggs and buckets, can only be stacked up to a maximum of 16. Items like tools cannot be stacked at all. Hover over any item in your inventory and its name will appear.

OFF-HAND SLOT
Your off-hand slot can be equipped to hold a second item, which will enable you to dual-wield. You will automatically use the item in your off-hand slot when there is no item in your main slot. You can't use weapons when they're in your off-hand slot, but it's ideal for items like arrows, food or torches.

KEY

Throughout this book you'll see symbols that represent different items, values or properties – they cover everything from causes of damage to mob drops. Refer back to this page when you spot them to check what they mean.

GENERAL

MOJANG STUFF

This super-exclusive info has come directly from the developers at Mojang.

∞

Indicates that this item is an unlimited drop, while the mob in question is alive.

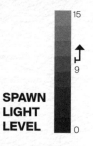

SPAWN LIGHT LEVEL

15

9

0

Indicates the light level at which a mob spawns. In this example, the mob spawns at a light level of 9 or higher.

Mob does not die when the sun rises.

HOSTILITY

Indicates the hostility level of a mob – yellow is passive, orange is neutral and red is hostile.

	Blow it up with TNT
	Disable mob spawner with 5 torches
	Drink milk to neutralise poison effects
	Enemy player attack
	Falling anvil
	Fire
	Force it into cacti
	Force it into lava

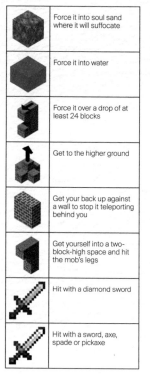

	Force it into soul sand where it will suffocate
	Force it into water
	Force it over a drop of at least 24 blocks
	Get to the higher ground
	Get your back up against a wall to stop it teleporting behind you
	Get yourself into a two-block-high space and hit the mob's legs
	Hit with a diamond sword
	Hit with a sword, axe, spade or pickaxe

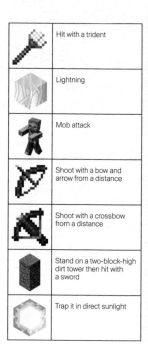

	Hit with a trident
	Lightning
	Mob attack
	Shoot with a bow and arrow from a distance
	Shoot with a crossbow from a distance
	Stand on a two-block-high dirt tower then hit with a sword
	Trap it in direct sunlight

ITEMS, BLOCKS AND EFFECTS

Armour	Enchanted book	Music disc	Raw rabbit
Arrow	Ender pearl	Mushroom (brown)	Raw salmon
Bamboo	Experience point	Mushroom (red)	Redstone
Bone	Feather	Naturally-spawned equipment	Rotten flesh
Bow	Fireball, fire charge or ender acid ball	Paper	Saddle
Bowl	Glass bottle	Phantom membrane	Scute
Carpet	Glowstone dust	Picked-up equipment	Seagrass
Carrot	Gold ingot	Potato	Skeleton head
Chest	Golden nugget	Potion of invisibility	Slimeball
Clownfish	Gunpowder	Prismarine crystal	Spider eye
Cooked chicken	Horse armour	Prismarine shard	Steak
Cooked cod	Illager banner	Pufferfish	Stick
Cooked mutton	Ink sac	Rabbit hide	String
Cooked porkchop	Iron axe	Rabbit's foot	Sugar
Cooked rabbit	Iron ingot	Raw beef	Totem of undying
Cooked salmon	Iron shovel	Raw chicken	Trident
Creeper head	Lead	Raw cod	Wet sponge
Crossbow	Leather	Raw mutton	Wool
Egg	Milk bucket	Raw porkchop	Zombie head
Emerald			

BEFORE YOU SPAWN

This guide assumes you are playing alone in Survival mode. Before you start your first game (and 'spawn' into the world you've created), there are a few things to understand about the mysterious world of Minecraft.

WORLD SEED

This is the string of numbers or characters that generates every Minecraft world and determines what it will look like. People often share the best seeds online. The world seed is set automatically, but you can set it manually if there's a particular seed you'd like to try – go to 'create new world' then 'more world options' to enter the seed.

BLOCKS

The Minecraft landscape is made of naturally-generated blocks, but you can also craft blocks yourself. Blocks can be placed on top of other blocks and used for building. Some are opaque, others transparent, and they can be liquid or solid. Many blocks also have a function, e.g. torches provide a light source and cake restores food points.

ITEMS

Items can't be placed in the Minecraft world, but can be held and dropped for other players to pick up. They generally have a function, e.g. tools, and can often be combined with other items to craft blocks, e.g. gunpowder.

MOBS

Mob is short for 'mobile' and refers to all living, moving creatures. Mobs can be passive, neutral or hostile. Some mobs are tameable, and two are categorised as utility mobs since they can help to defend you.

BREAKING BLOCKS

You need to break blocks to collect them. Some, e.g. wood, can be broken by hand or with a tool. Other blocks can only be broken with a specific tool, such as a pickaxe. Some tools allow you to break certain blocks more quickly – for example, a spade breaks sand, grass and gravel the fastest.

HEALTH POINTS AND DEATH

As we know, in Survival mode your health points decrease if you take damage and if you don't eat. If you lose all 20 health points you will find yourself back at the respawn screen. The contents of your inventory will be dropped at the site of your demise – if you're quick you can run back and pick everything up.

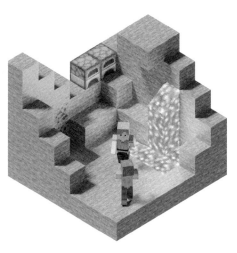

DAY AND NIGHT CYCLE

A complete day/night cycle lasts 20 minutes – 10 minutes of day followed by 10 minutes of night. The sun and moon rise and fall in the sky, so check their position to give you an idea of how much day or night is left.

LEVELS AND EXPERIENCE

Experience points are earned through mining, defeating mobs and players, using furnaces and breeding animals. Experience orbs will appear and you'll automatically collect them if you're standing close enough. Gain enough points to increase your level, or use them to make enchanted tools, weapons and armour with new abilities.

COORDINATES

Coordinates are numbers that tell you where you are. The x axis is your distance east or west from your spawn point, the z axis is your distance north or south and the y axis shows how high or low you are. Check your coordinates on a PC or Mac by pressing F3, or by consulting a map item when playing on a console.

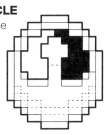

1

THE MINECRAFT LANDSCAPE

This section is all about the physical landscape of your Minecraft world. You'll learn about the different biomes you might spawn in and discover the pros and cons of settling in each. You'll also learn where to search for fascinating naturally-generated structures and valuable loot that will help you on your journey.

BIOMES

BADLANDS

Rare badlands biomes are largely composed of terracotta and red sand. There are very few trees and no passive mobs to provide meat, so avoid this biome when you first spawn. Gold ore generates at all levels here.

BADLANDS VARIANTS

These variants contain flat, tree-covered areas and terracotta spikes respectively.

PLATEAU

ERODED BADLANDS

ABANDONED MINESHAFT

Abandoned mineshafts generate at surface level, giving you access to rare ores.

DARK FOREST

Dark forest biomes have a dense covering of dark oak trees and huge mushrooms that block out most of the sunlight.

HOSTILE MOBS

Hostile mobs often spawn during the day due to the low light level, so this is not a biome for beginners to settle in.

WOODLAND MANSION

These rare structures are packed with loot, but crawling with dangerous mobs.

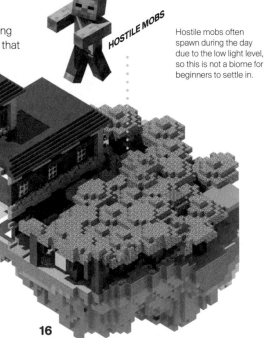

DESERT

Desert biomes are barren and inhospitable. Most passive mobs don't spawn here, and rain doesn't fall, so finding and growing food is difficult. Visit deserts to collect resources but build your base in a more hospitable biome.

DID YOU KNOW?

Look out for fossils when mining in desert biomes – they generate 15-24 blocks below the surface and are made of bone blocks. It's thought they are the remains of giant, extinct creatures ...

DESERT WELL

Desert wells can sometimes be found, too – these are largely decorative but can also be used as a water source.

DESERT TEMPLE

CACTUS

Desert temples and villages are common features. Both are a great source of materials and also contain loot chests in which you can find more valuable items and blocks.

There are no trees to provide wood – the surface is covered with sand, dead bushes and cacti.

FOREST

Forests are an ideal spawn point as they provide lots of wood for crafting. The surface is covered with oak trees.

FOREST VARIANTS

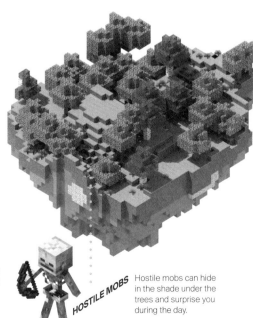

Flower forests have fewer trees but an abundance of colourful flowers.

BIRCH FOREST

FLOWER FOREST

The birch forest variant contains only birch trees.

HOSTILE MOBS

Hostile mobs can hide in the shade under the trees and surprise you during the day.

JUNGLE

Jungles are difficult to travel across and build in due to the dense covering of trees. Hostile mobs can spawn in the daytime as the tree canopy blocks out a lot of sunlight, so avoid settling here when you first spawn. This is the only biome in which you can find melons and cocoa.

JUNGLE VARIANT

Bamboo jungles have fewer trees but lots of bamboo. Pandas spawn here – see page 42 for more info.

BAMBOO JUNGLE

JUNGLE TEMPLE

Jungle temples contain trapped loot chests – see page 27 for more info.

Ocelots and parrots spawn exclusively in jungles. See pages 38 and 43 for more info.

PASSIVE MOBS

MOUNTAINS

Mountains are impressive to look at, but building is difficult due to the lack of flat ground, and exploring is dangerous as you can fall from the cliffs.

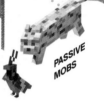

EMERALD ORE

Emerald ore only generates in mountains, so it's a good biome for mining.

LLAMA

Llamas spawn in herds in the mountains – see page 41 for more info.

MUSHROOM FIELDS

The rare mushroom fields biome can be found in the middle of the ocean. It's a mixture of hills and plains, covered in mycelium. Mushroom fields are one of only two biomes in which huge mushrooms grow naturally. The biome is a safe refuge for beginners, but trees don't grow here so you'll need to move on if you want to craft useful items.

Mooshrooms are the only mob that spawns here – there are no hostile mobs.

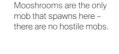

MOOSHROOM

MYCELIUM

Mycelium is a block on which mushrooms and huge mushrooms grow at any light level.

OCEAN

There are four kinds of ocean biome: warm, lukewarm, cold and frozen. They're teeming with life – you'll meet everything from friendly dolphins to deadly drowned mobs. There are plenty of fish to provide food, too. They're also laden with loot, so keep an eye out for underwater ruins and shipwrecks.

Treasure-laden monuments generate in deep areas of ocean and are patrolled by dangerous guardians and elder guardians.

OCEAN MONUMENT

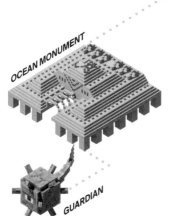

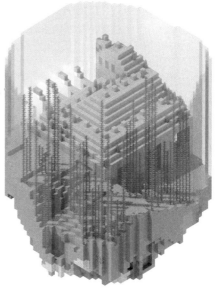

GUARDIAN

PLAINS

Plains are flat and grassy, with only a sparse covering of trees. Villages are commonly found here, and they're one of only a few biomes in which horses spawn naturally. They're relatively easy to build in so they're great for beginners and for settling long-term.

PASSIVE MOBS

Plains are a great source of food due to the abundance of passive mobs.

PLAINS VARIANT

SUNFLOWER PLAINS

This rare variant of the plains biome is covered in sunflowers, all pointing east to help you get your bearings.

SAVANNA

Savannas are arid, flat biomes covered with dry grass and acacia trees. Farming can be difficult due to lack of water. Horses and llamas spawn frequently in savannas.

HORSE

LLAMA

VILLAGE

Villages are common in savannas, so they're a good biome in which to gather resources.

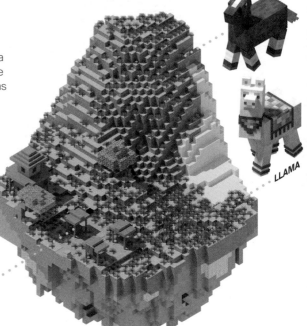

SNOWY TUNDRA

Snowy tundras are flat, snowy biomes in which all exposed water sources have frozen to ice. Sugar cane is often found here, but farming is difficult since water freezes. There aren't many trees, so it's not ideal for beginners.

SNOWY TUNDRA VARIANT

In this variant biome you'll find large spikes of ice. Some can reach over 50 blocks in height.

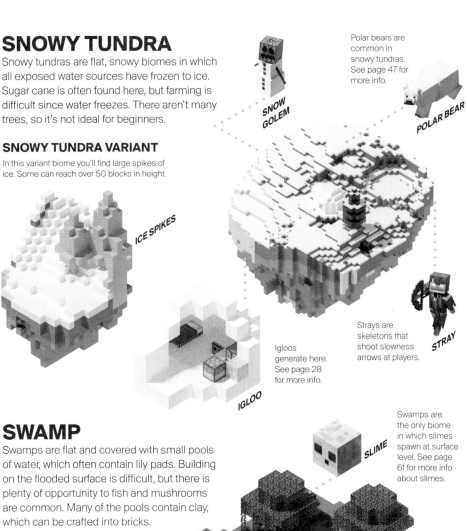

SNOW GOLEM

Polar bears are common in snowy tundras. See page 47 for more info.

POLAR BEAR

ICE SPIKES

Igloos generate here. See page 28 for more info.

Strays are skeletons that shoot slowness arrows at players.

STRAY

IGLOO

SWAMP

Swamps are flat and covered with small pools of water, which often contain lily pads. Building on the flooded surface is difficult, but there is plenty of opportunity to fish and mushrooms are common. Many of the pools contain clay, which can be crafted into bricks.

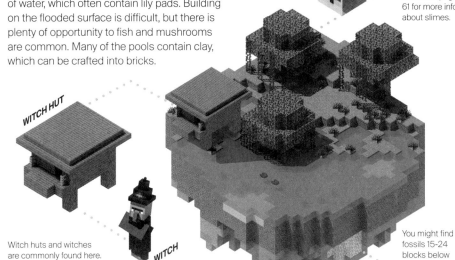

Swamps are the only biome in which slimes spawn at surface level. See page 61 for more info about slimes.

SLIME

WITCH HUT

Witch huts and witches are commonly found here. See page 60 for more info on witches.

WITCH

You might find fossils 15-24 blocks below the surface of swamps.

TAIGA

Taiga biomes are a great source of wood due to the abundance of spruce trees, making them a good starting point for beginners. You'll find wolves, rabbits and foxes here, as well as villages.

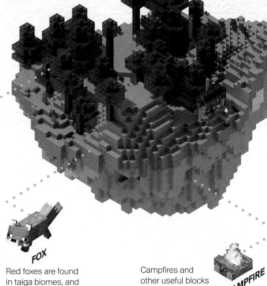

TAIGA VARIANT

This sub-biome is covered in a type of dirt called podzol and has giant trees.

GIANT TREE TAIGA

FOX

Red foxes are found in taiga biomes, and white foxes appear in the snowy taiga variant.

CAMPFIRE

Campfires and other useful blocks can be found in taiga villages.

THE NETHER

You'll never spawn here, but more advanced players will want to visit the Nether – a hellish dimension filled with new and terrifying hostile mobs. The Nether is a great source of unique materials such as glowstone, which can be used as a light source, and Nether quartz, which can be turned into quartz for building.

HOSTILE MOBS

Nether mobs drop an array of useful items, many of which are needed for potions.

NETHER FORTRESS

Nether fortresses are the only naturally-generated structure in the Nether. They contain several useful materials including Nether wart, which you'll need for potions.

NETHER PORTAL

The Nether is accessed via a portal that you'll build from obsidian then set alight to activate.

THE END

The End is composed of several islands floating in the Void. Only the most advanced players dare venture there ...

ENDER DRAGON

MAIN ISLAND

The main island is accessed via an End portal in a stronghold in the Overworld – see page 30 for more info. If you want to get out of there alive and visit the outer islands you'll need to defeat the ultimate boss mob – the ender dragon.

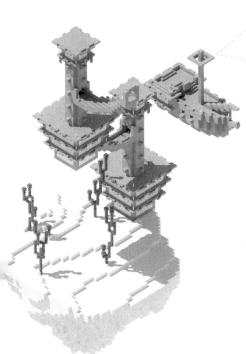

OUTER ISLANDS

For those skilful enough to defeat the dragon, you must then find a way to the outer islands. There you'll find unique blocks, as well as rare items such as elytra (wings that allow you to glide), a decorative dragon head and a new hostile mob – the shulker.

MOJANG STUFF

As in the Nether, sleeping in a bed in the End will cause it to explode. One speedrun challenge in Hardcore mode is to find a way of placing beds during the climactic battle so that you are partly shielded from the explosion, but inflict maximum damage to the dragon as it swoops in. Timing is everything!

NATURALLY-GENERATED STRUCTURES

If you know where to look you'll find naturally-generated structures all around you. These structures contain valuable materials and sometimes loot chests, too, but they're dangerous and often contain traps. Proceed with caution.

ABANDONED MINESHAFT

Usually found underground, abandoned mineshafts are an excellent place to mine for ores.

Beware of cave spider spawners, which are surrounded by a heavy layer of cobwebs. Cave spiders are venomous and can soon overpower you in the narrow corridors.

Watch out for lava streams and pools, which are common underground.

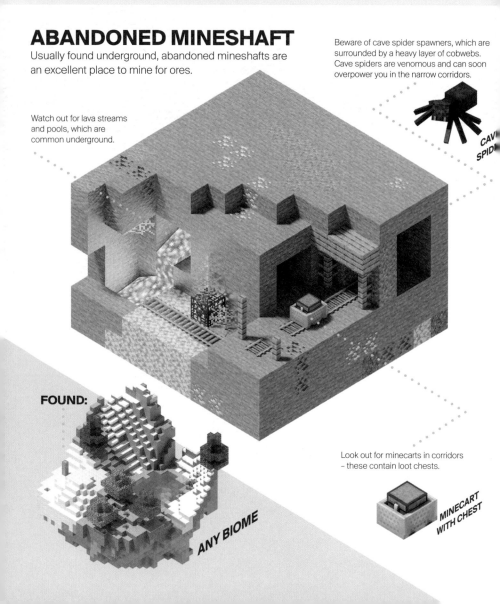

CAV[E]
SPID[ER]

FOUND:

ANY BIOME

Look out for minecarts in corridors – these contain loot chests.

MINECART
WITH CHEST

DESERT TEMPLE

Desert temples are found in desert biomes. They are constructed from various sandstone blocks, with decorative blocks of orange and blue terracotta. You can mine these blocks for use in your own constructions.

Desert temples may be partially buried in sand and can be difficult to spot. Look out for sandstone and orange terracotta, or a tower protruding from the landscape.

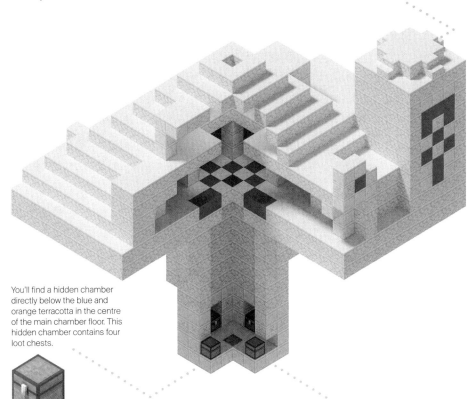

You'll find a hidden chamber directly below the blue and orange terracotta in the centre of the main chamber floor. This hidden chamber contains four loot chests.

LOOT CHEST

FOUND:

DESERT

The pressure plate in the centre of the chests is rigged to a TNT block and will detonate if you step or fall directly onto it. Descend carefully.

TNT

DUNGEON

Dungeons are small rooms built out of mossy cobblestone and cobblestone. They usually generate underground, and you can wander into them fairly easily. Keep an eye out for mossy cobblestone or flames flickering in the darkness when mining.

You'll find a zombie, skeleton or spider spawner in the centre of the dungeon, which you can disable by placing torches around and on top of it. Alternatively, you could use the spawner for combat practice.

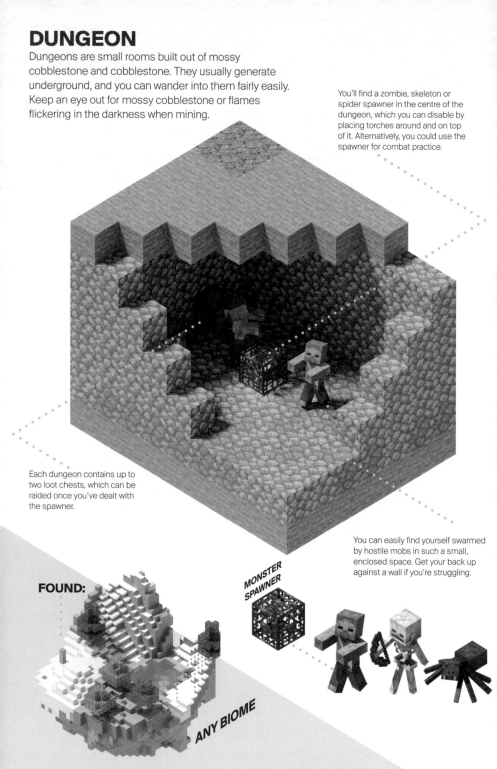

Each dungeon contains up to two loot chests, which can be raided once you've dealt with the spawner.

You can easily find yourself swarmed by hostile mobs in such a small, enclosed space. Get your back up against a wall if you're struggling.

FOUND:

MONSTER SPAWNER

ANY BIOME

JUNGLE TEMPLE

Built from cobblestone, mossy cobblestone and chiselled stone bricks, mysterious jungle temples have three floors and can be accessed via an entrance at ground level.

Down in the basement you'll find three levers. When pulled in the right order they'll reveal a secret chamber back on the ground floor which contains a loot chest.

The top floor is empty but can be mined for mossy cobblestone.

MOSSY COBBLESTONE

Once you've collected the loot, you can mine the trap mechanisms and redstone for your own use.

FOUND:

JUNGLE

Further along the corridor from the levers you'll find two dispensers filled with arrows. Find a way to pass without walking through the tripwire and you'll be rewarded with another loot chest at the end of the corridor.

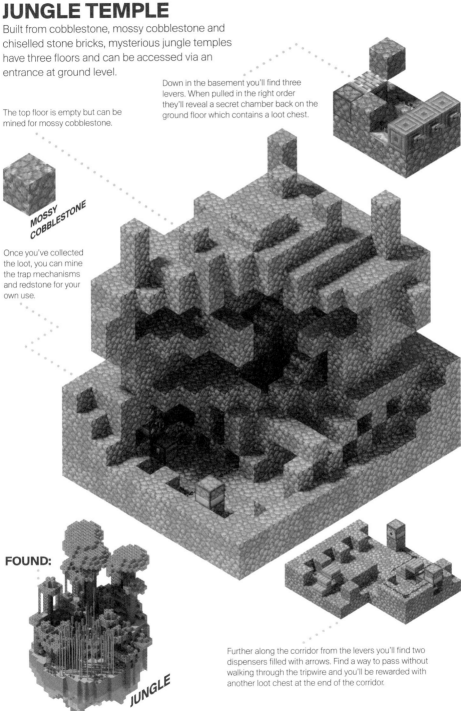

IGLOO

Igloos are small structures composed of snow blocks. They make useful emergency shelters.

Inside you'll find carpet, a bed, a crafting table and a furnace.

Half of igloos also contain a basement, accessed via a trapdoor under the carpet.

The basement contains a brewing stand, a loot chest, a cauldron and two cells imprisoning a villager and a zombie villager. Mine the brewing stand and cauldron with a pickaxe – you'll need them to brew potions.

FOUND:

SNOWY TUNDRA / COLD TAIGA

Watch out for silverfish in the basement – some of the wall blocks are actually monster eggs.

VILLAGE

Home to your friendly local villagers, villages contain a variety of structures with different functions, from houses and farms to a blacksmith and libraries.

Watch out for zombie villagers, especially in small villages with no iron golem.

Villagers spawn in the building relating to their profession. During the day they leave their buildings and wander around the village.

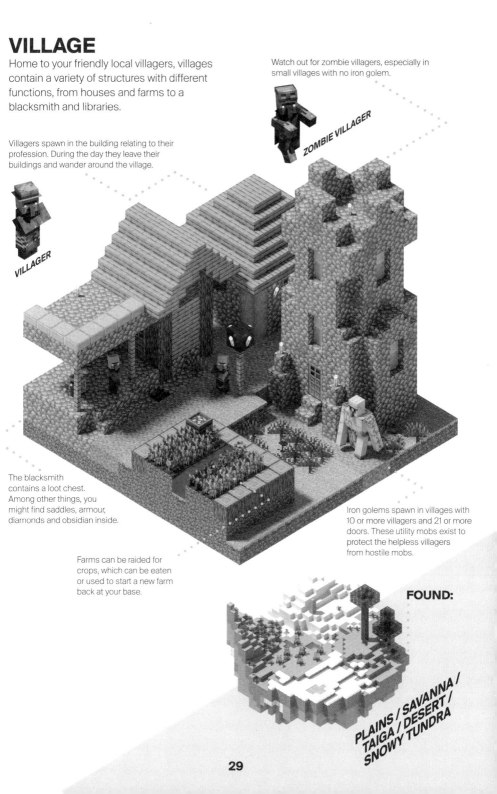

ZOMBIE VILLAGER

VILLAGER

The blacksmith contains a loot chest. Among other things, you might find saddles, armour, diamonds and obsidian inside.

Iron golems spawn in villages with 10 or more villagers and 21 or more doors. These utility mobs exist to protect the helpless villagers from hostile mobs.

Farms can be raided for crops, which can be eaten or used to start a new farm back at your base.

FOUND:

PLAINS / SAVANNA / TAIGA / DESERT / SNOWY TUNDRA

STRONGHOLD

Strongholds are found underground, and sometimes underwater. You'll need to find a stronghold if you want to visit the End.

Throw eyes of ender to locate your nearest stronghold. Each eye will travel a short distance in the right direction. When they stop travelling and fall onto the same spot, dig down to find the stronghold.

Strongholds vary in size. They are composed of several rooms, connected by a maze of corridors and staircases. It's easy to get lost in large strongholds as you search for the End portal room.

Look out for loot chests as you explore. These may contain everything from enchanted books to diamond horse armour.

FOUND:

ANY BIOME

The End portal room contains an incomplete End portal and a silverfish spawner. You'll need to fill the empty End portal frames with eyes of ender to activate it, then jump through to be transported to the End.

PILLAGER OUTPOST

Pillager outposts generate around 100-150 blocks away from villages. They're home to hostile pillagers who like to carry out raids on the villages.

IRON GOLEM

Iron golems can be found in cages around some towers.

The main structure looks like a watchtower.

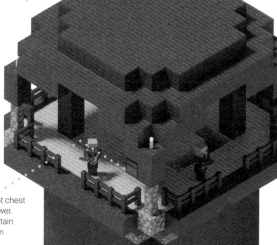

You'll find a loot chest in the watchtower. This could contain everything from carrots to an enchanted book.

There will usually be other structures around the tower.

FOUND:

PLAINS / SAVANNA / TAIGA / DESERT / SNOWY TUNDRA

WOODLAND MANSION

Woodland mansions are a rare sight in dark forest biomes. Built from wood and cobblestone, they have several floors, many rooms and offer an abundance of useful resources. Sound too good to be true? Unfortunately they're also home to some of Minecraft's most dangerous mobs.

In addition to the usual hostile mobs, vindicator, evoker and vex mobs spawn inside the mansion. These boss-like mobs are highly dangerous and only skilled players should attempt to take them on. See pages 62-63 to learn more.

VINDICATOR   EVOKER   VEX

You may find several farming areas on the ground floor, including a tree farm, mushroom farm and pumpkin and melon patches.

FOUND:

DARK FOREST

DID YOU KNOW? ↗

Explorer maps are handy items that help you track down woodland mansions – see page 45 to learn how to get your hands on one.

Several rooms have a more homely feel – dining rooms contain tables, flower pots and bookshelves, and you might find many bedrooms, too.

DID YOU KNOW? ↗

The most dedicated explorers are likely to find secret areas inside mansions, some of which contain valuable loot.

Among the more sinister structures you might find are altar-style constructs, strange platforms and prison cells. There might also be a map room, which suggests the vindicators and evokers are plotting something.

2

MOBS

You're not alone in this mysterious new world. In this section you'll discover the differences between passive, neutral and hostile mobs. You'll learn where to find them, how to defend yourself from neutral and hostile mob attacks and, most importantly, what each mob drops when defeated.

PASSIVE MOBS

As you explore the Overworld you'll come across a variety of passive mobs that can easily be defeated with a tool or weapon. Most drop useful items, including meat, which will be cooked if they are defeated when on fire.

SPAWN LOCATION

ANY BIOME

CHICKEN

BEHAVIOUR
Chickens spawn in grassy areas. They wander around, clucking and laying eggs every 5-10 minutes.

SPECIAL SKILLS
When falling, chickens slow their descent by flapping their wings so they don't take damage.

DROPS WHEN DEFEATED

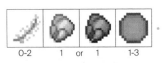

| 0-2 | 1 or 1 | 1-3 |

DROPS WHEN ALIVE

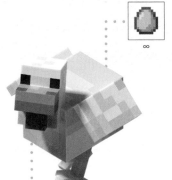

∞

SPAWN LIGHT LEVEL

15

9

0

BAT

BEHAVIOUR
Bats spawn in caves across the Overworld. They hang upside-down when idle, but otherwise can be seen flying around erratically.

SPECIAL SKILLS
Bats are the only passive mob that spawns in the dark and that can fly.

DROPS WHEN DEFEATED

0

MOJANG STUFF

The high-pitched squeak the bat makes was toned down several times after players said it hurt their ears.

SPAWN LIGHT LEVEL

15

3

0

PIG

BEHAVIOUR
Pigs roam the Overworld in groups of 3-4, oinking randomly. They will follow any player that is within 5 blocks of them and is holding a carrot, a carrot on a stick, a potato or beetroot.

See page 75 for a fishing rod recipe. Carrots can be found in village farms and can be dropped by zombies.

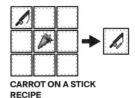

CARROT ON A STICK RECIPE

SPECIAL SKILLS
Pigs can be ridden, although they aren't very fast. You'll need to saddle them first, then lead them around using a carrot on a stick. They will eat the carrot over time so you'll need to keep an eye on its durability bar. Saddles can be found in naturally-generated chests. A saddled pig will drop its saddle upon death.

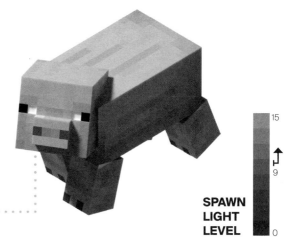

DROPS WHEN DEFEATED

| 1-3 | or | 1-3 | 0-1 | 1-3 |

SPAWN LIGHT LEVEL

15

9

0

SHEEP

DROPS WHEN ALIVE

1-3

BEHAVIOUR
Sheep wander around, bleating occasionally and eating grass blocks.

SPECIAL SKILLS
Sheep drop 1 wool when they die, but 1-3 wool if you shear them while they're alive. The wool will grow back after shearing. You can also dye a sheep before you shear it to permanently change the wool's colour. Dyes can be crafted from flowers, lapis lazuli, cocoa beans and ink sacs, among other items.

DROPS WHEN DEFEATED

| 1 | 1-2 | or | 1-2 | 1-3 |

SPAWN LIGHT LEVEL

15

9

0

37

OCELOT

BEHAVIOUR
Ocelots creep through jungles, occasionally attacking chickens. They avoid players and hostile mobs.

SPECIAL SKILLS
Ocelots scare creepers away and are immune to fall damage. They can be bred by feeding them raw fish. Stand within 10 blocks of an ocelot, then wait for it to enter begging mode – it will walk right up to you and look at you. Don't make any sudden movements or you'll scare it off. Feed 2 ocelots raw fish and they will make a baby ocelot. Once you've fed an ocelot, it will trust you and stop running away.

SPAWN LOCATION

JUNGLE

DROPS WHEN DEFEATED

1-3

SPAWN LIGHT LEVEL

15

0

RABBIT

BEHAVIOUR
Rabbits hop around, avoiding players, hostile mobs and wolves. They seek out and eat mature carrot crops.

SPECIAL SKILLS
Rabbits will approach you if you're within 8 blocks and are holding carrots or dandelions. They will go over cliffs to reach carrots, but not through lava.

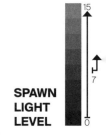

DID YOU KNOW?

Rabbits spawn in desert, flower forest, taiga and snowy tundra biomes and the hills variants of these biomes.

DROPS WHEN DEFEATED

| 0-1 | 0-1 or | 0-1 | 0-1 | 1-3 |

SPAWN LIGHT LEVEL

15

7

0

SQUID

BEHAVIOUR

Squid move through water using their tentacles. If attacked, they try to swim away. They suffocate if not in water.

SPECIAL SKILLS

Squid can swim against a current. They also have an impressive set of teeth, although they are harmless.

DROPS WHEN DEFEATED

1-3   1-3

SPAWN LOCATION

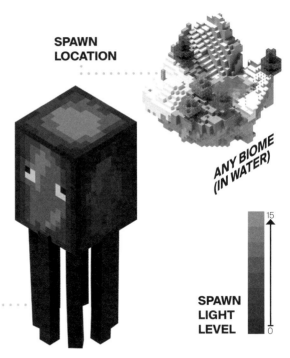

ANY BIOME (IN WATER)

SPAWN LIGHT LEVEL

15

0

HORSE

BEHAVIOUR

Horses roam in herds of 2-6. They can have one of 35 different colour and marking combinations. Donkeys are a smaller variant of horse. If a horse breeds with a donkey they will produce a mule.

SPECIAL SKILLS

Horses are one of the fastest methods of transport, but they need to be tamed first. Tame a horse by mounting it repeatedly until it stops throwing you off, then saddle it so it can be ridden. Saddles can be found in naturally-generated chests. Donkeys and mules can also be equipped with chests and used to transport items. When defeated, horses will drop any equipment they have, and donkeys and mules will drop their chest, if equipped, plus its contents.

SPAWN LOCATION

SAVANNA/ PLAINS

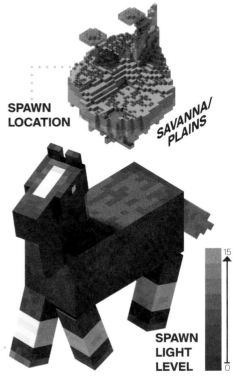

SPAWN LIGHT LEVEL

15

0

DROPS WHEN DEFEATED

0-2   0-1   0-1   0-1   1-3

COW

BEHAVIOUR
Cows travel in groups and can be heard mooing from quite some distance.

SPECIAL SKILLS
Cows can be milked by using a bucket on them. See page 73 for a bucket recipe. They also follow you if you're holding wheat within 10 blocks of them. They may drop leather when defeated, which can be used in several crafting recipes, and will drop meat, which will be cooked if they were killed by fire.

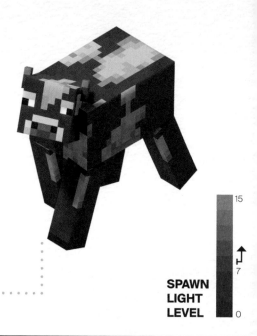

DROPS WHEN DEFEATED

| 0-2 | 1-3 | or | 1-3 | 1-3 |

SPAWN LIGHT LEVEL

15

7

0

MOOSHROOM

BEHAVIOUR
Mooshrooms can only be found in mushroom fields biomes. They wander around in herds of 4-8, avoiding danger such as cliffs and lava.

SPAWN LOCATION

MUSHROOM FIELDS

SPECIAL SKILLS
Mooshrooms can be milked by using a bucket on them. They can also be milked with a bowl to produce mushroom stew, and sheared for 5 mushrooms (red or brown depending on the type of mooshroom), which will turn them into regular cows. In all other respects they are very similar to cows – they may drop leather when defeated, and will drop 1-3 pieces of meat, which will be cooked if they were killed by fire.

DROPS WHEN ALIVE

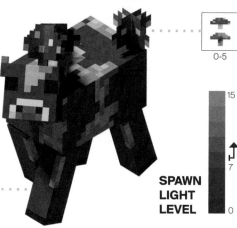

0-5

15

7

0

DROPS WHEN DEFEATED

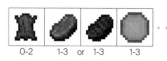

| 0-2 | 1-3 | or | 1-3 | 1-3 |

SPAWN LIGHT LEVEL

LLAMA

BEHAVIOUR

Llamas like to stay together in herds. If one llama is led by a player, nearby llamas will follow, forming a caravan. They are hostile towards wolves and will spit at them, dealing a small amount of damage. They will also spit at any player who attacks them.

SPECIAL SKILLS

Tame a llama by riding it a few times with an empty hand, until it stops throwing you off. Once tame you can equip a llama with a chest, and with a carpet to change the appearance of its saddle. It will drop any equipped items when defeated.

DROPS WHEN DEFEATED

0-2	0-1	0-1	1-3

SPAWN LOCATIONS

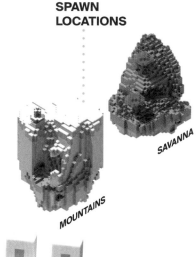

SAVANNA

MOUNTAINS

DID YOU KNOW?

Each llama has its own unique strength rating which determines how many items it can carry. They're all equally adorable, however.

SPAWN LIGHT LEVEL

15

7

0

CAT

BEHAVIOUR

These tameable mobs can be found wandering around villages as strays. They will have one of 11 different skins. Black cats can also spawn in witch huts in swamps.

SPECIAL SKILLS

Stray cats can be tamed by feeding them raw cod or raw salmon. Once tamed, they'll follow you around and will teleport to your side if separated. They'll also sleep when you sleep and will sometimes bring you gifts like rabbit's feet, feathers or raw chicken. Cats scare off creepers and phantoms. They can also see players who have taken a potion of invisibility.

SPAWN LOCATION

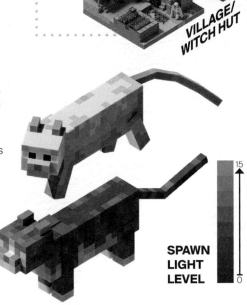

VILLAGE/ WITCH HUT

DROPS WHEN DEFEATED

0-2   1-3

15

SPAWN LIGHT LEVEL

0

PANDA

BEHAVIOUR

Pandas wander around bamboo jungles, searching for bamboo to eat. Some pandas are brown and white instead of black and white. Pandas will follow players within 16 blocks who are holding bamboo. Adult pandas also like to eat cake. If hurt by a player, adult pandas will attack once.

SPECIAL SKILLS

Pandas have different personalities and can be lazy, worried, playful, aggressive or weak. Baby pandas sometime sneeze, producing a slimeball and making nearby adult pandas jump. Baby pandas can also roll over. Pandas can drop bamboo when defeated.

SPAWN LOCATION

BAMBOO JUNGLE

DROPS WHEN DEFEATED

0-2   1-3

15

9

SPAWN LIGHT LEVEL

0

PARROT

BEHAVIOUR

These tameable birds can be found in jungles.
There are 5 different colours: red, blue, green,
cyan and grey. They can fly a little way above
the ground and can also swim. Parrots crowd
around other mobs, including hostile mobs.

SPECIAL SKILLS

Parrots can be tamed with seeds and will perch
on their player's shoulder. They can also copy
the sounds made by other mobs within 20
blocks, e.g. a creeper's hiss. Insert a music
disc in a jukebox and nearby parrots will dance.
Parrots will die if fed cookies.

DROPS WHEN DEFEATED

1-2   1-3

SPAWN LOCATION

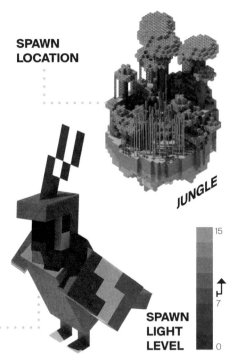

JUNGLE

15

7

0

SPAWN LIGHT LEVEL

TURTLE

BEHAVIOUR

Turtles can be seen swimming in the ocean, and also found
on warm, sandy beaches. They are fast swimmers but move
slowly on land. When it's time for turtles to lay their eggs,
they always return to their home beach – the beach where
they spawned.

SPECIAL SKILLS

Turtles follow players if they're holding seagrass. If 2 turtles are
fed seagrass they will breed. They lay 1-4 eggs on their home
beach. The eggs take a while to hatch and only hatch at
night. When baby turtles become adults, they drop a scute
– an item which can be crafted into a turtle shell. This piece
of headgear allows players to breathe underwater. Adult
turtles can drop seagrass but not scutes.

DROPS WHEN DEFEATED

0-2   1-3

DROPS WHEN ALIVE

1 (BABY)

SPAWN LOCATION

WARM BEACH

15

7

0

SPAWN LIGHT LEVEL

FOX

SPAWN LOCATION

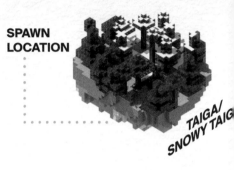

BEHAVIOUR

Foxes spawn in groups of 1-3. In regular taiga their fur is red, but in the snowy taiga it's white. They attack chickens, rabbits and baby turtles when on land, and fish if near water. They sleep during the day (unless there's a thunderstorm) and head to nearby villages to scavenge for food at night. They love to eat sweet berries – see page 77 for more info.

SPECIAL SKILLS

Foxes can spawn with items in their mouths. They can also pick up dropped items and hold them in their mouth. If you attach a baby fox to a lead and lead it away from its parents, it will trust you and never run away from you.

TAIGA/ SNOWY TAIGA

DROPS WHEN DEFEATED

0-2

SPAWN LIGHT LEVEL

15

0

WANDERING TRADER

BEHAVIOUR

You'll only ever see 1 wandering trader in your world at any time, and it could be anywhere. They have 2 leashed llamas and will despawn after 40-60 minutes. Sometimes wild llamas form a caravan behind the leashed llamas.

SPAWN LOCATION

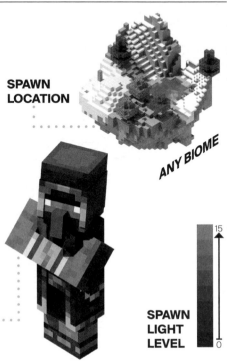

ANY BIOME

SPECIAL SKILLS

Wandering traders offer one of 6 random trades when you interact with them. All trades involve emeralds, either as the offered item or as payment. As the sun sets, they drink potion of invisibility to hide from dangerous mobs. At sunrise they drink milk to remove the effect.

DROPS WHEN DEFEATED

0-2   0-1

SPAWN LIGHT LEVEL

15

0

VILLAGER

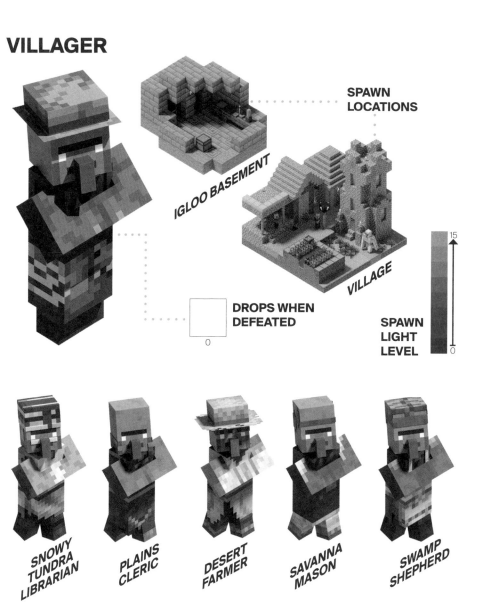

SPAWN
LOCATIONS

IGLOO BASEMENT

VILLAGE

DROPS WHEN
DEFEATED

0

SPAWN
LIGHT
LEVEL

15

0

SNOWY
TUNDRA
LIBRARIAN

PLAINS
CLERIC

DESERT
FARMER

SAVANNA
MASON

SWAMP
SHEPHERD

BEHAVIOUR

Villagers wander around villages, interacting with each other and performing tasks related to their profession. Each profession has a block related to their job – e.g. a lectern for a librarian, or a stonecutter for a stone mason. Their clothing varies depending on their job and the biome their village is in. You'll also find a villager in every igloo basement.

SPECIAL SKILLS

Villagers like to trade with players – they'll swap a number of useful items for emeralds, and vice versa. Interact with a villager to see what trades they're currently offering. Cartographers will trade explorer maps for emeralds – these rare and valuable maps will lead you to loot-laden woodland mansions and ocean monuments so you can stock up on loot.

NEUTRAL MOBS

Unfortunately, not all mobs are passive sources of food. A handful of mobs are classified as neutral, which means their behaviour varies and they can become hostile under certain circumstances. Keep an eye out for them – they drop some useful items that will aid your progress in different ways.

WOLF

HEALTH POINTS	8 IF UNTAMED	20 IF TAMED
ATTACK STRENGTH	3-6 IF UNTAMED	4 IF TAMED
HOW TO DEFEAT		
ITEMS DROPPED	1-3	

SPAWN LIGHT LEVEL

15
7
0

BEHAVIOUR

Wolves roam in packs of 4 and will attack foxes, rabbits, skeletons and sheep on sight. A wolf will become hostile towards any player or mob that attacks them, and any nearby wolves will become hostile, too. Hostile wolves have red eyes and growl.

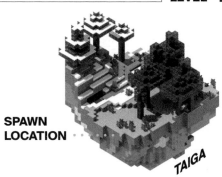

SPAWN LOCATION

TAIGA

SPECIAL SKILLS

Wolves can be tamed by feeding them bones. Once tame, they will wear a red collar and follow you around. Tamed wolves can teleport to their owner and will attack any mob that you attack, with the exception of creepers.

ATTACK METHOD

A hostile wolf will pounce on you, inflicting damage with each hit.

POLAR BEAR

HEALTH POINTS	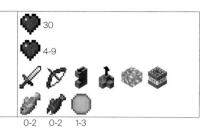	30
ATTACK STRENGTH		4-9
HOW TO DEFEAT		
ITEMS DROPPED		0-2 0-2 1-3

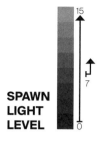

SPAWN LIGHT LEVEL

BEHAVIOUR

Adult polar bears are neutral but will become hostile if attacked by a player or if they have cubs and a player gets too close to them. Cubs are passive and will run away if attacked, but all the adults within a 41 x 21 x 41 area will become hostile and attack you in retaliation.

SPECIAL SKILLS

Polar bears are fast swimmers. They may drop fish when defeated.

SPAWN LOCATIONS

ICE SPIKES/ SNOWY MOUNTAINS/ SNOWY TUNDRA

ATTACK METHOD

Polar bears will rear up onto their back legs and strike you from above with their front paws.

SPIDER

HEALTH POINTS	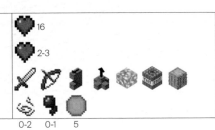 16	
ATTACK STRENGTH	2-3	
HOW TO DEFEAT		
ITEMS DROPPED	0-2 0-1 5	

SPAWN
LIGHT
LEVEL

BEHAVIOUR

Spiders are hostile to players and iron golems if the light level is 11 or lower. If the light level is higher, they won't attack unless provoked. Once hostile they will continue to pursue you, even if the light level increases.

SPECIAL SKILLS

Spiders can climb over obstacles and up walls. They are immune to poison.

ATTACK METHOD

Spiders will pounce on their opponent, inflicting damage with each hit.

SPAWN LOCATIONS

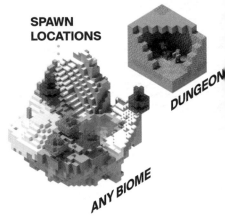

DUNGEON

ANY BIOME

VARIANT: CAVE SPIDER

SPECIAL SKILLS

Cave spiders inflict venom, poisoning you over time. They can fit through spaces that are 1 block wide and half a block tall.

HOW TO DEFEAT	

SPAWN LOCATION

ABANDONED MINESHAFT

CAVE SPIDER

DID YOU KNOW?

Occasionally a regular spider spawns with a skeleton rider. These horrifying spider jockeys have the speed and agility of a spider combined with the archery skills of a skeleton, making them truly formidable.

ENDERMAN

HEALTH POINTS	❤ 40			
ATTACK STRENGTH	❤ 4-10			
HOW TO DEFEAT	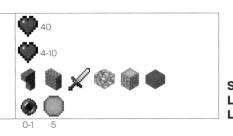			
ITEMS DROPPED				

0-1   5

SPAWN LIGHT LEVEL

15
7
0

BEHAVIOUR

Endermen are not hostile towards players unless provoked by attack or by a player looking directly at their head. Once provoked they will shake and scream, then launch themselves at you to attack. Endermen will also attack endermites on sight.

SPAWN LOCATIONS

THE OVERWORLD

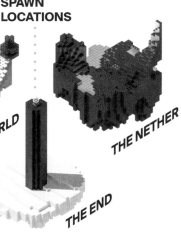
THE NETHER

THE END

SPECIAL SKILLS

Endermen teleport to avoid danger. They drop ender pearls which, when thrown, will teleport you. They can also pick up and place certain blocks.

ATTACK METHOD

Endermen will teleport to you and hit you, inflicting damage.

TIP

Wear a carved pumpkin on your head and an enderman will remain neutral even if you look at it. See page 89 to discover how to equip armour.

MOJANG STUFF

Endermen hate endermites, so you can use the nasty little bugs as a handy distraction. You can, for instance, put an endermite into a minecart and set it rolling past endermen, using it to lure them away, or, if you are particularly well-prepared, into a pit.

HOSTILE MOBS

Hostile mobs can make your life incredibly difficult and easily send you back to the respawn screen. They can be particularly dangerous if you encounter them in a small space or whilst mining underground, but, like neutral mobs, they drop some useful items if you manage to defeat them.

ZOMBIE

HEALTH POINTS	❤ 20	
ATTACK STRENGTH	❤ 2-5	
HOW TO DEFEAT	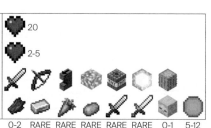	
ITEMS DROPPED		

0-2   RARE   RARE   RARE   RARE   RARE   0-1   5-12

SPAWN LIGHT LEVEL

15

7

0

SPAWN LOCATION

ANY BIOME

BEHAVIOUR

Zombies spawn in groups of 4, at light levels of 7 or less. Some zombies spawn wearing armour, which they may then drop upon death. They can't spawn on transparent blocks like glass. They shamble around slowly, with their arms outstretched, making a moaning noise. They catch fire in the sun, so will try to seek shade when the sun rises in the morning.

DID YOU KNOW?

Unlike naturally-spawned equipment, zombies never fail to drop the equipment that they have picked up when defeated. Evidence of a guilty conscience, perhaps ...

SPECIAL SKILLS

Zombies can break through wooden doors if your difficulty level is set to hard. They can pick up items from the ground, including weapons and tools which they will use, and armour which they will put on. When wearing helmets, zombies are safe from burning in the sun.

USEFUL DROPS

Zombies drop 0-2 pieces of rotten flesh, which you can eat in an emergency but you might get food poisoning as a result. You can also use rotten flesh to breed and heal tamed wolves. Zombies also drop any equipment they have picked up, such as weapons, tools and armour, and will drop their head if killed by a charged creeper's explosion.

ATTACK METHOD

Zombies will pursue players, villagers and iron golems on sight, from 40 blocks away. They aren't a big threat unless you encounter a large group of them – they'll bump into you, inflicting damage and knocking you backwards with each hit, potentially into lava or over a cliff.

ZOMBIE VARIANTS

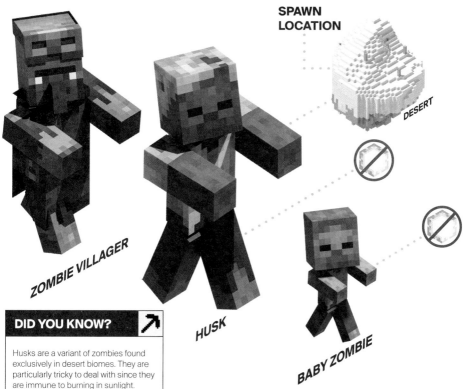

SPAWN LOCATION

DESERT

ZOMBIE VILLAGER

HUSK

BABY ZOMBIE

DID YOU KNOW?

Husks are a variant of zombies found exclusively in desert biomes. They are particularly tricky to deal with since they are immune to burning in sunlight.

CREEPER

HEALTH POINTS	♥ 20	
ATTACK STRENGTH	♥ 49	
HOW TO DEFEAT	⚔ 🏹 🧱 🔲 🔲 🔲	
ITEMS DROPPED	● ● 🔲 ⚪	

0-2   0-1   0-1   5

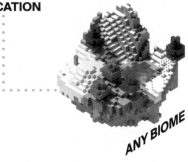

SPAWN LIGHT LEVEL

15
7
0

BEHAVIOUR
Creepers move around almost silently, searching for players to target. They have a TNT core that detonates when they are close enough to a player.

SPAWN LOCATION

ANY BIOME

SPECIAL SKILLS
Creepers are immune to burning in sunlight, and continue to creep around in search of players after the sun has risen. They also have the ability to climb up ladders and vines and can do so when pursuing their targets.

ATTACK METHOD
When they're within 3 blocks of a player, creepers will hiss and flash before exploding. Once they begin to hiss you have 1.5 seconds to get out of the blast radius (7 blocks) if you want to stop the explosion.

USEFUL DROPS

Creepers drop gunpowder, needed to craft TNT, and will drop a music disc if killed by a skeleton's arrow. You'll need a jukebox to play a music disc. Jukeboxes can be crafted from any wood planks.

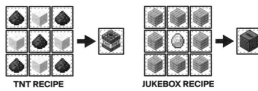

TNT RECIPE

JUKEBOX RECIPE

VARIANT: CHARGED CREEPER

SPAWN LOCATION

When lightning strikes within 3-4 blocks of a regular creeper.

LIGHTNING

ANY BIOME

SPECIAL SKILLS

The charged creeper's explosion is twice as powerful as that of a regular creeper. This explosion will cause any zombies, skeletons or regular creepers unfortunate enough to be in the vicinity to drop their heads. These rare blocks can be used for decoration or worn instead of a helmet. Wearing a mob head will reduce the chance of that mob recognising you as a player and attacking.

SKELETON

HEALTH POINTS	❤ 20					
ATTACK STRENGTH	❤ 1-5					
HOW TO DEFEAT						
ITEMS DROPPED						

0-2   0-2   RARE   RARE   0-1   5-8

SPAWN LIGHT LEVEL

15 — 7 — 0

BEHAVIOUR

Skeletons rattle as they move around, searching for players to attack. They seek out shade at sunrise to avoid burning.

ATTACK METHOD

Skeletons will pursue you on sight. Once they're within 8 blocks they'll shoot you with arrows, circling you at the same time to make it difficult for you to hit them.

SPAWN LOCATIONS

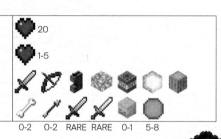

NETHER FORTRESS

ANY BIOME

DUNGEON

SPECIAL SKILLS AND USEFUL DROPS

Skeletons can climb ladders. They can pick up items including tools, weapons and armour, which they will equip/use. They may also spawn wearing armour. Upon death they will drop anything they have picked up, and may drop any naturally-spawned equipment.

VARIANT: STRAY

Strays only appear in snowy biomes. They shoot tipped arrows that inflict slowness for 30 seconds. They may also drop 1 tipped arrow upon death.

SPAWN LOCATIONS

ICE SPIKES

SNOWY MOUNTAINS

SNOWY TUNDRA

SKELETON HORSEMAN

HEALTH POINTS	❤ 30
ATTACK STRENGTH	❤ 1-10
HOW TO DEFEAT	🏹
ITEMS DROPPED	🦴 🏹 ⬤

0-2 0-2 5

SPAWN LIGHT LEVEL

15
10
0

BEHAVIOUR

Skeleton horsemen move very fast, and circle their opponent in the same way a skeleton does. If you kill a skeleton horseman, the horse will become tame and you can saddle and ride it.

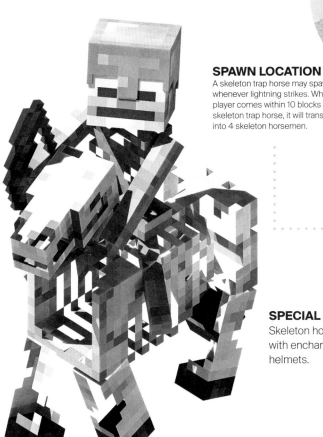

LIGHTNING

SPAWN LOCATION

A skeleton trap horse may spawn whenever lightning strikes. When a player comes within 10 blocks of a skeleton trap horse, it will transform into 4 skeleton horsemen.

ANY BIOME

SPECIAL SKILLS

Skeleton horsemen spawn with enchanted bows and helmets.

ATTACK METHOD

Skeleton riders attack on sight, shooting players with their bows.

DROWNED

HEALTH POINTS	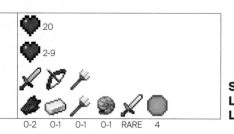 20					
ATTACK STRENGTH	2-9					
HOW TO DEFEAT						
ITEMS DROPPED						
	0-2	0-1	0-1	0-1	RARE	4

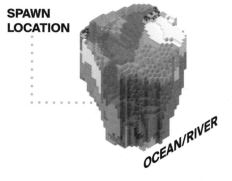

SPAWN
LIGHT
LEVEL

15
7
0

BEHAVIOUR

Drowned spawn in oceans and rivers at light levels of 7 or lower. If a zombie drowns it will become a drowned. They come up onto land at night and are hostile towards players, villagers, wandering traders, iron golems, baby turtles and turtle eggs.

SPAWN LOCATION

OCEAN/RIVER

ATTACK METHOD

Like zombies, drowned attack with their hands, dealing damage when they touch you. If holding a trident, they will throw it at their target. They will also stamp on turtle eggs in an attempt to destroy them.

SPECIAL SKILLS

Drowned are similar to zombies in many ways but they can breathe underwater. This makes them even more dangerous - you never know whre you might bump into one.

USEFUL DROPS

Drowned may drop their trident, if they have one. Find out more about this weapon on page 91. They may also drop a nautilus shell or a gold ingot.

56

PHANTOM

HEALTH POINTS	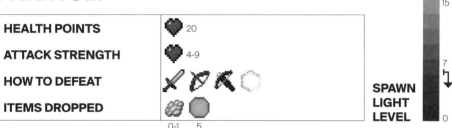 20	
ATTACK STRENGTH	4-9	
HOW TO DEFEAT		
ITEMS DROPPED	0-1 5	

SPAWN
LIGHT
LEVEL

15

7

0

BEHAVIOUR

Phantoms only spawn when a player hasn't slept in a bed for 3 in-game days. They appear at night or during thunderstorms in groups of 1-6. Like other undead mobs, they will burn if exposed to sunlight.

ATTACK METHOD

Phantoms can spot players from some distance away. They swoop quickly to attack, hitting their target to deal damage.

SPECIAL SKILLS

Phantoms produce a trail of grey smoke as they move. If they're hit with a splash potion of invisibility, their eyes and smoke trail will still be visible.

SPAWN LOCATION

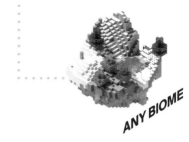

ANY BIOME

USEFUL DROPS

Phantoms may drop a phantom membrane. This strange item can be used to repair elytra – wearable wings that allow you to glide, only found in the End dimension. You can also use a phantom membrane to brew a potion of slow falling. This makes you fall at the same speed as a chicken, which stops you taking damage.

SILVERFISH

HEALTH POINTS		8
ATTACK STRENGTH		1
HOW TO DEFEAT		
ITEMS DROPPED		

5

SPAWN LIGHT LEVEL

15

11

0

BEHAVIOUR

When not spawning directly from monster spawners in strongholds, idle silverfish live in monster egg blocks and emerge when a player mines the block.

SPECIAL SKILLS

Silverfish can call other silverfish to their aid when they are being attacked. They can see you through walls and will use this ability to find a path to you.

ATTACK METHOD

Silverfish run towards you and inflict damage, knocking you backwards upon contact. You can easily find yourself swarmed.

SPAWN LOCATIONS

Silverfish spawn when monster egg blocks are broken in strongholds, igloo basements and in mountains biomes. They also appear from monster spawners in strongholds.

MOUNTAINS

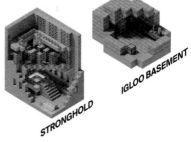

STRONGHOLD

IGLOO BASEMENT

DID YOU KNOW? ↗

If you're quick and defeat a silverfish in a single hit with a diamond sword, nearby silverfish won't be alerted.

ENDERMITE

HEALTH POINTS	 8
ATTACK STRENGTH	2-3
HOW TO DEFEAT	
ITEMS DROPPED	3

SPAWN
LIGHT
LEVEL

15

0

BEHAVIOUR

Endermites are the smallest mob. They occasionally spawn when an ender pearl is thrown. They scuttle about, leaving a trail of purple particles behind them, and attack players within 16 blocks. When not attacking players they sometimes try to burrow into blocks.

SPECIAL SKILLS

Endermites will despawn after two minutes. If one endermite is attacked, all nearby endermites will retaliate.

ATTACK METHOD

Endermites run towards you and inflict damage by bumping into you. As with silverfish, you can easily find yourself swarmed.

SPAWN LOCATIONS

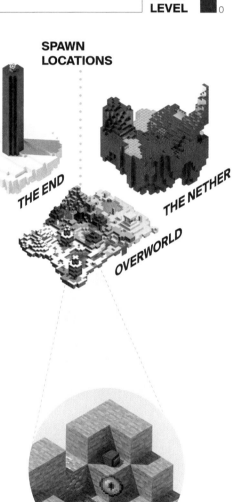

THE END

THE NETHER

OVERWORLD

WITCH

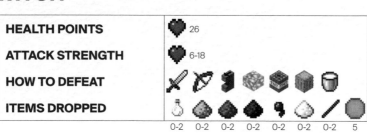

HEALTH POINTS	❤ 26							
ATTACK STRENGTH	❤ 6-18							
HOW TO DEFEAT	🗡 🏹 ▮ ◈ ▩ ▦ 🪣							
ITEMS DROPPED	🧪 ◆ ◆ ◆ 🔥 ◇ ╱ ◯							
	0-2	0-2	0-2	0-2	0-2	0-2	0-2	5

SPAWN LIGHT LEVEL

15

7

0

BEHAVIOUR

Witches wander around, searching for players. Their cackle will alert you to their presence.

USEFUL DROPS

Witches may drop up to three different items, from the ITEMS DROPPED list, but no more than two of each unique item.

ATTACK METHOD

Witches throw harmful splash potions (poison, slowness, weakness and harming) at you, whilst drinking helpful potions to heal themselves.

SPAWN LOCATIONS

Witches can also spawn when lightning strikes within 3-4 blocks of a villager.

ANY BIOME

LIGHTNING

WITCH HUT

DID YOU KNOW? ↗

Witches aren't great at multitasking – they can't attack and drink helpful potions at the same time. Get some hits in when you see them start to heal themselves.

MOJANG STUFF 🖸

For a long time, witches had no sound effects. When they were finally implemented, the developers forgot to tell anyone. Players creeping through caves suddenly heard unfamiliar and alarming sounds emanating from the dark. Some were convinced the game was haunted!

SLIME

HEALTH POINTS	❤	1-16
ATTACK STRENGTH	❤	0-6
HOW TO DEFEAT	🗡 🏹 🧱 🔲 🔲 🔲	
ITEMS DROPPED	⚪ ⚪	
	0-2 1-4	

SPAWN LIGHT LEVEL

15

7

0

BEHAVIOUR
Slimes come in three sizes: big, small and tiny. They bounce around searching for players to attack and are also hostile towards iron golems.

SPECIAL SKILLS
Slimes can swim in water. They also have the ability to duplicate – if you defeat a big slime, it will split into small slimes, and if you defeat a small slime it will split into tiny slimes. All slimes drop experience points, but tiny slimes also drop slimeballs which can be used in a number of crafting recipes including sticky pistons and leads.

SPAWN LOCATIONS
Slimes spawn below level 40 in all biomes. In swamps they spawn between layers 50 and 70 when the light level is 7 or lower.

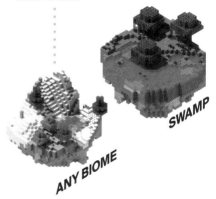

SWAMP

ANY BIOME

ATTACK METHOD
Slimes will bounce into you, inflicting damage when they make contact.

ILLAGER

Illagers look similar to villagers but are dressed in dark robes and their skin has an unhealthy grey hue. There are two variants – the vindicator and the evoker. They can be found in woodland mansions and also spawn as part of raids (attacks on villages triggered by cursed players).

SPAWN LOCATION

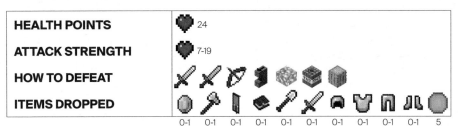

DARK FOREST

WOODLAND MANSION

SPAWN LIGHT LEVEL

15

0

VARIANT: VINDICATOR

HEALTH POINTS	24
ATTACK STRENGTH	7-19
HOW TO DEFEAT	
ITEMS DROPPED	0-1 0-1 0-1 0-1 0-1 0-1 0-1 0-1 0-1 0-1 5

BEHAVIOUR
Vindicators spawn in groups of 2-3. They are hostile towards players and villagers and will pursue them on sight.

ATTACK METHOD
Vindicators will move quickly towards their target, brandishing their axe as a weapon then using it to deal damage.

USEFUL DROPS
Vindicators may drop emeralds when defeated which can be used to trade with their passive cousins in villages. They may also drop an enchanted book, as well as iron tools and weapons or iron armour.

VARIANT: EVOKER

HEALTH POINTS	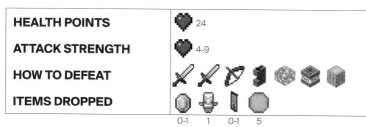 24
ATTACK STRENGTH	4-9
HOW TO DEFEAT	
ITEMS DROPPED	

0-1 1 0-1 5

BEHAVIOUR
Evokers spawn alone in woodland mansions and as part of raids. They're hostile towards players and villagers.

ATTACK METHOD
The evoker has a special fang attack – it summons a stream of sharp teeth, which rise up out of the floor and bite the evoker's opponent. Evokers can also summon three vexes to join the fight.

USEFUL DROPS
When defeated, evokers drop a rare and powerful item – the totem of undying. When held, this object will prevent the owner from dying.

VEX

HEALTH POINTS	 14
ATTACK STRENGTH	5-13
HOW TO KILL	
ITEMS DROPPED	

3

BEHAVIOUR
Vexes are summoned by evokers. Armed with swords, they fly at the nearest player or regular villager and attack. They begin to take damage 30-119 seconds after spawning.

SPECIAL SKILLS
Vexes can fly through solid blocks and can often be seen disappearing through the floor.

ATTACK METHOD
Vexes fly at players or villagers and hit them with their sword.

PILLAGER

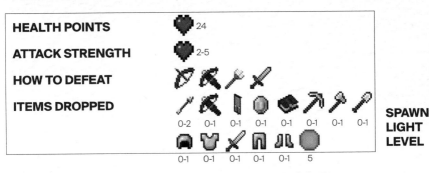

HEALTH POINTS	❤ 24						
ATTACK STRENGTH	❤ 2-5						
HOW TO DEFEAT							
ITEMS DROPPED							

0-2	0-1	0-1	0-1	0-1	0-1	0-1	0-1

0-1	0-1	0-1	0-1	0-1	5

SPAWN LIGHT LEVEL 15 — 0

BEHAVIOUR

Pillagers spawn in groups of 2-5, called patrols, 24-48 blocks away from players. They also spawn in and around pillage outposts, and as part of raids (attacks on villages by waves of pillagers, vindicators, evokers, ravagers and witches). Pillagers are hostile towards players, villagers, wandering traders and iron golems.

ATTACK METHOD

Pillagers are armed with crossbows and will shoot their targets. Their crossbows may be enchanted with an effect like multishot (fires 3 arrows at the cost of 1) or quick charge (decreases the crossbow loading time). Pillagers can also ride ravagers.

SPECIAL SKILLS

Each raid has a captain. It could be a pillager, vindicator or evoker, and it will be wearing an ominous banner on its head. If a player defeats the captain, it will drop its banner and the player will be inflicted with the bad omen status effect. If the player then enters a village, this will trigger the start of a raid.

USEFUL DROPS

Pillagers may drop arrows and their crossbow. They can also drop a variety of weapons and armour, as well as emeralds.

SPAWN LOCATION

ANY BIOME

RAVAGER

HEALTH POINTS	100
ATTACK STRENGTH	7-18
HOW TO DEFEAT	
ITEMS DROPPED	1 20

SPAWN
LIGHT
LEVEL

BEHAVIOUR

Up to 5 ravagers can spawn as part of raids, in or near to villages. Like pillagers, they are hostile towards players, villagers, wandering traders and iron golems. Some ravagers spawn with pillagers or evokers riding them.

SPAWN LOCATION

VILLAGE

ATTACK METHOD

Ravagers use their head to ram their targets, dealing damage and knocking the target backwards. Their powerful roar also deals 6 points of damage.

SPECIAL SKILLS

Ravagers can destroy certain blocks by ramming into them – for example, pumpkins, flowers and sugar canes.

USEFUL DROPS

Ravagers drop a saddle when defeated, which can be used to ride horses, donkeys, mules and pigs.

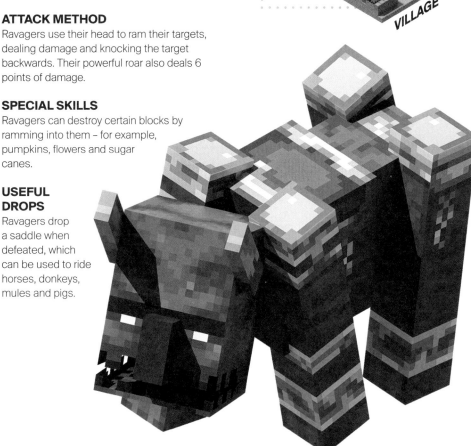

65

3

SURVIVAL

Now that you're familiar with the Minecraft landscape and its mobs, it's time to start your first game. In this section you'll learn how to find food and materials to keep yourself safe. You'll discover how to build a shelter and a farm, how to mine for materials and how to defend yourself in combat as you explore.

YOUR FIRST DAY

When you first spawn it's a race against time to gather resources before night falls and the hostile mobs come looking for you. Every adventure is different, but this step-by-step guide is one option that will keep you safe until day two.

FIRST DAY

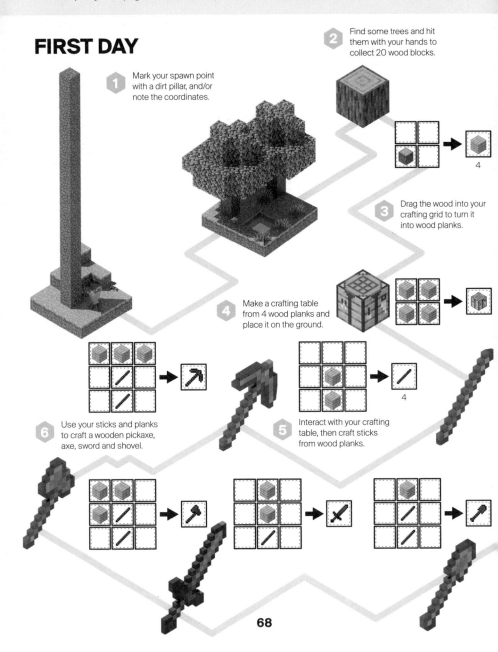

2 Find some trees and hit them with your hands to collect 20 wood blocks.

1 Mark your spawn point with a dirt pillar, and/or note the coordinates.

3 Drag the wood into your crafting grid to turn it into wood planks.

4 Make a crafting table from 4 wood planks and place it on the ground.

6 Use your sticks and planks to craft a wooden pickaxe, axe, sword and shovel.

5 Interact with your crafting table, then craft sticks from wood planks.

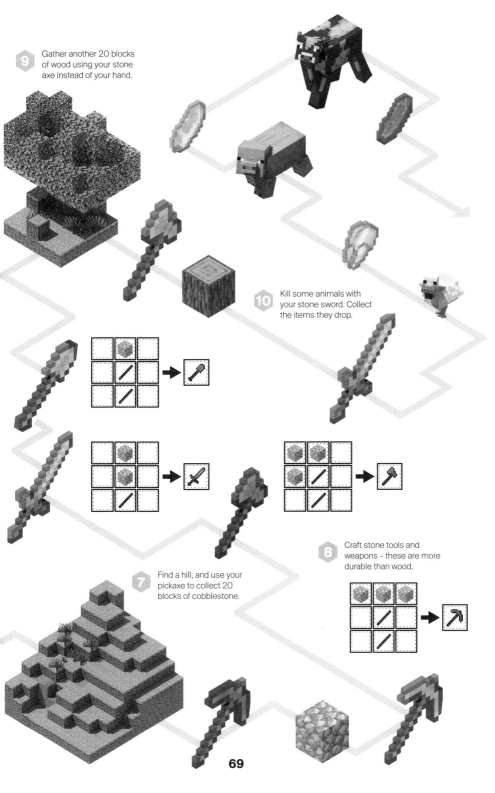

9 Gather another 20 blocks of wood using your stone axe instead of your hand.

10 Kill some animals with your stone sword. Collect the items they drop.

8 Craft stone tools and weapons – these are more durable than wood.

7 Find a hill, and use your pickaxe to collect 20 blocks of cobblestone.

69

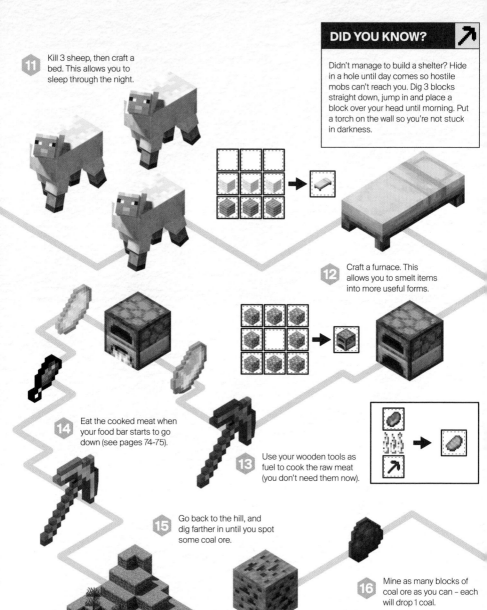

11 Kill 3 sheep, then craft a bed. This allows you to sleep through the night.

DID YOU KNOW? ↗

Didn't manage to build a shelter? Hide in a hole until day comes so hostile mobs can't reach you. Dig 3 blocks straight down, jump in and place a block over your head until morning. Put a torch on the wall so you're not stuck in darkness.

12 Craft a furnace. This allows you to smelt items into more useful forms.

14 Eat the cooked meat when your food bar starts to go down (see pages 74-75).

13 Use your wooden tools as fuel to cook the raw meat (you don't need them now).

15 Go back to the hill, and dig farther in until you spot some coal ore.

16 Mine as many blocks of coal ore as you can – each will drop 1 coal.

DID YOU KNOW? ↗

No coal ore in sight? Charcoal can be used instead of coal to make torches. Place wood in both furnace slots to create charcoal.

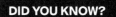

21 Light up your hole using torches to prevent hostile mobs spawning overnight. Shut the door and either sleep in your bed or wait until morning. Hide round the corner, out of sight of the door.

MOJANG STUFF

First day too easy for you? Try something like The 404 Challenge, which became really popular in the early days of Minecraft. The name refers to the world seed number 404 which, at the time, spawned you on a large gravel plane with a huge cave just beneath the surface. You have a day to collect resources above ground, then survive the night inside the cave. The seed no longer works so have fun finding a new one!

DID YOU KNOW?

If you don't manage to make a bed before sunset, use the night to cook any raw food and craft more equipment (see the next page for ideas). You could also start mining beneath your shelter if you're feeling brave ...

20 Craft a wooden door and place it on your shelter from the outside.

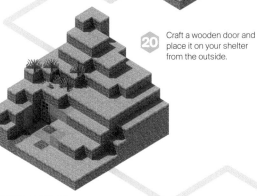

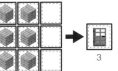
3

19 Expand the hole into an L-shape shelter, so you can hide round the corner.

18 Now you can use coal in your furnace – it'll smelt more items.

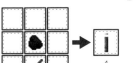
4

17 Craft torches. These can be placed on other blocks to provide light.

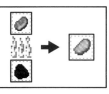

YOUR SECOND DAY

Congratulations – you've made it to day two! Now's the time to fill your inventory with supplies, deal with any resilient hostile mobs that are still lurking and craft more items. Here are some useful crafting recipes to get you started.

CHEST

A chest has 27 slots and is used to store blocks and items. Place two single chests next to each other in your shelter to create a double chest, and transfer materials from your inventory to free up some valuable space.

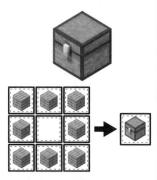

LADDER

Ladders help you ascend and descend quickly and safely. They come in handy when you encounter steep cliffs and when you start mining deeper into the ground. Just place them on the side of the blocks you wish to climb.

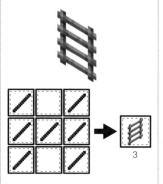

BOAT

Boats allow you to travel across water more quickly – they're a great investment if you live near an ocean and will be essential when the time comes for you to explore new biomes further from home.

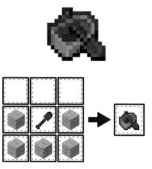

MOJANG STUFF

Pick up a chest and its contents will spill out onto the ground. If you want to carry your stuff around with you, craft a shulker box from shulker shells and a chest.

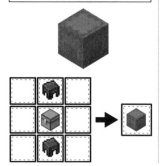

TRAPDOOR

If you start a mine underneath your base it's a good idea to place a trapdoor on the entrance to prevent hostile mobs from coming up. You'll need to attach the trapdoor to the block by the side of your entrance.

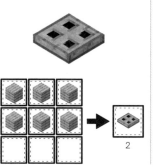

BOWL

You'll need a bowl if you want to cook rabbit stew, mushroom stew or beetroot soup. See pages 76-77 for more information. Bowls can also be used on mooshrooms for instant mushroom stew.

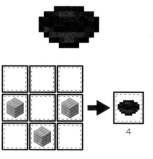

IRON ORE

Your next priority is to find iron ore, which can be smelted into iron ingots and used to make a variety of tools and weapons. Iron ore can be found at sea level and below, in veins of up to 8 blocks. Look out for orange flecks among the stone, then mine as many blocks as you can with your stone pickaxe. Once mined you'll need to smelt iron ore in your furnace to make usable iron ingots, then use it in the crafting recipes below.

IRON TOOLS AND WEAPONS

Upgrade your tools and weapons – use the recipes on page 69 but replace the cobblestone with iron ingots.

IRON ORE

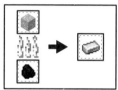

DID YOU KNOW?

You can make gold and diamond tools and weapons – replace the iron ingots with gold ingots or diamonds. Gold equipment wears out quickly but is the easiest to enchant, and diamond equipment is the most durable. See pages 86-87 for tips on how to find gold and diamond.

IRON DOOR

Unlike a wooden door, zombies will never be able to break down an iron door. They're more complicated than wooden doors, though, so you'll need to place buttons on the inside and outside to activate them.

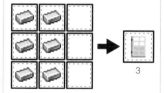

BUCKET

Buckets are tools that allow you to pick up and carry water and lava. You can then place the contents in a new location. Buckets can also be used to milk cows and mooshrooms.

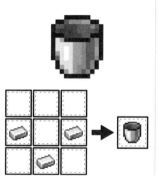

FLINT AND STEEL

Flint and steel creates fire when used on top of a solid block. You'll need it to light TNT and activate Nether portals. It's crafted from an iron ingot and flint (sometimes dropped by gravel). See page 53 for the TNT recipe.

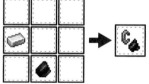

SHEARS

Shears can be used to remove wool from sheep without killing them – and there'll be more of it if you shear rather than kill them. Shears also come in handy when exploring jungle biomes as they quickly destroy leaves.

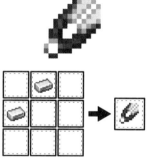

HEALTH AND FOOD

In Survival mode you'll need to keep an eye on your health and food bars, which sit just above your hotbar. It's important to eat frequently and heal when you take damage, otherwise your health bar will reach zero and you'll die.

HEALTH POINTS

When you first spawn in Survival mode you'll have a full 20 health points (10 hearts) and a full 20 food points (10 shanks). As you play, you'll take damage, use energy and lose points. To restore your health points you'll need to eat and avoid taking damage for a while. Your food bar shows you how hungry you are – when it's full you won't be able to eat any more.

You lose health points through:

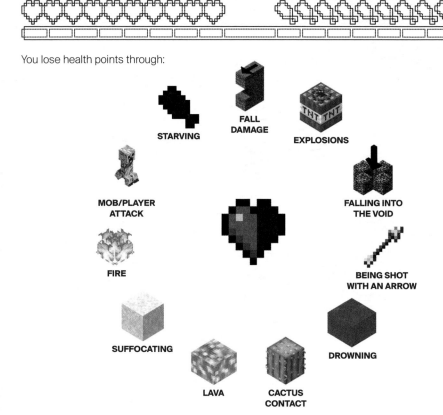

STARVING

FALL DAMAGE

EXPLOSIONS

MOB/PLAYER ATTACK

FALLING INTO THE VOID

FIRE

BEING SHOT WITH AN ARROW

SUFFOCATING

DROWNING

LAVA

CACTUS CONTACT

You lose health points rapidly during combat so it's a good idea to keep food in a hotbar slot. Different types of food restore different amounts of food points – read on for more details.

RAW BEEF
3 food points

 STEAK
8 food points

 **RAW PORKCHOP**
3 food points

 COOKED PORKCHOP
8 food points

 RAW CHICKEN
2 food points

 COOKED CHICKEN
6 food points

 **RAW MUTTON**
2 food points

 COOKED MUTTON
6 food points

 **RAW RABBIT**
3 food points

 COOKED RABBIT
5 food points

MEAT

Most animals drop raw meat when defeated. This meat will be cooked if they were killed by fire. Meat is an excellent food source as it restores more food points than fruit and vegetables. Cooked meat restores more food points than raw meat.

FISH

If you have a fishing rod and access to water, raw fish are an unlimited resource and an excellent food source. Raw fish can also be obtained by defeating polar bears (see page 47). Cooking fish in a furnace will increase its food points. Use your fishing rod to cast it into the water. When the bobber dips, reel it back in to see what you've caught.

TIP

Fishing doesn't just catch you fish – there's a probability that you'll get junk items and, occasionally, really valuable items like enchanted books. You can put enchantments on your fishing rod, too – that'll increase your chance of snagging the good stuff.

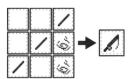

FISHING ROD RECIPE

 TROPICAL FISH
1 food point

 COOKED COD
5 food points

 RAW COD
2 food points

 COOKED SALMON
6 food points

 RAW SALMON
2 food points

FRUIT AND VEGETABLES

Fruit and vegetables don't restore as many food points as meat, but they are a good alternative if you can't find any animals. They are readily available all over the Overworld, if you know where to look, and several can be crafted into more useful items.

DID YOU KNOW?

Carrots, potatoes and mushrooms can be crafted into rabbit stew, which restores 10 food points.

1 Potatoes can be found in village farms, and zombies occasionally drop potatoes when defeated. A potato can be baked in a furnace to increase its food points.

A potato restores 1 food point, a baked potato restores 5 food points.

2 Beetroot can be found in village farms. It can be eaten immediately or crafted into beetroot soup.

Beetroot restores 1 food point, beetroot soup restores 6 food points.

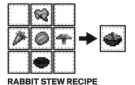

RABBIT STEW RECIPE

3 Carrots can be found in village farms. Zombies occasionally drop carrots when they die.

A carrot restores 3 food points.

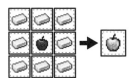

BEETROOT SOUP RECIPE

4 Apples can be obtained by destroying oak and dark oak leaves, and can be found in naturally-generated chests. Villagers may also sell apples for emeralds.

An apple restores 4 food points.

5 In addition to restoring food points, a golden apple provides an effect known as 'absorption I', which absorbs damage for 2 minutes, as well as 'regeneration II', which heals damage for 5 seconds. Golden apples can be found in naturally-generated chests.

A golden apple restores 4 food points.

GOLDEN APPLE RECIPE

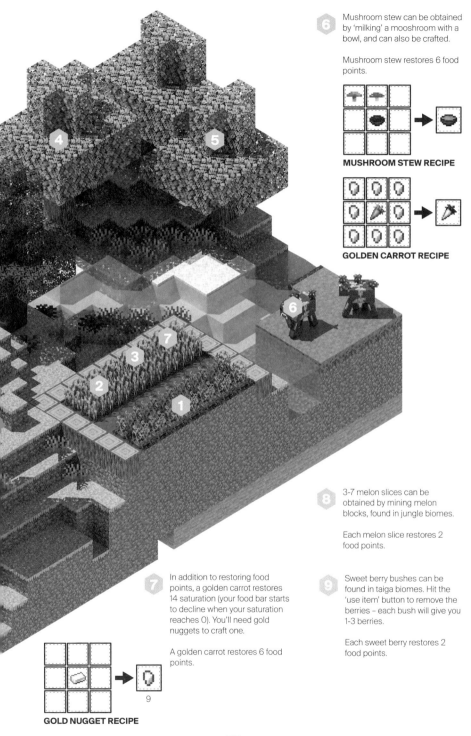

Mushroom stew can be obtained by 'milking' a mooshroom with a bowl, and can also be crafted.

Mushroom stew restores 6 food points.

MUSHROOM STEW RECIPE

GOLDEN CARROT RECIPE

3-7 melon slices can be obtained by mining melon blocks, found in jungle biomes.

Each melon slice restores 2 food points.

Sweet berry bushes can be found in taiga biomes. Hit the 'use item' button to remove the berries – each bush will give you 1-3 berries.

Each sweet berry restores 2 food points.

In addition to restoring food points, a golden carrot restores 14 saturation (your food bar starts to decline when your saturation reaches 0). You'll need gold nuggets to craft one.

A golden carrot restores 6 food points.

9

GOLD NUGGET RECIPE

BAKED GOODS

With the right ingredients you can craft a variety of more complex 'baked' goods to top up your food points and add a little variety to your diet. Here's a quick guide to locating and collecting the necessary items.

1 Have a look for some wheat in a village farm. You can also hunt for it in loot chests in dungeons, igloos or woodland mansions.

Bread can be found in naturally-generated chests. Villager farmers will sell 2-4 bread for an emerald.

Bread restores 5 food points.

BREAD RECIPE

2 Sugar cane is often found near water. Harvest some, then place it in your crafting grid to make sugar.

SUGAR RECIPE

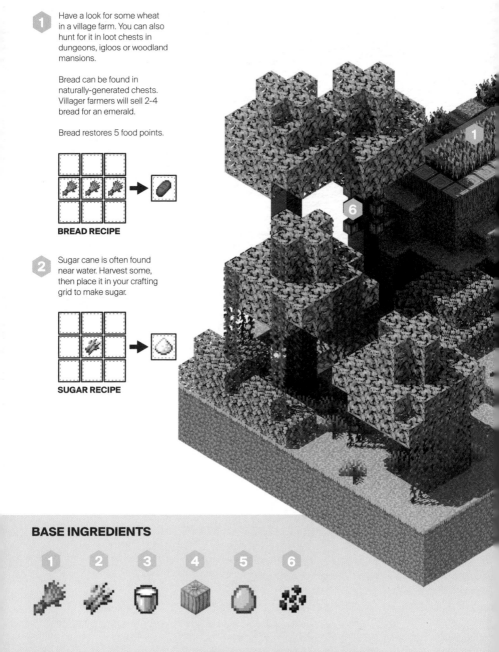

BASE INGREDIENTS

1   2   3   4   5   6

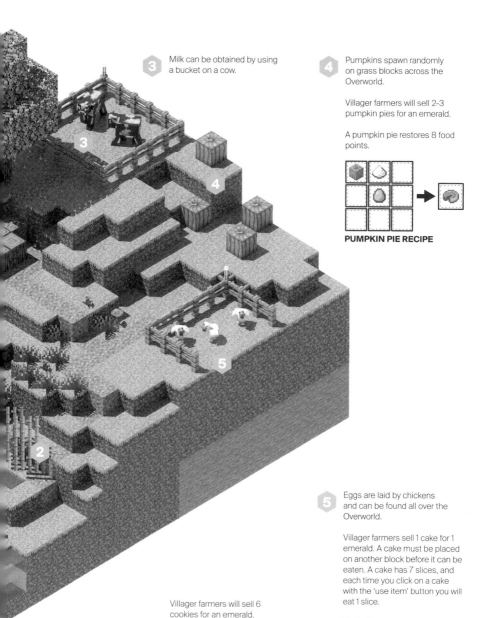

3 Milk can be obtained by using a bucket on a cow.

4 Pumpkins spawn randomly on grass blocks across the Overworld.

Villager farmers will sell 2-3 pumpkin pies for an emerald.

A pumpkin pie restores 8 food points.

PUMPKIN PIE RECIPE

5 Eggs are laid by chickens and can be found all over the Overworld.

Villager farmers sell 1 cake for 1 emerald. A cake must be placed on another block before it can be eaten. A cake has 7 slices, and each time you click on a cake with the 'use item' button you will eat 1 slice.

Each slice restores 2 food points – 14 food points in total.

Villager farmers will sell 6 cookies for an emerald.

A cookie restores 2 food points.

6 Cocoa beans can be harvested from cocoa growing on the side of jungle trees.

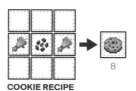

8

COOKIE RECIPE

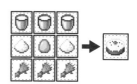

CAKE RECIPE

79

SETTING UP YOUR OWN FARM

Although you can find sources of food throughout the Overworld, life will be a lot easier if you set up a crop and animal farm next to your shelter. That way you'll have a sustainable source of food right on your doorstep.

BREEDING ANIMALS

As you know, animals have many uses, so an animal farm is a profitable investment. You'll need to stock up on the food each animal responds to, then build a pen and lead them inside to breed.

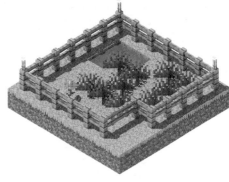

 Choose a suitable grassy spot for your pen, near to your shelter. It should be at least 10 x 10 blocks and well-lit to prevent hostile mobs spawning inside.

WOOD FENCE RECIPE

3

Hunt some animals. If you have string and slime, craft leads so you can easily manoeuvre the animals into the pen. If not, lead two of each animal into the pen by holding the food item they respond to.

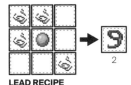

LEAD RECIPE

2

Feed 2 of the same animal when they are within 8 blocks of each other and they will enter love mode. After a moment a baby animal will appear.

FOODS FOR BREEDING

RABBIT
Dandelions
Carrots
Golden carrots

PIG
Carrots
Potatoes
Beetroot

HORSE
Golden apples
Golden carrots

SHEEP
Wheat

CAT
Raw cod
Raw salmon

COW
Wheat

MOOSHROOM
Wheat

TAMED WOLF
Any raw meat
Any cooked meat
Rotten flesh

LLAMA
Hay bales

CHICKEN
Wheat seeds
Pumpkin seeds
Melon seeds
Beetroot seeds
Nether wart

TIP ↗

Bored of white wool? You can dye your
sheep before breeding them to create
more coloured sheep. The baby sheep
will be the colour of one of its parents,
or it will be a combination, if the colours
can mix. Many flowers can be used
as dyes, as well as cactus, lapis lazuli,
cocoa beans and ink sacs.

CROP FARMING

Different crops require different conditions to grow, and it's important to create the right environment. Choose a flat area of dirt, then follow the steps below to create a crop farm.

CARROTS, POTATOES, BEETROOT AND WHEAT

1 Collect carrots, potatoes, beetroot and wheat from village farms. Wheat seeds can also be collected by destroying tall grass.

2 Craft a hoe – you'll need this to till dirt blocks into farmland.

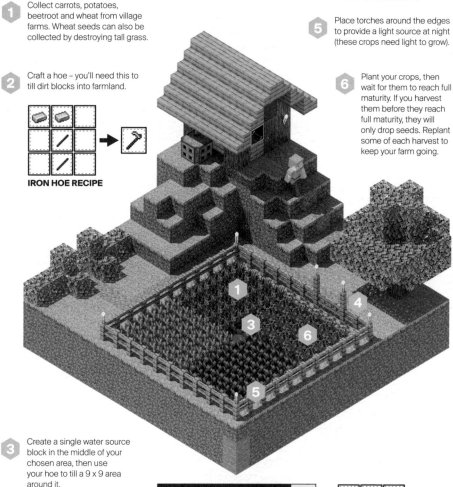

IRON HOE RECIPE

4 Surround your farm with fences and a gate to protect it from hungry animals.

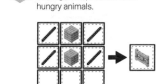

WOOD GATE RECIPE

5 Place torches around the edges to provide a light source at night (these crops need light to grow).

6 Plant your crops, then wait for them to reach full maturity. If you harvest them before they reach full maturity, they will only drop seeds. Replant some of each harvest to keep your farm going.

3 Create a single water source block in the middle of your chosen area, then use your hoe to till a 9 x 9 area around it.

TIP

Bone meal is a fantastic fertiliser. Use it on your crops to bring them to full maturity immediately.

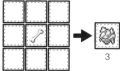

BONE MEAL RECIPE

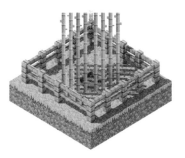

SUGAR CANE

Sugar cane must be planted on dirt, grass or sand that is right next to a water block. It doesn't need light to grow. You'll need sugar cane to make sugar for baking and paper for making books for bookcases. Bookcases will come in useful when you start enchanting items.

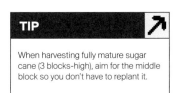

TIP ↗

When harvesting fully mature sugar cane (3 blocks-high), aim for the middle block so you don't have to replant it.

MELONS AND PUMPKINS

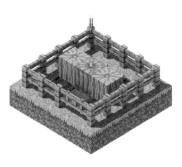

Melons and pumpkins don't need water to grow – just farmland. Till some dirt and make sure there's a block of space to the side, then plant melon or pumpkin seeds. A stem will grow, eventually producing a melon or pumpkin in the adjacent block. When you harvest the melon/pumpkin, the stem will remain and the growth process will begin again.

MELON SEEDS RECIPE

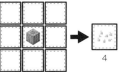

PUMPKIN SEEDS RECIPE

Melon seeds can be crafted from melon slices, and can sometimes be found in chests.

Pumpkin seeds can be crafted from a pumpkin, and can sometimes be found in chests.

MUSHROOMS

Mushrooms only grow in areas where the light level is 12 or lower, unless planted on mycelium or podzol (podzol is a type of dirt found exclusively in giant tree taiga biomes). Once planted, mushrooms will spread to nearby blocks that meet their light requirement, as long as there aren't more than 4 mushrooms of that type in a 9 x 9 area.

MYCELIUM   **PODZOL**

MINING

Mining is a tricky business, but it's essential if you want to get your hands on rare and useful materials. Many of the rarest items are found beneath the surface of your world, and can only be mined with certain tools.

THE GOLDEN RULES

Follow these golden rules to stay safe as you descend below ground and ensure you return to the surface laden with the supplies you need.

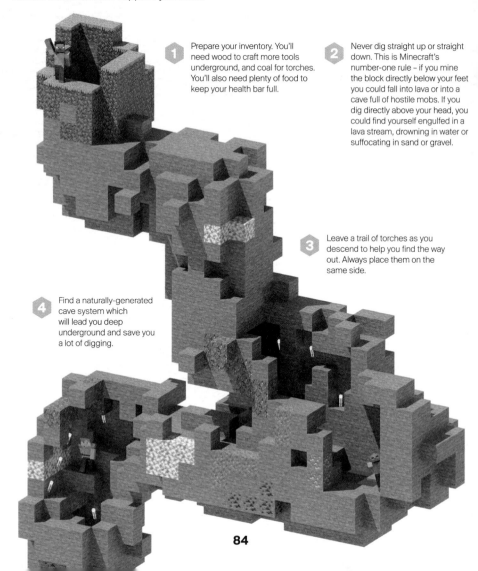

1 Prepare your inventory. You'll need wood to craft more tools underground, and coal for torches. You'll also need plenty of food to keep your health bar full.

2 Never dig straight up or straight down. This is Minecraft's number-one rule – if you mine the block directly below your feet you could fall into lava or into a cave full of hostile mobs. If you dig directly above your head, you could find yourself engulfed in a lava stream, drowning in water or suffocating in sand or gravel.

3 Leave a trail of torches as you descend to help you find the way out. Always place them on the same side.

4 Find a naturally-generated cave system which will lead you deep underground and save you a lot of digging.

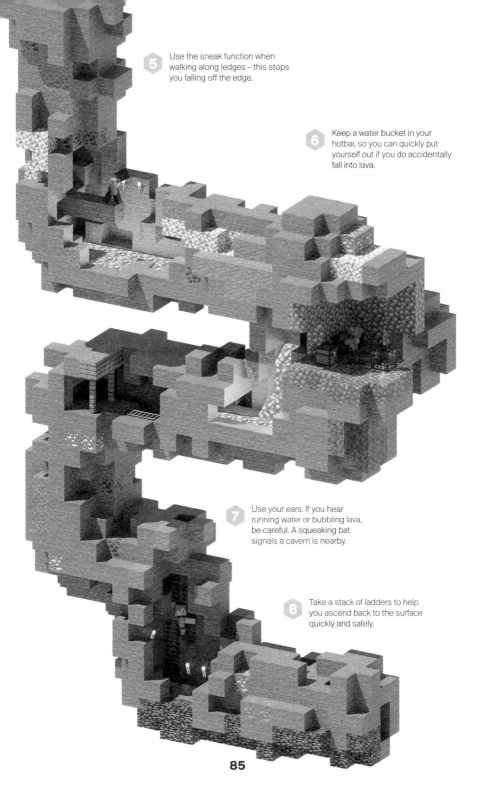

Use the sneak function when walking along ledges – this stops you falling off the edge.

Keep a water bucket in your hotbar, so you can quickly put yourself out if you do accidentally fall into lava.

Use your ears. If you hear running water or bubbling lava, be careful. A squeaking bat signals a cavern is nearby.

Take a stack of ladders to help you ascend back to the surface quickly and safely.

MINING FOR ORES

Minecraft's most valuable blocks are found deep underground, near the bottom of the world. Rare ores generate below level 32, where hostile mobs spawn freely in the dark and lava is a serious hazard. You'll need an iron pickaxe or better to mine most ores.

TIP

The best level at which to mine for ores is y=10 to y=15 since all ores generate within this band. Remember to check your coordinates as you descend.

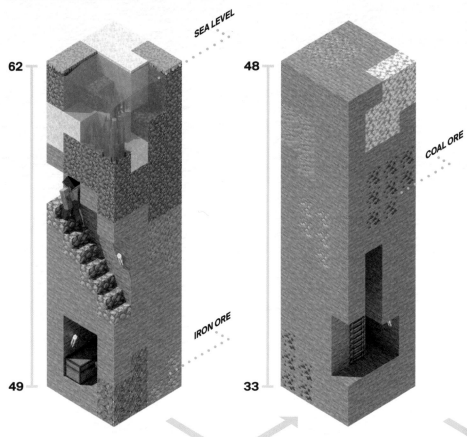

GOLD ORE

Found in veins of 4-8 blocks, at layer 32 and under, gold ore drops itself when mined. You'll need to smelt it in a furnace to turn it into gold ingots. Gold can be used to craft armour, tools and weapons as well as golden apples, clocks and powered rails.

REDSTONE ORE

Redstone ore is found in veins of 4-8 blocks, at layer 16 and under. When mined, each block drops 4-5 redstone. Redstone can be used like a wire to transmit power, and to craft various items, for example, clocks, compasses and powered rails.

LAPIS LAZULI ORE

Lapis lazuli ore is found in veins of 1-10 blocks, at layer 31 and under. When mined with a stone pickaxe or better, each block drops 4-8 pieces of lapis lazuli. Lapis lazuli can be used in enchanting and as a dye.

DIAMOND ORE

Found in veins of 1-10 blocks, at layer 16 and under, each block of diamond ore will drop 1 diamond. Diamonds can be used to craft the most durable tools, weapons and armour, as well as jukeboxes and enchantment tables.

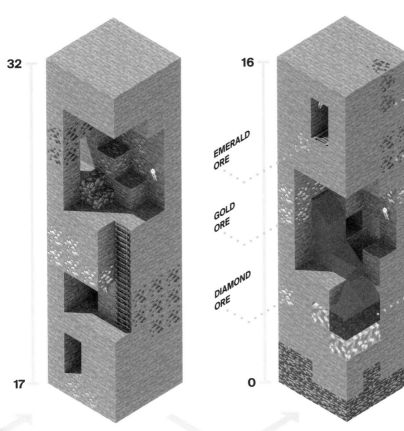

32

16

17

0

LAPIS LAZULI ORE

REDSTONE ORE

EMERALD ORE

GOLD ORE

DIAMOND ORE

OBSIDIAN

BEDROCK

EMERALD ORE

Found in single blocks between layers 4 and 32 in mountain biomes, emerald ore drops 1 emerald when mined. Emeralds can be used in villager trading. See page 45 for more info. They can also be crafted into decorative blocks of emerald.

DID YOU KNOW?

Obsidian is often found towards the bottom of the world where flowing water hits a lava source. It's the toughest mineable block in Survival mode, and is the only block that can only be mined with a diamond pickaxe. You'll need it to make a Nether portal and an enchantment table.

COMBAT

Unless you choose the peaceful option, Survival mode requires you to fight for your life. Pro Minecrafters use potions and enchantments to improve their performance, but here's a guide to basic combat to get you started.

BASIC COMBAT

You'll need a few key items to defend yourself from hostile mobs or enemy players. These crafting recipes will give you a fighting chance.

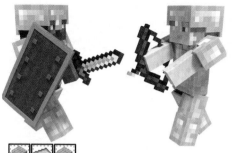

Craft a wood, stone, iron, gold or diamond sword and hit your opponent to inflict damage.

An axe does more damage per hit than a sword, but takes longer to recover.

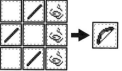

SHIELD RECIPE

A shield allows you to block attacks, reducing the damage you take, but you'll slow to sneaking pace.

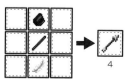

BOW RECIPE

ARROWS RECIPE

4

You can attack hostile mobs or enemy players from a safe distance with a bow and arrows.

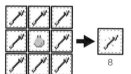

8

TIPPED ARROWS RECIPE

Tipped arrows are arrows that have been combined with lingering potions and administer the potion's effect upon contact. You can brew potions and they are sometimes dropped by witches when they die.

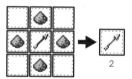

2

SPECTRAL ARROWS RECIPE

Spectral arrows give the glowing effect for 10 seconds, so your target is visible through solid blocks. Glowstone dust can be found in the Nether and is sometimes dropped by witches.

ARMOUR

To help protect yourself from damage you can craft a full set of armour – a helmet, chestplate, leggings and boots – from 24 units of leather, iron, gold or diamond. Each substance gives you a different level of protection: leather is the weakest, and diamond is the strongest.

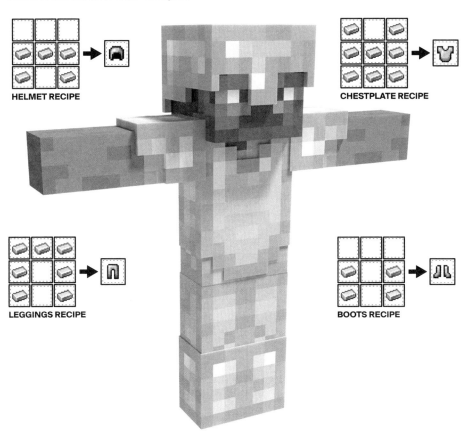

HELMET RECIPE

CHESTPLATE RECIPE

LEGGINGS RECIPE

BOOTS RECIPE

Once you've crafted your armour, open your inventory and locate the four armour slots. Equip your armour here and it will appear on your body, and an armour bar will appear above your health points. Keep an eye on it to check how much durability is left – it will decrease as the armour absorbs damage, and eventually you'll need to craft a new set or repair on an anvil.

ARMOUR WILL PROTECT AGAINST:

CROSSBOW

Once you've had some experience with a bow and arrows, you can upgrade to a crossbow. This powerful weapon deals more damage than a bow, and shoots further. It takes longer to load than a bow and uses arrows or firework rockets as ammunition.

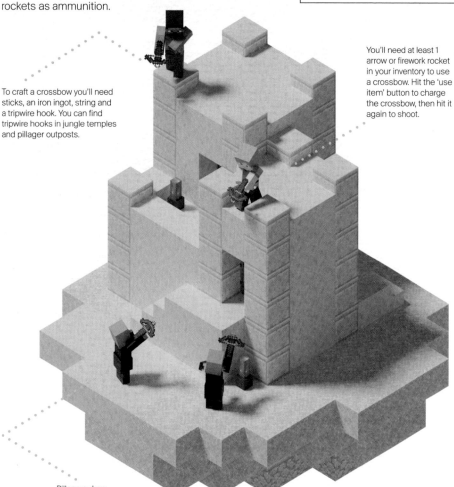

You'll need at least 1 arrow or firework rocket in your inventory to use a crossbow. Hit the 'use item' button to charge the crossbow, then hit it again to shoot.

To craft a crossbow you'll need sticks, an iron ingot, string and a tripwire hook. You can find tripwire hooks in jungle temples and pillager outposts.

Pillagers drop crossbows when defeated, and they can also be found in pillager outpost chests.

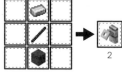

TRIPWIRE HOOK RECIPE

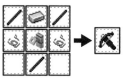

CROSSBOW RECIPE

TRIDENT

These powerful weapons can be used for melee (hand-to-hand) combat, or for ranged attacks if you throw them at your target.

Hold down the 'use item' button for a few seconds to charge your trident, then aim it at your target. When you release the button, the trident will fly towards your target.

If the trident makes contact with a mob or player it will bounce off them and fall to the ground nearby. If it makes contact with a block, it will become embedded in that block.

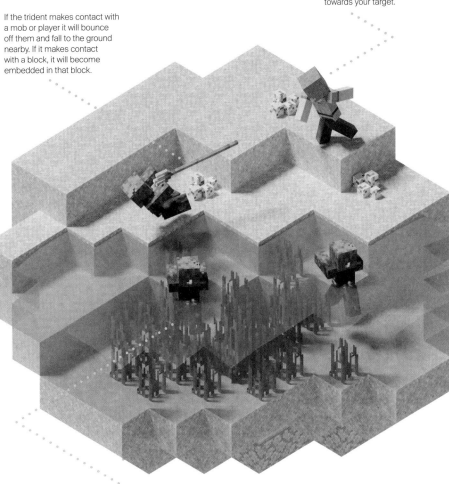

Tridents are rare – drowned mobs may drop them when defeated, but they can't be crafted.

MOJANG STUFF

We recommend enchanting your trident with Loyalty, because it'll come back to you! The higher its level, the faster it'll return.

UPGRADE YOUR SHELTER

So all that mining and mob combat paid off and your inventory is packed with useful blocks and items just waiting to be used. Now it's time to upgrade your shelter so you have a secure base from which to prepare for your next adventure.

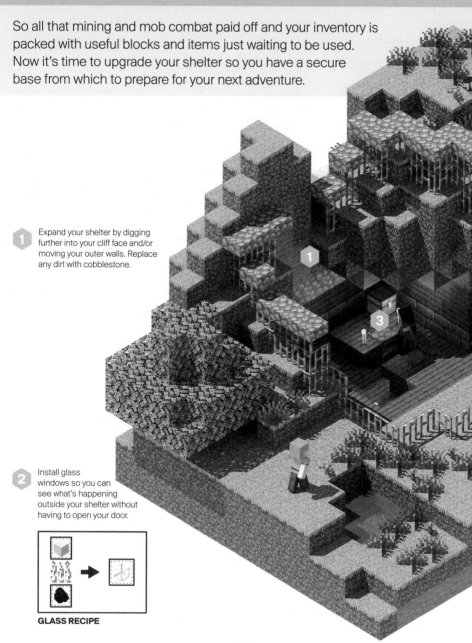

1. Expand your shelter by digging further into your cliff face and/or moving your outer walls. Replace any dirt with cobblestone.

2. Install glass windows so you can see what's happening outside your shelter without having to open your door.

GLASS RECIPE

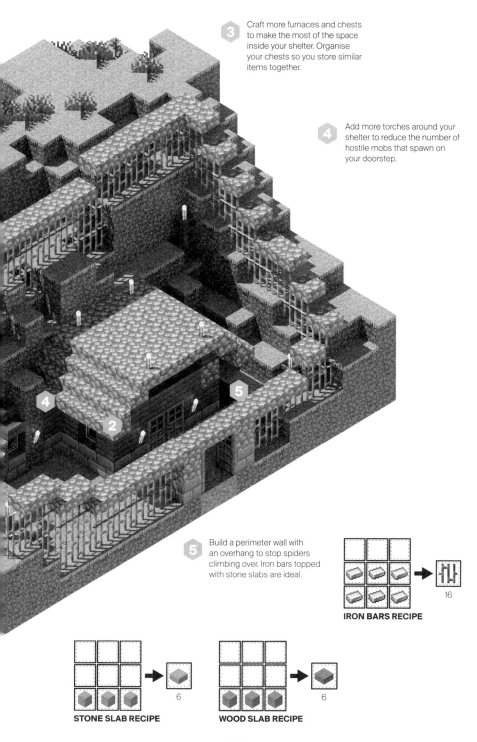

Craft more furnaces and chests to make the most of the space inside your shelter. Organise your chests so you store similar items together.

Add more torches around your shelter to reduce the number of hostile mobs that spawn on your doorstep.

Build a perimeter wall with an overhang to stop spiders climbing over. Iron bars topped with stone slabs are ideal.

16

IRON BARS RECIPE

6

STONE SLAB RECIPE

6

WOOD SLAB RECIPE

NAVIGATING

There's a whole world waiting to be explored beyond the horizon - exciting new biomes full of resources and rare loot, and mobs you've never seen before. It's easy to get lost on long journeys, so make sure you're prepared before you set off.

1 Mark your shelter with a beacon and remember to make a note of your coordinates to help you find your way back.

2 A compass will point to your spawn point, which will help you get back home if you built your shelter nearby.

COMPASS RECIPE

3 A map shows you what's in the immediate area and will help you decide which way you'd like to go.

MAP RECIPE

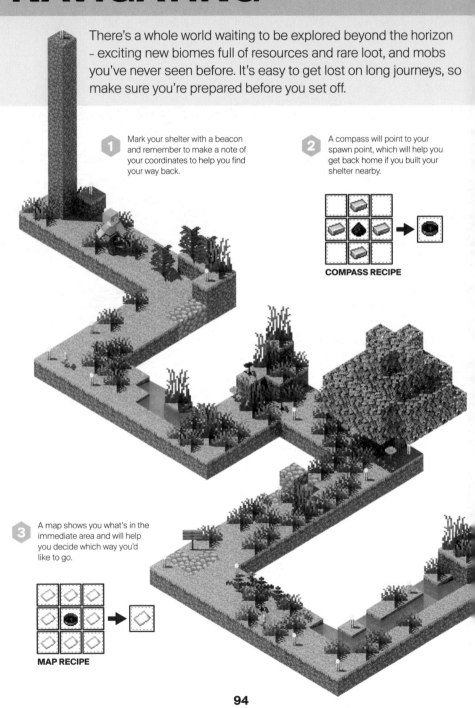

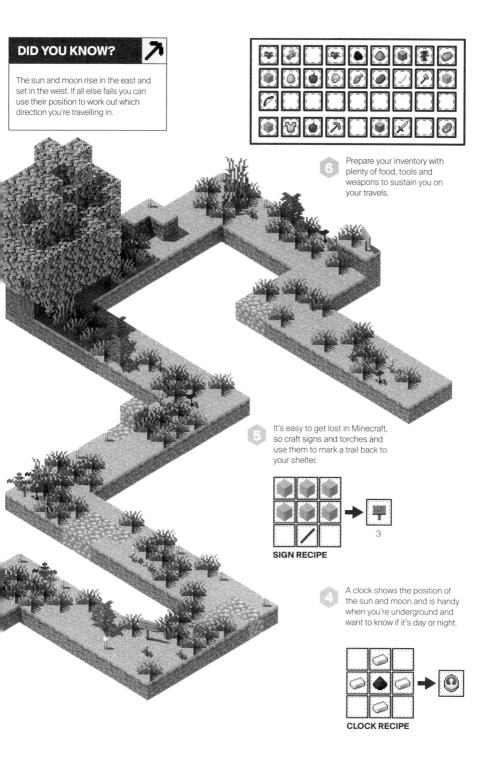

DID YOU KNOW?

The sun and moon rise in the east and set in the west. If all else fails you can use their position to work out which direction you're travelling in.

6 Prepare your inventory with plenty of food, tools and weapons to sustain you on your travels.

5 It's easy to get lost in Minecraft, so craft signs and torches and use them to mark a trail back to your shelter.

3

SIGN RECIPE

4 A clock shows the position of the sun and moon and is handy when you're underground and want to know if it's day or night.

CLOCK RECIPE

95

First published in Great Britain 2017 by Egmont UK Limited.
This edition published in 2020 by Dean, an imprint of Egmont UK Limited,
2 Minster Court, 10th Floor, London EC3R 7BB

Written by Craig Jelley
Additional material by Marsh Davies
Designed by Joe Bolder and Andrea Philpots
Illustrations by Ryan Marsh
Cover designed by John Stuckey
Production by Louis Harvey
Special thanks to Lydia Winters, Owen Jones, Junkboy,
Martin Johansson, Marsh Davies and Jesper Öqvist.

ISBN 978 0 6035 7928 8

71019/001

Printed in China

ONLINE SAFETY FOR YOUNGER FANS

Spending time online is great fun! Here are a few simple rules to help younger fans stay safe and
keep the internet a great place to spend time:

- Never give out your real name – don't use it as your username.
- Never give out any of your personal details.
- Never tell anybody which school you go to or how old you are.
- Never tell anybody your password except a parent or a guardian.
- Be aware that you must be 13 or over to create an account on many sites. Always check the
site policy and ask a parent or guardian for permission before registering.
- Always tell a parent or guardian if something is worrying you.

Stay safe online. Any website addresses listed in this book are correct at the time of going
to print. However, Egmont is not responsible for content hosted by third parties. Please be
aware that online content can be subject to change and websites can contain content that is
unsuitable for children. We advise that all children are supervised when using the internet.

Egmont takes its responsibility to the planet and its inhabitants very seriously.
We aim to use papers from well-managed forests run by responsible suppliers.

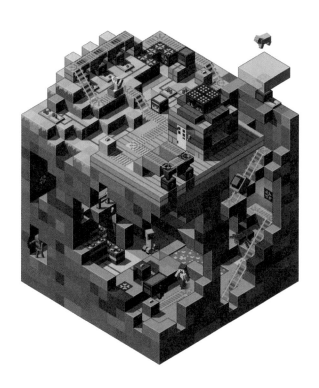

GUIDE TO:

CONTENTS

INTRODUCTION

Welcome to our Guide to Redstone – Minecraft's answer to electronics! Lay down redstone dust like electrical wire, add a few simple components, and you can build clever computers or crafty combination locks, trigger human catapults or trap mischievous mobs. It's powerful and versatile! So versatile, in fact, that we're often gobsmacked by the stuff the community makes – everything from pixel-art editors to massive walking mechs. We hope this guide gives you the know-how to unleash your imagination and build the next thing that leaves us gawping!

MARSH DAVIES
THE MOJANG TEAM

1

THE BASICS

Before we start building incredible contraptions, we're going to look at the different redstone components, what they do and how we can use them in simple creations that you can build straight away. Learning the basics first will ensure you become a true redstone expert, capable of building awesome mechanisms.

FINDING REDSTONE

Redstone is a mysterious substance that is used to power mechanisms and traps. In its rawest form, it's an ore found underground, but it can be mined and refined into redstone dust. As well as forming the basis for redstone circuits, it's also an important crafting ingredient for redstone components.

REDSTONE LOCATIONS

When hunting for redstone, you'll want to focus on certain Overworld locations. Let's take a look at where redstone naturally occurs.

REDSTONE ORE

REDSTONE DUST

1 Redstone dust can be found in woodland mansions, though the deadly illagers protect the chests in which it is found.

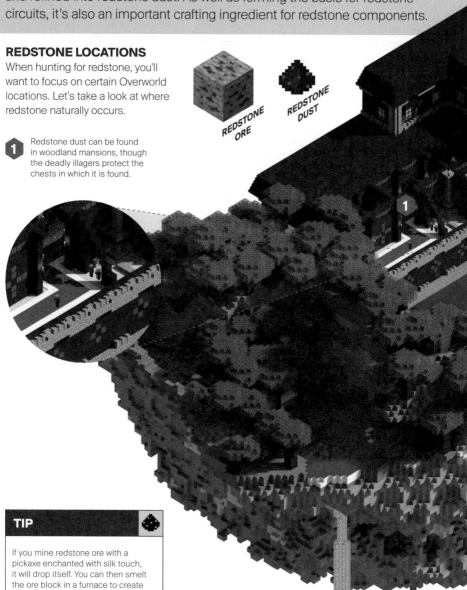

TIP

If you mine redstone ore with a pickaxe enchanted with silk touch, it will drop itself. You can then smelt the ore block in a furnace to create redstone dust.

2 When defeated, witches will drop stacks of up to six pieces of redstone. Hunt them down in swamp biomes.

2

3 Redstone dust can be found in chests in other naturally generated structures too – dungeons, strongholds and abandoned mineshafts will all have some.

3

4

4 Redstone ore generates naturally underground, within 1 to 16 blocks from the bedrock layer. When mined, the ore will drop 4-5 redstone dusts.

REDSTONE DUST

So what does redstone dust actually do? Well, it has the ability to transmit a redstone signal from a power source to a redstone component, allowing for an almost infinite number of possible mechanisms and circuits. It's really very useful!

When placed, redstone dust lies flat on the ground and is initially dark red in colour. When it's activated, it will glow a bright red and emit particles. When powered, the redstone signal will travel a maximum of 15 blocks, unless it is powered again along the way.

DEACTIVATED · ACTIVATED

REDSTONE DUST BEHAVIOUR

In its most basic behaviour, redstone will interact with redstone in adjacent blocks, stretching out and connecting with it.

If the redstone is placed beside an existing line of redstone, then it will curve sideways, creating a turn in the circuit.

If redstone is placed on both sides of an existing line then it will fork in multiple directions, which can split a redstone signal.

A split signal can be brought back around and joined together again with more redstone dust, creating a signal loop.

Additional redstone can be placed inside a loop to create a grid, which can be used to power a group of blocks simultaneously.

Redstone can link with redstone placed a level higher or lower. It can also form loops, curves and grids with redstone on other levels.

TICKS AND TIMING

Time passing in Minecraft is measured as 'ticks' and there are 20 ticks per second. Redstone signals are measured in the same way. You'll see the term 'redstone tick', or just 'tick', a lot in this book – each redstone tick is the length of two game ticks, meaning there are 10 redstone ticks per second. You don't need to know too much about how or why it works, but the lower the number of ticks, the faster a redstone signal will travel.

POWER AND STRENGTH

Sometimes we'll refer to strength of redstone signals in this book. The strength ranges from 1 (lowest) to 15 (highest). The signal strength can depend on the power source that is being used. You'll see a lot more later on in the book about how power sources produce different signal strengths, and how the signal strength can be altered.

REDSTONE POWER SOURCES

There are lots of ways to power a circuit. Each power source offers a different combination of signal strength and interaction with other redstone components. Let's take a look at your options so you can decide which is right for your build.

MANUAL ACTIVATORS

The simplest power sources in Minecraft are buttons and levers, easily crafted from wood or stone. They will need to be manually activated by a player, and, even at this simple level, have different characteristics that make them more appropriate for certain build types.

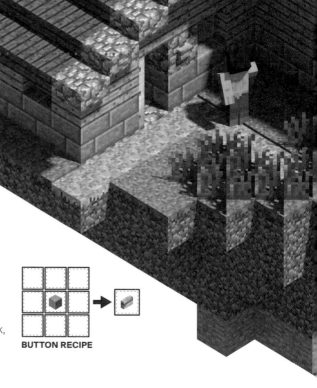

Here we see the button in its simplest usage. Placed beside an iron door, the button will send power through the solid block it's placed on when pushed, opening the door for a brief time.

BUTTON

Buttons are crafted from a single block of stone or wood planks. When pushed they provide a temporary redstone signal at maximum strength. They can be placed on any side of a solid block, including the top and bottom.

BUTTON RECIPE

LEVER

Crafted by combining a stick and cobblestone, levers also produce the maximum redstone signal. However, unlike buttons, they are switchable sources, which means that the redstone signal will toggle on and off each time it is used.

LEVER RECIPE

In this example, the lever will open up the trapdoor on the adjacent block when interacted with once. It will stay open until the lever is activated once again.

TRAP ACTIVATORS

These power sources are perfect for players who like to build sneaky traps. Most of them look innocent enough, or can't be seen at all, which is why they're so perfect. Your target won't know they've activated a cunning contraption until it's too late.

PRESSURE PLATES

Pressure plates can be made with wood or stone, and are often used in simple, non-trap builds too. Each sends a temporary redstone signal at the maximum strength through solid blocks or redstone components. They can be activated by players or mobs stepping on them, however, the wooden pressure plate will also produce an output when an item is dropped on it.

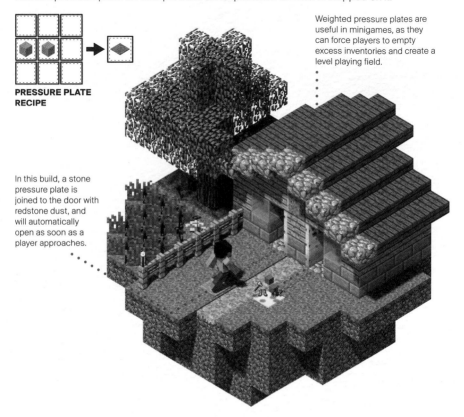

PRESSURE PLATE RECIPE

Weighted pressure plates are useful in minigames, as they can force players to empty excess inventories and create a level playing field.

In this build, a stone pressure plate is joined to the door with redstone dust, and will automatically open as soon as a player approaches.

WEIGHTED PRESSURE PLATES

Weighted pressure plates come in a light variety (made with gold ingots), and heavy variety (made with iron ingots). The signal strength they produce depends on the number of 'entities' on them (this includes players, mobs and dropped items). The light plate requires 57 items to create maximum signal strength, whereas at least 598 are needed to do the same with the heavy variety.

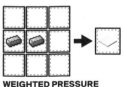

WEIGHTED PRESSURE PLATE (HEAVY) RECIPE

TRIPWIRE

The nearly-invisible tripwire is a particularly crafty way to activate a trap. Tripwire hooks need to be attached together by string, but can be placed up to 40 blocks apart. When the tripwire is broken by a mob or player, each hook will output a maximum signal to adjacent blocks.

Tripwires won't break when activated, so players and mobs will repeatedly activate them. This makes it perfect for a security system – link it up to redstone lamps to get notified whenever someone enters your HQ.

TRIPWIRE HOOK RECIPE

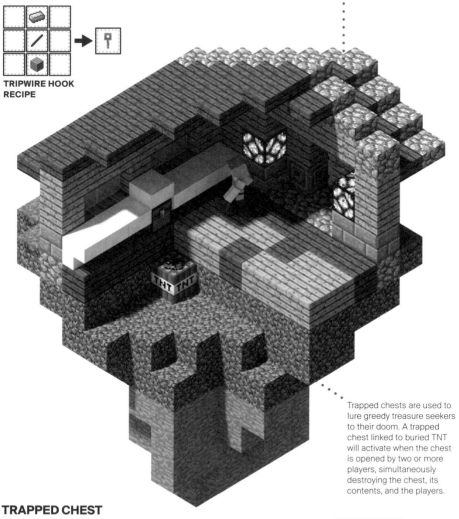

Trapped chests are used to lure greedy treasure seekers to their doom. A trapped chest linked to buried TNT will activate when the chest is opened by two or more players, simultaneously destroying the chest, its contents, and the players.

TRAPPED CHEST

The trapped chest is almost indistinguishable from its regular counterpart, except for a red band around the clasp. They can be used for regular storage, as long as any redstone traps are disabled before opening. The output depends on how many people are viewing the chest's contents – the more people trying to steal from the trapped chest, the more powerful the signal.

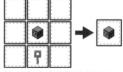

TRAPPED CHEST RECIPE

CONSTANT ACTIVATORS

In some situations you'll want a constant power source that doesn't require any interaction to generate a signal. This is where constant activators come in handy – they are permanently on, or alter their output depending on other external factors. Here's a guide to using them effectively.

REDSTONE TORCH

As well as being a source of light, redstone torches also provide a maximum redstone signal of 15. Redstone torches can be inverted in redstone circuits, so that they are constantly off rather than on.

Placing another redstone torch under the first will invert the signal and turn off the first redstone torch. They can also be placed on the side of blocks, to provide power through solid blocks above, and redstone components on horizontally adjacent blocks.

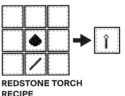

REDSTONE TORCH RECIPE

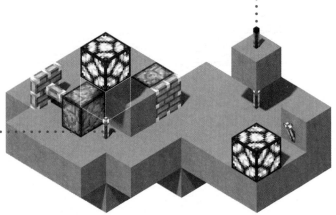

This build shows the behaviour of a redstone signal from a redstone torch. It can travel upwards through a solid block, or power redstone components directly beside it, however, it won't travel through a solid block beside it.

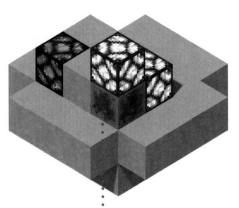

The redstone block consistently powers two redstone lamps, one to the side and one above. The redstone block won't provide power through adjacent solid blocks, and it will also deactivate other power sources like the redstone torch.

REDSTONE BLOCK

Redstone blocks are made from, and can produce, nine pieces of redstone dust, which makes them great for storing excess redstone. When placed, they can power redstone components on adjacent blocks in all directions, as well as mechanisms like doors and pistons.

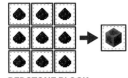

REDSTONE BLOCK RECIPE

DAYLIGHT SENSOR

Daylight sensors produce different levels of power depending on the sunlight in the world – more when it's daytime, less at night, though weather also has an effect. They can also be inverted by interacting with the block, so that they produce more power when the world is darker.

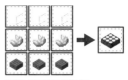

DAYLIGHT SENSOR RECIPE

Daylight sensors are handy for creating automatic lighting systems. This room has two daylight sensors on the roof, one regular and one inverted, which are linked to redstone lamps beneath. At least one of the lamps will be on at any point during the day.

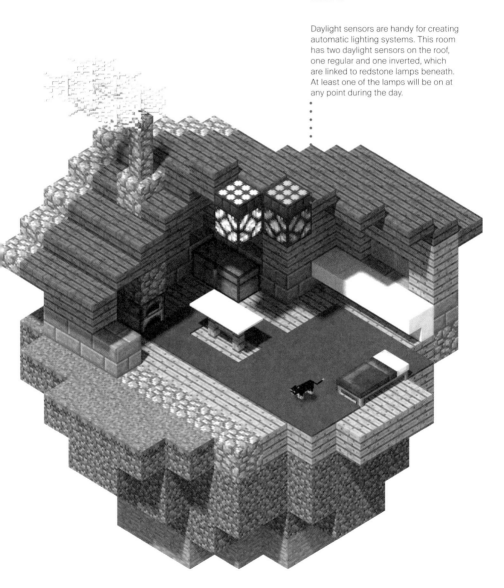

OBSERVERS

The observer block is the newest addition to the redstone repertoire, and produces a signal when it detects an update in the block it's monitoring. It can fully replace a BUD (block-update detection) circuit, which is quite complex and detects a more exclusive range of updates.

BLOCK FACES

The observer has two functional faces – the observer face, which monitors the block directly ahead, and an output face, which produces the redstone signal in the opposite direction. Observers can be placed to monitor blocks in all directions.

The observer is made from cobblestone, redstone dust and Nether quartz. It's not affected by external redstone sources, so it can't be inverted as redstone torches can. When activated, the observer will output the maximum redstone signal too.

OBSERVER FACE   OUTPUT FACE

OBSERVER RECIPE

DETECTION VARIETY

So what exactly can an observer block detect? Among other things, it will observe the activation of powered rails, pistons extending, and the spreading of grass to dirt (and vice-versa). In this example, when the daylight sensor inverts or senses a change in light, the observer will detect it and power the circuit, activating a sound from the note block.

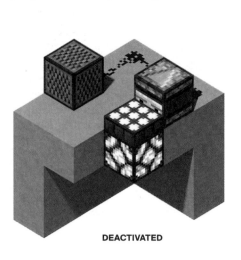

DEACTIVATED

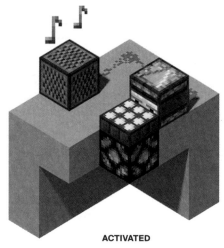

ACTIVATED

UPDATING OBSERVERS

Observers can also be moved within a circuit. When they're pushed or pulled by a piston, this will also count as a block update, but it will only output a signal when it reaches its new position.

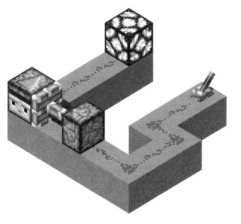
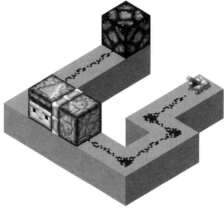

BUD CIRCUIT

For those block updates that an observer isn't capable of detecting, you'll need to use a BUD circuit instead. Among other things, it can detect a furnace beginning to smelt, changes in redstone power levels, and the placement or removal of blocks, like the crafting table that's been added in the examples below.

MANIPULATION

We've seen that there are plenty of ways to power a circuit and provide it with a signal, but that's just the beginning of what you can do with redstone. The blocks that we'll look at in this section manipulate the strength and flow of the signal, set the speed that it travels at, and even influence non-redstone elements.

REDSTONE REPEATERS

You've learnt how to power circuits using different power sources, so let's look at how you can use blocks to adapt circuits to suit your needs. The first block you'll need is the redstone repeater, which is shown to the right.

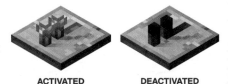

ACTIVATED   **DEACTIVATED**

REPEATER FUNCTIONS

1

Repeaters can amplify redstone signals back up to full strength.

2

Repeaters can combine with other repeaters to create 'locks' in circuits.

3

Repeaters ensure signals only move one way through a circuit.

4

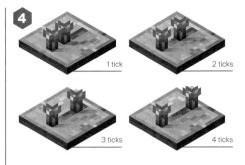

1 tick   2 ticks

3 ticks   4 ticks

Repeaters can delay signals by 1-4 ticks depending on the chosen setting.

HOW REPEATERS ARE USED

Let's explore how each of these functions can be applied to help create a variety of circuits that perform different tasks. You'll see as we go through the book how repeater functions are used in actual contraptions.

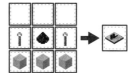

REDSTONE REPEATER RECIPE

AMPLIFICATION

Place a repeater on the fifteenth block of a circuit, when the redstone signal is down to its •••••••••••••• lowest strength (1), and it will amplify the signal back up to its maximum strength (15).

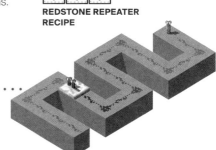

LOCK FUNCTION

Both lamps are powered by the same lever. When one of the side-facing repeaters is powered by ••••••••••••• the lever on the left, it locks one repeater and blocks the signal reaching the redstone lamp.

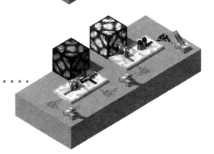

ONE-WAY MOVEMENT

When the circuit is active and the lever is pulled, a signal remains in the left of the circuit. This causes •••••••••••••• the piston to pull the other piston back. The repeaters stop the signal reaching the right of the circuit.

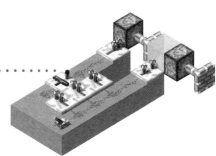

DELAY FUNCTION

When the lever is pulled, the lamp on the right lights up first. The circuit leading to the lamp •••••••••••• on the left has a repeater set to 4 ticks, delaying the signal and creating a staggered activation.

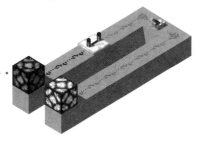

REDSTONE COMPARATORS

A redstone comparator is a component that compares up to three redstone signals and outputs a signal accordingly. You'll see it has three redstone torches on top of the block and an arrow facing in the output direction. The torches at the back of the block indicate if it is outputting a signal, and the front torch indicates which 'mode' it's in.

The comparator has two modes, which can be changed by interacting with it. This will turn the front torch on and off – if it's off, the comparator is in 'comparison mode', which compares a signal from the back to the side inputs. If the torch is on, then the comparator is in 'subtraction mode', which means that the side inputs are subtracted from the strength of the rear input.

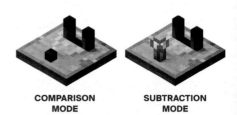

COMPARISON MODE   **SUBTRACTION MODE**

COMPARATOR FUNCTIONS

1

A comparator sustains a signal flowing into it, and outputs a signal of the same strength.

2

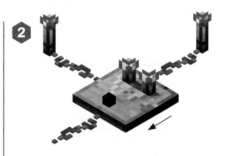

A comparator compares a signal going through the rear input to a signal going into the side.

3

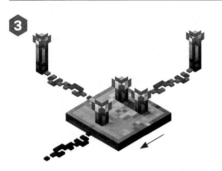

In subtraction mode, comparators output a signal equal to the rear input minus side input.

4

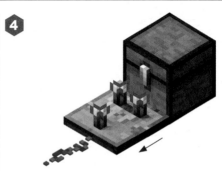

Comparators detect the fullness of storage items and output a corresponding signal.

HOW COMPARATORS ARE USED

The comparator is just as useful and versatile as the redstone repeater. Here are some examples to show each of its functions in action. You'll see more of how the comparator's functions work in later builds too.

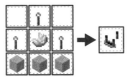

REDSTONE COMPARATOR RECIPE

 MAINTAINING A SIGNAL

The comparator and a repeater are in the same position in parallel circuit strands. The comparator ·············· doesn't increase the signal, which limits the signal's reach, so the redstone lamp on its strand is off.

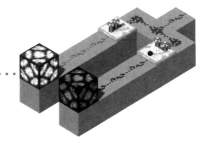

 COMPARING SIGNALS

If the signal entering the side of the comparator is weaker than the one entering the rear, then the signal is ········· maintained and output through the front. If the side input is stronger when compared, there will be no output. It can compare up to two inputs, one entering each side of the comparator.

Side input stronger

Side input weaker

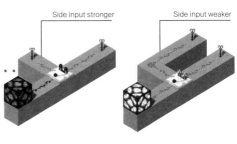

 SUBTRACTING SIGNALS

When switched to subtraction mode, the strength of the side signal is subtracted from the rear ··············· signal, and a reduced redstone signal is output, which leaves the redstone lamp deactivated. It can subtract up to two inputs, one from each side of the comparator.

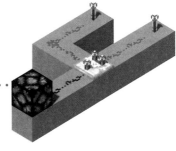

 MEASURING STORAGE

Comparators in these circuits measure how much is in each of the chests. When completely ········· full with stacks of 64 items, comparators output a maximum strength signal, when empty they won't output a signal at all.

Full

Half-full

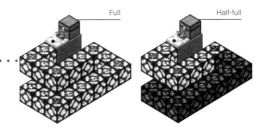

PISTONS, STICKY PISTONS AND SLIME BLOCKS

Now that you've grasped the basics of redstone circuitry, we can take a look at how circuits can be used to physically move blocks around. With the help of pistons and slime blocks, your circuits are able to push, pull, drag, break and even bounce blocks.

PISTON

The primary function of the piston is to physically move blocks around in a circuit. When powered, the head of the piston extends to push a block directly in front of it by a single block space. When the signal stops, the head retracts back to its original position.

DEACTIVATED   **ACTIVATED**

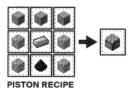

PISTON RECIPE

STICKY PISTON

Pistons are able to push a maximum of 12 blocks at a time. Sticky pistons are even more useful – they stick to blocks when extended, and pull them backwards when they retract. This is shown in action below.

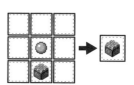

STICKY PISTON RECIPE

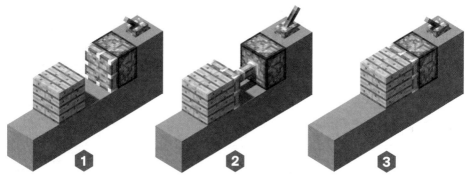

SLIME BLOCK

Crafted from slimeballs, slime blocks can be used in circuits to grab and move blocks. They're treated as a transparent block as they let light through, but, unlike most transparent blocks, you can also place blocks on them.

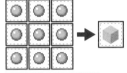

SLIME BLOCK RECIPE

Slime blocks are also bouncy! They can be used as platforms to bounce items and entities up in the air, or combined with pistons to create a forceful pushing mechanism.

The slime block's sticky quality allows it to pick up adjacent blocks, and push or pull them providing there are no more than 12. Because it can pick up blocks in all directions, a slime block attached to a piston allows a lot more possibilities than sticky pistons.

OBSIDIAN

There are some blocks in Minecraft that have extremely high blast resistance and others that are completely immovable by pistons or slime blocks. Obsidian possesses both of these qualities, which makes it an incredibly handy tool for your redstone arsenal.

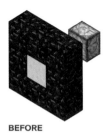

BEFORE

AFTER

BEFORE

AFTER

Obsidian is particularly useful when you're creating redstone contraptions in which slime blocks or sticky pistons are in danger of moving critical parts of the redstone circuit. The images above show what happens when you use obsidian instead of clay with a sticky slime block.

SECRET PISTON PASSAGE

We've discovered quite a few redstone components so far, so now we're going to create our first simple build – a secret passage that's cleverly activated by sticky pistons. It can be used to hide an entrance to a treasure stash or perhaps a top secret mine.

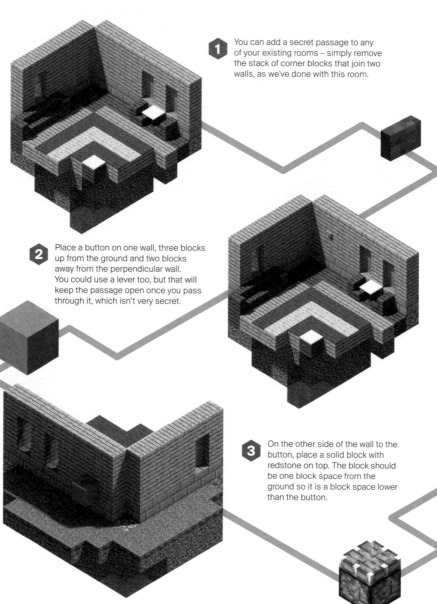

1 You can add a secret passage to any of your existing rooms – simply remove the stack of corner blocks that join two walls, as we've done with this room.

2 Place a button on one wall, three blocks up from the ground and two blocks away from the perpendicular wall. You could use a lever too, but that will keep the passage open once you pass through it, which isn't very secret.

3 On the other side of the wall to the button, place a solid block with redstone on top. The block should be one block space from the ground so it is a block space lower than the button.

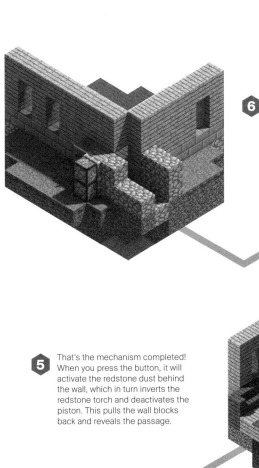

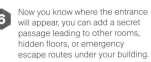
6 Now you know where the entrance will appear, you can add a secret passage leading to other rooms, hidden floors, or emergency escape routes under your building.

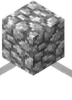

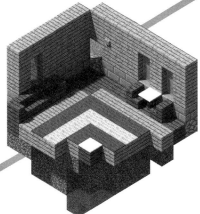

5 That's the mechanism completed! When you press the button, it will activate the redstone dust behind the wall, which in turn inverts the redstone torch and deactivates the piston. This pulls the wall blocks back and reveals the passage.

4 Place a redstone torch on the front of the solid block, then stack two sticky pistons beside it, facing the wall, one on top of the other. The sticky pistons will instantly activate and extend to touch the wall.

OUTPUT

So we can power redstone circuits and we can control what they do, now it's time to look at what they can produce. Many functions of pistons can be considered output, but there are some blocks that specialise in the effects that they can produce, which we'll look at in this section.

DISPENSERS, DROPPERS AND HOPPERS

The first output group contains dispensers, droppers and hoppers. All of them contain storage for items, and have the ability to move those items in different ways and for different purposes.

DISPENSERS

Dispensers are created with cobblestone, bows and redstone dust, and are able to produce an output facing any direction. They can hold nine stacks of items and will eject an item, sometimes activated, when powered.

Dispensers activate once after a two-tick delay, so would need to be repeatedly activated, manually or in a circuit, to create repetition. It also has a tick delay on reactivation, so rapid output isn't easy to achieve.

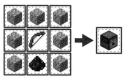

DISPENSER RECIPE

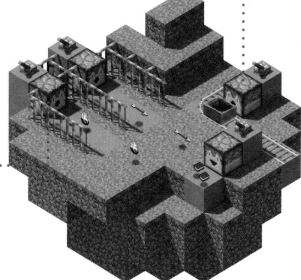

Dispensers can be used to fire arrows and fireballs using fire charges, deploy minecarts to rails, and place blocks like jack o'lanterns.

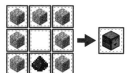

DROPPER RECIPE

DROPPERS

The dropper is so called as it performs a similar function to dropping items from your inventory. Unlike dispensers, it can't activate items, but merely throws them forward.

Both the dispenser and the dropper have a special interface for storing items. Each has nine slots to put items in, but no way of selecting a slot to output. If there are multiple item types in the slots, a random item will be chosen to output. Hoppers have just five storage slots instead of nine.

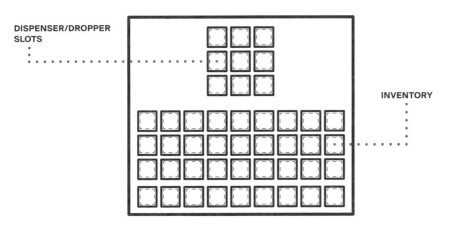

DISPENSER/DROPPER SLOTS

INVENTORY

HOPPERS

Hoppers are more similar to droppers as they also only have the ability to move items. The hopper has a unique function that can be used to siphon items from one object to another. This can be used to collect drops from a mob-infested cave, or move items from one chest to another.

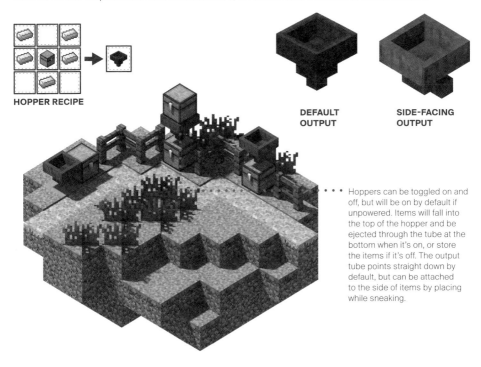

HOPPER RECIPE

DEFAULT OUTPUT

SIDE-FACING OUTPUT

Hoppers can be toggled on and off, but will be on by default if unpowered. Items will fall into the top of the hopper and be ejected through the tube at the bottom when it's on, or store the items if it's off. The output tube points straight down by default, but can be attached to the side of items by placing while sneaking.

AUTOMATIC FIREWORK DISPLAY

We're going to use our new-found knowledge of dispensers to create an awesome automatic firework display. This build also utilises repeaters to cause a delayed redstone signal to certain dispensers so it creates staggered explosions in the display.

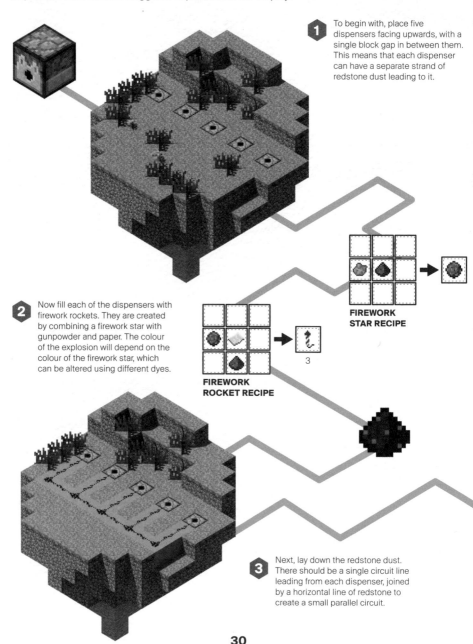

1 To begin with, place five dispensers facing upwards, with a single block gap in between them. This means that each dispenser can have a separate strand of redstone dust leading to it.

FIREWORK STAR RECIPE

2 Now fill each of the dispensers with firework rockets. They are created by combining a firework star with gunpowder and paper. The colour of the explosion will depend on the colour of the firework star, which can be altered using different dyes.

FIREWORK ROCKET RECIPE

3

3 Next, lay down the redstone dust. There should be a single circuit line leading from each dispenser, joined by a horizontal line of redstone to create a small parallel circuit.

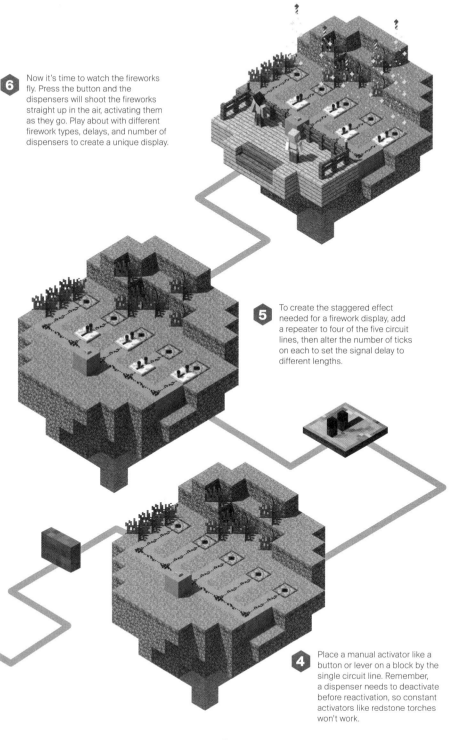

6 Now it's time to watch the fireworks fly. Press the button and the dispensers will shoot the fireworks straight up in the air, activating them as they go. Play about with different firework types, delays, and number of dispensers to create a unique display.

5 To create the staggered effect needed for a firework display, add a repeater to four of the five circuit lines, then alter the number of ticks on each to set the signal delay to different lengths.

4 Place a manual activator like a button or lever on a block by the single circuit line. Remember, a dispenser needs to deactivate before reactivation, so constant activators like redstone torches won't work.

ACTIVATOR, POWERED AND DETECTOR RAILS

There are a number of specialised redstone rails in Minecraft that can work as part of a circuit. These cross the spectrum of functions that we've already seen – they can output power, and detect storage, while others still will interact with a minecart that passes over the rail.

DETECTOR RAIL

Detector rails work in a similar way to pressure plates – they detect when a minecart passes over them, and output a full redstone signal to adjacent blocks and components.

 Combined with comparators, detector rails can measure how full minecarts with hoppers or chests are, and output a corresponding signal. If storage is full, the signal will be at its maximum, but if it's almost empty, it will only produce a weak signal.

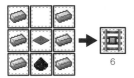

DETECTOR RAIL RECIPE

POWERED RAIL

Powered rails accelerate minecarts along a route. They require a redstone signal to provide the boost, otherwise they may actually slow down minecarts. Activated powered rails will conduct a signal to eight adjacent powered rails.

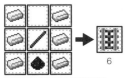

POWERED RAIL RECIPE

 Detector and powered rails can be used to provide continuous momentum along a track. By placing a detector rail in front of a powered rail, passing carts will activate a boost. If this is done all along a track, then movement should be continuous.

ACTIVATOR RAIL

The final redstone rail is the activator rail. It can be powered by the detector rail or any other redstone power source and has a number of functions, which depend on its activation state and the type of minecart that is passing over it.

ACTIVATOR RAIL RECIPE

6

4 Activator rails can also begin the detonation of a minecart with TNT. This is particularly useful for mining as all rails are immune to the blast. This makes it easy to send multiple TNT minecarts in quick succession to mine a large area.

5 The final activator rail function can be seen when an entity in a minecart passes over the activator rail. The activator rail will eject the mob or player in the cart!

3 When the activator rail is deactivated, it can activate a minecart with a hopper, allowing it to pick up items along its route, until it is full or deactivated. Conversely, when it's activated it will deactivate the same minecart, stopping it from collecting items.

TIP ♣

Redstone-enabled rails are unable to curve like normal rails. They must be used as straight track.

REDSTONE INTERSECTION

Building a working redstone rail system makes it much easier to travel across the vast expanse of your world. This redstone intersection will give you complete control over your route and allow you to change your intended direction without ever leaving your minecart.

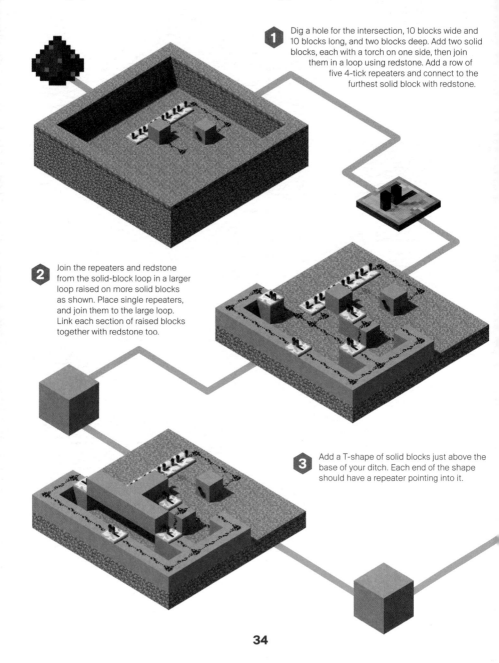

1 Dig a hole for the intersection, 10 blocks wide and 10 blocks long, and two blocks deep. Add two solid blocks, each with a torch on one side, then join them in a loop using redstone. Add a row of five 4-tick repeaters and connect to the furthest solid block with redstone.

2 Join the repeaters and redstone from the solid-block loop in a larger loop raised on more solid blocks as shown. Place single repeaters, and join them to the large loop. Link each section of raised blocks together with redstone too.

3 Add a T-shape of solid blocks just above the base of your ditch. Each end of the shape should have a repeater pointing into it.

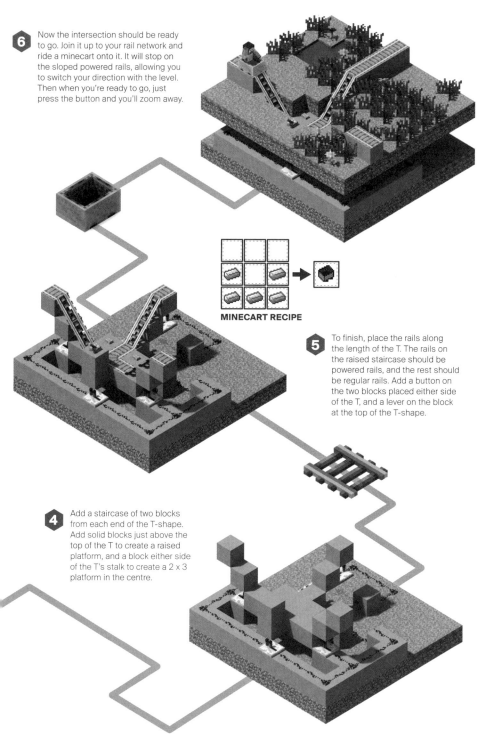

6 Now the intersection should be ready to go. Join it up to your rail network and ride a minecart onto it. It will stop on the sloped powered rails, allowing you to switch your direction with the level. Then when you're ready to go, just press the button and you'll zoom away.

MINECART RECIPE

5 To finish, place the rails along the length of the T. The rails on the raised staircase should be powered rails, and the rest should be regular rails. Add a button on the two blocks placed either side of the T, and a lever on the block at the top of the T-shape.

4 Add a staircase of two blocks from each end of the T-shape. Add solid blocks just above the top of the T to create a raised platform, and a block either side of the T's stalk to create a 2 x 3 platform in the centre.

NOTE BLOCK AND REDSTONE LAMPS

The final redstone output components are the ones that produce light and sound. Note blocks can play different types of sound at different pitches, while redstone lamps are similar in appearance to glowstone, though they have the advantage of being switchable.

NOTE BLOCK

Each note block can be made with wood planks of any sort and a single piece of redstone dust. When a redstone signal passes through them they will produce a sound dependent on the block that it is standing on. The diagram below shows the block needed to produce each sound.

NOTE BLOCK RECIPE

The spectrum of a note block covers two octaves, which is a total of 24 notes. To tune your note blocks, simply interact with the block to raise the pitch by one note.

The depth of customisation, along with a simple redstone circuit can be used to create everything from nursery rhymes to versions of popular songs. You can use repeater delays to create the correct rhythm of songs too.

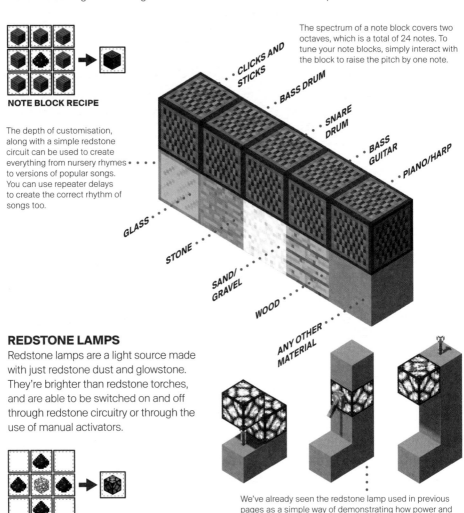

CLICKS AND STICKS

BASS DRUM

SNARE DRUM

BASS GUITAR

PIANO/HARP

GLASS

STONE

SAND/GRAVEL

WOOD

ANY OTHER MATERIAL

REDSTONE LAMPS

Redstone lamps are a light source made with just redstone dust and glowstone. They're brighter than redstone torches, and are able to be switched on and off through redstone circuitry or through the use of manual activators.

REDSTONE LAMP RECIPE

We've already seen the redstone lamp used in previous pages as a simple way of demonstrating how power and manipulation blocks work. It can be powered from all sides so it is versatile enough to be used in walls, floors, ceilings, and specialised lighting objects.

SECURITY LOOP

Note blocks and redstone lamps serve a useful function as alert items. This build incorporates both types of items to create sound and lights that trigger when an intruder enters a building.

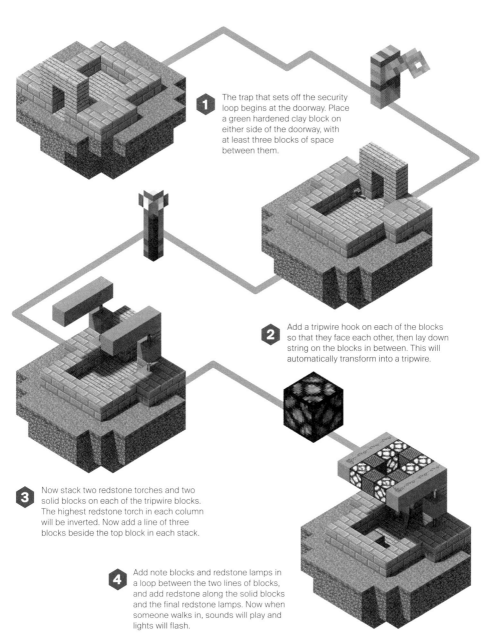

1 The trap that sets off the security loop begins at the doorway. Place a green hardened clay block on either side of the doorway, with at least three blocks of space between them.

2 Add a tripwire hook on each of the blocks so that they face each other, then lay down string on the blocks in between. This will automatically transform into a tripwire.

3 Now stack two redstone torches and two solid blocks on each of the tripwire blocks. The highest redstone torch in each column will be inverted. Now add a line of three blocks beside the top block in each stack.

4 Add note blocks and redstone lamps in a loop between the two lines of blocks, and add redstone along the solid blocks and the final redstone lamps. Now when someone walks in, sounds will play and lights will flash.

2

SIMPLE CIRCUITS

Now we have all the tools and redstone knowledge we need to progress to creating circuits. The circuits featured in this section are some of the easiest you can make, but you'll see from the example builds that it only takes a simple circuit to create a really cool mechanism.

CLOCK CIRCUITS

We're going to start off with the simplest circuit we can make – the clock circuit. Clock circuits conduct a signal that repeatedly triggers and travels through all the components, creating an infinite loop of activation for any attached mechanisms.

CLOCK CREATION

There are numerous ways to create a clock circuit, and even more ways that we can change its behaviour. On this spread we're going to look at types we can create with different components, so you can choose the one that's easiest for you.

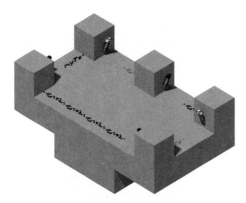

TORCH CLOCK

The simplest clock circuit utilises redstone torches. It requires an odd number of torches, and uses their ability to invert to repeatedly turn sections on and off. The torch clock above shows a 5-tick clock, which is the shortest stable clock that can be made, and takes 5 redstone ticks for the signal to loop.

REPEATER CLOCK

Repeater clocks are common as it's easy to amend the delay on redstone repeaters, and they can be rapid. This repeater clock is a 1-tick version, with no delay on the repeaters, which face alternate directions. The only thing to remember is to place the torch last, otherwise the signal will get stuck and stay on constantly.

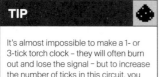

> **TIP**
>
> It's almost impossible to make a 1- or 3-tick torch clock – they will often burn out and lose the signal – but to increase the number of ticks in this circuit, you can add pairs of torches in the same fashion, or replace the redstone with repeaters to delay the signal.

> **TIP**
>
> You can destroy the torch once the clock signal is set in the repeater clock, but not in the comparator clock.

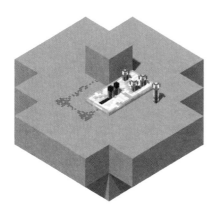

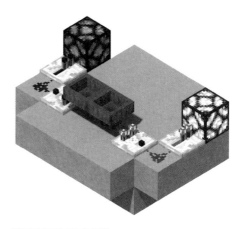

COMPARATOR CLOCK

Comparator clocks use a comparator set to subtraction mode to repeat a signal. It faces a solid block, from which redstone dust loops into the side of the comparator via a repeater, so the redstone doesn't join. The redstone torch behind the comparator provides a signal of 15, so when the side input is subtracted, it still results in an output and a repeating loop.

HOPPER CLOCK

Each hopper's output tube faces the other to create an alternating clock. Placing an item in one hopper will cause it to be passed back and forth indefinitely. The comparator beside each hopper measures the storage of each, which alternates between zero and one item, causing a small redstone signal output, which is then amplified by the repeater.

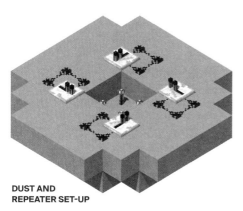

**DUST AND
REPEATER SET-UP**

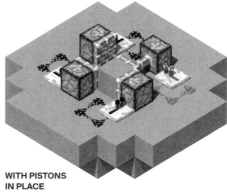

**WITH PISTONS
IN PLACE**

PISTON CLOCK

Unlike the other clock circuits, piston clocks have the advantage of being switchable, so they will only trigger when you want them to. This clock uses pistons to push a block around, which the redstone torches will pass a signal through, powering one of the four outer loops in turn.

MOB FARM TRAP

We're going to use the piston clock circuit as the basis for a handy mob farm, which lures in sunlight-hating mobs. It uses some of the outer loops of the piston clock to initiate different parts of the trap, and collect all the drops in easily accessible chests.

YOU WILL NEED:

138   16   12   20   65   8   4   7   4   4

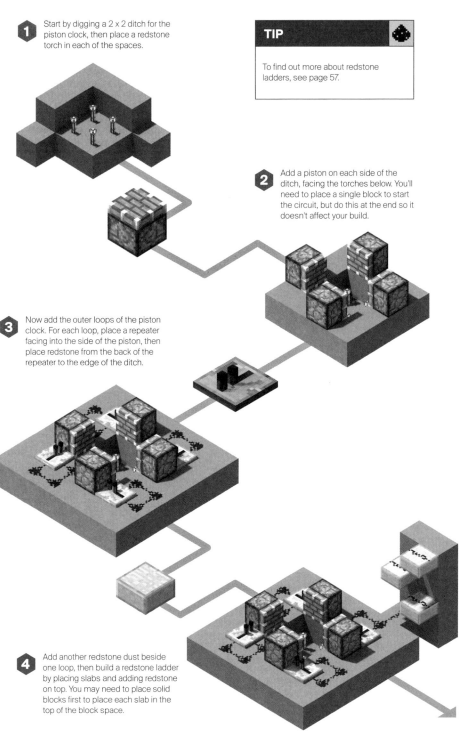

1. Start by digging a 2 x 2 ditch for the piston clock, then place a redstone torch in each of the spaces.

TIP ♠

To find out more about redstone ladders, see page 57.

2. Add a piston on each side of the ditch, facing the torches below. You'll need to place a single block to start the circuit, but do this at the end so it doesn't affect your build.

3. Now add the outer loops of the piston clock. For each loop, place a repeater facing into the side of the piston, then place redstone from the back of the repeater to the edge of the ditch.

4. Add another redstone dust beside one loop, then build a redstone ladder by placing slabs and adding redstone on top. You may need to place solid blocks first to place each slab in the top of the block space.

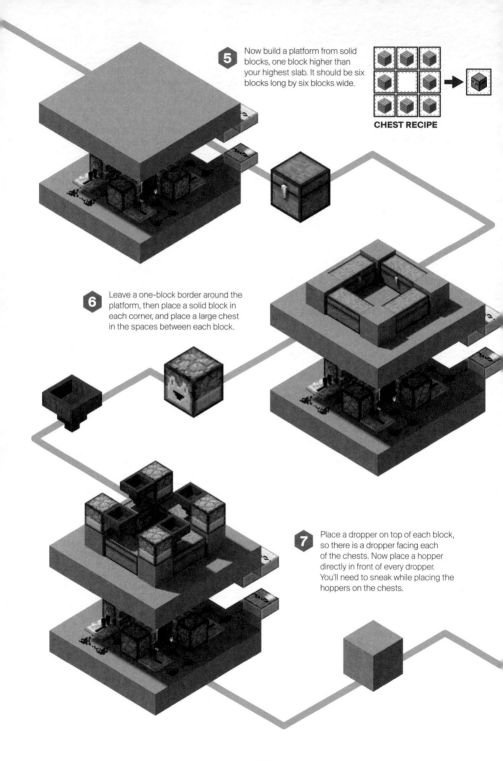

5 Now build a platform from solid blocks, one block higher than your highest slab. It should be six blocks long by six blocks wide.

CHEST RECIPE

6 Leave a one-block border around the platform, then place a solid block in each corner, and place a large chest in the spaces between each block.

7 Place a dropper on top of each block, so there is a dropper facing each of the chests. Now place a hopper directly in front of every dropper. You'll need to sneak while placing the hoppers on the chests.

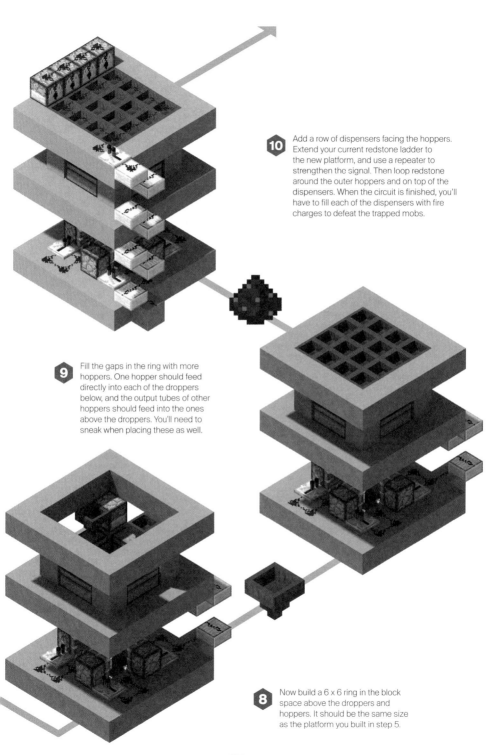

10 Add a row of dispensers facing the hoppers. Extend your current redstone ladder to the new platform, and use a repeater to strengthen the signal. Then loop redstone around the outer hoppers and on top of the dispensers. When the circuit is finished, you'll have to fill each of the dispensers with fire charges to defeat the trapped mobs.

9 Fill the gaps in the ring with more hoppers. One hopper should feed directly into each of the droppers below, and the output tubes of other hoppers should feed into the ones above the droppers. You'll need to sneak when placing these as well.

8 Now build a 6 x 6 ring in the block space above the droppers and hoppers. It should be the same size as the platform you built in step 5.

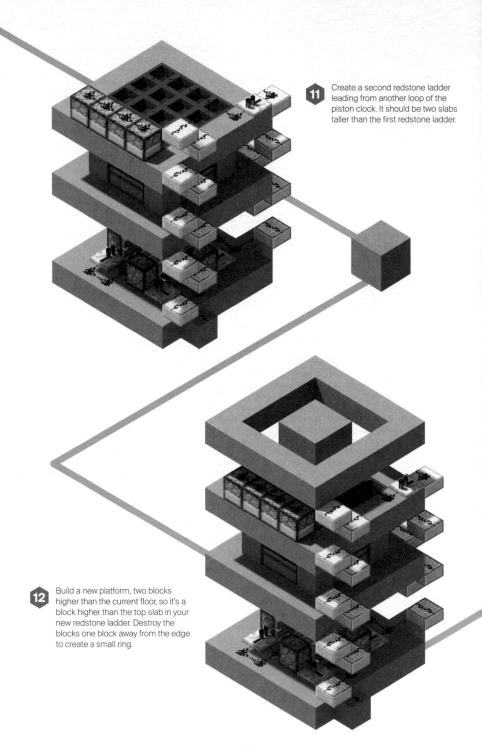

11 Create a second redstone ladder leading from another loop of the piston clock. It should be two slabs taller than the first redstone ladder.

12 Build a new platform, two blocks higher than the current floor, so it's a block higher than the top slab in your new redstone ladder. Destroy the blocks one block away from the edge to create a small ring.

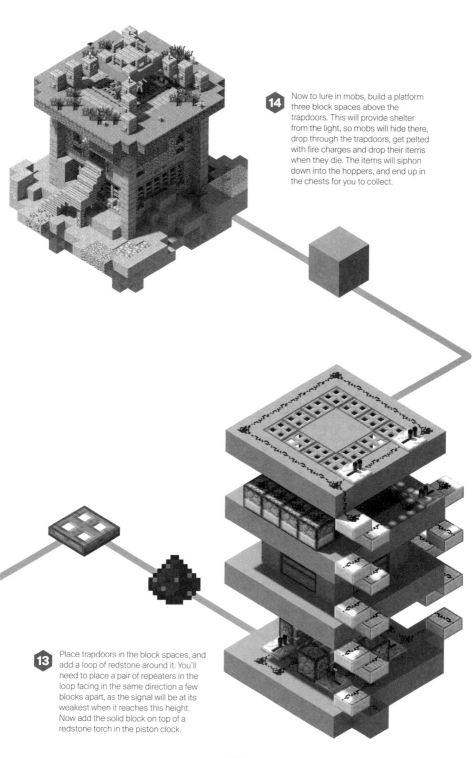

14 Now to lure in mobs, build a platform three block spaces above the trapdoors. This will provide shelter from the light, so mobs will hide there, drop through the trapdoors, get pelted with fire charges and drop their items when they die. The items will siphon down into the hoppers, and end up in the chests for you to collect.

13 Place trapdoors in the block spaces, and add a loop of redstone around it. You'll need to place a pair of repeaters in the loop facing in the same direction a few blocks apart, as the signal will be at its weakest when it reaches this height. Now add the solid block on top of a redstone torch in the piston clock.

PULSE CIRCUIT

The next circuit type is the pulse circuit, which focuses less on multiple triggers, and more on adapting signal duration as it travels through a circuit. This allows redstone mechanisms to stay active for a determined length of time.

PULSE CREATION

Like clock circuits, there are many different ways to create pulse circuits. However, pulse circuits are made from multiple elements, as featured here, that can be included and combined to make a truly customisable contraption.

TIP

Some pulses may be too lengthy to pass through a multiplier – they won't end before the second pulse reaches its destination. Run long pulses through a limiter first if this happens.

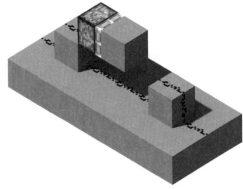

PULSE GENERATOR

All pulse circuits begin with a generator, which creates the initial pulse. In this one, a single lever controls two adjacent repeaters, one of which powers a third repeater, causing it to lock. When the lever is pulled again, the repeaters deactivate, releasing the lock on the final repeater. This in turn releases a built-up redstone pulse into a circuit.

LIMITER

The limiter reduces the length of a pulse. It raises redstone dust by one block on both sides of a three-block dip, with a sticky piston and solid block positioned above. When the pulse travels over the first raised block, the piston pushes the block and severs the redstone. When it deactivates, the redstone reattaches, allowing the reduced pulse through.

EXTENDER

This extender is highly customisable and can adapt a pulse to last hundreds of ticks! The item in the dropper is passed to the hopper and back, alternating whether the first comparator measures any storage. A pulse is then sent via a repeater, through a block, beginning the passage of items between the final hoppers. The pulse will last as long as it takes to pass all items back and forth, so you can lengthen the pulse by adding more items. Another comparator and repeater are situated between the two sets of hoppers to resupply the item to the dropper and reset the system.

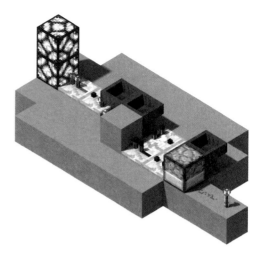

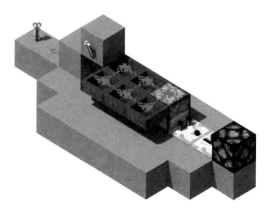

MULTIPLIER

Multipliers take a single pulse input and increase the number of pulses they emit, quickly activating a mechanism twice or more. The signal first passes through a solid block, powering the redstone lamps, and along the loop next to it, passing the signal to the comparator set to subtraction mode. It passes through the solid block once again, but won't reach the comparator as the signal strength has been reduced by the first subtraction.

COUNTER

The opposite to a multiplier, the counter emits a pulse only when it has reached the required number of pulse inputs. This counter requires six pulse inputs before it will output a signal, which it achieves by passing a single item around the hoppers in a loop, until it reaches the dropper. The comparator then detects the item and outputs a pulse. Note that the output tube of each hopper faces into the next one, and the final hopper's output tube faces into the dropper.

COMBINATION LOCK

This circuit combines generators, an extender and a counter into one simple contraption that can protect your base or storage area. It uses a wall of dummy buttons so that only people who know the right combination can enter.

YOU WILL NEED:

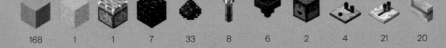

| 168 | 1 | 1 | 7 | 33 | 8 | 6 | 2 | 4 | 21 | 20 |

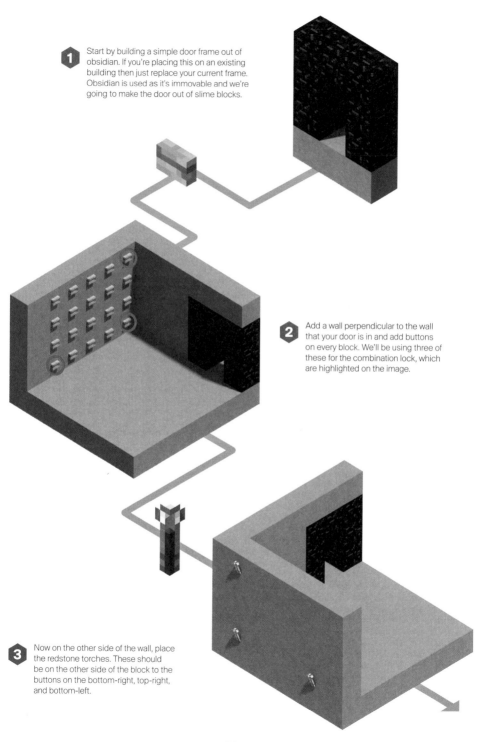

1 Start by building a simple door frame out of obsidian. If you're placing this on an existing building then just replace your current frame. Obsidian is used as it's immovable and we're going to make the door out of slime blocks.

2 Add a wall perpendicular to the wall that your door is in and add buttons on every block. We'll be using three of these for the combination lock, which are highlighted on the image.

3 Now on the other side of the wall, place the redstone torches. These should be on the other side of the block to the buttons on the bottom-right, top-right, and bottom-left.

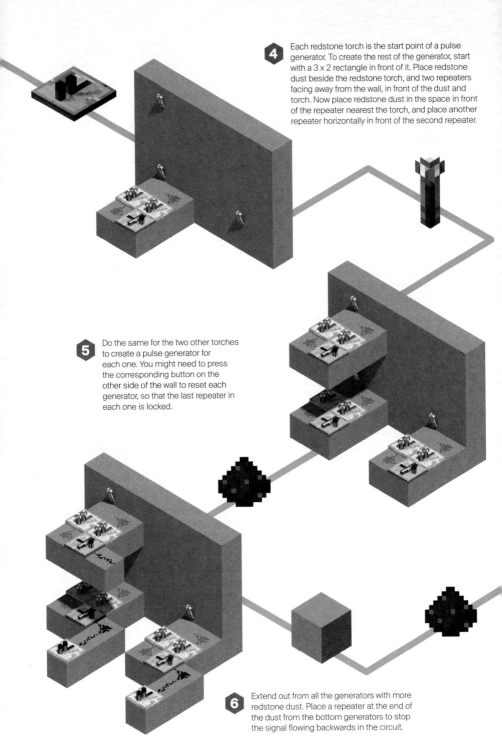

4 Each redstone torch is the start point of a pulse generator. To create the rest of the generator, start with a 3 x 2 rectangle in front of it. Place redstone dust beside the redstone torch, and two repeaters facing away from the wall, in front of the dust and torch. Now place redstone dust in the space in front of the repeater nearest the torch, and place another repeater horizontally in front of the second repeater.

5 Do the same for the two other torches to create a pulse generator for each one. You might need to press the corresponding button on the other side of the wall to reset each generator, so that the last repeater in each one is locked.

6 Extend out from all the generators with more redstone dust. Place a repeater at the end of the dust from the bottom generators to stop the signal flowing backwards in the circuit.

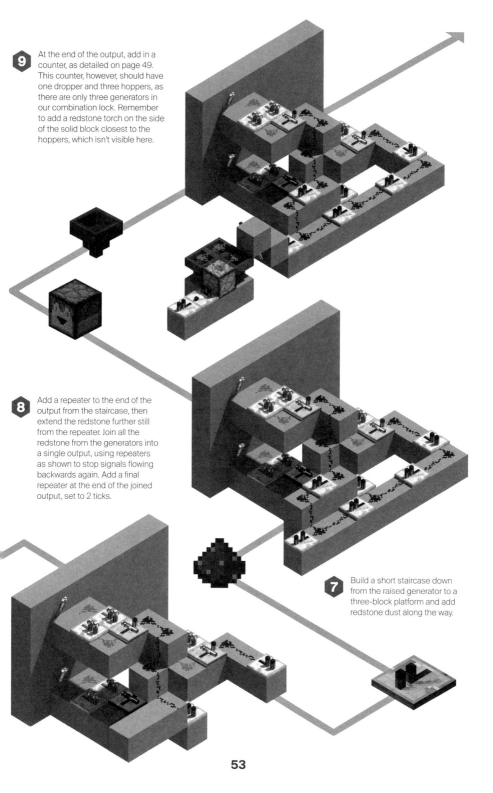

9 At the end of the output, add in a counter, as detailed on page 49. This counter, however, should have one dropper and three hoppers, as there are only three generators in our combination lock. Remember to add a redstone torch on the side of the solid block closest to the hoppers, which isn't visible here.

8 Add a repeater to the end of the output from the staircase, then extend the redstone further still from the repeater. Join all the redstone from the generators into a single output, using repeaters as shown to stop signals flowing backwards again. Add a final repeater at the end of the joined output, set to 2 ticks.

7 Build a short staircase down from the raised generator to a three-block platform and add redstone dust along the way.

53

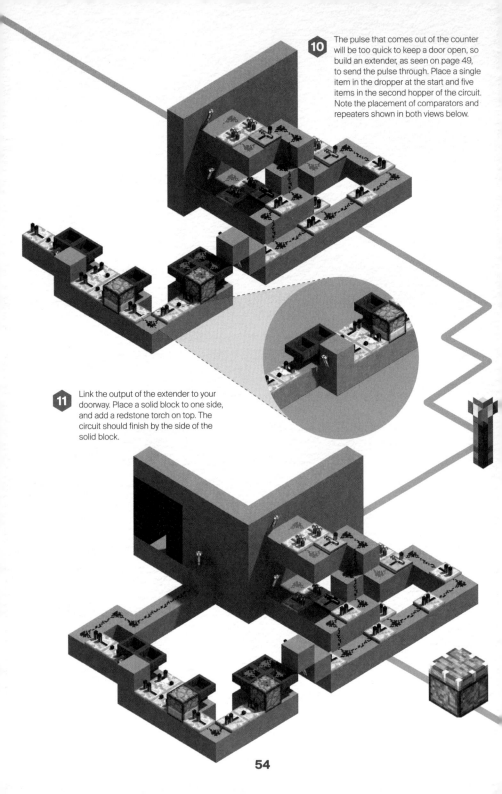

10 The pulse that comes out of the counter will be too quick to keep a door open, so build an extender, as seen on page 49, to send the pulse through. Place a single item in the dropper at the start and five items in the second hopper of the circuit. Note the placement of comparators and repeaters shown in both views below.

11 Link the output of the extender to your doorway. Place a solid block to one side, and add a redstone torch on top. The circuit should finish by the side of the solid block.

54

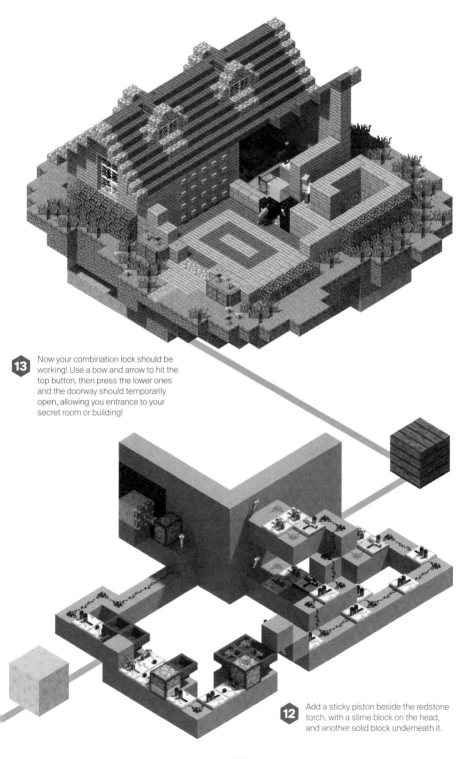

13 Now your combination lock should be working! Use a bow and arrow to hit the top button, then press the lower ones and the doorway should temporarily open, allowing you entrance to your secret room or building!

12 Add a sticky piston beside the redstone torch, with a slime block on the head, and another solid block underneath it.

VERTICAL TRANSMISSION

We've seen ways to create horizontal circuits, but often when creating redstone mechanisms, you'll need elements on different levels. Vertical transmission will enable your redstone to travel along a new third dimension.

VERTICAL CIRCUIT CREATION

Vertical transmission seems quite difficult, but is actually really easy when you know how. It can rely on the basic behaviours of redstone, or inversion of constant power sources, and can be used to send redstone signals up and down in contraptions.

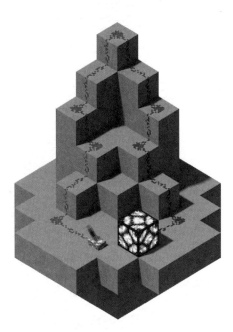

> **TIP**
>
> This build also shows how other redstone power sources can be used to turn off the bottom redstone torch, changing the order of inversion.

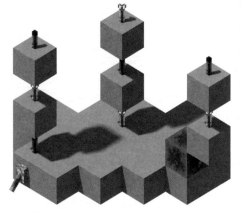

BASIC VERTICAL TRANSMISSION

The simplest way of building vertical transmission is to utilise redstone's inherent ability to join between blocks one space higher or lower. This takes up a lot of space if you're trying to create a compact build, but redstone will join up around corners travelling vertically, allowing spiral 'staircases'.

TORCH TOWER

This circuit uses inverted torches and minimal floor space to reach an elevated point. The redstone torch provides a signal through the block above, deactivating the torch on top, allowing the next torch to stay active, and so on. The necessity for pairs of redstone torches and solid blocks means it can lack precision.

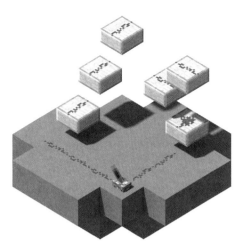

REDSTONE LADDER
Unlike full blocks, partial blocks such as slabs won't sever redstone dust if stacked in an alternating formation. This means they can be used to create ladders when placed in the top half of a block space. Other blocks that can be used to similar effect include hoppers and upside-down stairs.

STICKY PISTON TOWER
Sending signals downwards in a small space is harder to do, but still possible. This tower uses a redstone block placed on a sticky piston, facing downwards. When the block above the piston is powered, the piston extends, pushing the redstone block directly above the redstone dust, activating it in turn. This mechanism can also be stacked to pass a signal from great heights.

COMBINATION TRANSMISSION
Each transmission circuit has strengths and weaknesses; some take up lots of space, others will only stack at certain increments, while others still will only travel up or down. By combining the various systems, you can create unique circuits that compensate for a system's shortcomings with another's strength.

ARMOUR SWAPPER

To show vertical transmission in practice, we're going to build a clever wardrobe solution. With a few pulls of a lever, the armour swapper can cycle through your available armours, allowing you to choose one that suits your impending adventure.

YOU WILL NEED:

| 3 | 1 | 2 | 8 | 3 | 4 | 1 | 2 | 8 | 1 | 1 |

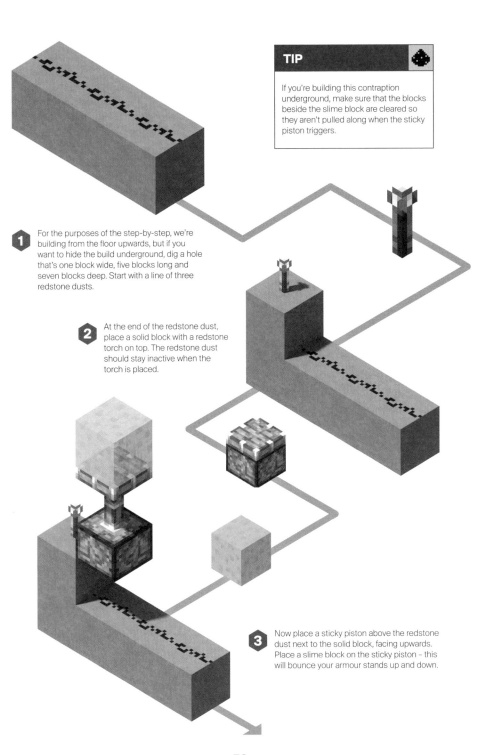

1 For the purposes of the step-by-step, we're building from the floor upwards, but if you want to hide the build underground, dig a hole that's one block wide, five blocks long and seven blocks deep. Start with a line of three redstone dusts.

2 At the end of the redstone dust, place a solid block with a redstone torch on top. The redstone dust should stay inactive when the torch is placed.

3 Now place a sticky piston above the redstone dust next to the solid block, facing upwards. Place a slime block on the sticky piston – this will bounce your armour stands up and down.

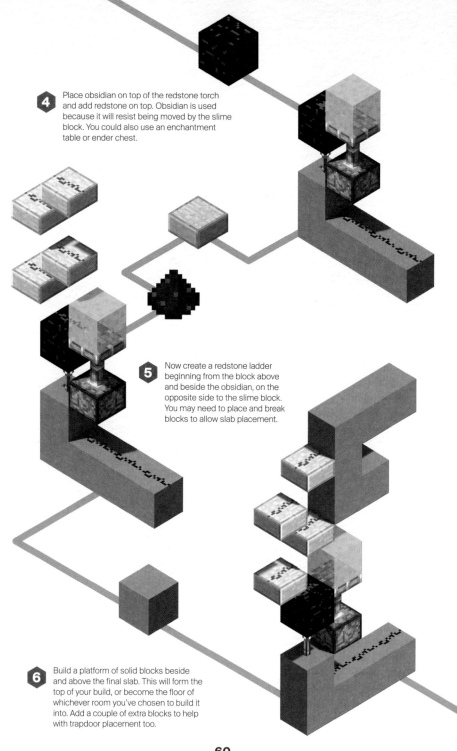

4 Place obsidian on top of the redstone torch and add redstone on top. Obsidian is used because it will resist being moved by the slime block. You could also use an enchantment table or ender chest.

5 Now create a redstone ladder beginning from the block above and beside the obsidian, on the opposite side to the slime block. You may need to place and break blocks to allow slab placement.

6 Build a platform of solid blocks beside and above the final slab. This will form the top of your build, or become the floor of whichever room you've chosen to build it into. Add a couple of extra blocks to help with trapdoor placement too.

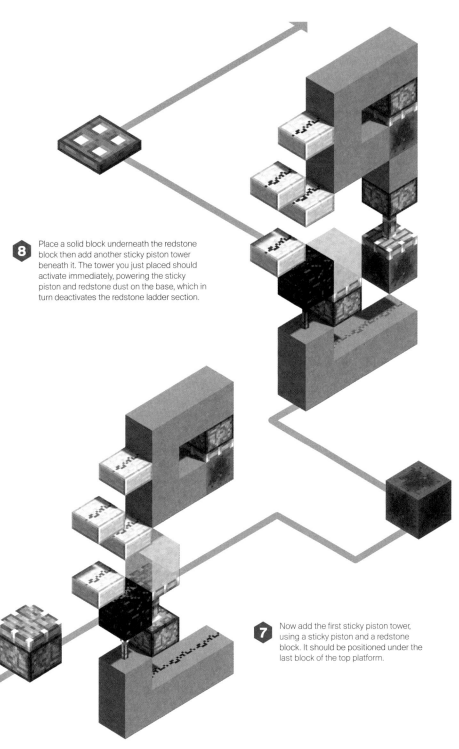

8 Place a solid block underneath the redstone block then add another sticky piston tower beneath it. The tower you just placed should activate immediately, powering the sticky piston and redstone dust on the base, which in turn deactivates the redstone ladder section.

7 Now add the first sticky piston tower, using a sticky piston and a redstone block. It should be positioned under the last block of the top platform.

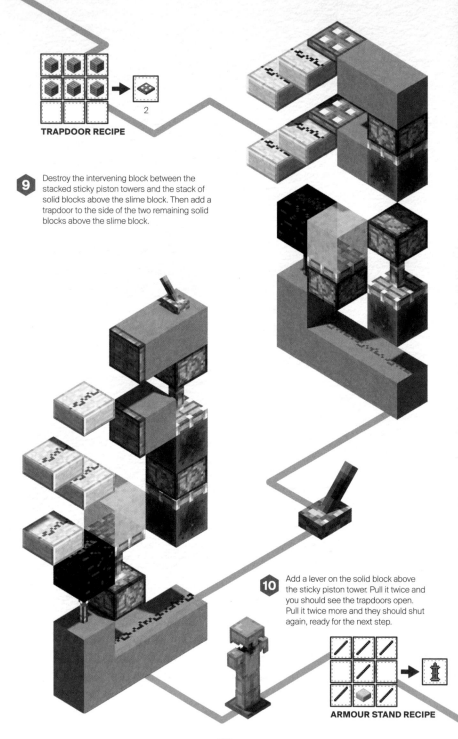

TRAPDOOR RECIPE

2

9 Destroy the intervening block between the stacked sticky piston towers and the stack of solid blocks above the slime block. Then add a trapdoor to the side of the two remaining solid blocks above the slime block.

10 Add a lever on the solid block above the sticky piston tower. Pull it twice and you should see the trapdoors open. Pull it twice more and they should shut again, ready for the next step.

ARMOUR STAND RECIPE

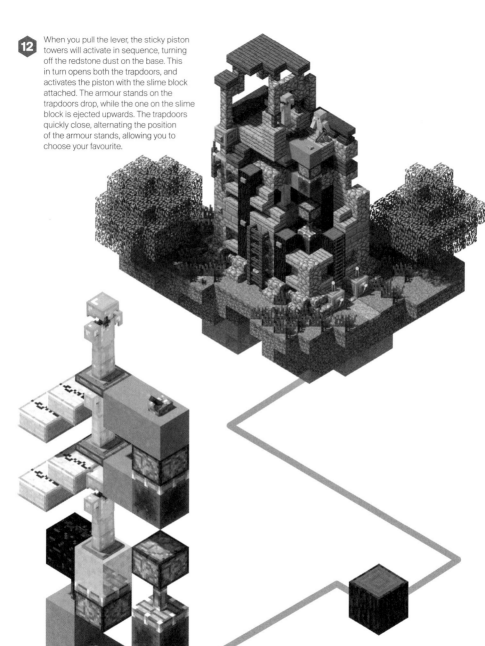

12 When you pull the lever, the sticky piston towers will activate in sequence, turning off the redstone dust on the base. This in turn opens both the trapdoors, and activates the piston with the slime block attached. The armour stands on the trapdoors drop, while the one on the slime block is ejected upwards. The trapdoors quickly close, alternating the position of the armour stands, allowing you to choose your favourite.

11 Now add the armour stands. Place one on top of the trapdoor – you will need to crouch while placing – and decorate with a set of armour. Pull the lever twice to make it disappear. Now do the same thing with two new armour stands. If it's worked correctly, you should now have your first set of armour in front of you.

3

BIG BUILDS

Now you're a redstone master, it's time to put all your new knowledge to good use. The final section features big projects, each of which incorporates various redstone components and different circuits that we've learned about in previous sections, and combines them to create something truly incredible!

PLATFORM ELEVATOR

The first of our big builds combines observer output, vertical transmission, slime blocks and obsidian to create a clever elevator that can travel up or down, and can be summoned whether you're standing at the top of a structure or at the bottom. It's perfect for adding to tall buildings like skyscrapers.

YOU WILL NEED:

9   6   2   2   5   2   2   16   47   1

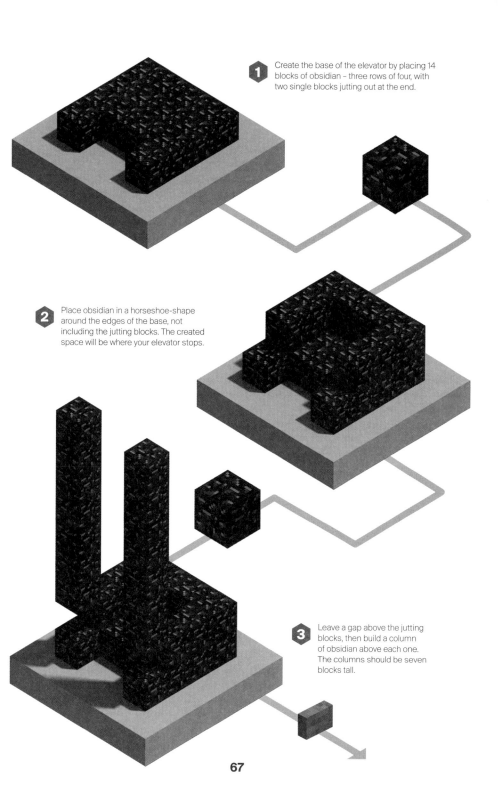

1 Create the base of the elevator by placing 14 blocks of obsidian – three rows of four, with two single blocks jutting out at the end.

2 Place obsidian in a horseshoe-shape around the edges of the base, not including the jutting blocks. The created space will be where your elevator stops.

3 Leave a gap above the jutting blocks, then build a column of obsidian above each one. The columns should be seven blocks tall.

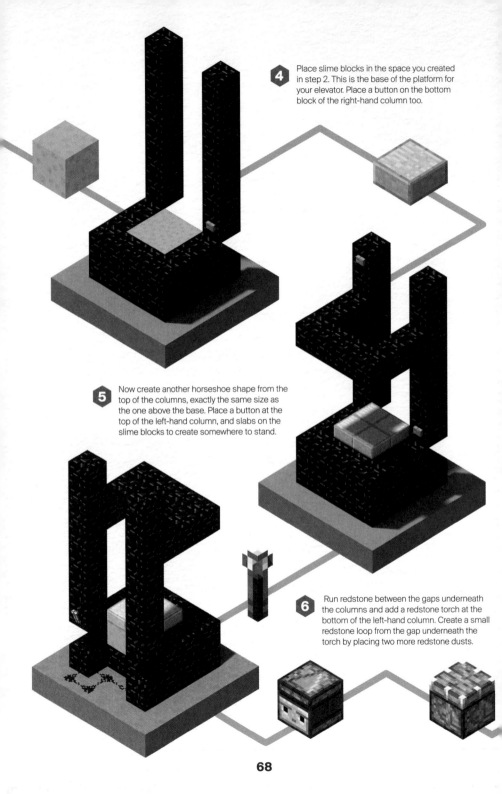

4 Place slime blocks in the space you created in step 2. This is the base of the platform for your elevator. Place a button on the bottom block of the right-hand column too.

5 Now create another horseshoe shape from the top of the columns, exactly the same size as the one above the base. Place a button at the top of the left-hand column, and slabs on the slime blocks to create somewhere to stand.

6 Run redstone between the gaps underneath the columns and add a redstone torch at the bottom of the left-hand column. Create a small redstone loop from the gap underneath the torch by placing two more redstone dusts.

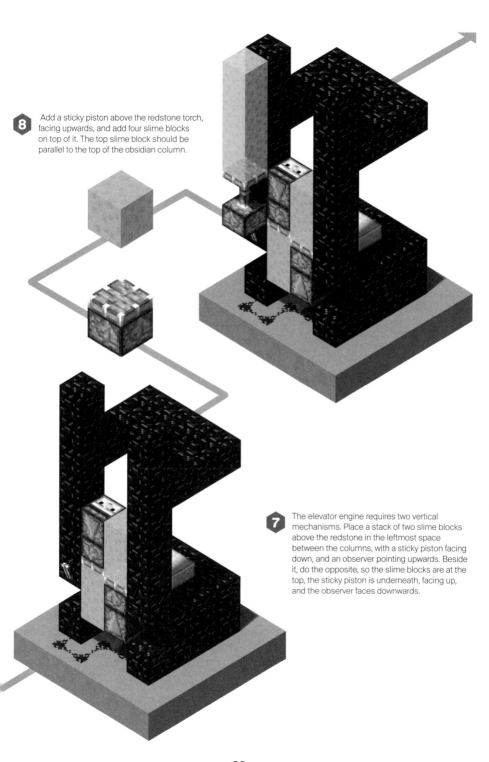

8 Add a sticky piston above the redstone torch, facing upwards, and add four slime blocks on top of it. The top slime block should be parallel to the top of the obsidian column.

7 The elevator engine requires two vertical mechanisms. Place a stack of two slime blocks above the redstone in the leftmost space between the columns, with a sticky piston facing down, and an observer pointing upwards. Beside it, do the opposite, so the slime blocks are at the top, the sticky piston is underneath, facing up, and the observer faces downwards.

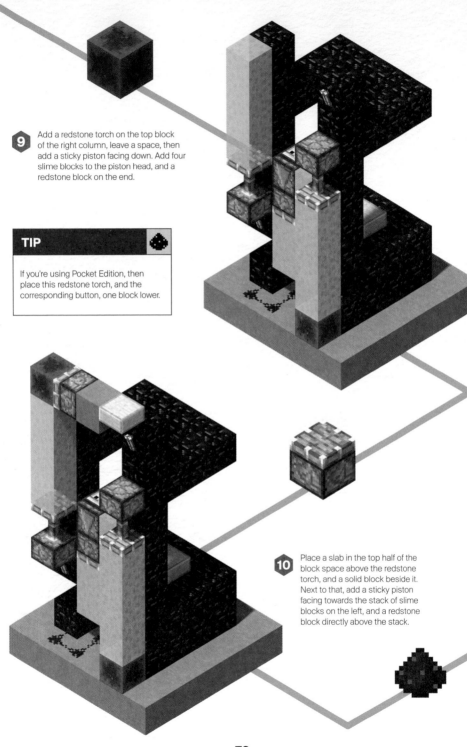

9 Add a redstone torch on the top block of the right column, leave a space, then add a sticky piston facing down. Add four slime blocks to the piston head, and a redstone block on the end.

TIP

If you're using Pocket Edition, then place this redstone torch, and the corresponding button, one block lower.

10 Place a slab in the top half of the block space above the redstone torch, and a solid block beside it. Next to that, add a sticky piston facing towards the stack of slime blocks on the left, and a redstone block directly above the stack.

12 The elevator is now in service. Stand on the platform and press the button. The downward-facing observer detects the change in the state of the redstone dust, which extends the piston, pushing the slime blocks repeatedly upwards, carrying you along with it. At the top, when the button is pressed, the upward-facing observer detects that the piston has retracted, causing the same process in the opposite direction.

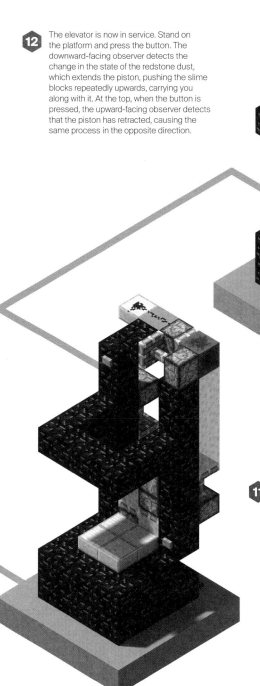

11 Add redstone dust on the slab, solid block and the top obsidian block of the left column. On the opposite obsidian column, add a sticky piston facing inwards. It should extend immediately. Add an obsidian block on the piston head too.

TIP

You can make the elevator a lot taller by stacking the sticky piston towers on each side. Just make sure that each piston is pushing a maximum of 11 slime blocks and one redstone block.

ELYTRA LAUNCHER

Gliding across the Minecraft world is one of the fastest ways to travel. This elytra launcher combines a vertical transmission circuit with slime blocks, dispensers and TNT to hurl you in the air so you can easily float to your destination.

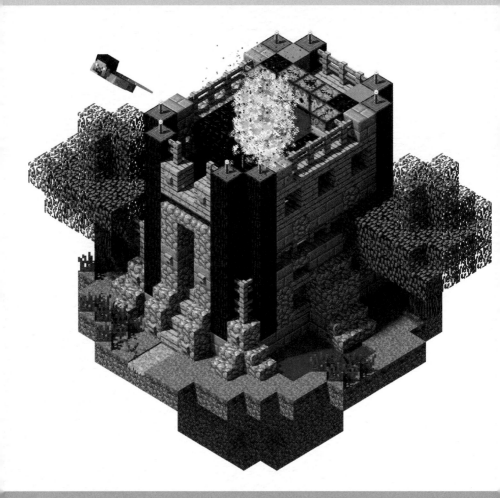

YOU WILL NEED:

| 25 | 8 | 5 | 1 | 1 | 1 | 1 | 1 | 10 | 45 | 42 |

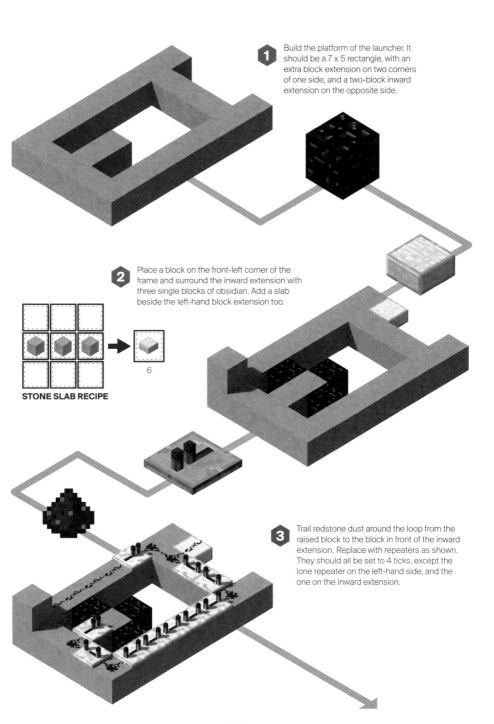

1 Build the platform of the launcher. It should be a 7 x 5 rectangle, with an extra block extension on two corners of one side, and a two-block inward extension on the opposite side.

2 Place a block on the front-left corner of the frame and surround the inward extension with three single blocks of obsidian. Add a slab beside the left-hand block extension too.

STONE SLAB RECIPE

6

3 Trail redstone dust around the loop from the raised block to the block in front of the inward extension. Replace with repeaters as shown. They should all be set to 4 ticks, except the lone repeater on the left-hand side, and the one on the inward extension.

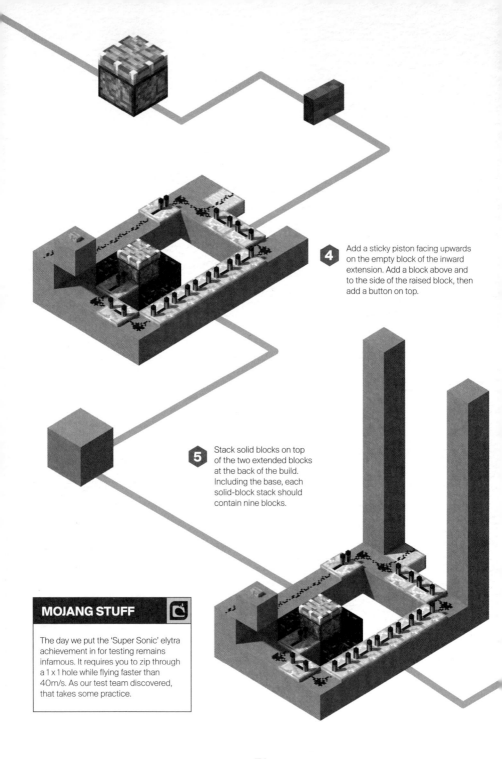

4 Add a sticky piston facing upwards on the empty block of the inward extension. Add a block above and to the side of the raised block, then add a button on top.

5 Stack solid blocks on top of the two extended blocks at the back of the build. Including the base, each solid-block stack should contain nine blocks.

MOJANG STUFF

The day we put the 'Super Sonic' elytra achievement in for testing remains infamous. It requires you to zip through a 1 x 1 hole while flying faster than 40m/s. As our test team discovered, that takes some practice.

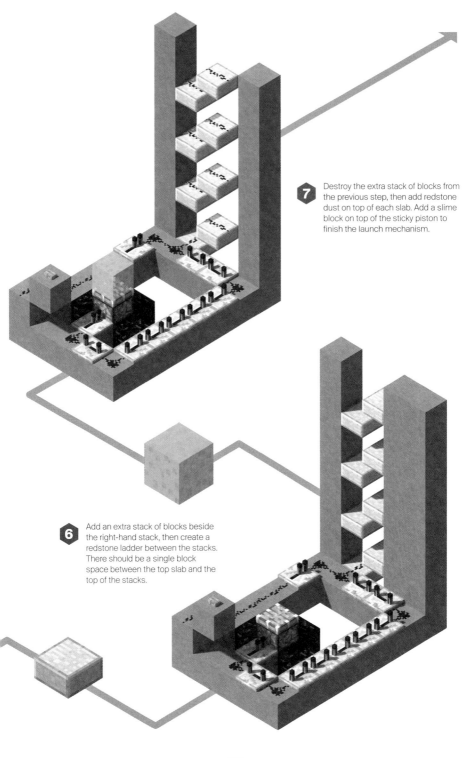

7 Destroy the extra stack of blocks from the previous step, then add redstone dust on top of each slab. Add a slime block on top of the sticky piston to finish the launch mechanism.

6 Add an extra stack of blocks beside the right-hand stack, then create a redstone ladder between the stacks. There should be a single block space between the top slab and the top of the stacks.

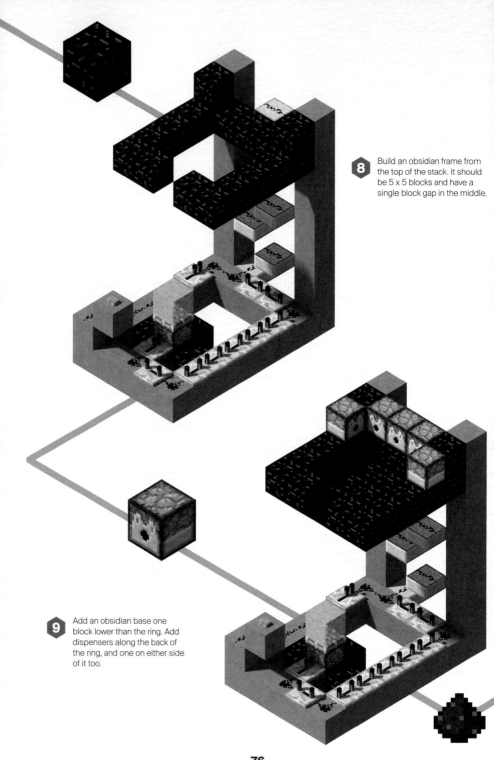

8 Build an obsidian frame from the top of the stack. It should be 5 x 5 blocks and have a single block gap in the middle.

9 Add an obsidian base one block lower than the ring. Add dispensers along the back of the ring, and one on either side of it too.

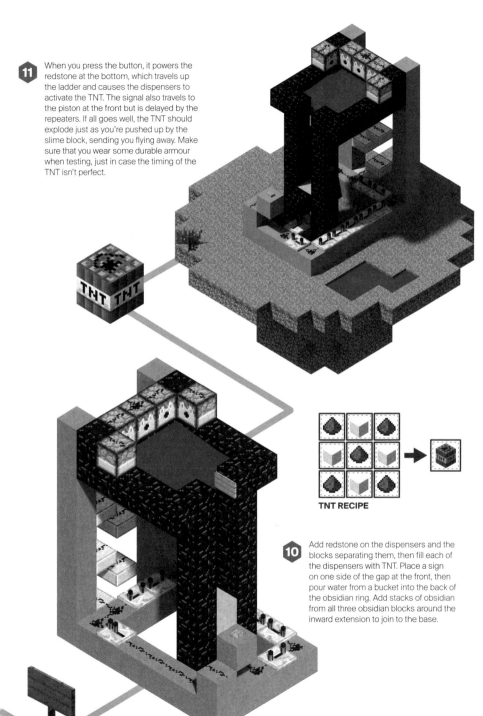

11 When you press the button, it powers the redstone at the bottom, which travels up the ladder and causes the dispensers to activate the TNT. The signal also travels to the piston at the front but is delayed by the repeaters. If all goes well, the TNT should explode just as you're pushed up by the slime block, sending you flying away. Make sure that you wear some durable armour when testing, just in case the timing of the TNT isn't perfect.

TNT RECIPE

10 Add redstone on the dispensers and the blocks separating them, then fill each of the dispensers with TNT. Place a sign on one side of the gap at the front, then pour water from a bucket into the back of the obsidian ring. Add stacks of obsidian from all three obsidian blocks around the inward extension to join to the base.

PISTON SQUISHER

An excellent example of a redstone trap, the piston squisher uses pressure plates to activate two sets of pistons, above and below, connected by a redstone tower. The result is a claustrophobic, nigh-on inescapable chamber.

YOU WILL NEED:

| 27 | 179 | 48 | 16 | 4 | 16 |

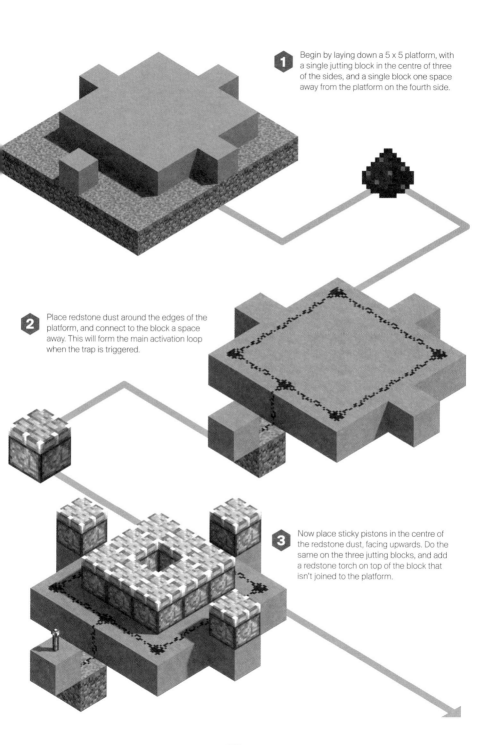

1. Begin by laying down a 5 x 5 platform, with a single jutting block in the centre of three of the sides, and a single block one space away from the platform on the fourth side.

2. Place redstone dust around the edges of the platform, and connect to the block a space away. This will form the main activation loop when the trap is triggered.

3. Now place sticky pistons in the centre of the redstone dust, facing upwards. Do the same on the three jutting blocks, and add a redstone torch on top of the block that isn't joined to the platform.

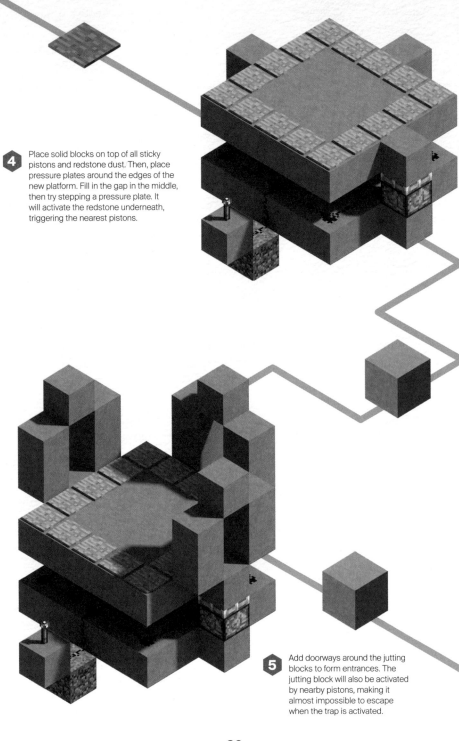

4 Place solid blocks on top of all sticky pistons and redstone dust. Then, place pressure plates around the edges of the new platform. Fill in the gap in the middle, then try stepping a pressure plate. It will activate the redstone underneath, triggering the nearest pistons.

5 Add doorways around the jutting blocks to form entrances. The jutting block will also be activated by nearby pistons, making it almost impossible to escape when the trap is activated.

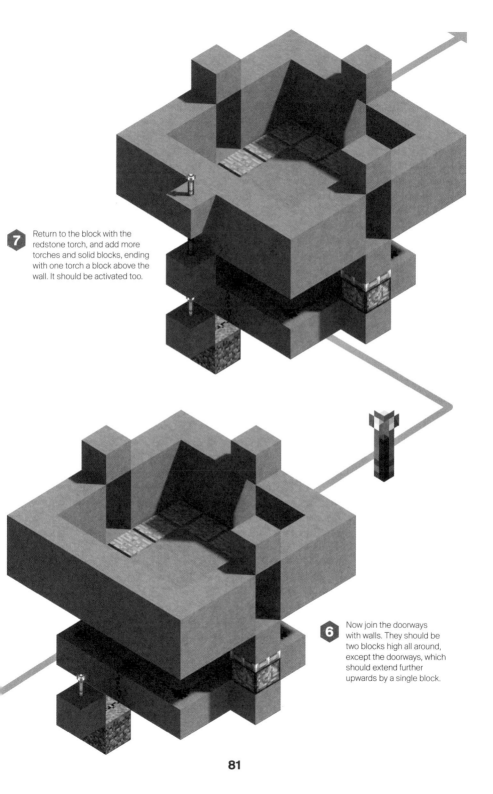

7 Return to the block with the redstone torch, and add more torches and solid blocks, ending with one torch a block above the wall. It should be activated too.

6 Now join the doorways with walls. They should be two blocks high all around, except the doorways, which should extend further upwards by a single block.

81

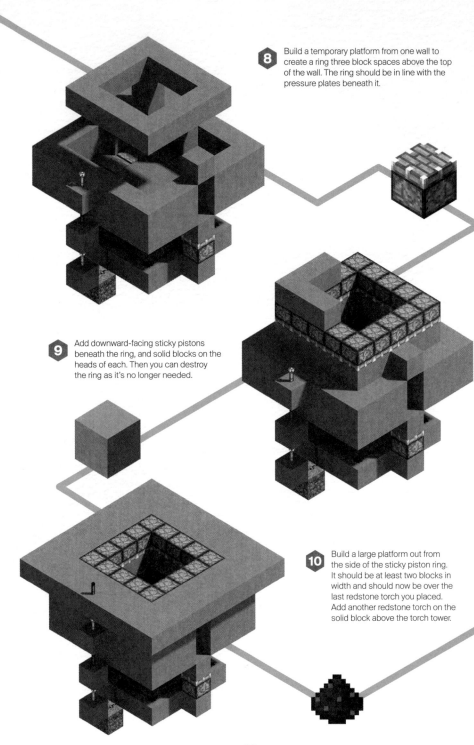

8 Build a temporary platform from one wall to create a ring three block spaces above the top of the wall. The ring should be in line with the pressure plates beneath it.

9 Add downward-facing sticky pistons beneath the ring, and solid blocks on the heads of each. Then you can destroy the ring as it's no longer needed.

10 Build a large platform out from the side of the sticky piston ring. It should be at least two blocks in width and should now be over the last redstone torch you placed. Add another redstone torch on the solid block above the torch tower.

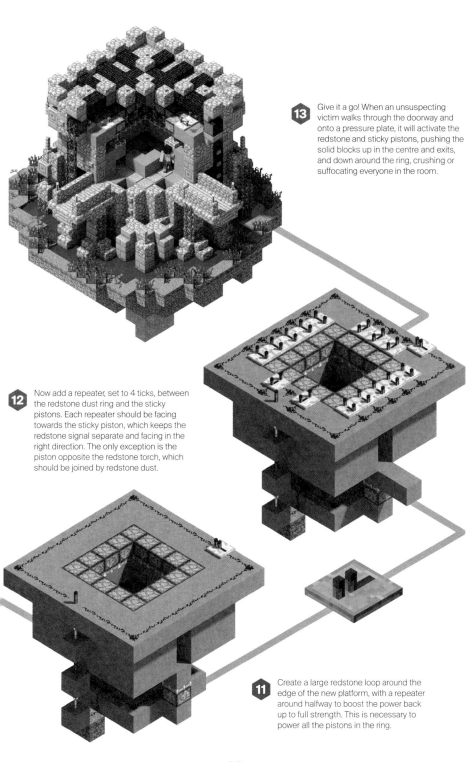

13 Give it a go! When an unsuspecting victim walks through the doorway and onto a pressure plate, it will activate the redstone and sticky pistons, pushing the solid blocks up in the centre and exits, and down around the ring, crushing or suffocating everyone in the room.

12 Now add a repeater, set to 4 ticks, between the redstone dust ring and the sticky pistons. Each repeater should be facing towards the sticky piston, which keeps the redstone signal separate and facing in the right direction. The only exception is the piston opposite the redstone torch, which should be joined by redstone dust.

11 Create a large redstone loop around the edge of the new platform, with a repeater around halfway to boost the power back up to full strength. This is necessary to power all the pistons in the ring.

AUTOMATIC BREWER

Brewing potions is very handy, but can be a nightmare if you need to collect dozens of ingredients. This handy redstone workshop uses dispensers to gather the necessary items and automatically feed them into a brewing stand, taking the work out of brewing.

YOU WILL NEED:

3	8	4	1	2	17	2	14	15	11	7

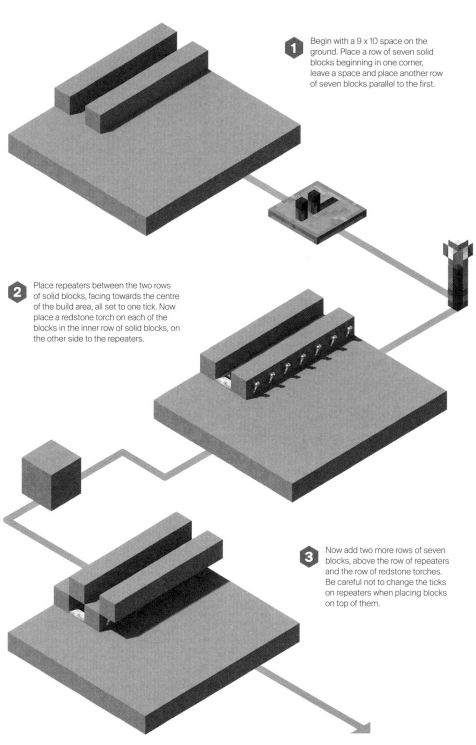

1 Begin with a 9 x 10 space on the ground. Place a row of seven solid blocks beginning in one corner, leave a space and place another row of seven blocks parallel to the first.

2 Place repeaters between the two rows of solid blocks, facing towards the centre of the build area, all set to one tick. Now place a redstone torch on each of the blocks in the inner row of solid blocks, on the other side to the repeaters.

3 Now add two more rows of seven blocks, above the row of repeaters and the row of redstone torches. Be careful not to change the ticks on repeaters when placing blocks on top of them.

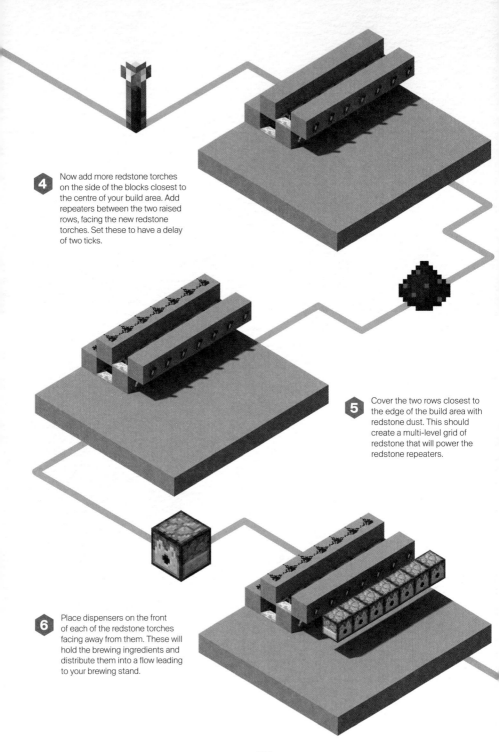

4 Now add more redstone torches on the side of the blocks closest to the centre of your build area. Add repeaters between the two raised rows, facing the new redstone torches. Set these to have a delay of two ticks.

5 Cover the two rows closest to the edge of the build area with redstone dust. This should create a multi-level grid of redstone that will power the redstone repeaters.

6 Place dispensers on the front of each of the redstone torches facing away from them. These will hold the brewing ingredients and distribute them into a flow leading to your brewing stand.

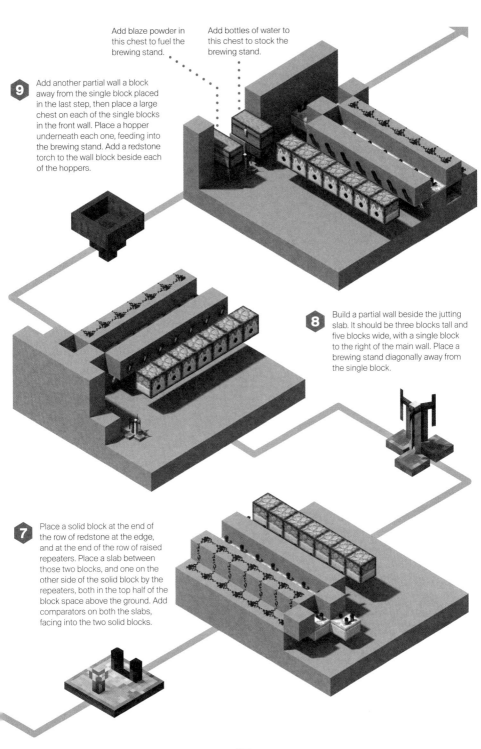

Add blaze powder in this chest to fuel the brewing stand.

Add bottles of water to this chest to stock the brewing stand.

9 Add another partial wall a block away from the single block placed in the last step, then place a large chest on each of the single blocks in the front wall. Place a hopper underneath each one, feeding into the brewing stand. Add a redstone torch to the wall block beside each of the hoppers.

8 Build a partial wall beside the jutting slab. It should be three blocks tall and five blocks wide, with a single block to the right of the main wall. Place a brewing stand diagonally away from the single block.

7 Place a solid block at the end of the row of redstone at the edge, and at the end of the row of raised repeaters. Place a slab between those two blocks, and one on the other side of the solid block by the repeaters, both in the top half of the block space above the ground. Add comparators on both the slabs, facing into the two solid blocks.

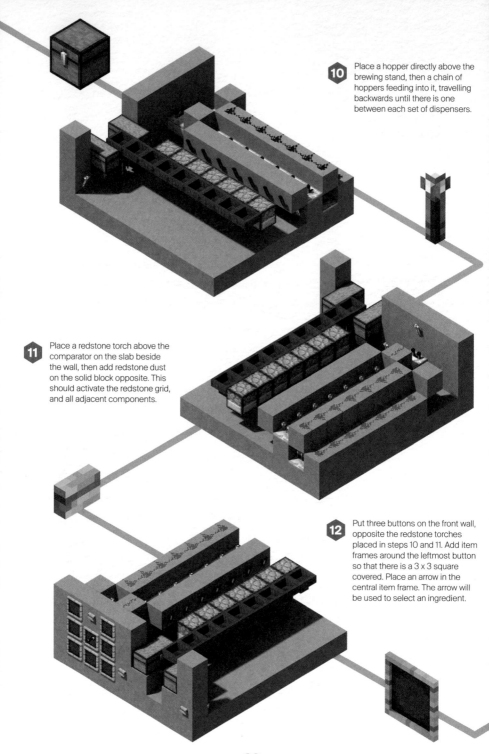

10 Place a hopper directly above the brewing stand, then a chain of hoppers feeding into it, travelling backwards until there is one between each set of dispensers.

11 Place a redstone torch above the comparator on the slab beside the wall, then add redstone dust on the solid block opposite. This should activate the redstone grid, and all adjacent components.

12 Put three buttons on the front wall, opposite the redstone torches placed in steps 10 and 11. Add item frames around the leftmost button so that there is a 3 x 3 square covered. Place an arrow in the central item frame. The arrow will be used to select an ingredient.

14 Now you're ready! Press each of the buttons either side of the brewing stand to fill with bottles of water and fuel with blaze powder. Now rotate the arrow until it is pointing at the item you want to add. The comparator on the other side of the frame will detect the direction of the item in the frame and produce a varying signal, powering the correct dispenser, which passes the ingredient down the hoppers and into the brewing stand.

TIP

In this build the comparator detects the direction of the arrow in the item frame. Comparators can also detect how many pieces of a cake are left, which record is playing on a jukebox, or whether an end portal frame block contains an eye of ender.

13 Place an ingredient on each of the item frames, then stock the corresponding dispenser with stacks of the item. Refer to the numbering for an indication of which position will activate each dispenser.

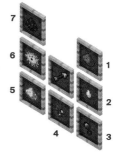

1 - GUNPOWDER	5 - GLOWSTONE DUST
2 - GHAST TEAR	6 - PUFFERFISH
3 - SPIDER EYE	7 - REDSTONE DUST
4 - NETHER WART	

REDSTONE LIGHTHOUSE

For the final build, we're going to combine a simple torch clock with vertical transmission to make a grand lighthouse, visible from miles around. It's the perfect mechanism to mark your territory and light the way for visitors.

YOU WILL NEED:

24   54   5   12   97

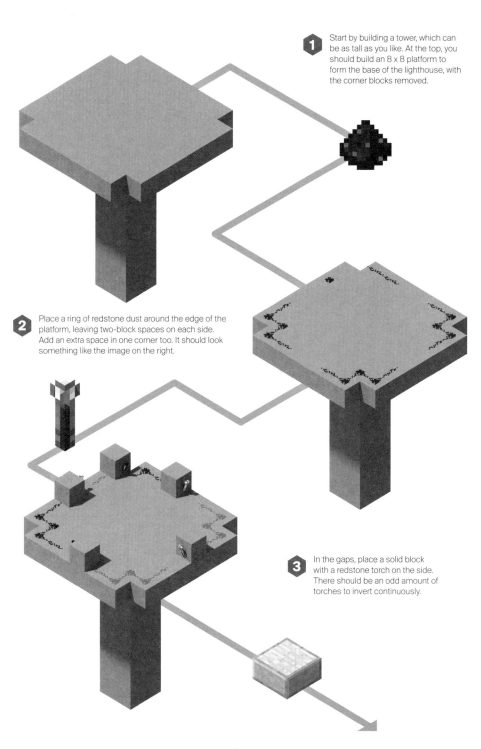

1 Start by building a tower, which can be as tall as you like. At the top, you should build an 8 x 8 platform to form the base of the lighthouse, with the corner blocks removed.

2 Place a ring of redstone dust around the edge of the platform, leaving two-block spaces on each side. Add an extra space in one corner too. It should look something like the image on the right.

3 In the gaps, place a solid block with a redstone torch on the side. There should be an odd amount of torches to invert continuously.

91

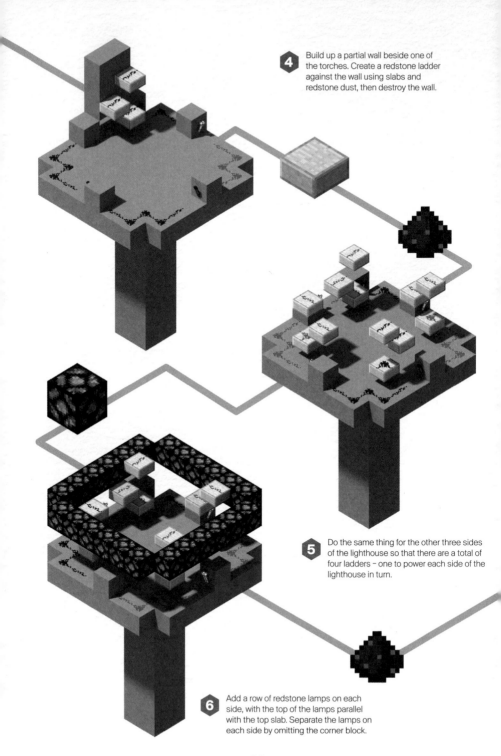

4 Build up a partial wall beside one of the torches. Create a redstone ladder against the wall using slabs and redstone dust, then destroy the wall.

5 Do the same thing for the other three sides of the lighthouse so that there are a total of four ladders – one to power each side of the lighthouse in turn.

6 Add a row of redstone lamps on each side, with the top of the lamps parallel with the top slab. Separate the lamps on each side by omitting the corner block.

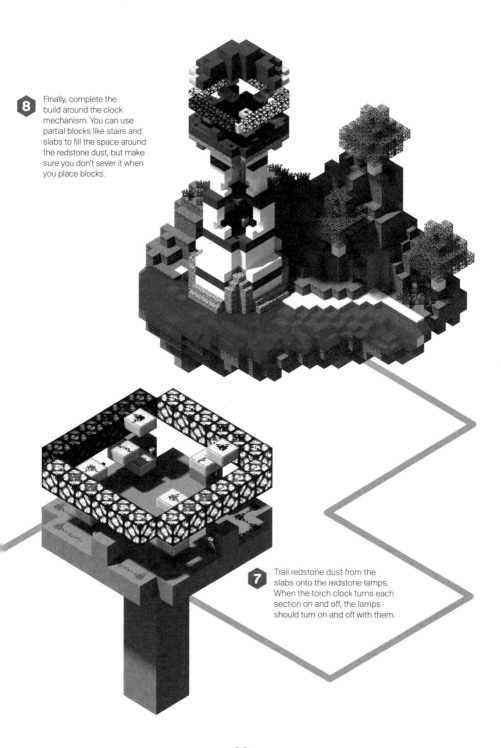

8 Finally, complete the build around the clock mechanism. You can use partial blocks like stairs and slabs to fill the space around the redstone dust, but make sure you don't sever it when you place blocks.

7 Trail redstone dust from the slabs onto the redstone lamps. When the torch clock turns each section on and off, the lamps should turn on and off with them.

FINAL WORDS

P hew! You made it. Hopefully you can now tell your comparators from your repeaters, pulse circuits from clock circuits and how to fix up an effective hopper, dropper or swapper. With any luck, you can combine this elite wisdom to assemble devices capable of the most devious computation, propelling players to new heights, or setting imaginations (and mobs) alight.

The choice is yours and the possibilities are wide open. What will you build? We can't wait to see!

MARSH DAVIES
THE MOJANG TEAM

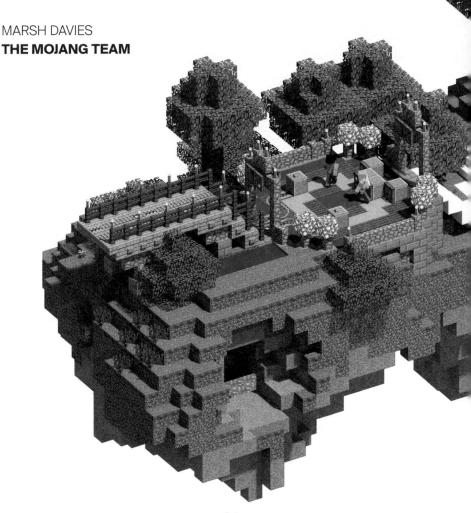

First published in Great Britain 2017 by Egmont UK Limited.
This edition published in 2020 by Dean, an imprint of Egmont UK Limited,
2 Minster Court, 10th Floor, London EC3R 7BB

Written by Stephanie Milton
Additional material by Owen Jones and Marsh Davies
Designed by Andrea Philpots, Joe Bolder and John Stuckey
Illustrations by Ryan Marsh and James Bale
Cover designed by John Stuckey
Production by Louis Harvey
Special thanks to Lydia Winters, Owen Jones, Junkboy,
Martin Johansson, Marsh Davies and Jesper Öqvist.

ISBN 978 0 6035 7928 8

71019/001

Printed in China

ONLINE SAFETY FOR YOUNGER FANS

Spending time online is great fun! Here are a few simple rules to help younger fans stay safe and
keep the internet a great place to spend time:

- Never give out your real name – don't use it as your username.
- Never give out any of your personal details.
- Never tell anybody which school you go to or how old you are.
- Never tell anybody your password except a parent or a guardian.
- Be aware that you must be 13 or over to create an account on many sites. Always check the
site policy and ask a parent or guardian for permission before registering.
- Always tell a parent or guardian if something is worrying you.

Stay safe online. Any website addresses listed in this book are correct at the time of going
to print. However, Egmont is not responsible for content hosted by third parties. Please be
aware that online content can be subject to change and websites can contain content that is
unsuitable for children. We advise that all children are supervised when using the internet.

Egmont takes its responsibility to the planet and its inhabitants very seriously.
We aim to use papers from well-managed forests run by responsible suppliers.

GUITE TO:

◉ **THE NETHER & THE END**

CONTENTS

1. THE NETHER

2. THE END

INTRODUCTION

Welcome, bold adventurers, clever crafters and worldly wanderers! Are you ready for an even greater challenge, with even greater rewards, than anything found in the grassy plains and craggy mountains of Minecraft's Overworld? You soon will be! In these pages we'll dig through the secrets of the Nether – a place of roiling lava lakes and black caverns – and the strange reality of the End, with its pale islands, floating in an inky void. Ghasts! Shulkers! Such foes you will learn to face as you conquer the furthest reaches of the world. So, be sure to pack this book before stepping through a portal – and good luck!

MARSH DAVIES
THE MOJANG TEAM

KEY

Throughout the pages of this book you'll see symbols that represent different items, values or properties. Refer back to this page when you spot them to check what they mean.

GENERAL

MOJANG STUFF

This super-exclusive info has come directly from the developers at Mojang.

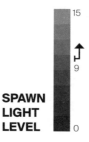

SPAWN LIGHT LEVEL

15

9

0

Indicates the light level at which a mob spawns. In this example, the mob spawns at a light level of 9 or higher.

HOSTILITY

Indicates the hostility level of a mob – yellow is passive, orange is neutral and red is hostile.

	Block projectiles with your shield
	Block projectiles with your sword
	Disable mob spawner with 5 torches
	Drink a potion of fire resistance
	Drink a potion of healing

	Drink a potion of strength
	Get yourself into a two block-high space and hit the mob's legs
	Hit with enchanted diamond sword
	Pelt with snowballs
	Reel in with fishing rod

	Shoot with enchanted bow and arrows
	Stand on two block-high tower and hit them with a sword
	Stand on a three block-high tower and hit them with a sword
	Throw a splash potion of healing at it
	Use a bed then step backwards quickly to avoid the explosion

	Blaze powder		Glass		Pumpkin
	Blaze rod		Glowstone dust		Redstone
	Bones		Gold ingot		Redstone torch
	Bowl		Gold nugget		Rotten flesh
	Coal		Gold sword		Sand
	Cobblestone		Gunpowder		Shulker shell
	Cocoa beans		Iron ingot		Slimeball
	Diamond		Magma cream		Stick
	Dragon egg		Milk		Stone
	Egg		Mushroom (brown)		Stone pressure plate
	Ender pearl		Mushroom (red)		String
	Experience point		Nether brick		Sugar
	Eye of ender		Nether quartz		Wood planks
	Feather		Nether star		Wood slab
	Flint		Obsidian		Wheat
	Ghast tear		Popped chorus fruit		Wither skeleton skull

1

THE NETHER

After the rolling green hills and lush forests of the Overworld, the Nether is a dramatic change of scene. In this section you'll discover what awaits you on the other side of your Nether portal, how to defeat the Nether's hellish hostile mobs and where to look for valuable blocks and items.

THE NETHER ENVIRONMENT

The perilous Nether dimension is partially submerged in lava and inhabited by five dangerous hostile mobs that you won't have seen before. It's also home to many useful materials that are essential to your progress. Let's take a look at the environment.

1 The majority of the terrain is netherrack – a substance that burns indefinitely when it comes into contact with fire.

2 The terrain is surrounded by vast oceans of lava. Lava cascades pour from the ceiling, and more lava is hidden behind many netherrack blocks, so mining is dangerous.

3 You won't find any of the Overworld ores in the Nether, but veins of Nether quartz ore are a common sight. When mined with a pickaxe it will drop Nether quartz as well as experience points.

4 Patches of soul sand occur frequently. If you walk across soul sand it will cause you to sink a little way into it and slow your movement. It's also needed to grow Nether wart.

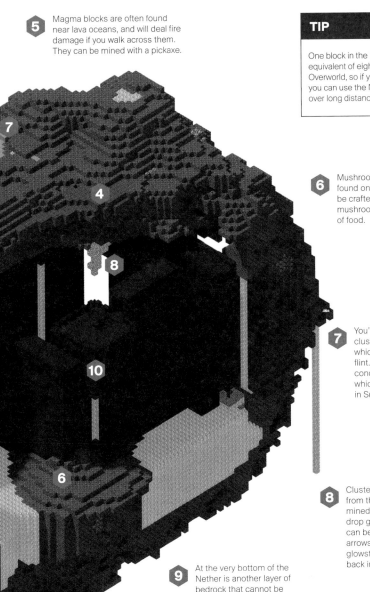

5 Magma blocks are often found near lava oceans, and will deal fire damage if you walk across them. They can be mined with a pickaxe.

TIP

One block in the Nether is the equivalent of eight blocks in the Overworld, so if you're in a bit of a hurry you can use the Nether as a shortcut over long distances in the Overworld.

6 Mushrooms are commonly found on the ground and can be crafted with a bowl to make mushroom stew if you run out of food.

7 You'll see the occasional cluster of gravel blocks, which can be mined for flint. The netherrack ceiling conceals a bedrock layer which cannot be penetrated in Survival mode.

8 Clusters of glowstone hang from the Nether ceiling. When mined, these blocks break and drop glowstone dust which can be used to craft spectral arrows and firework stars. 4 glowstone dust can be crafted back into a block of glowstone.

9 At the very bottom of the Nether is another layer of bedrock that cannot be mined in Survival mode.

DID YOU KNOW?

Some items don't work in the Nether. You'll be able to place a bed, but, if you attempt to sleep in it you'll get an explosive surprise. Maps also don't work, and you can't place water anywhere except in a cauldron.

10 Nether fortresses are fairly common – they are large structures composed of Nether brick, containing several interesting features including loot chests and blaze spawners. See pages 34-35 for more info on Nether fortresses.

NETHER BLOCKS AND THEIR USES

If you're skilled enough to navigate the Nether's many dangers and collect the unique materials found there, a host of new crafting recipes will become available to you. Here are some examples of how you can put your Nether spoils to good use back in the Overworld.

NETHERRACK

Due to its ability to burn indefinitely, netherrack can be used to make fireplaces. You can also use it on perimeter walls to deter enemy players from raiding your base.

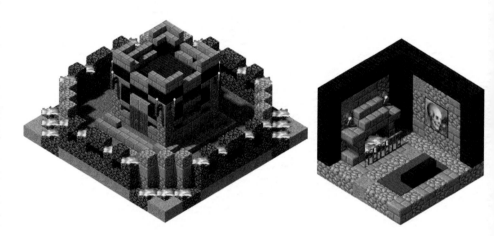

GLOWSTONE

Glowstone has a luminance of 15 – the highest possible light level – so it's an ideal block to use in light fixtures.

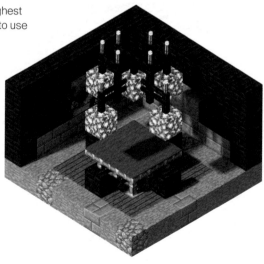

SOUL SAND

Soul sand can be used to make endermite and silverfish traps. Due to their small size, both mobs will suffocate in it. Soul sand is also used to grow Nether wart – an important potion ingredient – and is necessary to craft the wither, one of Minecraft's boss mobs.

NETHER BRICK

Nether brick has the same blast resistance as cobblestone but looks much more polished and dramatic. It's an excellent construction material for bases.

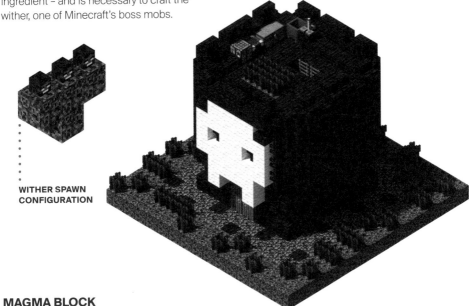

WITHER SPAWN CONFIGURATION

MAGMA BLOCK

Since magma blocks deal fire damage and Overworld mobs are not immune, they are ideal for use in Overworld base defences and traps.

NETHER QUARTZ

Nether quartz is a key ingredient in several redstone crafting recipes, and can be combined into decorative blocks of quartz for use in construction. A block of quartz only has a blast resistance of 4 (compared to cobblestone and Nether brick, which have a blast resistance of 30) so it's best used for base details rather than entire builds.

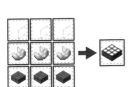

DAYLIGHT SENSOR RECIPE

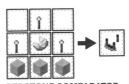

REDSTONE COMPARATOR RECIPE

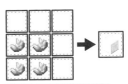

QUARTZ BLOCK RECIPE

PREPARING FOR A TRIP TO THE NETHER

So you've convinced yourself that a trip to the Nether is necessary. But if you want to make it back alive with an inventory full of useful supplies, you'll need to arm yourself with the right equipment. Here's a definitive guide to what you'll need to take with you.

WEAPONS AND DEFENSIVE ITEMS

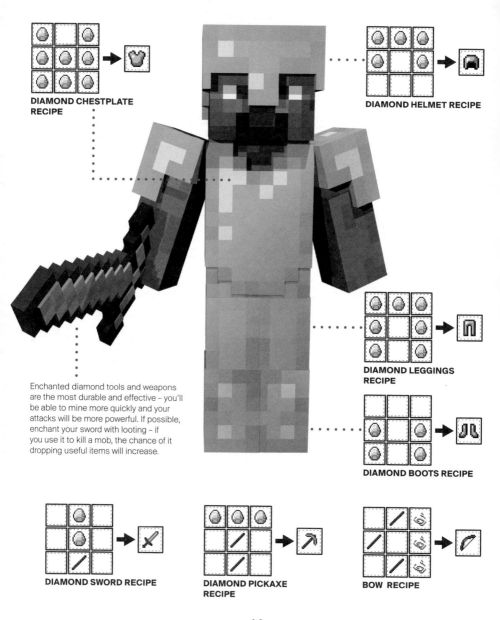

DIAMOND CHESTPLATE RECIPE

DIAMOND HELMET RECIPE

DIAMOND LEGGINGS RECIPE

DIAMOND BOOTS RECIPE

Enchanted diamond tools and weapons are the most durable and effective – you'll be able to mine more quickly and your attacks will be more powerful. If possible, enchant your sword with looting – if you use it to kill a mob, the chance of it dropping useful items will increase.

DIAMOND SWORD RECIPE

DIAMOND PICKAXE RECIPE

BOW RECIPE

Snowballs are essential for blaze combat as they deal 3 damage per hit. Breaking snow blocks with a shovel will give you snowballs.

Drinking helpful potions will counteract the damage you take and keep your health up – fire resistance and healing potions are ideal but you'll need to be set up for brewing first. Witches sometimes drop potions when defeated.

You'll be safest in enchanted diamond armour. Fire protection and blast protection enchantments will come in particularly handy.

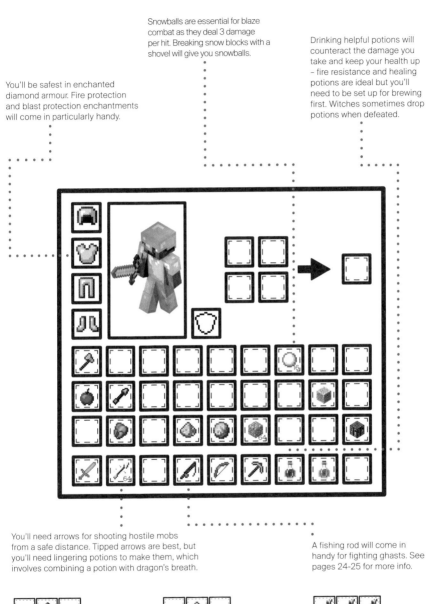

You'll need arrows for shooting hostile mobs from a safe distance. Tipped arrows are best, but you'll need lingering potions to make them, which involves combining a potion with dragon's breath.

A fishing rod will come in handy for fighting ghasts. See pages 24-25 for more info.

ARROW RECIPE   4

SPECTRAL ARROW RECIPE   2

POISON ARROW RECIPE   8

OTHER TOOLS AND BLOCKS

1 The chance of your Nether portal being damaged by ghast fireballs is extremely high. Make sure you have spare obsidian blocks to rebuild it and a flint and steel to relight it.

LADDER RECIPE

2 Ladders will help you to navigate the Nether's many cliffs more safely.

3 Wood doesn't generate naturally in the Nether, so take a stack of unrefined wood for crafting replacement tools and weapons.

4 You'll need plenty of good-quality food, such as steak, to refill your health and hunger bars.

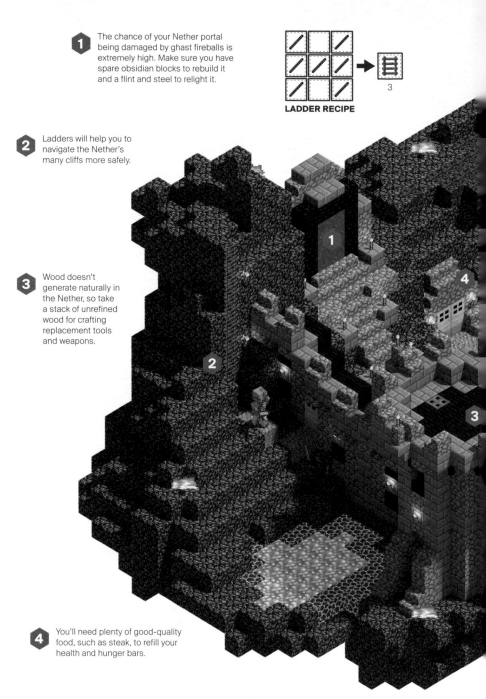

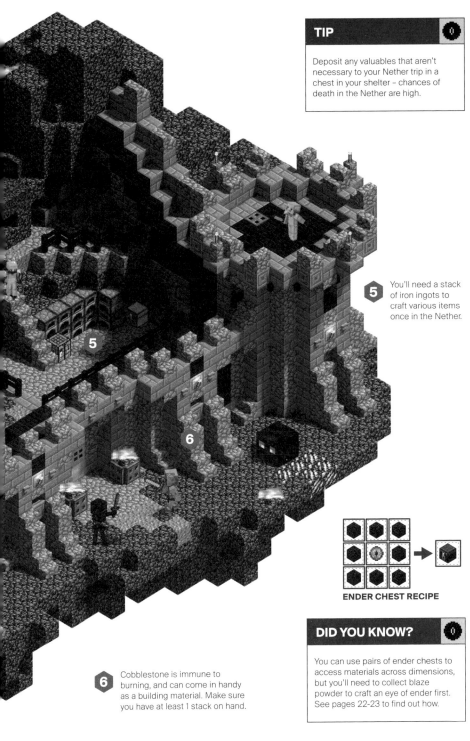

TIP

Deposit any valuables that aren't necessary to your Nether trip in a chest in your shelter – chances of death in the Nether are high.

5 You'll need a stack of iron ingots to craft various items once in the Nether.

ENDER CHEST RECIPE

DID YOU KNOW?

You can use pairs of ender chests to access materials across dimensions, but you'll need to collect blaze powder to craft an eye of ender first. See pages 22-23 to find out how.

6 Cobblestone is immune to burning, and can come in handy as a building material. Make sure you have at least 1 stack on hand.

NETHER PORTALS

There is no naturally-occuring gateway between the Overworld and the Nether – you'll need to build a Nether portal. This portal enables you to travel back and forth between the two dimensions, as long as it remains activated. Let's look at how to create a standard Nether portal using the minimum number of obsidian blocks.

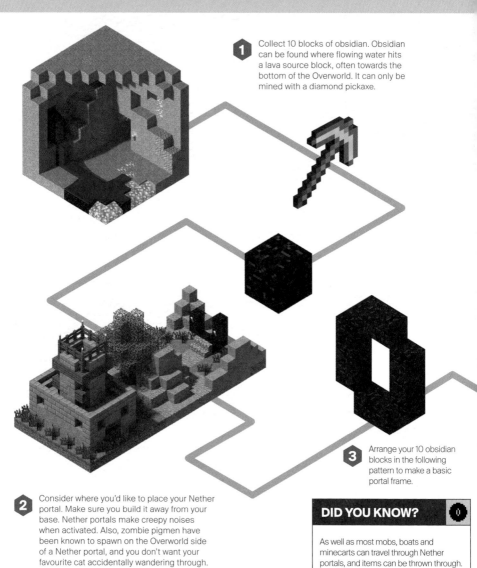

1 Collect 10 blocks of obsidian. Obsidian can be found where flowing water hits a lava source block, often towards the bottom of the Overworld. It can only be mined with a diamond pickaxe.

3 Arrange your 10 obsidian blocks in the following pattern to make a basic portal frame.

2 Consider where you'd like to place your Nether portal. Make sure you build it away from your base. Nether portals make creepy noises when activated. Also, zombie pigmen have been known to spawn on the Overworld side of a Nether portal, and you don't want your favourite cat accidentally wandering through.

DID YOU KNOW?

As well as most mobs, boats and minecarts can travel through Nether portals, and items can be thrown through.

Though for a long time Nether portals needed to be built to a very strict design, you can now make portals at larger sizes and different dimensions, just as long as it remains an oblong space enclosed in obsidian. Whatever shape and size you go for, though, the exit portal in the Nether is always generated at the default 4 x 5 scale. You can rebuild it, but be warned: unless the shapes on either end match, it can be tricky to work out where you'll emerge.

7 Be very careful when exiting your portal on the Nether side. There's no way to control where it comes out, and if you're really unlucky it might be floating in mid-air over a sea of lava.

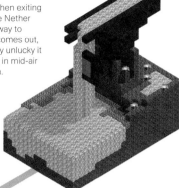

TIP

If you find that you've emerged on a floating island or over a lava ocean, try building out from the portal using cobblestone. Use the sneak function to ensure you don't fall over the edge.

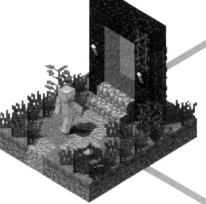

6 Stand in this vortex for 4 seconds and you'll be transported into the Nether.

4 If you'd prefer a proper rectangle you can also fill in the corners, but it'll work without them and save you 4 blocks of obsidian.

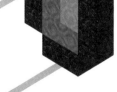

5 Use a flint and steel on the space in the obsidian frame to activate the portal – portal blocks will appear.

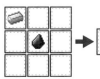

FLINT AND STEEL RECIPE

SURVIVAL AND EXPLORATION

Surviving in the Nether is no easy task. There's lava everywhere, treacherous cliffs to negotiate and terrifying new hostile mobs to deal with. Plus, the terrain doesn't have many distinguishing features so it's very easy to get lost. Follow these steps to give yourself the best chance of surviving as you explore.

1 Build a shelter around your portal. For now, make it out of cobblestone with an iron door – you can upgrade to Nether brick later. This will protect it from being destroyed by ghast fireballs and leaving you trapped in the Nether.

2 Once safely inside your portal shelter, take a moment to scan the area around you for immediate threats – mobs, lava streams, cliffs and magma blocks.

3 Make a crafting table and a chest for your shelter so that you're set up to make more equipment if necessary. Store some wood and iron ingots in here.

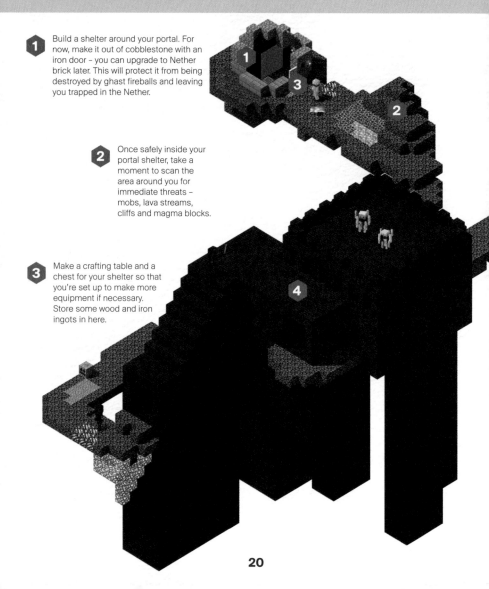

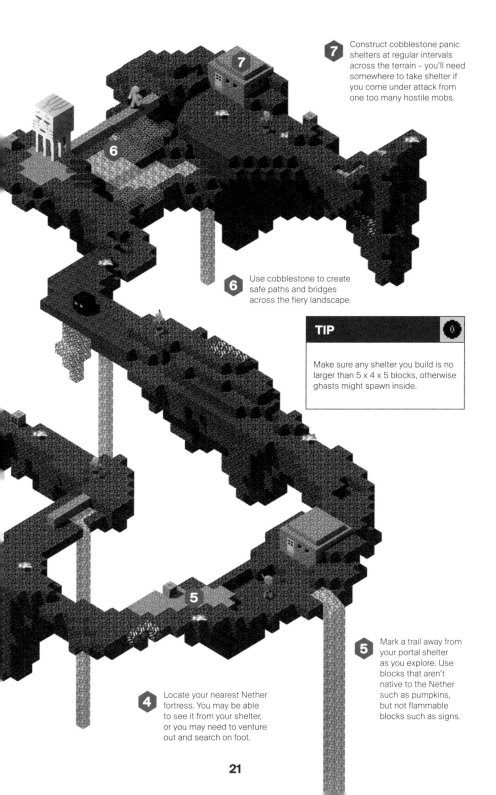

7 Construct cobblestone panic shelters at regular intervals across the terrain – you'll need somewhere to take shelter if you come under attack from one too many hostile mobs.

6 Use cobblestone to create safe paths and bridges across the fiery landscape.

TIP

Make sure any shelter you build is no larger than 5 x 4 x 5 blocks, otherwise ghasts might spawn inside.

5 Mark a trail away from your portal shelter as you explore. Use blocks that aren't native to the Nether such as pumpkins, but not flammable blocks such as signs.

4 Locate your nearest Nether fortress. You may be able to see it from your shelter, or you may need to venture out and search on foot.

NETHER MOBS

The Nether is crawling with powerful, flame-retardant hostile mobs and they do not appreciate you trespassing on their territory. Many can be found freely wandering the terrain, others prefer to stick to the Nether fortresses. Let's take a look at how they can be defeated and the useful items they might drop.

BLAZE

HOSTILITY

HEALTH POINTS	♥ 20
ATTACK STRENGTH	♥ 4-9
HOW TO DEFEAT	
ITEMS DROPPED	0-1 10

SPAWN LIGHT LEVEL

15
11
0

SPAWN LOCATION
Anywhere in Nether fortresses, at light levels of 11 or lower and from monster spawners in the fortresses.

MONSTER SPAWNER

NETHER FORTRESS

BEHAVIOUR
Blazes hover just above the ground when idle, but will fly when whey find a target to attack. They produce smoke as they move, and blaze rods orbit their core. A metallic grinding noise will alert you to their presence.

ATTACK METHOD

Blazes pursue players within 48 blocks and shoot fireballs at their targets from up to 16 blocks away. These fireballs deal damage upon contact. Blazes will hit their targets when they are within 2 blocks of them, dealing damage.

SPECIAL SKILLS

Like all Nether mobs, blazes are immune to fire and lava so they have an immediate advantage. If they take damage from a player they will quickly alert all other blazes within 48 blocks, and they will all attack you in retaliation.

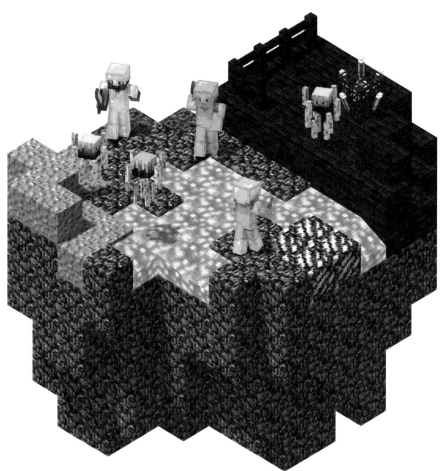

HOW TO DEFEAT

It's best to keep a safe distance when fighting a blaze. Throw snowballs at it to inflict damage, or shoot it with a bow and arrow. You should also drink a potion of fire resistance and try to disable the blaze spawner with five torches as soon as possible. If desperate, hit them with your sword.

USEFUL DROPS

Blazes may drop a blaze rod when defeated. Blaze rods are initially required to craft a brewing stand. They are also necessary to fuel the brewing stand but must be broken down into blaze powder first. Blaze powder is also needed to craft an eye of ender.

GHAST

HEALTH POINTS	❤ 10
ATTACK STRENGTH	❤ 6-25
HOW TO DEFEAT	
ITEMS DROPPED	

0-2   0-1   5

SPAWN
LIGHT
LEVEL

15

0

SPAWN LOCATION
Any 5 x 4 x 5 space in the Nether at all light levels.

NETHER

BEHAVIOUR
Ghasts float slowly around the Nether. When idle, their eyes and mouth are closed as if they are sleeping, but they are always on the lookout for targets within 16 blocks. They make the occasional strange, high-pitched sound.

ATTACK METHOD

You'll know a ghast is about to attack when it opens its red eyes and mouth. It makes a chirp-like sound when shooting fireballs. These fireballs have infinite range and deal damage upon contact with their target.

SPECIAL SKILLS

Ghasts are one of the largest mobs – their bodies are 4 x 4 x 4 blocks and they have 9 tentacles hanging from their underside. They also have an extremely long search radius and can target players from up to 100 blocks away.

DID YOU KNOW?

If you manage to destroy a ghast by deflecting its own fireball back at it, you'll earn the achievement Return to Sender.

HOW TO DEFEAT

If you have good aim, deflect the ghast's fireballs back at it with your sword. You can also shoot it from a distance with an enchanted bow and arrows, or reel it towards you on a fishing rod and finish it off with your sword.

USEFUL DROPS

Ghasts may drop up to 2 pieces of gunpowder, which is needed to craft TNT and fire charges. They may also drop a single ghast tear, which is needed to make mundane potion, potion of regeneration and End crystals.

MAGMA CUBE

HEALTH POINTS	♥ 1-16	
ATTACK STRENGTH	♥ 3-6	
HOW TO DEFEAT	🧊 🏹 🗡	
ITEMS DROPPED	⚙ ⬤	
	0-1 1-4	

SPAWN LIGHT LEVEL

15

0

DID YOU KNOW?

Magma cubes come in three delightful sizes: big, small and tiny. They all begin life as big magma cubes, but will divide into several smaller cubes when damaged, and then into several more tiny cubes before finally perishing.

BEHAVIOUR

Magma cubes can spawn anywhere in the Nether, but their spawn rate seems to be higher inside Nether fortresses. They bounce around when idle, searching for players to attack within a 16-block radius.

SPAWN LOCATION

Anywhere in the Nether at all light levels.

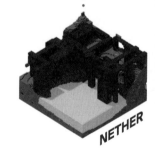

NETHER

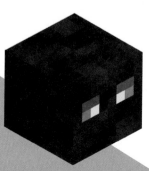

ATTACK METHOD

You will take damage simply from touching a magma cube, but they bounce towards their target and attempt to land on top of it to deal the maximum amount of damage possible. As the magma cube divides into smaller cubes its jump strength decreases.

SPECIAL SKILLS

As well as being immune to burning in fire and lava, magma cubes are actually able to swim quite fast in lava. They are also immune to fall damage. When damaged they can divide into smaller cubes and can travel twice as fast as most other mobs.

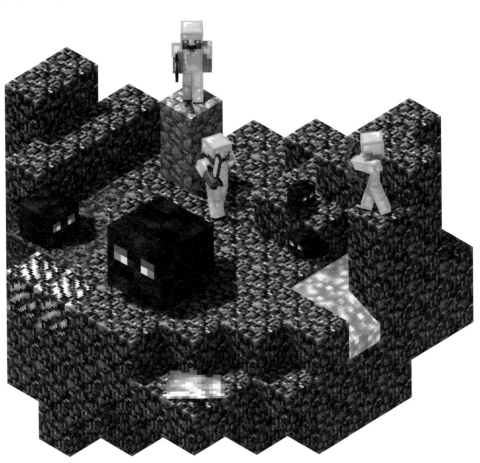

HOW TO DEFEAT

Stand on a two block-high pillar and hit the magma cube from above with a diamond sword. This will prevent them jumping on top of you. You can also shoot them from a safe distance with a bow and arrow.

USEFUL DROPS

Big and small magma cubes have a 25% chance of dropping 1 magma cream, but the chance increases if you use a looting sword. You need magma cream for mundane potion, potion of fire resistance and magma blocks.

WITHER SKELETON

HEALTH POINTS	20				
ATTACK STRENGTH	4-10				
HOW TO DEFEAT					
ITEMS DROPPED	0-1	0-2	0-1	5	RARE

SPAWN LIGHT LEVEL

15

7

0

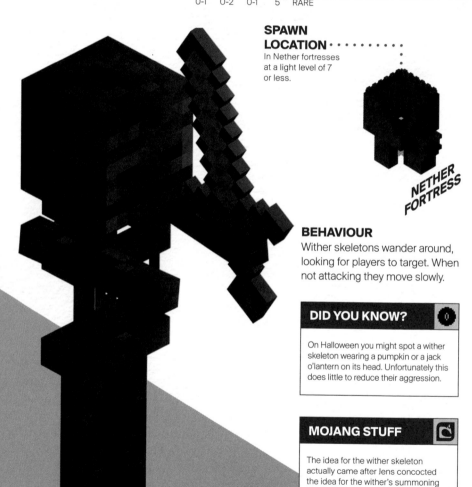

SPAWN LOCATION

In Nether fortresses at a light level of 7 or less.

NETHER FORTRESS

BEHAVIOUR

Wither skeletons wander around, looking for players to target. When not attacking they move slowly.

DID YOU KNOW?

On Halloween you might spot a wither skeleton wearing a pumpkin or a jack o'lantern on its head. Unfortunately this does little to reduce their aggression.

MOJANG STUFF

The idea for the wither skeleton actually came after Jens concocted the idea for the wither's summoning ritual. He had to make getting the ingredients a challenge. Naturally enough, wither skeletons don't give up their heads easily!

ATTACK METHOD

Wither skeletons sprint towards players and hit them with their stone sword on sight. They also inflict the wither effect for ten seconds. This effect turns the health bar black and drains it by 1 health point every 2 seconds.

SPECIAL SKILLS

Wither skeletons are immune to burning in fire or lava. They may pick up any weapons or armour they find lying on the ground. Like all undead mobs, they are healed by potion of harming, and harmed by potion of healing.

HOW TO DEFEAT

Use the wither skeleton's height against it – get yourself into a 2-block-high space and hit it through the gap with an enchanted diamond sword. You can also stand on a 3-block-high pillar and hit it from above, and throw a splash potion of healing at it.

USEFUL DROPS

Wither skeletons may drop 1 coal, and up to 2 bones which can be crafted into bone meal. Very rarely they will drop their skull – you need 3 wither skeleton skulls to craft the wither boss. See pages 32-33 for more info. They may also drop their sword.

ZOMBIE PIGMAN

HOSTILITY

HEALTH POINTS	20	
ATTACK STRENGTH	5-13	
HOW TO DEFEAT		
ITEMS DROPPED		

0-1 0-1 0-1 0-1 5

SPAWN LIGHT LEVEL

15

0

SPAWN LOCATIONS
Anywhere in the Nether.

NETHER

NETHER PORTAL

In the Overworld, when lightning strikes within 4 blocks of a pig.

OVERWORLD

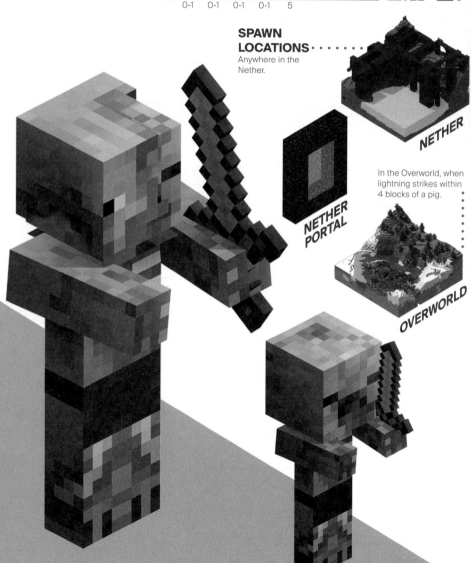

BEHAVIOUR

Zombie pigmen are the Nether's only neutral mob. When neutral they move slowly and don't do much until they are attacked. The pig-like sounds they make will alert you to their presence.

ATTACK METHOD

Zombie pigmen will leave you alone until you attack, then every pigman in the area will retaliate, hitting you with their swords. Their movement speeds up when aggravated and you can easily find yourself cornered by a large group of them.

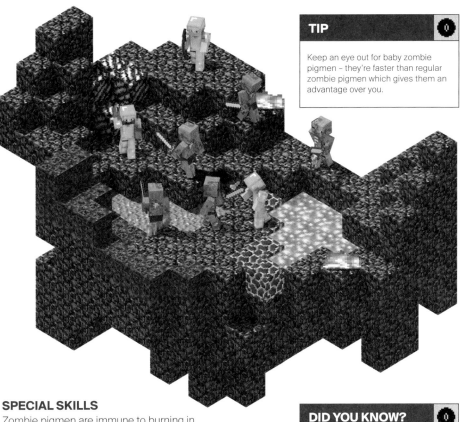

TIP

Keep an eye out for baby zombie pigmen – they're faster than regular zombie pigmen which gives them an advantage over you.

SPECIAL SKILLS

Zombie pigmen are immune to burning in fire and lava. They have the ability to pick up weapons and items. 5% of zombie pigmen will spawn as baby zombie pigmen, and 5% of baby zombie pigmen will be pigman jockeys. Zombie pigmen are immune to poison.

DID YOU KNOW?

Like their Overworld counterparts, zombie pigmen may bang on wooden doors, and can break them down if your difficulty is set to hard.

HOW TO DEFEAT

Pick zombie pigmen off one-by-one to reduce your chances of being swarmed. Shoot them with a bow and arrow from a distance, throw a splash potion of healing at them or stand on a 2-block-high dirt pillar and hit them from above with your sword.

USEFUL DROPS

Zombie pigmen may drop rotten flesh when defeated, which can be used to breed and heal tamed wolves and lead them around. They may also drop a gold nugget or a gold ingot which can be used for crafting, or their golden sword, which may be enchanted.

THE WITHER

HEALTH POINTS		300
ATTACK STRENGTH		5-12
HOW TO DEFEAT		
ITEMS DROPPED		

1   50

SPAWN LIGHT LEVEL

15

0

TIP

Snow golems are your friend when fighting the wither – they fire snowballs at it and distract the wither from attacking you. Craft a small army of snow golems to increase your chances of success.

SPAWNS · · · · · · · · · · · · · · · · · · ·

When crafted by the player, using 4 blocks of soul sand and 3 wither skeleton skulls. The last block placed must be a wither skeleton skull for the wither to spawn.

DID YOU KNOW?

You won't be able to spawn the wither in peaceful mode – the blocks will simply sit there, devoid of life.

TIP

There's a clue to the wither's crafting recipe in one of Minecraft's paintings.

BEHAVIOUR

Once spawned, the wither will flash blue and increase in size as its health bar fills. At this stage the wither is invulnerable and will not move or attack you. At the end of this process the wither creates a very large explosion, which destroys any nearby blocks and mobs. The wither will begin to attack after this explosion. The wither is hostile to players and all mobs except for undead mobs (skeletons, zombies, zombie pigmen, wither skeletons, husks, strays and other withers).

SPECIAL SKILLS

The wither is immune to fire, lava, drowning and suffocation. It also has 300 health points – that's 100 more than the ender dragon.

ATTACK METHOD

Each of its three heads can launch wither skull projectiles so it can attack three players or mobs at the same time. When these skulls make contact with a player they will be inflicted with the wither effect – a health-draining effect that lasts for 40 seconds.

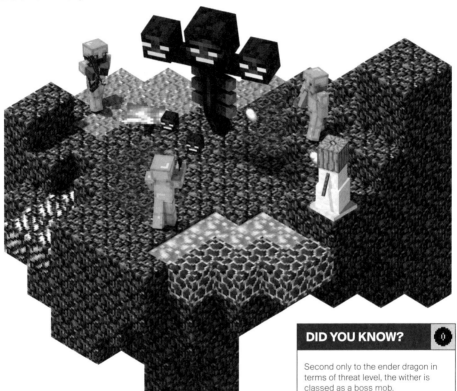

DID YOU KNOW?

Second only to the ender dragon in terms of threat level, the wither is classed as a boss mob.

HOW TO DEFEAT

Move backwards when it begins to flash blue so you don't get caught in the explosion. Once it has exploded, shoot it with an enchanted bow and arrows whilst drinking potions of strength and healing. Like other undead mobs, it's harmed by healing potions so you can throw splash potions of healing at it. You can also hit it with an enchanted diamond sword.

USEFUL DROPS

The wither will drop 1 Nether star if you manage to defeat it. This star will remain on the ground and never despawn until it is picked up. You'll need a Nether star to make a beacon – a useful block that can be placed on top of power pyramids to provide status buffs and a powerful light source. See page 75 for more info.

NETHER FORTRESSES

Nether fortresses are large, naturally generated structures that appear in strips along the z-axis (north-south). They're built from Nether brick and are partially buried in netherrack in several places. They're a great source of materials and loot, if you can negotiate your way past the hostile mobs. Let's take a closer look at the structure.

1 BRIDGES
Several bridges run around the periphery of the fortress. Follow one of these and it will eventually lead you to the interior.

2 BALCONIES
Exterior balconies provide vantage points from which to scan the surrounding area for threats. They're enclosed by Nether brick fence so you won't fall off the edge.

3 LAVA WELL ROOM
These rooms contain nothing except a small lava well – they mark the entry to the inside of the fortress and are found at the end of an exterior bridge.

CORRIDORS

4 Much of the interior of the fortress is made up of corridors. Hostile mobs wander these corridors freely and they are very dimly lit, so be careful when turning corners.

LOOT CHEST

5 Around a third of all Nether fortress corridors contain a loot chest, inside which you might find everything from obsidian to diamond horse armour.

NETHER WART STAIRCASES

6 Nether wart is an important potions ingredient, and it can be found growing at the side of staircases in patches of soul sand.

BLAZE SPAWNER PLATFORMS

7 Blaze spawners sit on raised platforms, accessed by stairs. They regularly produce blazes so you'll want to disable the spawner as quickly as possible.

EXPANDING AND FORTIFYING A NETHER FORTRESS

The existing structure of the Nether fortress can provide a foundation from which to build an impenetrable base, but you'll need to clear out the hostile mobs and make a few fortifications first. Follow these steps to turn it into a secure and intimidating fortress.

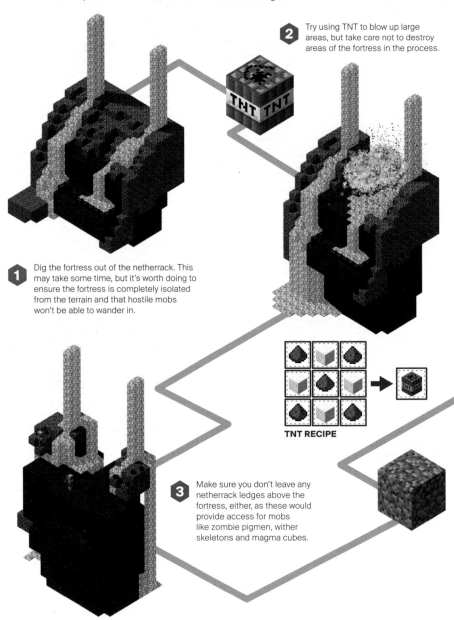

2 Try using TNT to blow up large areas, but take care not to destroy areas of the fortress in the process.

1 Dig the fortress out of the netherrack. This may take some time, but it's worth doing to ensure the fortress is completely isolated from the terrain and that hostile mobs won't be able to wander in.

TNT RECIPE

3 Make sure you don't leave any netherrack ledges above the fortress, either, as these would provide access for mobs like zombie pigmen, wither skeletons and magma cubes.

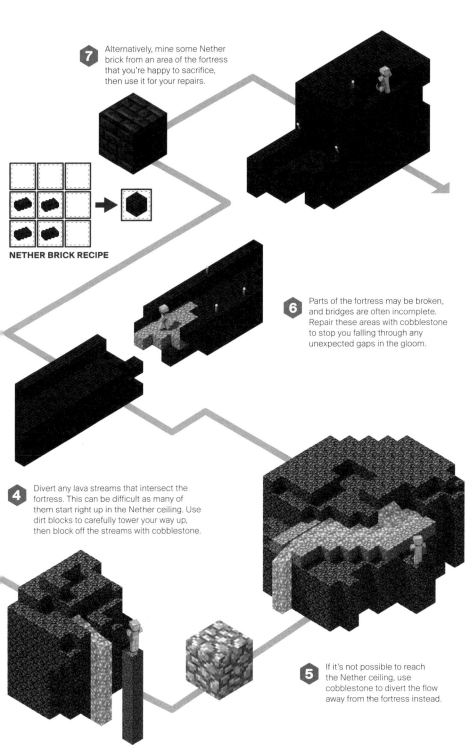

7 Alternatively, mine some Nether brick from an area of the fortress that you're happy to sacrifice, then use it for your repairs.

NETHER BRICK RECIPE

6 Parts of the fortress may be broken, and bridges are often incomplete. Repair these areas with cobblestone to stop you falling through any unexpected gaps in the gloom.

4 Divert any lava streams that intersect the fortress. This can be difficult as many of them start right up in the Nether ceiling. Use dirt blocks to carefully tower your way up, then block off the streams with cobblestone.

5 If it's not possible to reach the Nether ceiling, use cobblestone to divert the flow away from the fortress instead.

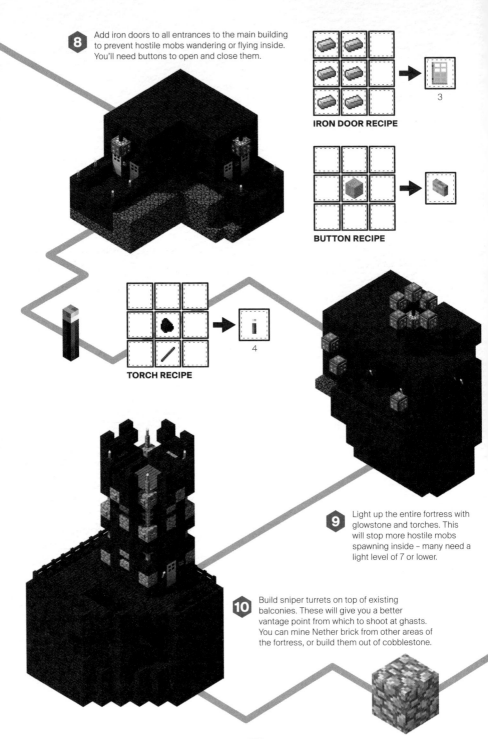

8 Add iron doors to all entrances to the main building to prevent hostile mobs wandering or flying inside. You'll need buttons to open and close them.

IRON DOOR RECIPE

3

BUTTON RECIPE

TORCH RECIPE

4

9 Light up the entire fortress with glowstone and torches. This will stop more hostile mobs spawning inside – many need a light level of 7 or lower.

10 Build sniper turrets on top of existing balconies. These will give you a better vantage point from which to shoot at ghasts. You can mine Nether brick from other areas of the fortress, or build them out of cobblestone.

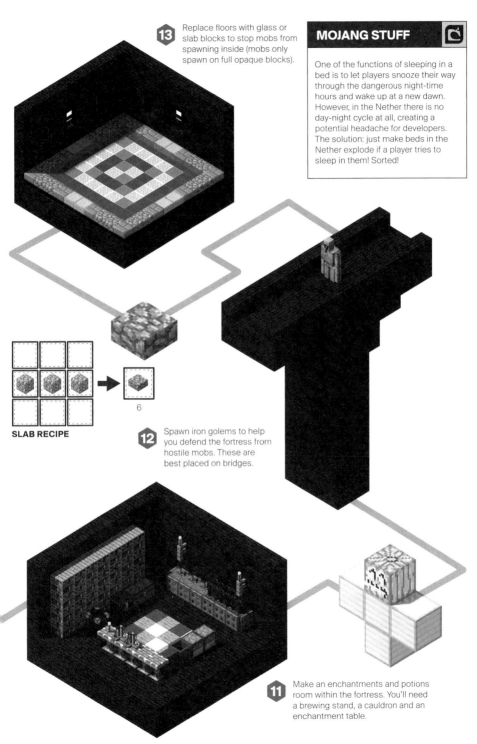

13 Replace floors with glass or slab blocks to stop mobs from spawning inside (mobs only spawn on full opaque blocks).

6

SLAB RECIPE

12 Spawn iron golems to help you defend the fortress from hostile mobs. These are best placed on bridges.

11 Make an enchantments and potions room within the fortress. You'll need a brewing stand, a cauldron and an enchantment table.

MINECART SYSTEM

An enclosed minecart system will allow you to travel quickly around your fortress and back and forth to your portal, without being swarmed by mobs. Follow these steps to create a fireproof minecart system that can also double up as a fun rollercoaster.

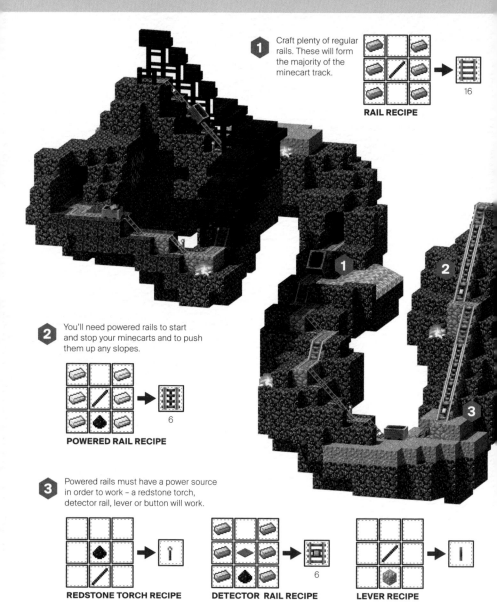

1 Craft plenty of regular rails. These will form the majority of the minecart track.

16

RAIL RECIPE

2 You'll need powered rails to start and stop your minecarts and to push them up any slopes.

6

POWERED RAIL RECIPE

3 Powered rails must have a power source in order to work – a redstone torch, detector rail, lever or button will work.

REDSTONE TORCH RECIPE

6

DETECTOR RAIL RECIPE

LEVER RECIPE

40

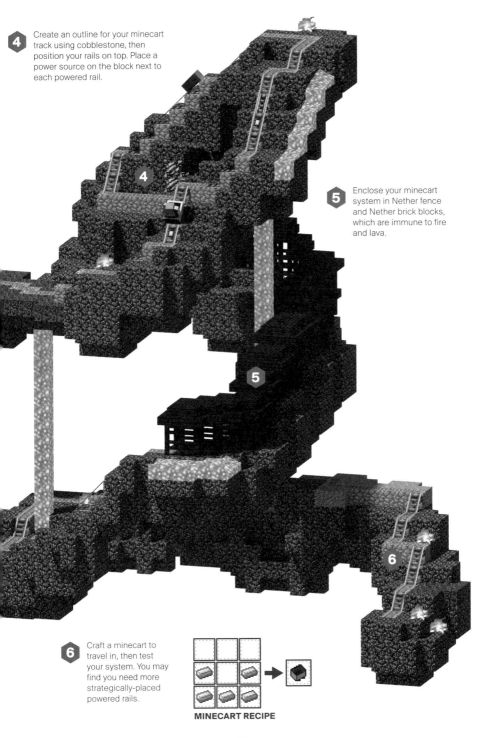

4 Create an outline for your minecart track using cobblestone, then position your rails on top. Place a power source on the block next to each powered rail.

5 Enclose your minecart system in Nether fence and Nether brick blocks, which are immune to fire and lava.

6 Craft a minecart to travel in, then test your system. You may find you need more strategically-placed powered rails.

MINECART RECIPE

41

FARMING

Mushrooms are the only source of food that grows naturally in the Nether and you can't place water. But that doesn't mean you can't grow your own food – follow these steps to set up a sustainable farm and you'll be able to spend as much time as you like in the Nether without risk of starvation.

TREES

Plant tree saplings to provide you with wood for crafting. You'll just need dirt blocks and a light source. Make sure you leave plenty of space between saplings to ensure that they grow. Oak trees may also drop apples which can be eaten as they are or crafted with gold ingots to make golden apples. Jungle trees can be used to grow cocoa – see page 45.

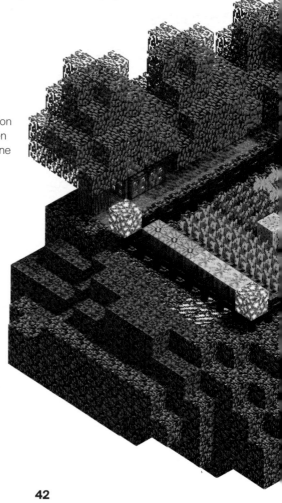

WHEAT, CARROTS, POTATOES AND BEETROOT

Wheat, carrots, potatoes and beetroot will also grow without water – it'll just take longer. Bring dirt across from the Overworld, place it in your desired location then use a hoe to till it into farmland, then plant seeds immediately. Place glowstone blocks along the side to provide light to enable growth.

MELONS AND PUMPKINS

Melons and pumpkins will grow without water – they just need light and an adjacent block to grow into.

DID YOU KNOW?

Wet sponge can be used to provide crops with water in the Nether. Just place blocks next to your farmland to hydrate it. Wet sponge can be found in ocean monuments.

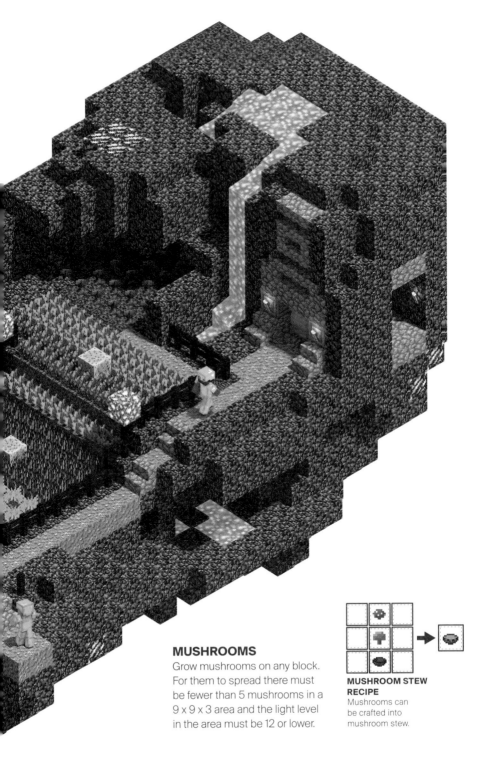

MUSHROOMS

Grow mushrooms on any block. For them to spread there must be fewer than 5 mushrooms in a 9 x 9 x 3 area and the light level in the area must be 12 or lower.

MUSHROOM STEW RECIPE
Mushrooms can be crafted into mushroom stew.

CHICKEN FARMING

Chicken eggs can easily be imported into the Nether. Simply throw them into a pen and approximately 1 in 8 will spawn a chicken. Your pen should be indoors to protect the chickens.

LEADING OTHER ANIMALS INTO THE NETHER

You can lead other animals such as cows, sheep, pigs and horses into the Nether through your portal, but this is tricky, especially if your fortress is some way away from your portal. Consider constructing a new portal at your fortress so you can more easily lead animals across to their new home. The safest way to bring animals across is to attach leads to them first.

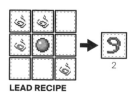

LEAD RECIPE

BAKERY

Importing a few key ingredients from the Overworld will allow you to set up a bakery within your fortress. With cake, bread, cookies and pumpkin pies available your chances of survival just got a lot higher!

You'll need to import buckets of milk if you don't have any cows in the Nether.

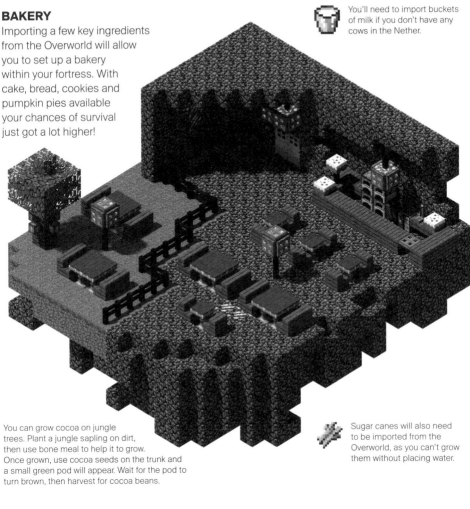

You can grow cocoa on jungle trees. Plant a jungle sapling on dirt, then use bone meal to help it to grow. Once grown, use cocoa seeds on the trunk and a small green pod will appear. Wait for the pod to turn brown, then harvest for cocoa beans.

Sugar canes will also need to be imported from the Overworld, as you can't grow them without placing water.

BAKERY RECIPES

Once you've collected all these ingredients you can craft the items shown to the right, which will restore higher levels of food points.

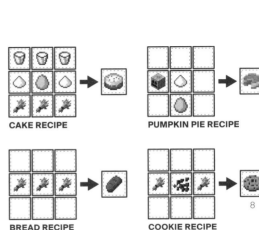

CAKE RECIPE

PUMPKIN PIE RECIPE

BREAD RECIPE

COOKIE RECIPE

TIP

As with farming in the Overworld, you can use bone meal to speed up crop growth in the Nether.

45

THE END

Now that you've conquered the Nether you can brew potions and prepare for the ultimate challenge. In this section you'll learn how to get to the dangerous End dimension, what to do when faced with the ultimate boss mob – the ender dragon – and where to look for the rarest blocks and items if you manage to defeat it.

THE END ENVIRONMENT

The End is a cluster of islands surrounded by a vast nothingness known simply as The Void. There is no day or night, just perpetual darkness. For many players it's the ultimate adventure: with barely any resources and Minecraft's boss mob, the ender dragon, living there, it's the ultimate survival challenge.

 All the islands are composed of End stone. This substance has a higher blast resistance than regular stone and can be mined with a pickaxe.

 The main island in the centre is home to the ender dragon. There's not much there, except for a small podium and several obsidian pillars with ender crystals on top, some of which are protected by iron bars. The obsidian and iron bars can be mined once you've defeated the dragon, but you'll need to destroy the crystals. See pages 56-59 for more info.

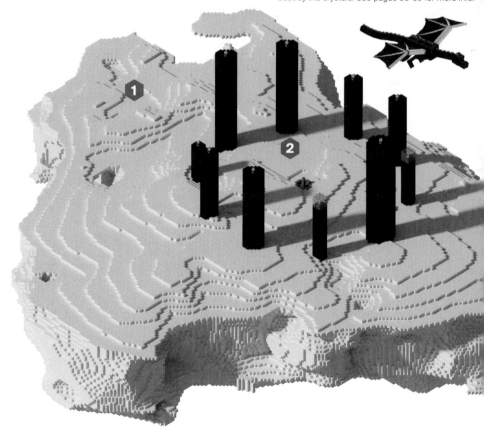

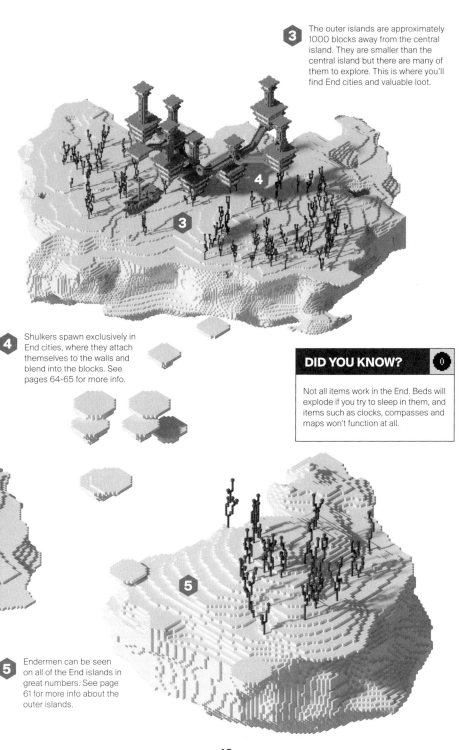

3 The outer islands are approximately 1000 blocks away from the central island. They are smaller than the central island but there are many of them to explore. This is where you'll find End cities and valuable loot.

4 Shulkers spawn exclusively in End cities, where they attach themselves to the walls and blend into the blocks. See pages 64-65 for more info.

DID YOU KNOW?

Not all items work in the End. Beds will explode if you try to sleep in them, and items such as clocks, compasses and maps won't function at all.

5 Endermen can be seen on all of the End islands in great numbers. See page 61 for more info about the outer islands.

PREPARING FOR A TRIP TO THE END

Given the danger that awaits, you must take special care to prepare for a trip to the End. It's not just the ender dragon you need to worry about, there are also endermen and shulkers, and the danger of falling into the Void. Let's look at what you'll need to take with you if you hope to survive.

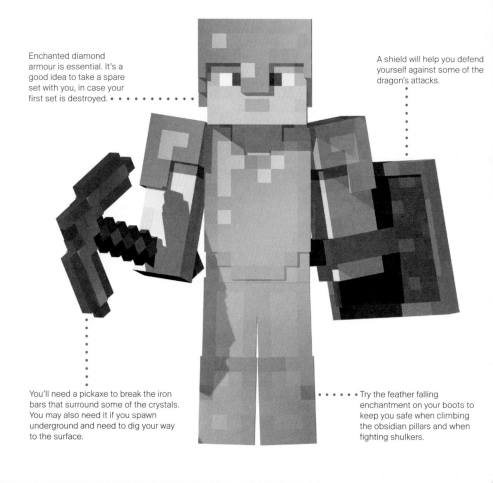

Enchanted diamond armour is essential. It's a good idea to take a spare set with you, in case your first set is destroyed.

A shield will help you defend yourself against some of the dragon's attacks.

You'll need a pickaxe to break the iron bars that surround some of the crystals. You may also need it if you spawn underground and need to dig your way to the surface.

Try the feather falling enchantment on your boots to keep you safe when climbing the obsidian pillars and when fighting shulkers.

 A pumpkin can be worn instead of a helmet to stop endermen becoming hostile if you look directly at them. Just be aware it won't provide any protection.

 Eyes of ender are necessary to locate a stronghold and repair the End portal. See pages 52-53.

 You'll need an enchanted bow and arrows of harming to deal damage to the ender dragon.

 You may spawn on a platform a short distance away from the main island, so you'll need ender pearls to teleport. You'll also need them once you've defeated the dragon.

 An enchanted diamond sword is the best choice of weapon for close-combat with the dragon.

 Take several stacks of good-quality food such as steak and cake to keep your food and health bars topped up.

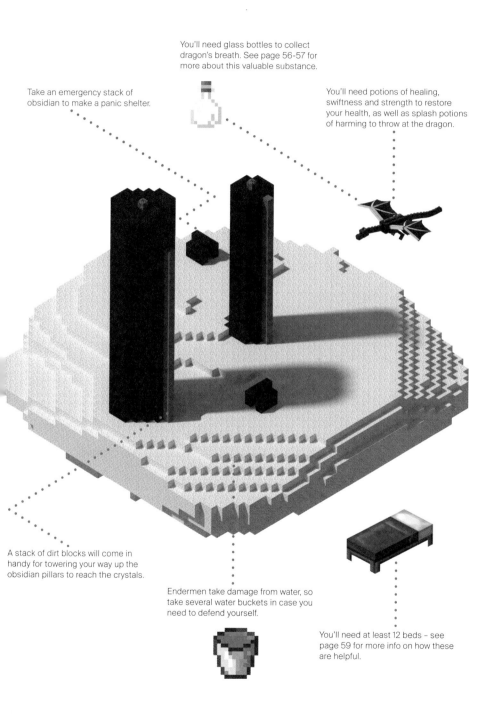

You'll need glass bottles to collect dragon's breath. See page 56-57 for more about this valuable substance.

Take an emergency stack of obsidian to make a panic shelter.

You'll need potions of healing, swiftness and strength to restore your health, as well as splash potions of harming to throw at the dragon.

A stack of dirt blocks will come in handy for towering your way up the obsidian pillars to reach the crystals.

Endermen take damage from water, so take several water buckets in case you need to defend yourself.

You'll need at least 12 beds – see page 59 for more info on how these are helpful.

LOCATING A STRONGHOLD

A stronghold is a naturally generated structure that contains a gateway to the End dimension. There are only a limited number per world (128) and they're hidden underground. Follow these steps to locate your nearest stronghold.

1 Craft eyes of ender. You'll need several to locate the stronghold, and then up to 12 more to activate the portal. They're crafted from ender pearls (dropped by endermen) and blaze powder (made from blaze rods, which are dropped by blazes in the Nether).

EYE OF ENDER RECIPE

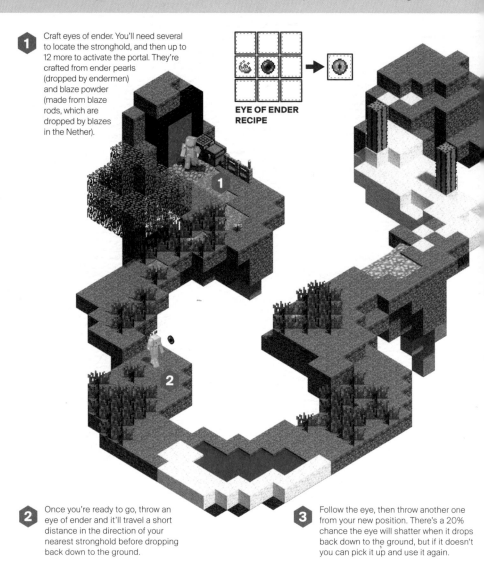

2 Once you're ready to go, throw an eye of ender and it'll travel a short distance in the direction of your nearest stronghold before dropping back down to the ground.

3 Follow the eye, then throw another one from your new position. There's a 20% chance the eye will shatter when it drops back down to the ground, but if it doesn't you can pick it up and use it again.

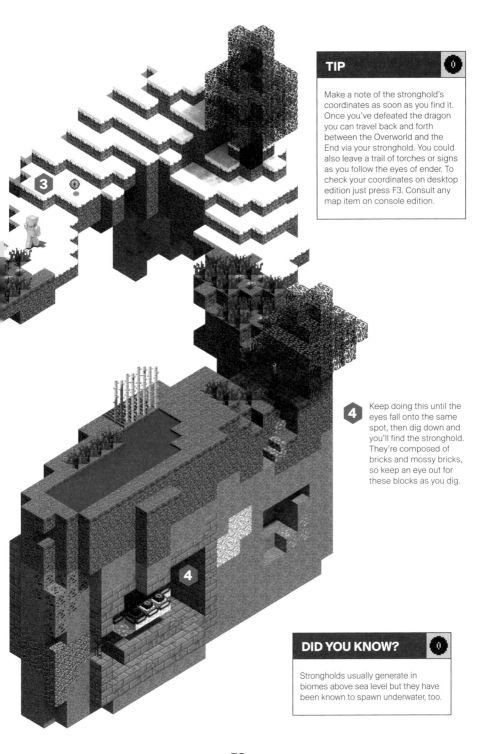

TIP

Make a note of the stronghold's coordinates as soon as you find it. Once you've defeated the dragon you can travel back and forth between the Overworld and the End via your stronghold. You could also leave a trail of torches or signs as you follow the eyes of ender. To check your coordinates on desktop edition just press F3. Consult any map item on console edition.

4 Keep doing this until the eyes fall onto the same spot, then dig down and you'll find the stronghold. They're composed of bricks and mossy bricks, so keep an eye out for these blocks as you dig.

DID YOU KNOW?

Strongholds usually generate in biomes above sea level but they have been known to spawn underwater, too.

NAVIGATING THE STRONGHOLD

Strongholds are sprawling structures with several rooms linked by corridors and stairs. Each stronghold has a unique layout, and they vary in size, but they always contain an End portal room. As its name suggests, this room is where you'll find the portal that will transport you to the End.

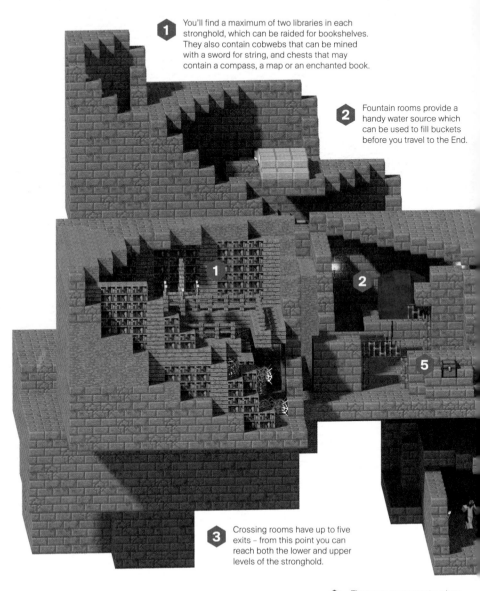

1 You'll find a maximum of two libraries in each stronghold, which can be raided for bookshelves. They also contain cobwebs that can be mined with a sword for string, and chests that may contain a compass, a map or an enchanted book.

2 Fountain rooms provide a handy water source which can be used to fill buckets before you travel to the End.

3 Crossing rooms have up to five exits – from this point you can reach both the lower and upper levels of the stronghold.

4 There are many empty prison cells which can be raided for iron bars and buttons.

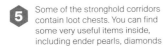 Some of the stronghold corridors contain loot chests. You can find some very useful items inside, including ender pearls, diamonds and horse armour.

TIP

The portal will deposit you either on, or near, the End's main island so you'll need to be prepared for immediate combat.

6 The End portal room usually contains an incomplete portal, except for rare cases where all 12 portal frames contain eyes of ender. It also contains a silverfish spawner and two lava pools. To activate an incomplete portal you'll need to place eyes of ender in the empty frames, then jump through.

7 There's a realistic chance that the ender dragon will defeat you, so you should be prepared to respawn. Before you enter the End for the first time, place a chest full of backup supplies in the portal room so that you can quickly return for round two. Make sure it includes a full set of armour, a pumpkin, weapons, potions, food and ender pearls.

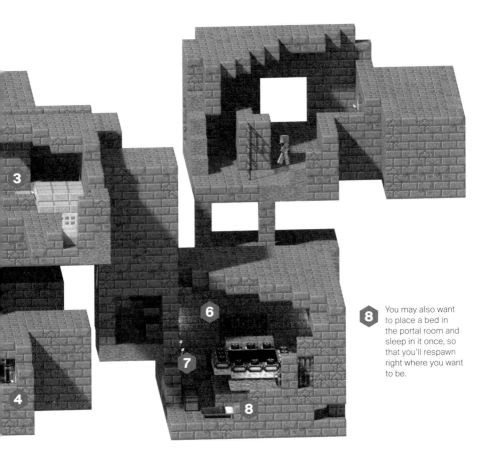

8 You may also want to place a bed in the portal room and sleep in it once, so that you'll respawn right where you want to be.

THE ENDER DRAGON

The ender dragon is Minecraft's deadliest boss mob. With an intimidating number of health points and some devastating attack methods, defeating it is no easy task. Let's take a look at what you're dealing with.

HEALTH POINTS	200
ATTACK STRENGTH	6-15
HOW TO DEFEAT	
ITEMS DROPPED	0-1 12,000

HOSTILITY

SPAWN · · · · · · · · · · · · · · · · · ·
LOCATION
As the player enters the End dimension for the first time, on the main island.

THE END

DID YOU KNOW?

You can respawn the ender dragon after defeating it, by placing four ender crystals on top of the exit portal.

MOJANG STUFF

As you might have guessed from the name, your battle with the ender dragon was meant to be the finale of the game. But who wants to stop playing Minecraft? Now you can respawn ender dragons and capture their breath to make lingering potions. You only get a dragon egg the first time you defeat one, though.

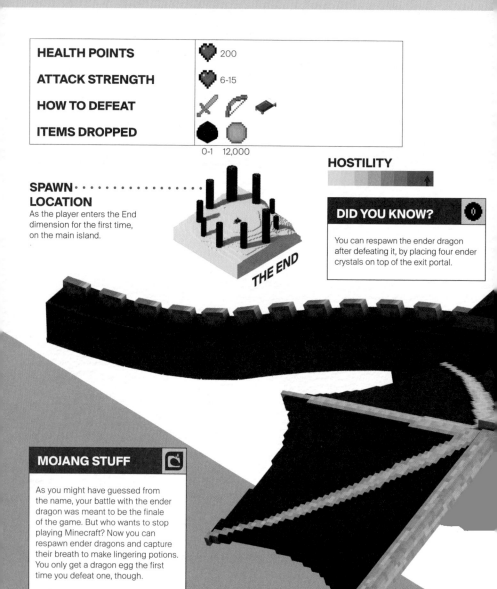

BEHAVIOUR

The ender dragon spends its life circling the main island. It seems to be protective of the podium in the centre, and when not attacking the player it flies down and perches on this podium.

SPECIAL SKILLS

In addition to its enormous size and high number of health points, the dragon has the ability to recharge its health by drawing power from the crystals on top of each obsidian pillar on the main island.

ATTACK METHOD

The dragon will charge, attacking its target with its breath and with ender charges – fireballs that emit harmful purple clouds on contact.

FIGHTING THE DRAGON

Once you step foot in the End there's no way out unless you defeat the ender dragon, or die trying. And defeating the dragon is arguably the most difficult thing you'll ever do in Minecraft, so you must be prepared. These combat tips will give you the best chance of success.

 As soon as you arrive in the End, drink a potion of regeneration. Take a moment to look around for the dragon, but don't underestimate the endermen's ability to seriously ruin your day. Consider wearing a pumpkin instead of a helmet so they don't become hostile if you look at them.

 The dragon draws power from the crystals on top of the obsidian pillars, so you'll need to destroy these before attempting to slay the dragon. Start with the crystals that aren't encased in iron bars – you can shoot them from the ground with arrows.

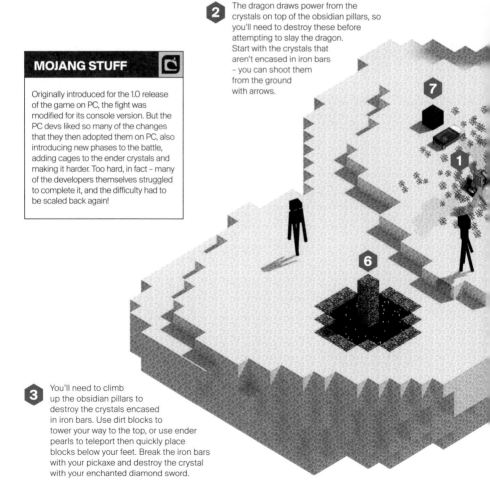

You'll need to climb up the obsidian pillars to destroy the crystals encased in iron bars. Use dirt blocks to tower your way to the top, or use ender pearls to teleport then quickly place blocks below your feet. Break the iron bars with your pickaxe and destroy the crystal with your enchanted diamond sword.

4 The crystals explode when destroyed, so you'll need to build a platform off the side of the pillar so you can step back and avoid taking damage. The dragon will swoop down to protect the pillars, so be careful it doesn't knock you off. If it does knock you off, try throwing an ender pearl as you fall or placing a bucket of water underneath you to cushion your landing.

5 Once all the crystals are destroyed you can proceed to attack the dragon directly. Keep an eye on its health bar and use your enchanted bow and arrows to shoot it when it's circling overhead. Don't waste arrows when it's far away – wait until it's a little closer and you're confident you can hit it.

6 The dragon will swoop down to land on the podium in the centre of the island every few seconds. It's immune to arrows when on the podium, but use your sword to hit its head, or throw a splash potion of harming at it.

7 To finish it off, place a bed on the ground in front of you, then try to sleep in it when it gets close enough. If you place a block of obsidian between yourself and the bed, it will protect you from some of the blast. You'll need to do this several times to defeat the dragon.

VICTORY

Victory is sweet! Once the dragon's health bar reaches zero it will explode, dropping an incredible 12,000 experience points. You'll also be rewarded with the highly coveted dragon egg which will appear on top of the exit portal which has materialised as if by magic in the centre of the island.

COLLECTING THE EGG

There's a catch: if you try to mine the egg it will unhelpfully teleport away.

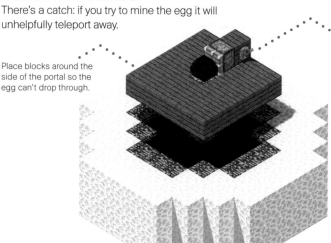

Place blocks around the side of the portal so the egg can't drop through.

Use a piston connected to a power source to push it off its plinth.

The egg will then drop as an item, so you can pick it up and take it back to the Overworld to display proudly in your home.

RESPAWNING THE DRAGON

Keen to stock up on dragon's breath for lingering potions? Then you'll need to respawn the dragon.

You'll need to place 4 ender crystals around the exit portal – one on each side. An ender crystal can be crafted from an eye of ender, a ghast tear and 7 glass blocks.

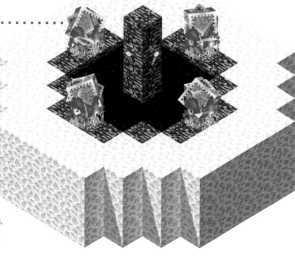

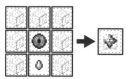

ENDER CRYSTAL RECIPE

Once the final crystal is placed it will regenerate the crystals on top of the pillars, and the dragon will appear. Be warned: if you respawn the dragon you won't be able to leave the End again until it is defeated.

WHERE NEXT?

Two portals appear when you defeat the dragon. The exit portal in the centre of the island will take you back to the Overworld, and a gateway portal will appear at the edge of the island – this leads to another gateway portal on the outer islands. If you choose the exit portal the End Poem will reveal itself to you before you arrive back in the Overworld. This intriguing text is worth a read.

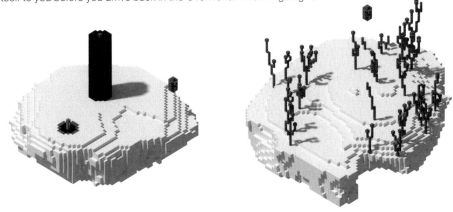

THE OUTER ISLANDS

The outer islands are approximately 1000 blocks away from the main island. As you'll see, the gateway portal that leads to the outer islands is only one block in size. To get through to the other side you'll need to throw an ender pearl into the portal and teleport across. The portal will transport you to one of the nearest outer islands, and from there you can explore the rest of the islands.

There are several useful materials to collect, but there are also endermen and shulkers to deal with. And it's easy to get lost as everything looks very similar.

You'll need to find a way to bridge the gaps between the outer islands so you don't fall into the Void. If you have enough cobblestone you can build cobblestone bridges between the islands so you can travel around safely.

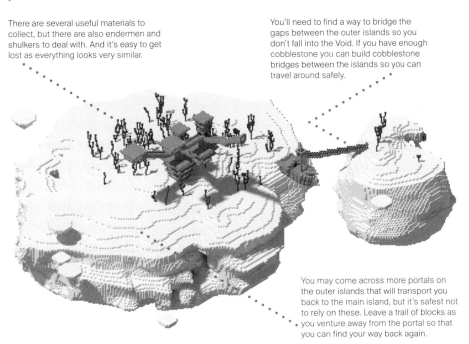

You may come across more portals on the outer islands that will transport you back to the main island, but it's safest not to rely on these. Leave a trail of blocks as you venture away from the portal so that you can find your way back again.

END CITIES

End cities are mysterious naturally generated structures found on the outer islands. They aren't a common sight so it can take a while to locate one. Let's take a look at the structures you'll find in End cities.

STRUCTURES

1 You'll typically see several towers – tall structures built from End stone brick and various purpur blocks. There may be several towers, and they are often linked by walkways.

2 Some tower rooms contain loot chests, inside which you might find everything from beetroot seeds to enchanted diamond equipment. They may also contain an ender chest.

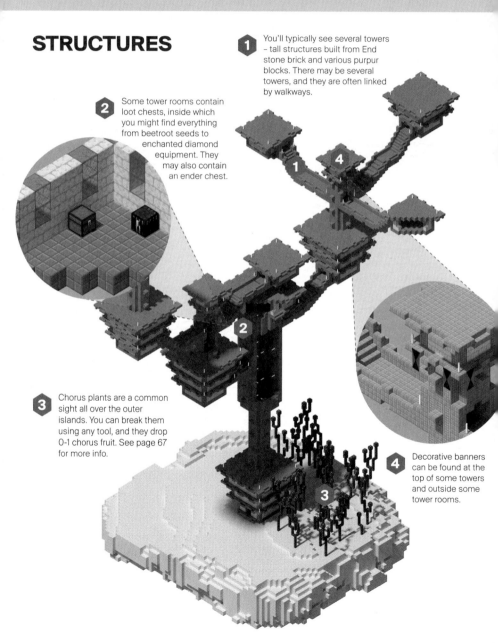

3 Chorus plants are a common sight all over the outer islands. You can break them using any tool, and they drop 0-1 chorus fruit. See page 67 for more info.

4 Decorative banners can be found at the top of some towers and outside some tower rooms.

TIP

End ships may be found at the end of piers in End cities. The easiest way to reach these floating ships is to walk to the end of the pier and throw an ender pearl to teleport across the gap.

5 There's a brewing room inside the ship, where you'll find a brewing stand and two potions of healing that may come in useful if you've taken a lot of damage. A staircase leads from the brewing room to the treasure room below.

6 End rods can be found all over End cities, and provide the only source of light on the outer islands. They can be mined with any tool. You'll also find a dragon head on the bow of the ship – the only place that this rare item generates.

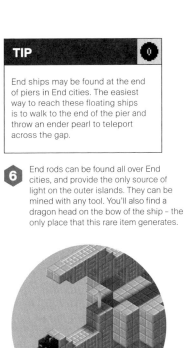

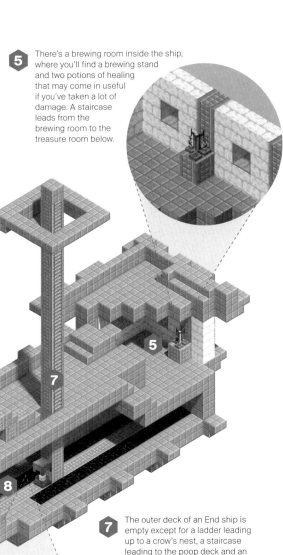

7 The outer deck of an End ship is empty except for a ladder leading up to a crow's nest, a staircase leading to the poop deck and an entrance to the cabin below.

8 Inside the treasure room you'll find two loot chests and elytra in an item frame (see pages 68-69 for more info). The floor is lined with obsidian. Unfortunately all of this is guarded by a shulker – see pages 64-65 for tips on how to deal with these creatures.

MOJANG STUFF

End cities were one of the first bits of architecture to be developed using structure blocks. These were originally an internal device used to save and load structures, but they were so useful that they were released to the community as a creative tool.

SHULKER

HEALTH POINTS	🖤 30	
ATTACK STRENGTH	🖤 4	
HOW TO DEFEAT		
ITEMS DROPPED		

0-1   5

SPAWN LIGHT LEVEL

15

0

MOJANG STUFF

The initial plans were to create a constructable, golem-like mob for End Cities, but the design just never came together in a fun way. Then, in a flash of inspiration, Jens had the idea of a mob that lived inside blocks!

SPAWN
LOCATION
In End cities attached to solid blocks, usually on the walls.

END CITY

BEHAVIOUR
Shulkers attach themselves to solid blocks. They generally lie dormant with their shell closed to blend in with the purpur blocks. Every so often they open their shell a little way to look for targets, revealing a vulnerable, fleshy creature inside.

ATTACK METHOD

When a shulker detects a target within 16 blocks they open their shell and shoot a projectile which follows the target and deals 4 health points of damage upon contact. It also administers the levitation effect for 10 seconds – when the effect wears off they fall back down to the ground, taking damage.

SPECIAL SKILLS

Shulkers camouflage themselves into the purpur blocks. They're immune to lava and fire and, when their shell is closed, they're immune to arrows. When one shulker is attacked any shulkers in the area will retaliate. When their health drops to less than half a heart they will teleport away to protect themselves.

SHULKER BOX RECIPE

HOW TO DEFEAT

Wait until the shulker opens its shell, then hit the creature inside with your enchanted diamond sword. You can also attempt to deflect the shulker's projectiles with a sword, a bow and arrow or your hands, or block them with your shield.

USEFUL DROPS

Shulkers may drop their shell when defeated, which can then be crafted with a chest to make a shulker box. These clever blocks have 27 storage slots and can store and transport items, and will even keep their items when broken with a pickaxe.

END BLOCKS & ITEMS & THEIR USES

Once you've dealt with the endermen and shulkers you can help yourself to the End city's unique blocks and items. Take a look at what you can do with these materials back in the Overworld.

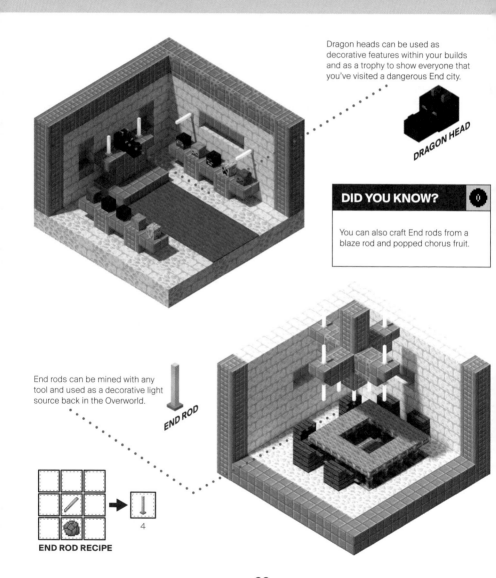

Dragon heads can be used as decorative features within your builds and as a trophy to show everyone that you've visited a dangerous End city.

DRAGON HEAD

DID YOU KNOW?

You can also craft End rods from a blaze rod and popped chorus fruit.

End rods can be mined with any tool and used as a decorative light source back in the Overworld.

END ROD

4

END ROD RECIPE

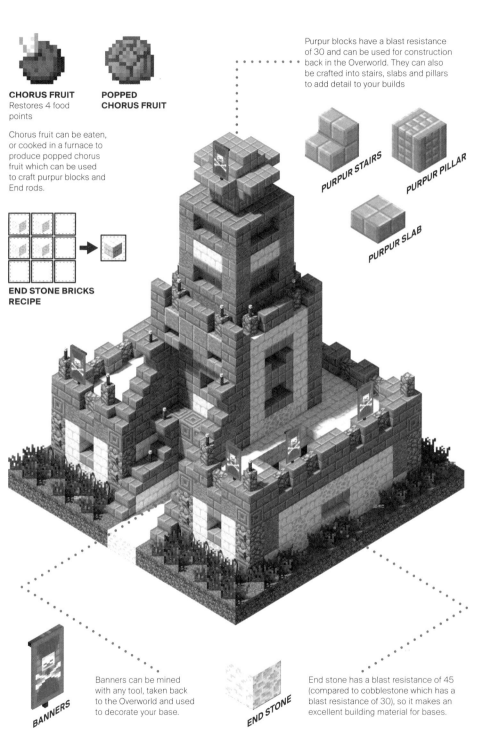

CHORUS FRUIT
Restores 4 food points

Chorus fruit can be eaten, or cooked in a furnace to produce popped chorus fruit which can be used to craft purpur blocks and End rods.

POPPED CHORUS FRUIT

END STONE BRICKS RECIPE

Purpur blocks have a blast resistance of 30 and can be used for construction back in the Overworld. They can also be crafted into stairs, slabs and pillars to add detail to your builds

PURPUR STAIRS

PURPUR PILLAR

PURPUR SLAB

BANNERS

Banners can be mined with any tool, taken back to the Overworld and used to decorate your base.

END STONE

End stone has a blast resistance of 45 (compared to cobblestone which has a blast resistance of 30), so it makes an excellent building material for bases.

ELYTRA

Elytra are wearable wings that allow you to glide through the air. Their default appearance is grey, but if you're wearing a cape they will cleverly adopt the cape's design. These wings are the closest you'll come to flying in Survival mode, so make sure you pick some up from your local End city.

HOW TO USE

Equip the elytra in your chestplate slot. When you're ready, jump from a height, e.g. off a cliff or building. Jump again when in mid-air to activate them. Once you're gliding, simply look left or right to change direction. Look up and down to change your speed and how quickly you descend.

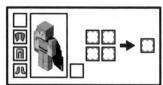

MOJANG STUFF

Elytra need to be activated after a jump or a fall, but this wasn't always the case. Back then you could also attach elytra to mobs, teleport them into the air and watch them swoop about - but by making the elytra activation-only, mobs just dropped like rocks! This would never do! By popular demand, elytra now automatically activate when attached to mobs.

DURABILITY

Elytra have a durability of 431, and this decreases by one point for each second they're in use. So, one pair of elytra will give you 7 minutes and 11 seconds of flight. When their durability reaches 1 they stop working.

REPAIR

Fortunately you can repair them – you can craft two damaged elytra together on an anvil or one elytra with leather. Each piece of leather repairs 108 durability points, so you'll need 4 pieces of leather to restore them to full durability.

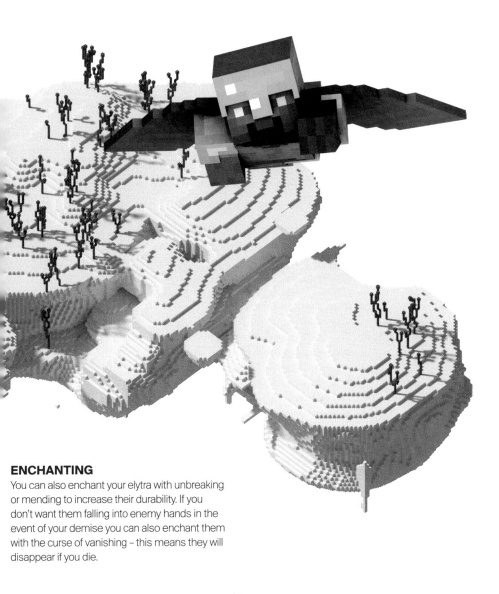

ENCHANTING

You can also enchant your elytra with unbreaking or mending to increase their durability. If you don't want them falling into enemy hands in the event of your demise you can also enchant them with the curse of vanishing – this means they will disappear if you die.

SETTLING IN THE END

Now that you've conquered the End you can make it into a permanent base of operations. Thanks to return portals (portals found near End cities that transport you back to the main island) you'll be able to travel back and forth between the islands, and back to the Overworld via your stronghold to import supplies.

MAIN ISLAND

Let's take a look at how you can develop the main island into a more permanent settlement.

1. Before you build anything, light up as much of the island as possible – this will reduce the number of endermen that spawn. Import glowstone and use it to create attractive lanterns.

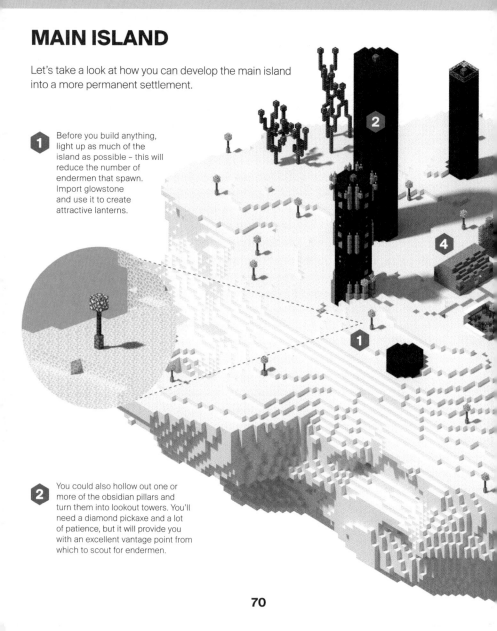

2. You could also hollow out one or more of the obsidian pillars and turn them into lookout towers. You'll need a diamond pickaxe and a lot of patience, but it will provide you with an excellent vantage point from which to scout for endermen.

3 Build a structure around the End portal to prevent you accidentally falling through to the Overworld. A small hut will do, but you could turn it into a larger build with other facilities inside such as a crafting, potions and enchanting area. After all, you've just earned an enormous amount of experience points that you'll be able to spend on new enchantments.

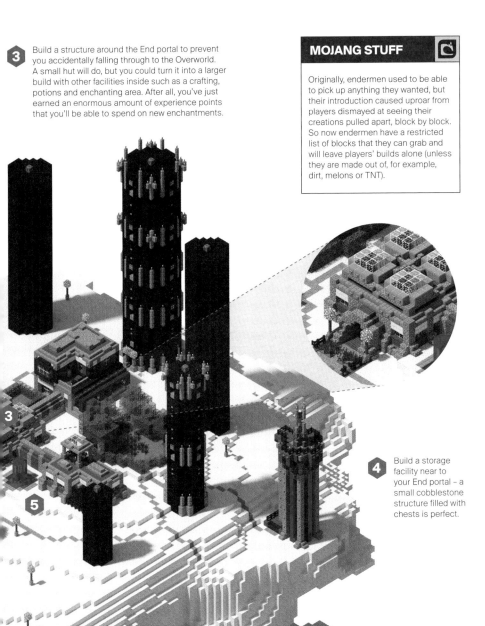

4 Build a storage facility near to your End portal – a small cobblestone structure filled with chests is perfect.

5 Create an infinite water source – you can use water for farming and to deter endermen. A fountain looks decorative as well as being functional.

71

OUTER ISLANDS

It makes sense to take advantage of the End's existing structures by expanding an End city settlement on one of the outer islands. There's plenty of flat, empty space around these cities, as well as an abundance of End stone that you can use for construction.

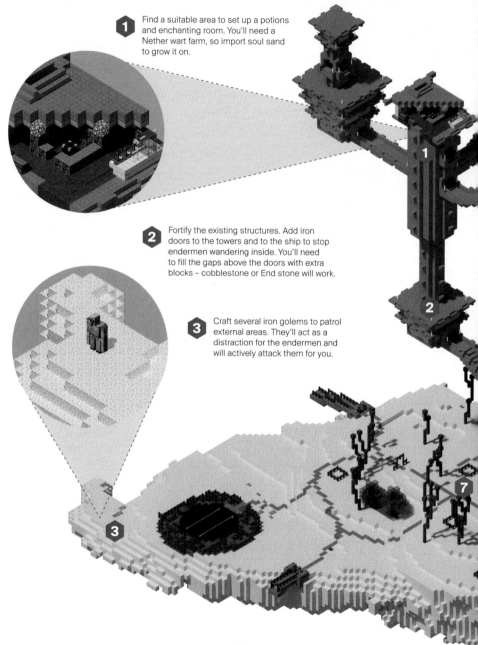

1 Find a suitable area to set up a potions and enchanting room. You'll need a Nether wart farm, so import soul sand to grow it on.

2 Fortify the existing structures. Add iron doors to the towers and to the ship to stop endermen wandering inside. You'll need to fill the gaps above the doors with extra blocks – cobblestone or End stone will work.

3 Craft several iron golems to patrol external areas. They'll act as a distraction for the endermen and will actively attack them for you.

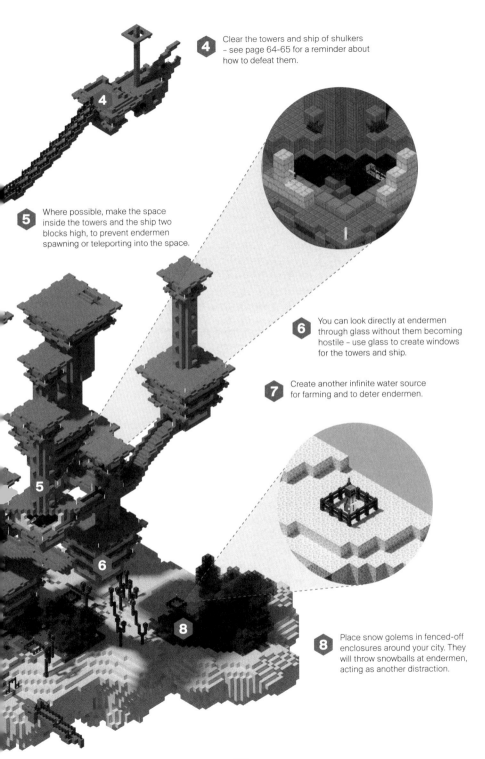

4 Clear the towers and ship of shulkers – see page 64-65 for a reminder about how to defeat them.

5 Where possible, make the space inside the towers and the ship two blocks high, to prevent endermen spawning or teleporting into the space.

6 You can look directly at endermen through glass without them becoming hostile – use glass to create windows for the towers and ship.

7 Create another infinite water source for farming and to deter endermen.

8 Place snow golems in fenced-off enclosures around your city. They will throw snowballs at endermen, acting as another distraction.

OUTER ISLANDS

1 If endermen are a real problem, make a secure underground base beneath one of the towers. The inside should only be two blocks high, so that endermen can't spawn inside.

3 Constructing a minecart system will make travel between the outer islands easier and reduce your risk of falling into the Void. See page 40-41 for a reminder about how to craft the necessary equipment.

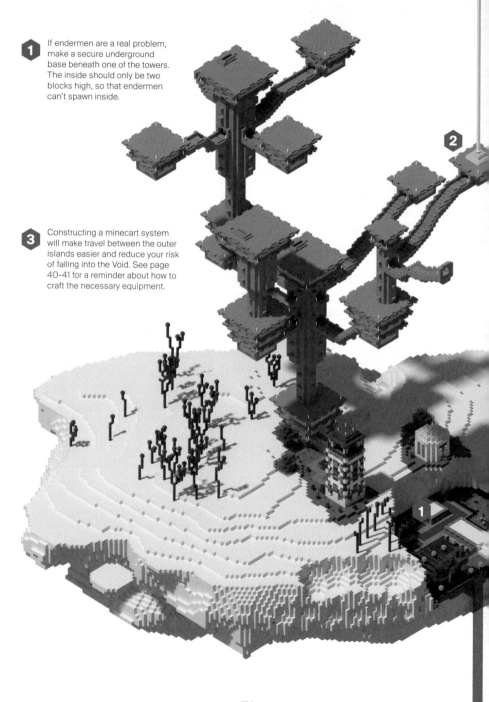

If you have the necessary resources you can build a power pyramid near the city and place a beacon block on top of it. This structure will provide you with special buffs when you're within a certain range. When placed, the beacon block will need an unobstructed view of the sky, and it must be on top of a pyramid, made of solid diamond, emerald, gold or iron blocks.

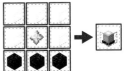

BEACON RECIPE

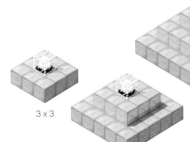

3 x 3

5 x 5

7 x 7

9 x 9

DID YOU KNOW?

There are four levels of pyramid: a level 1 pyramid is 3 x 3 blocks. To make a level 2 pyramid you can add a 5 x 5 base. A level 3 pyramid requires an additional 7 x 7 base and a level 4 pyramid requires an additional 9 x 9 base.

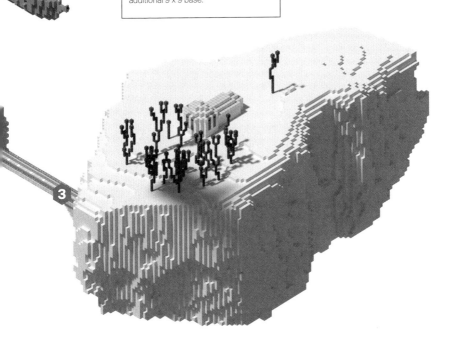

RESOURCES

If you'll be spending a significant amount of time in the End you'll need a supply of resources like food, wood and cobblestone. You can grow crops and breed chickens in the End and, unlike the Nether, you have the added bonus of being able to place water. Let's take a look at the resources you can produce.

WHEAT, BEETROOT, CARROTS AND POTATOES

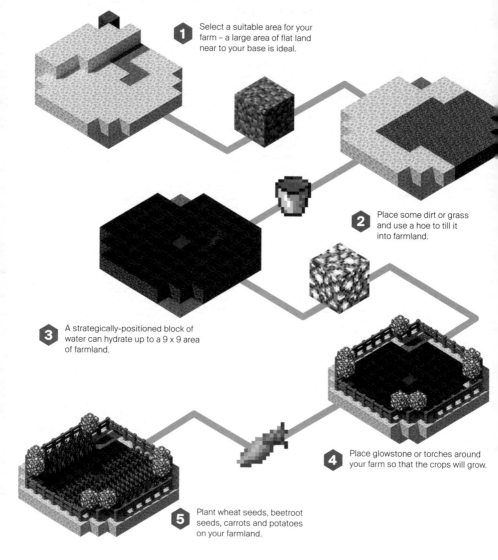

1 Select a suitable area for your farm – a large area of flat land near to your base is ideal.

2 Place some dirt or grass and use a hoe to till it into farmland.

3 A strategically-positioned block of water can hydrate up to a 9 x 9 area of farmland.

4 Place glowstone or torches around your farm so that the crops will grow.

5 Plant wheat seeds, beetroot seeds, carrots and potatoes on your farmland.

SUGAR CANES

Sugar canes can grow on grass, dirt or sand, as long as there's a water source on one side.

MELONS AND PUMPKINS

Melons and pumpkins just need farmland, light and an adjacent block to grow into.

TREE FARM

Cover a large area with dirt blocks and plant saplings 2 blocks apart. They need a light level of 8 or higher to grow, so place torches or glowstone lamps around your farm. Oak trees also provide you with apples if you destroy the leaves, and if you plant jungle tree saplings you can grow cocoa on their trunks.

TIP

Although it is possible to push mobs like cows and pigs through the End portal to get them into the End, it can be tricky. Instead, craft ender chests and set one up in the Overworld and one in the End city. Then you can place meat and other useful animal drops in the Overworld chest and access them in the End.

COBBLESTONE GENERATOR

Cobblestone is useful for building structures and for creating tools and weapons. It doesn't generate naturally in the End, but is created when a lava stream comes into contact with water. Create a ten-block long trench then place a water source block at one end and a lava source block at the other to make a cobblestone generator.

FLOWERS

The End is a barren, inhospitable place, so anything you can do to brighten it up will make you feel more at home. Import some colourful flowers from the Overworld and plant them around the city.

FINAL WORDS

Congratulations, 'crafter. With the knowledge contained in this book, you can be sure to face the terrors of the Nether and the End with confidence. Not too much confidence, mind you: these places are still among the most deadly Minecraft has to offer. Even the strongest, wisest warrior can come unstuck and take a tumble into a pond of molten rock. But you're as well equipped as you can be to overcome such peril, claim the great riches of these strange lands and journey on, finding new adventure. You may have beaten the End, but there's much more to see and do. Where will you go next? What will you build? We can't wait to see.

MARSH DAVIES
THE MOJANG TEAM

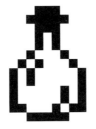

First published in Great Britain 2018 by Egmont UK Limited.
This edition first published in 2020 by Dean, an imprint of Egmont UK Limited,
2 Minster Court, 10th Floor, London EC3R 7BB

Written by Stephanie Milton
Additional material by Marsh Davies
Designed by Joe Bolder
Illustrations by Ryan Marsh and Joe Bolder
Cover designed by John Stuckey
Production by Louis Harvey
Special thanks to Lydia Winters, Owen Jones, Junkboy,
Martin Johansson, Marsh Davies and Jesper Öqvist.

ISBN 978 0 6035 7928 8

71019/001

Printed in China

ONLINE SAFETY FOR YOUNGER FANS

Spending time online is great fun! Here are a few simple rules to help younger fans stay safe and
keep the internet a great place to spend time:

- Never give out your real name - don't use it as your username.
- Never give out any of your personal details.
- Never tell anybody which school you go to or how old you are.
- Never tell anybody your password except a parent or a guardian.
- Be aware that you must be 13 or over to create an account on many sites. Always check the
site policy and ask a parent or guardian for permission before registering.
- Always tell a parent or guardian if something is worrying you.

Stay safe online. Any website addresses listed in this book are correct at the time of going
to print. However, Egmont is not responsible for content hosted by third parties. Please be
aware that online content can be subject to change and websites can contain content that is
unsuitable for children. We advise that all children are supervised when using the internet.

Egmont takes its responsibility to the planet and its inhabitants very seriously.
We aim to use papers from well-managed forests run by responsible suppliers.

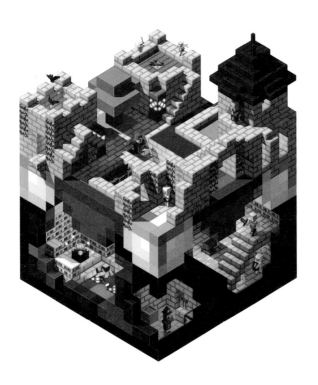

GUIDE TO:

ENCHANTMENTS & POTIONS

CONTENTS

INTRODUCTION

In theory, a bold adventurer can make their way through the world of Minecraft with little more than a pickaxe and a can-do attitude. In practice, though, such bold adventurers mostly end up as a pile of inventory items, bobbing in a dark pit surrounded by mobs – so it's probaly best to voyage into the unknown suitably equipped. That means learning how to affix your kit with arcane enchantments that let you deflect mighty blows, deal even more deadly damage, or even breathe underwater. A swig of a potion, meanwhile, can give you the power boost that means the difference between life and a lengthy trek back from your spawn point. Read on, and the mysteries of such magical arts will be revealed!

MARSH DAVIES
THE MOJANG TEAM

MOJANG STUFF

This super-exclusive info has come directly from the developers at Mojang.

1

ENCHANTMENTS

The mystical process of enchanting may seem daunting to beginners, but it's quite simple once you have the right equipment. Luckily, everything you need can be found in the Overworld. Let's take a look at the various methods of enchanting, the enchantments that are available for each item and when each enchantment will be most useful.

ENCHANTMENT MECHANICS

Enchantments are magical effects that improve the performance of your items, or provide them with extra abilities or uses. When used correctly they can really help to keep you alive in Survival mode. Enchanting is a fairly complicated process, so it's important to learn about the mechanics of the process before you begin.

MOJANG STUFF

As you play Minecraft you gain experience points, or XP. We should probably have called them enchantment points, however, as using them to power up your kit is really the only way you can spend them.

ENCHANTMENT METHODS

There are three methods you can use to enchant your items:

1 You can enchant items on an enchantment table, in exchange for experience levels and lapis lazuli. This only works for items with no existing enchantments. Three options are available each time you use an enchantment table.

2 You can combine two of the same item, each with a different enchantment, on an anvil. This will produce one item with two enchantments and costs experience levels.

3 You can combine an enchanted book with an unenchanted item on an anvil, imbuing the item with the enchantment from the book (or multiple enchantments if the book carries more than one). This also costs experience levels.

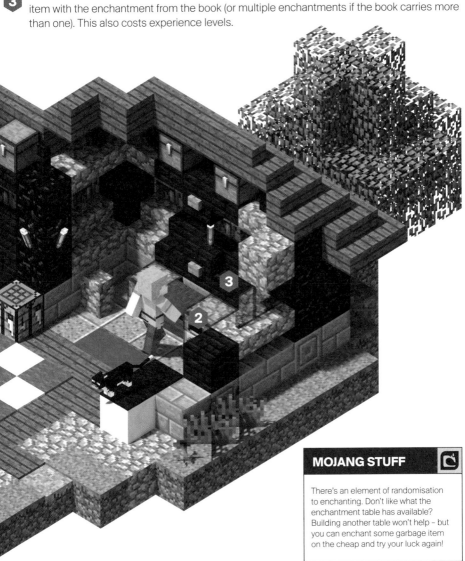

MOJANG STUFF

There's an element of randomisation to enchanting. Don't like what the enchantment table has available? Building another table won't help – but you can enchant some garbage item on the cheap and try your luck again!

WHAT CAN YOU ENCHANT?

You'll recognise enchanted items by their otherworldly purple glow. Enchantments can be added to most armour items, tools and weapons, and even books. Some items can be enchanted on a table or an anvil, others can only be enchanted on an anvil.

KEY

Can be enchanted on an enchantment table

Can be enchanted on an anvil

HELMET

CHESTPLATE

BOW

LEGGINGS/PANTS

BOOTS

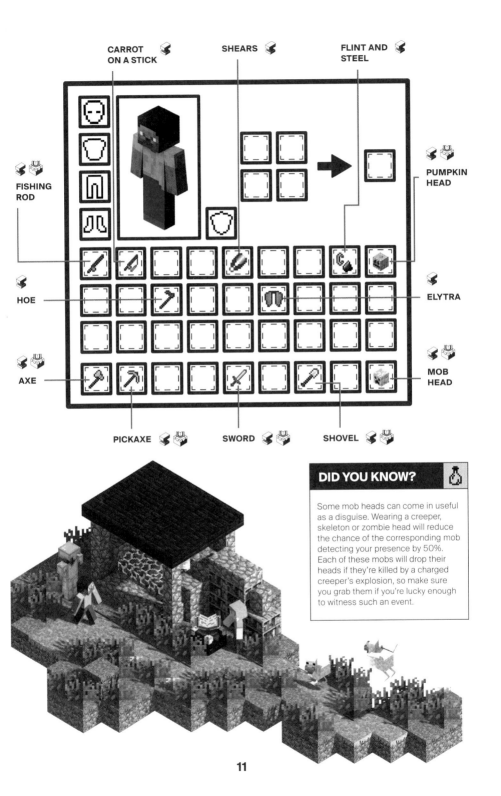

CARROT ON A STICK

SHEARS

FLINT AND STEEL

FISHING ROD

PUMPKIN HEAD

HOE

ELYTRA

AXE

MOB HEAD

PICKAXE   SWORD   SHOVEL

DID YOU KNOW?

Some mob heads can come in useful as a disguise. Wearing a creeper, skeleton or zombie head will reduce the chance of the corresponding mob detecting your presence by 50%. Each of these mobs will drop their heads if they're killed by a charged creeper's explosion, so make sure you grab them if you're lucky enough to witness such an event.

ENCHANTMENT POWER LEVEL

An enchantment's power level appears as a roman numeral next to its name. Some enchantments only have one power level (I), some three (III), others as many as five (V). The maximum power level for each enchantment is listed on pages 24-35.

The higher the power level, the more powerful the enchantment.

DIAMOND SWORD
FIRE ASPECT II
SMITE V

The power level will be visible in the enchantment's name – for example, Fire Aspect II is a power level 2 enchantment, and Smite V is a power level 5 enchantment.

ENCHANTMENT COST

Unfortunately, enchantments don't come for free – each has a different cost attached to it.

You pay for enchantments using your experience levels, which are an accumulation of the experience points you earn through mining, defeating mobs and other players, breeding, fishing and using furnaces.

You must be a certain experience level in order to access the enchantment in the first place. If an enchantment has a high level requirement it's a good indication that it will be a powerful enchantment, and that you will get multiple enchantments. It is not a guarantee, however, as there's also a random factor to the process.

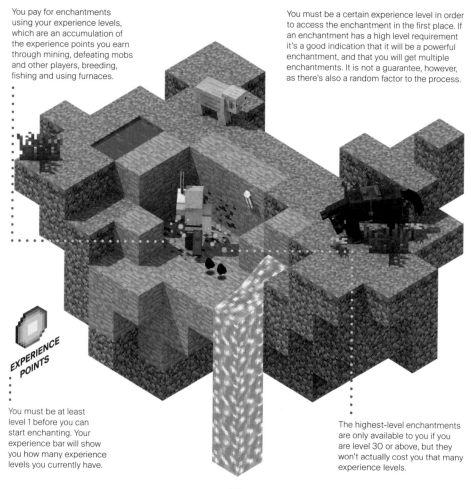

EXPERIENCE POINTS

You must be at least level 1 before you can start enchanting. Your experience bar will show you how many experience levels you currently have.

The highest-level enchantments are only available to you if you are level 30 or above, but they won't actually cost you that many experience levels.

The more experience levels you have, the more likely it is that higher-level enchantments will be available, although this isn't the only factor. See pages 20-21 to learn about the effect of bookshelves on an enchantment table.

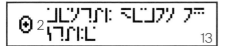

In this example you'll need 13 experience levels to be able to access the enchantment, but it will only cost you 2 experience levels (and 2 pieces of lapis lazuli).

ENCHANTMENT WEIGHT

Each enchantment has a weight, which tells you how likely it is to appear as an option when you enchant your items. The higher the weight of an enchantment, the more chance there is of it appearing. You can check the weight of each enchantment on pages 24-35.

PRIMARY AND SECONDARY ITEMS

Primary items can be enchanted in Survival mode via an enchantment table. Secondary items can't be enchanted on an enchantment table but can receive enchantments from enchanted books via an anvil. See pages 22-23 for more info.

ENCHANTABILITY

Different items and materials have different levels of enchantability. The higher the enchantability of an item, the greater the chance it will receive higher-level enchantments and multiple enchantments. This table shows the relative enchantability of various materials and items.

MATERIAL	ARMOUR ENCHANTABILITY	SWORD/TOOL ENCHANTABILITY
WOOD	N/A	15
LEATHER	15	N/A
STONE	N/A	5
IRON	9	14
CHAIN	12	N/A
DIAMOND	10	10
GOLD	25	22
BOOK	1	1

As you can see, gold has the highest enchantability and is the easiest material to enchant, but gold tools, weapons and armour are the least durable and wear out quickly. Diamond has a lower enchantability but is the most durable material and will last much longer than gold.

Chainmail armour can't be crafted, but armourer villagers may offer it as a trade.

TREASURE ENCHANTMENTS

Treasure enchantments are rare – they will never be available through an enchantment table, but you may find items carrying these enchantments on your travels, if you know where to look.

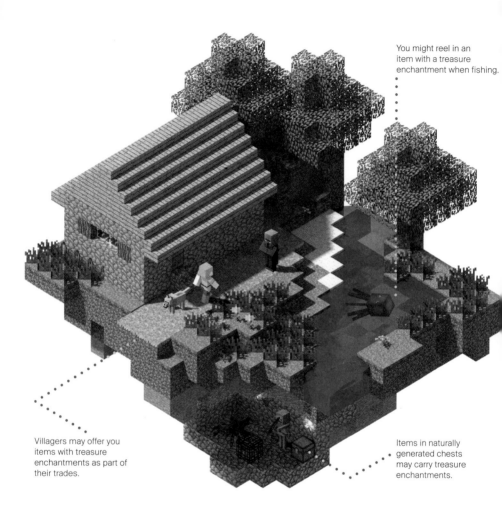

You might reel in an item with a treasure enchantment when fishing.

Villagers may offer you items with treasure enchantments as part of their trades.

Items in naturally generated chests may carry treasure enchantments.

MULTIPLE ENCHANTMENTS

There's a good chance you'll get more than one enchantment on an item when using an enchantment table, but you won't know exactly what additional enchantments you're getting until you perform the enchantment. The maximum number of enchantments that a single item can carry is five.

DIAMOND SWORD
FIRE ASPECT II
SMITE V
KNOCKBACK II
LOOTING III

CONFLICTING ENCHANTMENTS

Some enchantments conflict with other enchantments, which means they cannot both be applied to the same item. Bear in mind the following rules when enchanting to avoid disappointment.

1 Every enchantment conflicts with itself, so you can't add two of the same enchantment to one item.

2 All protection enchantments conflict with each other, so you can only choose one per item. The protection enchantments are Blast Protection, Feather Falling, Fire Protection, Projectile Protection and Protection.

3 All damage enchantments conflict with each other, so you can only choose one. Damage enchantments are Sharpness, Smite and Bane of Arthropods.

4 Silk Touch and Fortune conflict with each other.

5 Depth Strider and Frost Walker conflict with each other.

6 Mending and Infinity conflict with each other.

PROTECTION ENCHANTMENTS FOR ARMOUR

Each protection enchantment listed in the table below provides an enchantment protection factor, or EPF for short. When protection enchantments have been applied to several pieces of armour that are being worn simultaneously, these EPFs add up and will be capped when they reach a maximum of 20. At this level, the damage you take is reduced by the maximum amount, which is 80%.

This table shows the EPF for each level of each protection enchantment.

ENCHANTMENT	DAMAGE REDUCED FOR	EPF LEVEL I	EPF LEVEL II	EPF LEVEL III	EPF LEVEL IV
Protection	All	1	2	3	4
Fire Protection	Fire, lava and blaze fireballs	2	4	6	8
Blast Protection	Explosions	2	4	6	8
Projectile Protection	Arrows, ghast and blaze fireballs	2	4	6	8
Feather Falling	Fall damage	3	6	9	12

Want to save yourself some materials? You can achieve maximum protection against certain types of damage using just three pieces of armour. For example, you can wear two pieces of armour enchanted with Blast Protection IV (each offers an EPF of 8) and one enchanted with Protection IV (EPF 4), giving you a total of 20 EPF against explosions. See pages 24, 27, 28 and 32 for a full explanation of each protection enchantment.

THE ENCHANTMENT TABLE METHOD

The most popular method of enchanting an unenchanted item is using an enchantment table. This mysterious block is expensive to craft but worth the investment as it opens up a magical new world of opportunities.

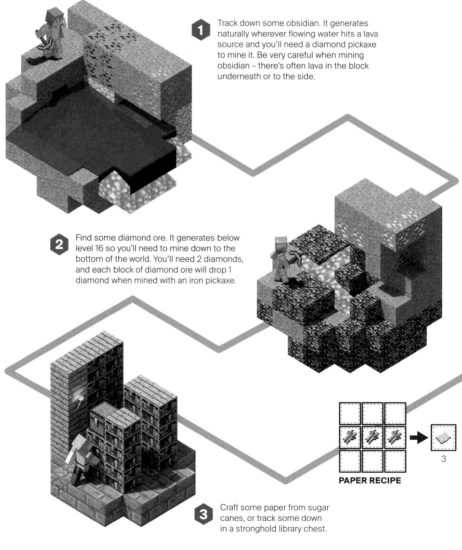

1 Track down some obsidian. It generates naturally wherever flowing water hits a lava source and you'll need a diamond pickaxe to mine it. Be very careful when mining obsidian – there's often lava in the block underneath or to the side.

2 Find some diamond ore. It generates below level 16 so you'll need to mine down to the bottom of the world. You'll need 2 diamonds, and each block of diamond ore will drop 1 diamond when mined with an iron pickaxe.

3

PAPER RECIPE

3 Craft some paper from sugar canes, or track some down in a stronghold library chest.

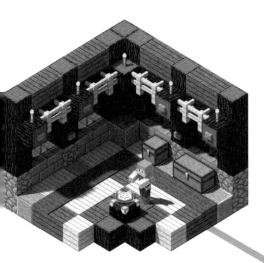

LAPIS LAZULI

You'll need a good supply of lapis lazuli to pay for your enchantments, so make sure you stock up before you begin. Lapis lazuli ore generates at level 31 and below. When mined with a stone pickaxe or better, each block will drop 4-8 pieces of lapis lazuli.

6 Find a home for your enchantment table in your base. Position it in an area with a few blocks' space on each side so you can surround it with bookshelves later to access the highest-level enchantments (see pages 20-21 for more info).

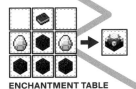

ENCHANTMENT TABLE RECIPE

5 Use your paper and leather to craft a book. Now you have everything you need to craft an enchantment table.

4 Collect some leather. Cows, mooshrooms, horses and llamas may drop leather upon death.

BOOK RECIPE

USING AN ENCHANTMENT TABLE

Now that your enchantment table is set up and you've mined all the lapis lazuli you can get your hands on, you're ready to start enchanting your items. Let's take a closer look at how this otherworldly block works.

When you interact with your enchantment table you'll be presented with an interface that looks like the one you can see below. Place the item you wish to enchant in the empty item slot, and three enchantment options will appear on the right for your consideration.

The enchantment options are written in the Standard Galactic Alphabet. Hover over them to see the name of one of the enchantments that will be applied if you choose that option. Although only one enchantment is visible, you may get more.

The required experience level (labelled as the 'enchantment level' when you hover over the enchantment if you have enough experience levels, or 'level requirement' if you don't) will be displayed to the right of each enchantment.

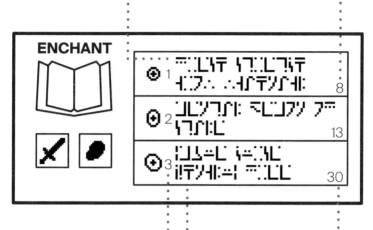

The number on the left of each enchantment tells you how many experience levels and pieces of lapis lazuli it costs.

You can only choose enchantments that are the same experience level or lower than your current experience level. Don't forget to check your experience bar to see which level you're currently at.

The lowest-level enchantment (always in the top slot) will cost 1 experience level and 1 lapis lazuli, the middle enchantment will cost 2 of each and the highest-level enchantment (always in the bottom slot) will cost 3.

Select one of the enchantment options that are available to you. You'll hear a strange noise and the lapis lazuli will disappear, along with the enchantment options. Drag your newly-enchanted item back into your inventory.

THE STANDARD GALACTIC ALPHABET

The Standard Galactic Alphabet is a series of cryptic runes that was first used in the Commander Keen games. The runes used to describe each enchantment are a random combination of 3-5 words. They aren't actually relevant to the enchantment chosen and are there for decoration.

BOOKSHELVES

Enchantment tables have the curious ability to draw power from nearby bookshelves and use it to access higher-level enchantments. Exactly how this works is a bit of a mystery. With no bookshelves, the experience level requirement for an enchantment will never be more than 8, but with bookshelves it can be as high as 30.

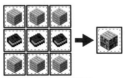

BOOKSHELF RECIPE

See page 17 for a reminder of how to craft books, then craft books together with wood planks to make bookshelves. To access the highest-level enchantments you'll need 15 bookshelves, arranged in the proper position. Try the bookshelf square or the bookshelf corner shown here.

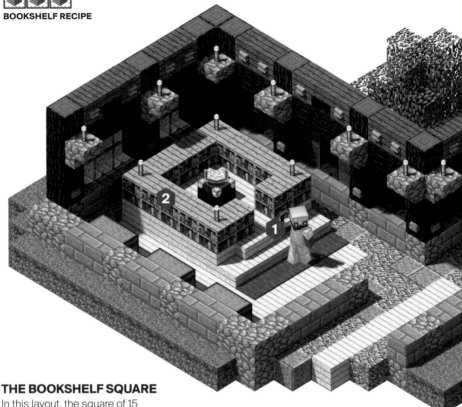

THE BOOKSHELF SQUARE
In this layout, the square of 15 bookshelves is 1 block high.

 There must be a block of air between each bookshelf and the enchantment table – even carpet will be enough to disable the effect of the bookshelves.

 You'll find bookshelves in some NPC village libraries, stronghold libraries and woodland mansions. When mined with an axe they'll drop their books, which can be crafted with wood planks to build new bookshelves.

THE BOOKSHELF CORNER

In this layout, 2 bookshelves are stacked on top of each other in each position, so the total number is 16. This is one more than is actually necessary to access the highest-level enchantments.

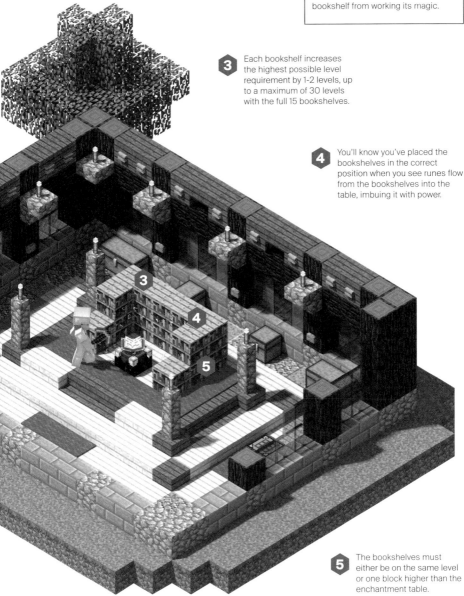

3 Each bookshelf increases the highest possible level requirement by 1-2 levels, up to a maximum of 30 levels with the full 15 bookshelves.

4 You'll know you've placed the bookshelves in the correct position when you see runes flow from the bookshelves into the table, imbuing it with power.

5 The bookshelves must either be on the same level or one block higher than the enchantment table.

21

THE ANVIL METHOD

There are two ways you can use an anvil to enchant items. You can combine an enchanted book with an unenchanted item, or you can combine two of the same item, each with different enchantments, to create one item that carries both.

Crafting an anvil will set you back 3 solid blocks of iron and an additional 4 iron ingots.

ANVIL

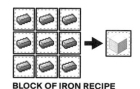

BLOCK OF IRON RECIPE

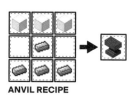

ANVIL RECIPE

1. COMBINING AN ENCHANTED BOOK WITH AN ITEM

An enchanted book is useful if you want a specific enchantment. You may come across enchanted books on your travels. If you don't have any items to enchant right now, but have lots of experience points, you might also choose to enchant a book and save it to apply to another item later.

ENCHANTED BOOK

You can enchant a regular book on an enchantment table. As with other items you'll be given three options and you may get multiple enchantments.

Make sure the enchantment on the enchanted book will work for the item you wish to enchant. For example, if the book is enchanted with Respiration, it will only work on a helmet. If there are multiple enchantments on the book, only the enchantments that work for that item will be applied. You can read about enchantments and the items they can be applied to in the next few pages.

Interact with your anvil and add the item you wish to enchant to the first slot, then add the enchanted book to the second slot. The enchanted item will appear in the output slot, and the cost (in experience points) will be displayed below.

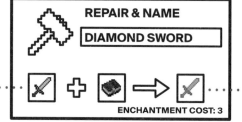

REPAIR & NAME

DIAMOND SWORD

ENCHANTMENT COST: 3

Select the enchantment and the book will disappear, leaving you with a newly-enchanted item.

Enchanted books may be found in chests in strongholds, jungle temples, desert temples, dungeons, abandoned mineshafts and woodland mansions. You might also reel in an enchanted book when fishing. Librarian villagers may also offer you an enchanted book as part of their trades, in exchange for emeralds.

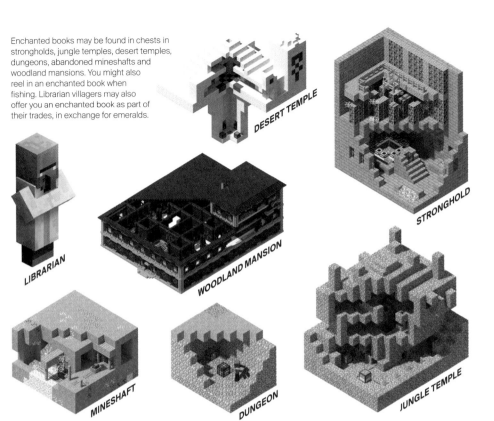

DESERT TEMPLE

STRONGHOLD

LIBRARIAN

WOODLAND MANSION

MINESHAFT

DUNGEON

JUNGLE TEMPLE

2. COMBINING TWO OF THE SAME ITEM WITH DIFFERENT ENCHANTMENTS

Once an item has been enchanted it can't be enchanted further using an enchantment table. That's where the anvil comes in handy yet again – it allows you to combine two of the same item with different enchantments. Add the items to the anvil slots and, if you have enough experience levels, the new item, carrying both enchantments, will appear in the output slot.

Slightly damaged anvil

Very damaged anvil

DID YOU KNOW?

Each time you use an anvil there's a chance that it will become damaged. Most anvils will last for 25 uses before being destroyed. Look for signs that your anvil is taking damage, and when it appears very damaged you'll know it's time to craft a new one.

REPAIRING ENCHANTED ITEMS

You can also repair enchanted items on an anvil, either by combining two of the same item (one will be sacrificed) or by using some of the material the item has been crafted from to repair it (e.g. iron ingots will repair an enchanted iron pickaxe). You can keep adding material such as iron ingots until the item is completely repaired, or just use one or two to slightly increase its remaining lifespan.

ENCHANTMENTS AND THEIR USES

So you have everything you need to start producing powerful enchanted tools, weapons and armour to give you a supernatural edge. Let's take a look at what each enchantment does and how it can help you.

AQUA AFFINITY

PRIMARY ITEMS	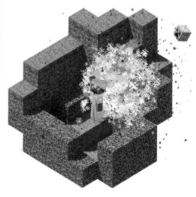
SECONDARY ITEMS	NONE
MAX POWER LEVEL	I
WEIGHT	2

Aqua Affinity increases the rate at which you can mine blocks when you're underwater. You'll be able to break blocks that are submerged in water at the same speed as if they were situated on land. This is particularly useful if you're mining large quantities of clay from river beds, or if you're mining in ocean monuments.

BANE OF ARTHROPODS

PRIMARY ITEMS	
SECONDARY ITEMS	
MAX POWER LEVEL	V
WEIGHT	5

This enchantment increases the damage to arthropod mobs – that means spiders, cave spiders, silverfish and endermites. It also inflicts Slowness IV on the mob which slows their movement. It lasts between 1 and 1.5 seconds at level I. The maximum duration will increase by half a second for each level, up to a maximum of 3.5 seconds at level V.

BLAST PROTECTION

PRIMARY ITEMS	
SECONDARY ITEMS	NONE
MAX POWER LEVEL	IV
WEIGHT	2

Blast Protection reduces the damage you'll take from explosions caused by TNT and creeper detonation. It also reduces the knockback caused by these explosions. It's a handy enchantment to use when you might come into contact with creepers, or enemy players.

CURSE OF BINDING

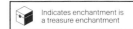

PRIMARY ITEMS	NONE
SECONDARY ITEMS	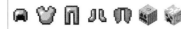
MAX POWER LEVEL	I
WEIGHT	1

When applied to an item, the Curse of Binding will prevent the item from being removed from a player once it's been equipped in an armour slot. The only way an item carrying this curse can be removed is if it's broken, or if the player wearing it dies and respawns. This may not sound terrible, but it comes in handy when you're fighting other players as it means you can trick your opponents into getting stuck wearing low durability leather armour or pumpkin heads during PVP (player versus player) battles.

CURSE OF VANISHING

PRIMARY ITEMS	NONE
SECONDARY ITEMS	
MAX POWER LEVEL	I
WEIGHT	1

The Curse of Vanishing enchantment causes the tool, weapon or piece of armour to be destroyed when the player dies. It's best used during PVP battles as it will prevent enemy players getting their hands on your best equipment. If you want to trade your Curse of Vanishing armour with a friend, you can drop it on the ground and they'll be able to pick it up in the usual way.

DEPTH STRIDER

PRIMARY ITEMS	
SECONDARY ITEMS	NONE
MAX POWER LEVEL	III
WEIGHT	2

Depth Strider increases a player's movement speed when they're underwater. Each level of the enchantment reduces the amount the water slows you down by a third, and if you use level III you'll be able to swim as fast as you would usually walk on dry land. This is another great enchantment to try out if you're planning to visit an ocean monument as it means you'll be able to navigate as quickly as possible.

EFFICIENCY

PRIMARY ITEMS	
SECONDARY ITEMS	
MAX POWER LEVEL	V
WEIGHT	10

The Efficiency enchantment increases your mining speed when you're mining blocks that drop an item rather than themselves, e.g. coal ore and glowstone. You must use the most efficient tool when mining the block in question, e.g. a shovel for gravel or an axe for wood. This is the perfect enchantment to use when you're out collecting large quantities of resources for crafting as it will save you valuable time.

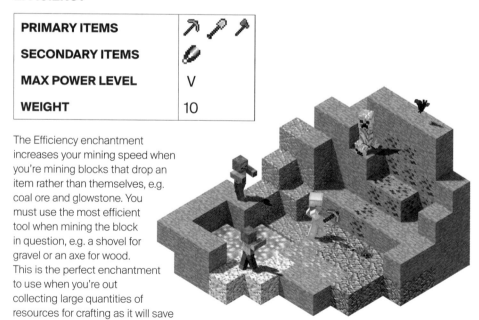

FEATHER FALLING

PRIMARY ITEMS	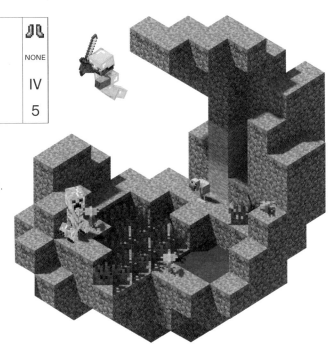
SECONDARY ITEMS	NONE
MAX POWER LEVEL	IV
WEIGHT	5

When applied to boots, the Feather Falling enchantment reduces the damage you take when you fall from a height, e.g. from a ledge when mining or off a cliff. It also reduces any damage you might take from teleporting using an ender pearl. It's a great all-purpose enchantment to use on your boots when exploring the world in Survival mode.

FIRE ASPECT

PRIMARY ITEMS	
SECONDARY ITEMS	NONE
MAX POWER LEVEL	II
WEIGHT	2

When you strike an enemy player or mob with a Fire Aspect sword, they will promptly be set on fire. Each level of the enchantment adds 80 fireticks – that's 4 seconds of burning time. Power level I will cause 3 points of damage, and power level II will cause 7. It's great for use in any dangerous situation, but if you kill an animal using a Fire Aspect sword it will drop cooked meat. Nether mobs are immune to burning so they won't take damage from this enchantment.

FIRE PROTECTION

PRIMARY ITEMS	
SECONDARY ITEMS	NONE
MAX POWER LEVEL	IV
WEIGHT	2

As its name suggests, the Fire Protection enchantment reduces the damage you take from lava or sources of fire. It also reduces the amount of time that you'll be on fire. Fire Protection is recommended for a trip to the Nether, and when mining at the bottom of the Overworld where lava is abundant.

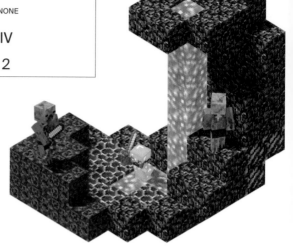

FLAME

PRIMARY ITEMS	
SECONDARY ITEMS	NONE
MAX POWER LEVEL	I
WEIGHT	2

Arrows fired from a bow enchanted with Flame will be flaming arrows. Each arrow deals 4 fire damage points to its target over the course of 5 seconds. Flaming arrows will only have an effect on mobs, players and TNT blocks and won't set wood or any other blocks ablaze. This enchantment is ideal for use on a bow for PVP battles or mob battles in the Overworld. Remember that Nether mobs are immune to burning so won't take any damage from a flame bow.

FORTUNE

PRIMARY ITEMS	
SECONDARY ITEMS	NONE
MAX POWER LEVEL	III
WEIGHT	2

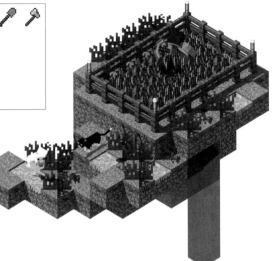

The Fortune enchantment will increase the chance of getting more drops from a block you're mining – this includes ores and crops. It will also increase the chance that leaf blocks will drop saplings and oak leaves will drop apples, so it's a great enchantment to use when you're out collecting resources.

FROST WALKER

PRIMARY ITEMS	NONE
SECONDARY ITEMS	
MAX POWER LEVEL	II
WEIGHT	2

The Frost Walker enchantment creates frosted ice blocks beneath your feet when you walk or run across water blocks, so it's very useful when you need to travel across large areas of water. It also prevents you taking damage from magma blocks in the Nether.

INFINITY

PRIMARY ITEMS	
SECONDARY ITEMS	NONE
MAX POWER LEVEL	I
WEIGHT	1

Infinity allows you to fire an infinite number of regular arrows from your bow, as long as you have 1 regular arrow in your inventory. Try it out when dealing with skeletons or during PVP combat. Unfortunately it doesn't work on tipped or spectral arrows.

KNOCKBACK

PRIMARY ITEMS	
SECONDARY ITEMS	NONE
MAX POWER LEVEL	II
WEIGHT	5

This enchantment increases the knockback of your sword (the amount a player or mob is pushed backwards, away from you, when hit). The effect of Knockback should not be underestimated – it's possible to knock players or mobs over cliffs or into lava. This is a great enchantment for any combat situation.

LOOTING

PRIMARY ITEMS	⚔️
SECONDARY ITEMS	NONE
MAX POWER LEVEL	III
WEIGHT	2

Looting causes an increase in mob drops. It increases the maximum number of common drops by 1 per power level and increases the chance of uncommon drops by causing a second attempt if the first fails. It also increases the chance of getting rare drops and equipment drops. It's best used when you need specific mob drops that are difficult to get, e.g. potion ingredients.

LUCK OF THE SEA

PRIMARY ITEMS	🎣
SECONDARY ITEMS	NONE
MAX POWER LEVEL	III
WEIGHT	2

The Luck of the Sea enchantment increases your luck when fishing. This means your chance of reeling in junk items and fish is lower than usual, whereas your chance of reeling in treasure items is higher. Treasure items include bows, enchanted books, fishing rods, name tags, saddles and lily pads, so this enchantment can provide you with some really useful items.

LURE

PRIMARY ITEMS	🎣
SECONDARY ITEMS	NONE
MAX POWER LEVEL	III
WEIGHT	2

The Lure enchantment increases the number of fish that will bite at your fishing rod. It also decreases the time you have to wait for a catch by 5 seconds per power level. Take this one with you on a fishing expedition and you'll soon have all the fish you could possibly need.

MENDING

PRIMARY ITEMS	NONE
SECONDARY ITEMS	
MAX POWER LEVEL	I
WEIGHT	2

When an item that's enchanted with Mending is held or worn it will be repaired using the experience points you earn. The rate of repair is 2 durability points per experience point. You won't accrue experience points while you're using this enchantment, but once the Mending item is fully repaired your experience points will begin to accrue again. This is a great enchantment to use when you're short on resources to craft more items.

POWER

PRIMARY ITEMS	🏹
SECONDARY ITEMS	NONE
MAX POWER LEVEL	V
WEIGHT	10

The Power enchantment increases arrow damage by 25% x (power level +1), rounded up to the nearest half heart. So, if your bow is Power level I, the damage is increased by 50% (25 x 2). For level II it's 75% (25 x 3), and so on. It's a great enchantment to use when fighting off hostile mobs or enemy players. You'll need an anvil if you want to apply level V.

PROJECTILE PROTECTION

PRIMARY ITEMS	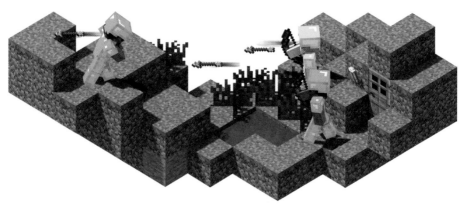
SECONDARY ITEMS	NONE
MAX POWER LEVEL	IV
WEIGHT	5

Projectile Protection reduces the damage you sustain from projectiles (arrows, ghast or blaze fireballs, fire charges). It's a great enchantment to use in PVP battles if your opponents have bows, when fighting skeletons, or in the Nether.

PROTECTION

PRIMARY ITEMS	
SECONDARY ITEMS	NONE
MAX POWER LEVEL	IV
WEIGHT	10

The Protection enchantment reduces all damage, except for hunger damage and damage sustained by falling into the Void. This is an all-purpose enchantment that is a valuable addition to your armour for any dangerous situation.

PUNCH

PRIMARY ITEMS	🏹
SECONDARY ITEMS	NONE
MAX POWER LEVEL	II
WEIGHT	2

The Punch enchantment increases the knockback effect of your bow and arrow, so mobs and players are knocked back further than they would usually be. It's a great enchantment for any combat situation where you're keen to keep your opponents as far away from you as possible.

RESPIRATION

PRIMARY ITEMS	🪖
SECONDARY ITEMS	NONE
MAX POWER LEVEL	III
WEIGHT	2

Respiration extends the amount of time you are able to survive underwater without breathing, by providing you with an additional 15 seconds per power level. It also improves your visibility. It's extremely useful if you plan to venture underwater, e.g. to visit an ocean monument.

SHARPNESS

PRIMARY ITEMS	🗡
SECONDARY ITEMS	⛏
MAX POWER LEVEL	V
WEIGHT	10

The Sharpness enchantment increases the damage dealt by your sword or axe, making it a more effective weapon for combat situations. It adds 1 extra point of damage for the first power level, and half a point for each additional power level. You'll need an anvil to apply power level V.

SILK TOUCH

PRIMARY ITEMS	⛏ 🪓 🔨
SECONDARY ITEMS	✂
MAX POWER LEVEL	III
WEIGHT	1

Silk Touch causes many blocks that would usually drop items to drop themselves instead. It can be used on coal ore, diamond ore, emerald ore, grass, huge mushrooms, ice, lapis lazuli ore, mycelium, packed ice, podzol, Nether quartz ore, redstone ore and cobwebs. Ender chests, bookshelves, glass and glass panes can only be retrieved by using Silk Touch once placed.

SMITE

PRIMARY ITEMS	⚔️
SECONDARY ITEMS	🔨
MAX POWER LEVEL	V
WEIGHT	5

Smite increases the damage your sword or axe does to undead mobs (skeletons, zombies, withers, wither skeletons and zombie pigmen). It's particularly handy for trips to the Nether. You'll need an anvil for Smite V.

SWEEPING EDGE

PRIMARY ITEMS	⚔️
SECONDARY ITEMS	NONE
MAX POWER LEVEL	III
WEIGHT	1

Sweeping Edge increases the sweeping attack damage of your sword. It's highly effective when battling hostile mobs or in PVP combat as it decreases the time it takes you to defeat your opponents.

THORNS

PRIMARY ITEMS	
SECONDARY ITEMS	
MAX POWER LEVEL	III
WEIGHT	1

Thorns inflicts damage on any player or mob that attacks you by melee (hand to hand) attack or projectile. It will reduce your armour's durability. You'll need an anvil to create Thorns III by combining two Thorns II enchantments, or trading for an enchanted book from a villager.

UNBREAKING

PRIMARY ITEMS	
SECONDARY ITEMS	
MAX POWER LEVEL	III
WEIGHT	5

Unbreaking increases the effective durability of your armour, tool or weapon. It's a great all-purpose enchantment that can be used when gathering resources or in combat situations.

NATURALLY-OCCURRING ENCHANTED ITEMS

If you find yourself without the necessary equipment or experience levels to enchant your items, don't despair. There are plenty of naturally-generated enchanted items just waiting to be discovered. Let's get hunting!

VILLAGER TRADING

Some villagers will offer enchanted items as part of their trades. Fishermen may offer enchanted fishing rods, librarians enchanted books, armourers pieces of enchanted armour etc. Villages can be found in desert, plains, savanna, taiga and ice plains biomes.

FISHING

There's even treasure hidden in the water – you might catch an enchanted book, bow or fishing rod when fishing.

MOB DROPS

Zombies, skeletons and zombie pigmen may drop items of enchanted armour or weapons when they die.

END CITY CHESTS

When visiting End cities on the outer islands you may find enchanted items of armour or enchanted tools or weapons in the loot chests.

2

POTIONS

Potions aren't just for witches – with your new-found knowledge of enchanting, you're ready to brave the Nether and collect the materials you need to brew your very own supply of potions. These drinkable items will give you even more of an edge in Survival mode.

BREWING EQUIPMENT

Brewing is the magical process of creating potions – drinkable items that provide you with temporary status effects. It's a complicated business, so before we get into the details of the process, let's take a look at the equipment you'll need.

 Potions are made on a brewing stand, which is crafted from a blaze rod and cobblestone. Blaze rods are dropped by blazes in the Nether when they die. Blazes spawn from spawners in Nether fortresses.

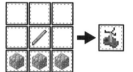

BREWING STAND RECIPE

 You'll need a cauldron, which you can craft from iron ingots. You might also find a cauldron in a witch hut, an igloo basement or a woodland mansion.

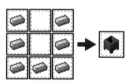

CAULDRON RECIPE

 TIP

Your cauldron will need to be refilled frequently so make sure you have a water source like a pond or lake nearby.

3 You'll need a water bucket to fill your cauldron.

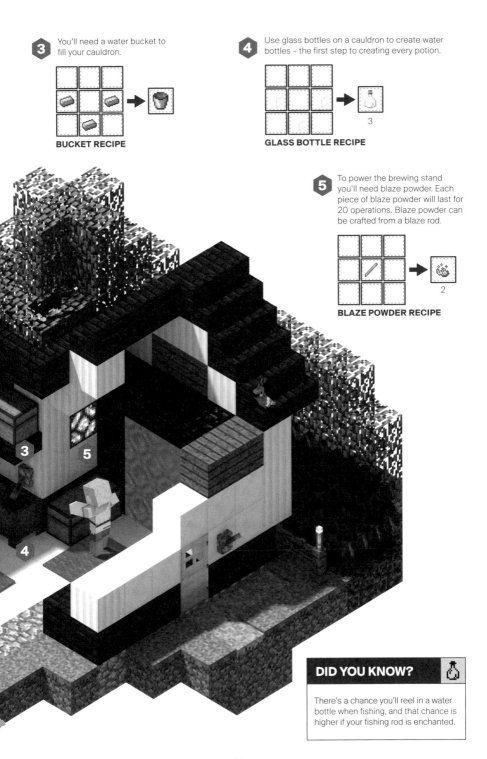

BUCKET RECIPE

4 Use glass bottles on a cauldron to create water bottles – the first step to creating every potion.

3

GLASS BOTTLE RECIPE

5 To power the brewing stand you'll need blaze powder. Each piece of blaze powder will last for 20 operations. Blaze powder can be crafted from a blaze rod.

2

BLAZE POWDER RECIPE

DID YOU KNOW?

There's a chance you'll reel in a water bottle when fishing, and that chance is higher if your fishing rod is enchanted.

INGREDIENTS

Before you can make usable potions you'll need to brew base potions by adding a single base ingredient to a water bottle. There are four base ingredients and four base potions. Mysteriously, only two of the base potions currently have a use . . .

BASE INGREDIENTS AND BASE POTIONS

NETHER WART

Nether wart is the base ingredient necessary to create most potions. It grows on soul sand under staircases in Nether fortresses and can also be found in loot chests in Nether fortresses.

AWKWARD POTION

When added to 3 water bottles, Nether wart makes 3 awkward potions. Awkward potion is the base for all potions except for potion of weakness.

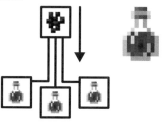

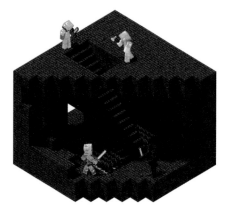

TIP	
Grab a few blocks of soul sand from the Nether and take them back to the Overworld, then you can set up your own Nether wart farm.	

GLOWSTONE DUST

Mine glowstone blocks in the Nether to get glowstone dust.

THICK POTION

When added to 3 water bottles, glowstone dust creates 3 thick potions. This potion currently has no use.

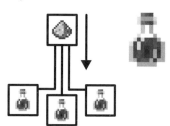

REDSTONE

Redstone can be obtained by mining redstone ore blocks which can be found at level 16 and below.

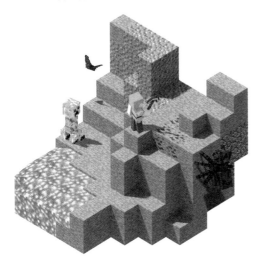

MUNDANE POTION

When added to 3 water bottles, redstone produces 3 mundane potions which currently have no use. Mundane potion can also be brewed from 3 water bottles and any secondary ingredient. See page 44-45 for a full list.

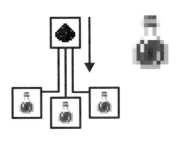

FERMENTED SPIDER EYE

A fermented spider eye can be crafted from a spider eye, sugar and a brown mushroom. Spiders may drop their eyes when killed.

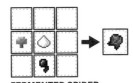

FERMENTED SPIDER EYE RECIPE

POTION OF WEAKNESS

Add a fermented spider eye to 3 water bottles to produce 3 potions of weakness. This potion reduces all melee attacks by 4 damage points and lasts for 1 minute 30 seconds.

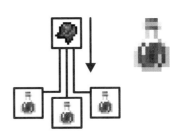

TIP

Potions don't stack in your inventory so make sure you clear some space before you start brewing.

SECONDARY INGREDIENTS AND MODIFIERS

Awkwardly, an awkward potion has no effect on its own; you'll need to brew it with a secondary ingredient to create a usable secondary potion. Secondary potions can then be brewed with a modifying ingredient to strengthen or change their effects. You'll need a good supply of all the ingredients you can see on this page.

SECONDARY INGREDIENTS

Sugar can be crafted from sugar canes. Witches sometimes drop sugar upon death.

SUGAR RECIPE

Pufferfish can be caught when fishing. Guardians and elder guardians will sometimes drop pufferfish when they die.

A rabbit's foot is a rare item that may be dropped by rabbits when they die.

GOLD NUGGET RECIPE

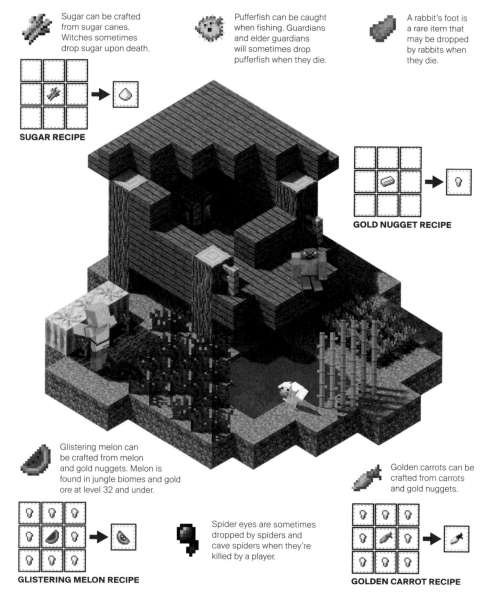

Glistering melon can be crafted from melon and gold nuggets. Melon is found in jungle biomes and gold ore at level 32 and under.

GLISTERING MELON RECIPE

Spider eyes are sometimes dropped by spiders and cave spiders when they're killed by a player.

Golden carrots can be crafted from carrots and gold nuggets.

GOLDEN CARROT RECIPE

Magma cream is sometimes dropped by big and small magma cubes in the Nether.

 Ghast tears are occasionally dropped by ghasts upon death.

 Blaze powder can be crafted from blaze rods, which may be dropped by blazes when they die.

MODIFIERS

 Brewing a secondary potion with redstone will make its effects last longer.

 Glowstone dust increases a potion's potency, so its effects are stronger.

Dragon's breath turns a regular potion into a lingering potion. See page 60-61 for more info.

 Fermented spider eye corrupts the effect of a potion – this usually means the effect is reversed to create a harmful potion. See page 43 for a reminder of the recipe.

 Brewing a secondary potion with gunpowder will turn it into a splash potion. See pages 58-59 for more info about splash potions. Gunpowder is sometimes dropped by creepers and ghasts when they die.

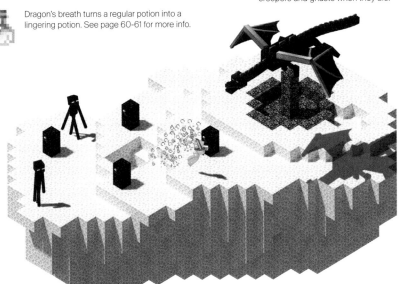

SECONDARY POTIONS

Now the real fun can begin – you're ready to start brewing secondary potions. These potions can have either helpful or harmful effects and can get you out of all sorts of tricky situations. Here's a rundown of each potion and its effects.

HELPFUL SECONDARY POTIONS

FIRE RESISTANCE

INGREDIENTS	Awkward potion & magma cream
STATUS EFFECT	Fire resistance
DURATION	3 minutes

Potion of fire resistance provides you with immunity against fire damage, lava damage and ranged blaze attacks. It's extremely useful for trips to the Nether.

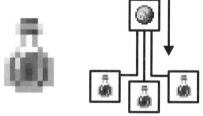

HEALING

INGREDIENTS	Awkward potion & glistering melon
STATUS EFFECT	Instant health
DURATION	Instant

A potion of healing will immediately restore 4 health points. This is a useful potion to keep in your inventory at all times in Survival mode.

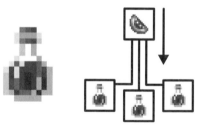

LEAPING

INGREDIENTS	Awkward potion & rabbit's foot
STATUS EFFECT	Jump boost
DURATION	3 minutes

Drink this potion and you'll be able to jump half a block higher than usual. This means you can clear obstacles like fences in a single leap.

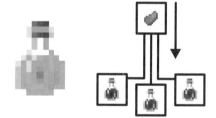

👁 NIGHT VISION

INGREDIENTS	Awkward potion & golden carrot
STATUS EFFECT	Night vision
DURATION	3 minutes

Drink this potion and everything will appear at maximum light level, including underwater areas. It's great for use at night, when mining and when swimming underwater.

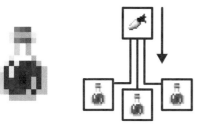

🖤 REGENERATION

INGREDIENTS	Awkward potion & ghast tear
STATUS EFFECT	Regeneration
DURATION	45 seconds

Regeneration restores your health over time (by around 2 health points every 2.4 seconds). It's particularly useful in situations where you might lose health points quite quickly.

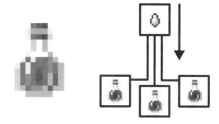

⚔ STRENGTH

INGREDIENTS	Awkward potion & blaze powder
STATUS EFFECT	Strength
DURATION	3 minutes

Potion of strength increases the damage you deal to your opponents through melee attacks by 3 health points. Drink this before battling other players or mobs.

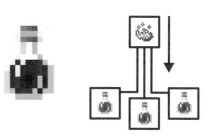

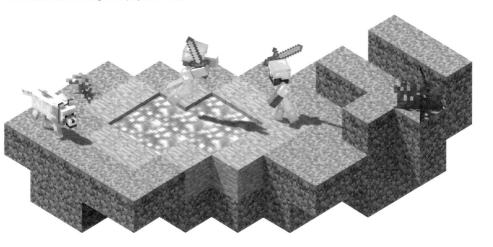

 SWIFTNESS

INGREDIENTS	Awkward potion & sugar
STATUS EFFECT	Speed
DURATION	3 minutes

Potion of swiftness increases your movement speed, sprinting speed and jumping length by around 20%. This is a good potion to drink if you're setting off on a long journey.

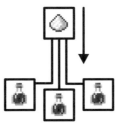

 WATER BREATHING

INGREDIENTS	Awkward potion & pufferfish
STATUS EFFECT	Water breathing
DURATION	3 minutes

Drink this potion to top up your oxygen bar for 3 minutes. This makes exploring underwater areas such as ocean monuments significantly easier.

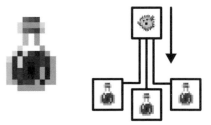

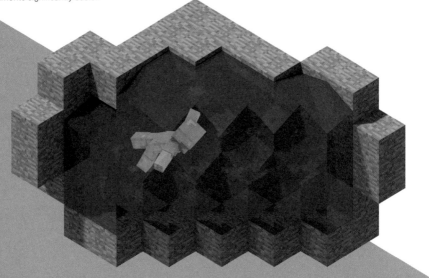

HARMFUL SECONDARY POTIONS

Unsurprisingly, harmful potions aren't going to do you any favours, so you're not going to want to drink them. Instead, they're best used as weapons against your opponents in the form of splash potions or lingering potions – see pages 58-61 to find out more.

POISON

INGREDIENTS	Awkward potion & spider eye
STATUS EFFECT	Poison
DURATION	45 seconds

This potion will poison a player, reducing their health by around 1 point every 1.5 seconds, to 1 point at most.

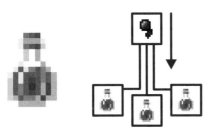

WEAKNESS (EXTENDED)

INGREDIENTS	Potion of weakness & redstone
STATUS EFFECT	Weakness
DURATION	4 minutes

The extended potion of weakness reduces all melee attacks by 4 damage points and lasts for 4 minutes.

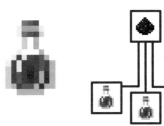

DID YOU KNOW?

A simple bucket of milk has the ability to remove any status effects that you may be under. Make sure you take one with you wherever you go so that you can cure yourself of any unwanted harmful status effects.

TERTIARY POTIONS

Tertiary potions are stronger versions of secondary potions – their effects last longer or they're more powerful. Favoured by pro Minecrafters, they're made by brewing a modifying ingredient either with a secondary potion or with another tertiary potion.

HELPFUL TERTIARY POTIONS

FIRE RESISTANCE (EXTENDED)

INGREDIENTS	Potion of fire resistance & redstone
STATUS EFFECT	Fire resistance
DURATION	8 minutes

This potion gives the drinker immunity to damage from fire, lava and ranged blaze attacks for 8 minutes. It's a popular choice for adventurers visiting the Nether.

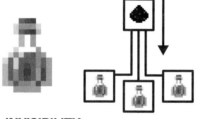

HEALING II

INGREDIENTS	Potion of healing & glowstone dust
STATUS EFFECT	Instant health II
DURATION	Instant

This restores 8 health points per potion (double the amount of regular potion of healing). It's great for any situation in which you're taking damage.

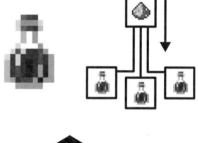

INVISIBILITY

INGREDIENTS	Potion of night vision & fermented spider eye
STATUS EFFECT	Invisibility
DURATION	3 minutes

Technically, this is the corrupted version of potion of night vision. The drinker will be invisible to mobs and other players, but any equipped or held items will still be visible.

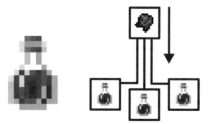

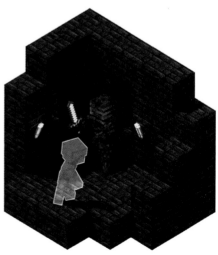

INVISIBILITY (EXTENDED)

INGREDIENTS	Potion of night vision (extended) & fermented spider eye
ALTERNATIVE RECIPE	Potion of invisibility & redstone
STATUS EFFECT	Invisibility
DURATION	8 minutes

The extended potion of invisibility will render the drinker invisible for 5 minutes longer than the regular version.

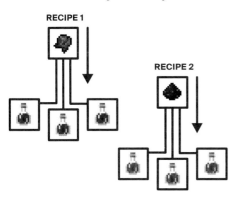

 # LEAPING (EXTENDED)

INGREDIENTS	Potion of leaping or potion of leaping II & redstone
STATUS EFFECT	Jump boost
DURATION	8 minutes

Drink this potion and you'll be able to jump half a block higher than usual. This means you can clear obstacles like fences in a single leap.

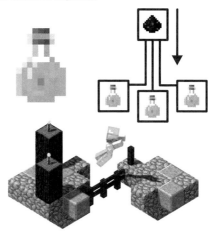

LEAPING II

INGREDIENTS	Potion of leaping & glowstone dust
STATUS EFFECT	Jump boost II
DURATION	1 minute 30 seconds

This potion enables the drinker to jump 1.5 blocks higher than usual. Note that the duration has decreased but the strength has increased.

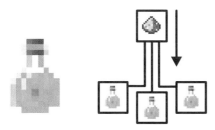

NIGHT VISION (EXTENDED)

INGREDIENTS	Potion of night vision & redstone
STATUS EFFECT	Night vision
DURATION	8 minutes

The extended potion of night vision lasts 5 minutes longer than the regular version. It makes everything appear to be at the maximum light level, including underwater areas.

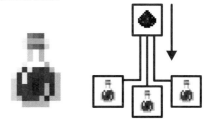

REGENERATION (EXTENDED)

INGREDIENTS	Potion of regeneration & redstone
STATUS EFFECT	Regeneration
DURATION	2 minutes

This restores the drinker's health over time by approximately 2 health points every 2.4 seconds. It lasts twice as long as the regular version.

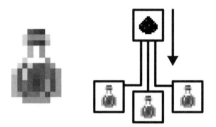

REGENERATION II

INGREDIENTS	Potion of regeneration & glowstone dust
STATUS EFFECT	Regeneration II
DURATION	22 seconds

The drinker's health is restored over time by around 2 health points every 1.2 seconds (that's more frequently than regular potion of regeneration).

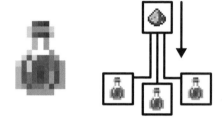

 STRENGTH (EXTENDED)

INGREDIENTS	Potion of strength & redstone
STATUS EFFECT	Strength
DURATION	8 minutes

The extended potion of strength increases the damage you deal through melee attacks by 3 health points, and lasts 5 minutes longer than the regular version.

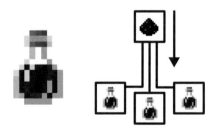

STRENGTH II

INGREDIENTS	Potion of strength & glowstone dust
STATUS EFFECT	Strength II
DURATION	1 minute 30 seconds

Strength II increases the damage you deal through melee attacks by 6 health points – that's double the amount of a regular potion of strength but doesn't last as long.

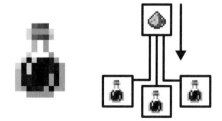

MOJANG STUFF

Originally the ingredients needed in brewing were going to be randomised every time you started a new world, so the result would always be a surprise when you combined ingredients. But this just wasn't as fun as we'd hoped it would be!

SWIFTNESS (EXTENDED)

INGREDIENTS	Potion of swiftness & redstone
STATUS EFFECT	Speed
DURATION	8 minutes

This increases a player's movement, sprinting speed and jumping length by approximately 20%, allowing for quicker travel across long distances.

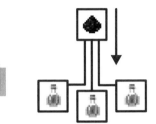

 # SWIFTNESS II

INGREDIENTS	Potion of swiftness & glowstone dust
STATUS EFFECT	Speed II
DURATION	1 minute 30 seconds

The drinker's movement, sprinting speed and jumping length will increase by around 40%, but it only lasts for a fraction of the time that the extended version lasts.

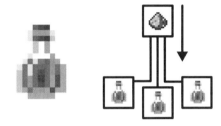

 # WATER BREATHING (EXTENDED)

INGREDIENTS	Potion of water breathing & redstone
STATUS EFFECT	Water breathing
DURATION	8 minutes

This potion ensures the player's oxygen bar doesn't deplete when they're underwater. It lasts 5 minutes longer than regular potion of water breathing.

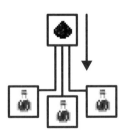

HARMFUL TERTIARY POTIONS

HARMING

INGREDIENTS	Potion of healing & fermented spider eye
ALTERNATIVE RECIPE	Potion of poison (base or extended) & fermented spider eye
STATUS EFFECT	Instant damage
DURATION	Instant

Technically, potion of harming is the reverted form of potion of healing or potion of poison. This potion inflicts 6 points of damage.

RECIPE 1

RECIPE 2

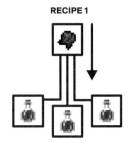

HARMING II

INGREDIENTS	Potion of healing II & fermented spider eye
ALTERNATIVE RECIPE	Potion of poison II & fermented spider eye
ALTERNATIVE RECIPE 2	Potion of harming & glowstone dust
STATUS EFFECT	Instant damage II
DURATION	Instant

This potion inflicts 12 points of damage on the recipient – that's double the amount of a regular potion of harming.

RECIPE 1

RECIPE 2

RECIPE 3

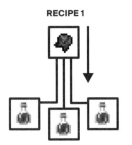
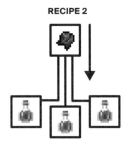
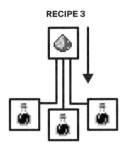

POISON (EXTENDED)

INGREDIENTS	Potion of poison & redstone
STATUS EFFECT	Poison
DURATION	2 minutes

This potion poisons the player, reducing their health to a minimum of 1 point, at a rate of approximately 1 point every 1.5 seconds.

POISON II

INGREDIENTS	Potion of poison & glowstone dust
STATUS EFFECT	Poison
DURATION	22 seconds

This potion poisons the player, reducing their health to a minimum of 1 point, at a rate of approximately 2 health points every 1.5 seconds.

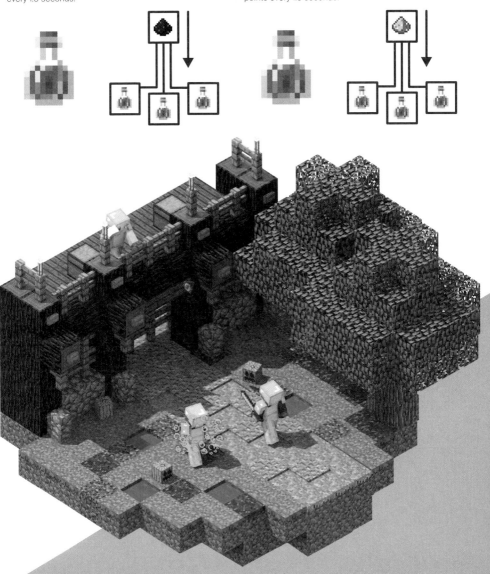

SLOWNESS

INGREDIENTS	Potion of swiftness & fermented spider eye
ALTERNATIVE RECIPE	Potion of leaping & fermented spider eye
STATUS EFFECT	Slowness
DURATION	1 minute 30 seconds

Slowness reduces the player's movement to a crouch (-15% speed).

RECIPE 1

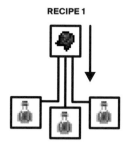

RECIPE 2

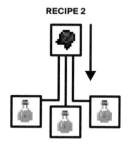

SLOWNESS (EXTENDED)

INGREDIENTS	Potion of slowness & redstone
ALTERNATIVE RECIPE	Potion of swiftness (extended) & fermented spider eye
ALTERNATIVE RECIPE 2	Potion of leaping (extended) & fermented spider eye
STATUS EFFECT	Slowness
DURATION	4 minutes

This slows the player's movement to a crouch (-15% speed) for twice as long as the regular potion of slowness.

RECIPE 1

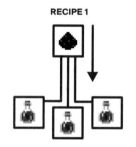

RECIPE 2

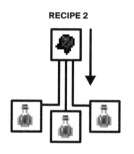

RECIPE 3

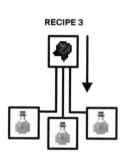

EFFICIENT BREWING

As we've seen, there's often more than one way to brew a potion. This chart shows the most efficient way to create each potion.

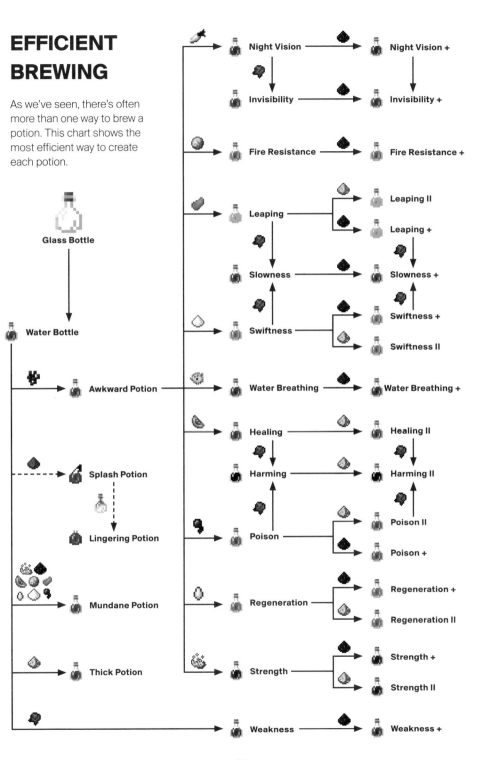

Glass Bottle

Water Bottle

Awkward Potion

Splash Potion

Lingering Potion

Mundane Potion

Thick Potion

Night Vision → **Night Vision +**

Invisibility → **Invisibility +**

Fire Resistance → **Fire Resistance +**

Leaping → **Leaping II**

Leaping +

Slowness → **Slowness +**

Swiftness → **Swiftness +**

Swiftness II

Water Breathing → **Water Breathing +**

Healing → **Healing II**

Harming → **Harming II**

Poison → **Poison II**

Poison +

Regeneration → **Regeneration +**

Regeneration II

Strength → **Strength +**

Strength II

Weakness → **Weakness +**

SPLASH POTIONS

Wouldn't it be great if you could trick your opponents into drinking harmful potions to bring about their own demise? Realistically that's not likely to happen, which is where splash potions come in useful – they can be thrown at mobs or other players so that they're forced into contact with the effect. Cunning!

HOW TO BREW AND USE

1 You'll need to combine a regular potion with gunpowder on your brewing stand to give it explosive properties. You can also combine water bottles with gunpowder to create splash water bottles which put out fires.

2 Once brewed, throw a splash potion to use it. Splash potions don't last as long as regular potions. When throwing them at mobs or players, aim for their head to ensure they last for the maximum duration.

3 When a splash potion hits its target (a player or block), it will explode, releasing its contents. Any mobs or players within an 8.25 x 8.25 x 4.25-block area centred on the impact spot will be affected. The splash potion bottle will break when used and you won't be able to retrieve it.

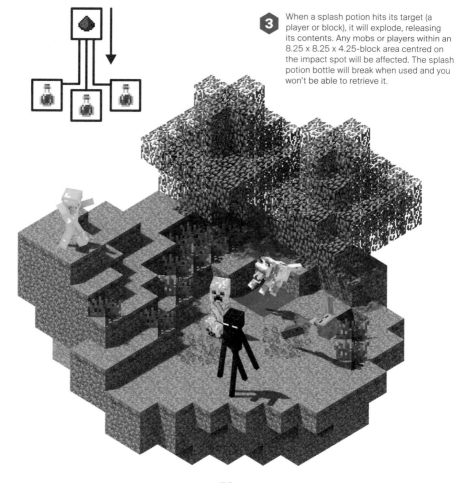

WHEN TO USE

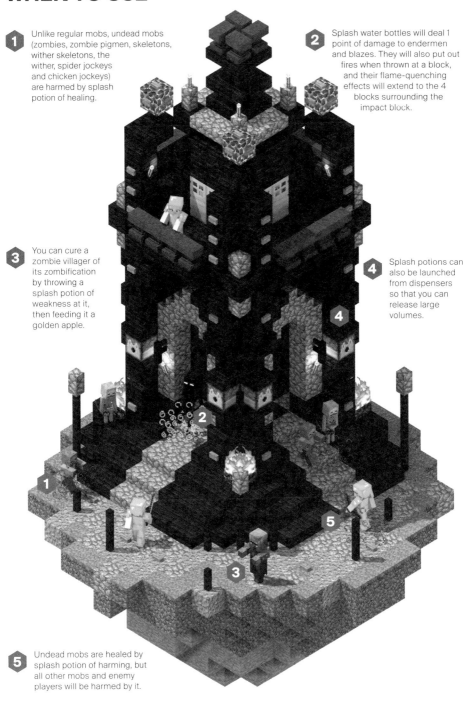

1 Unlike regular mobs, undead mobs (zombies, zombie pigmen, skeletons, wither skeletons, the wither, spider jockeys and chicken jockeys) are harmed by splash potion of healing.

2 Splash water bottles will deal 1 point of damage to endermen and blazes. They will also put out fires when thrown at a block, and their flame-quenching effects will extend to the 4 blocks surrounding the impact block.

3 You can cure a zombie villager of its zombification by throwing a splash potion of weakness at it, then feeding it a golden apple.

4 Splash potions can also be launched from dispensers so that you can release large volumes.

5 Undead mobs are healed by splash potion of harming, but all other mobs and enemy players will be harmed by it.

LINGERING POTIONS

True to its name, this variant of splash potion creates a cloud that lingers on the ground. Only the most advanced players will be able to brew lingering potions – the key ingredient is dragon's breath, which is incredibly difficult to get hold of.

HOW TO BREW AND USE

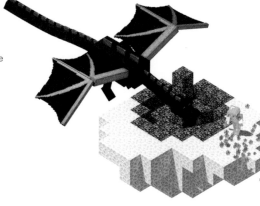

1 Collect dragon's breath by using a glass bottle when you're in or near to the ender dragon's breath attack. Be very careful – the dragon's breath will harm you.

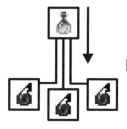

2 Brew 3 bottles of your chosen splash potion with the dragon's breath to create a lingering potion.

3 Throw your lingering potion and it will explode on impact with a solid block, creating a cloud of the potion's effect. On impact the cloud will extend to a radius of 3 blocks, eventually decreasing to 0 blocks over the course of 30 seconds. After 1 second, any player or mob that walks into the cloud will be imbued with the status effect of the potion. The amount of time the lingering potion effects will last for varies depending on the potion.

WHEN TO USE

1 Undead mobs will be harmed by lingering potions of healing, and other hostile mobs are harmed by lingering potions of harming.

2 Lingering potions can also be launched out of dispensers, which can be incorporated into your base defences.

3 Lingering potions can be crafted with arrows to create tipped arrows. These handy projectiles will imbue their target with the corresponding status effect. The effect of a tipped arrow only lasts one eighth of the amount of time the potion itself lasts.

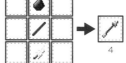

ARROW RECIPE

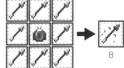

TIPPED ARROW OF SLOWNESS RECIPE

NATURALLY-OCCURRING BREWING EQUIPMENT

Having an 'off day'? Not feeling up to a trip to the Nether? Happily, some of the items you need for brewing potions can be found naturally in the Overworld and they're yours for the taking if you know where they're hidden.

WITCHES AND WITCH HUTS

You'll find a cauldron filled with a random potion in each witch hut in swamp biomes. Witches may drop a potion of healing, fire resistance, swiftness or water breathing, if they're killed whilst drinking that potion. Witches spawn in any biome at light levels of 7 or lower, and in witch huts.

IGLOOS

Igloos can be found in ice plains and cold taiga biomes. Half of igloos contain a basement, and if you venture down to explore you'll find a brewing stand containing a splash potion of weakness.

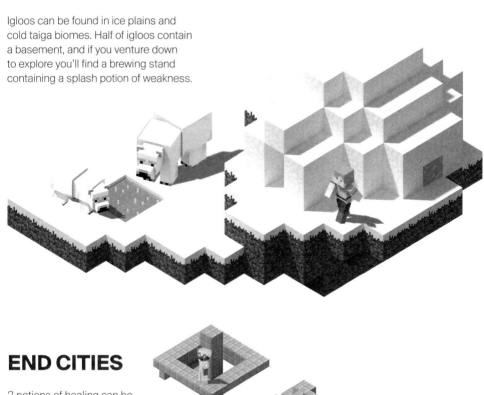

END CITIES

2 potions of healing can be found in a brewing stand on the ships in End cities. These cities generate on the outer islands of the End dimension.

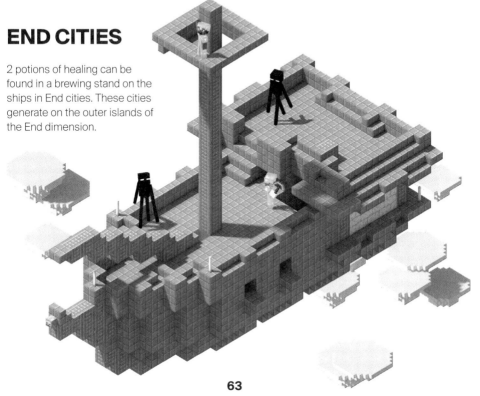

3

ADVANCED SORCERY

Congratulations – you're officially an advanced sorcerer. In this section you'll learn how to use enchantments and potions in clever combinations and discover how to build a suitably-impressive sorcerer's house from which to practise your craft.

COMBOS

Whether you're mining deep underground or visiting the End, there's a combination of enchantments and potions that will give you the upper hand. These clever combos are perfect for advanced players.

MINING

 • EFFICIENCY
• FORTUNE

 • UNBREAKING

 • FEATHER FALLING

HEALING   NIGHT VISION

EXPLORING

 • MENDING

 • FROST WALKER
• FEATHER FALLING

SWIFTNESS   LEAPING

MOB COMBAT

 ..... FIRE ASPECT
BANE OF ARTHROPODS

 ..... FLAME
INFINITY

 ..... UNBREAKING

HARMING   STRENGTH

PVP COMBAT

 ..... SMITE

 ..... KNOCKBACK
 POWER

 ..... PROTECTION

 ..... UNBREAKING

HEALING   STRENGTH

NIGHT

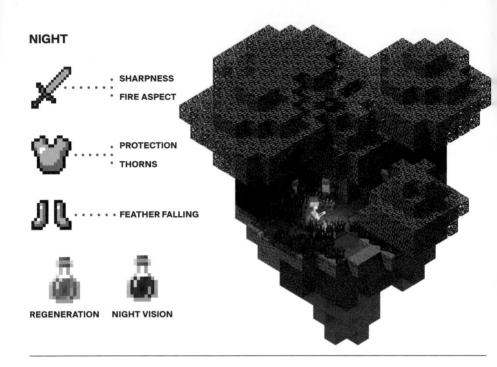

SHARPNESS
FIRE ASPECT

PROTECTION
THORNS

FEATHER FALLING

REGENERATION   NIGHT VISION

UNDERWATER

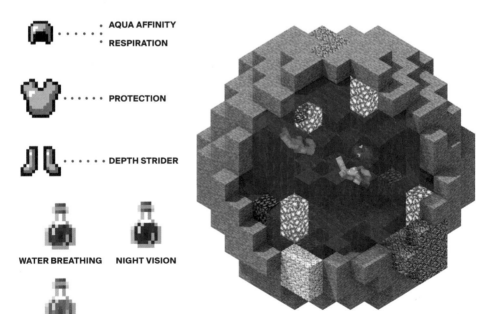

AQUA AFFINITY
RESPIRATION

PROTECTION

DEPTH STRIDER

WATER BREATHING   NIGHT VISION

REGENERATION

68

THE NETHER

  LOOTING
SMITE

 **MENDING**
FIRE PROTECTION

 PROJECTILE PROTECTION

FIRE RESISTANCE **INVISIBILITY**

THE END

 INFINITY
FLAME

 PROJECTILE PROTECTION

 FEATHER FALLING

STRENGTH **HEALING**

WATER

SORCERER'S HOUSE

This sorcerer's house is largely built from stone and wood blocks, but it's the smaller details that make it truly magical. Various Nether materials and swamp-like elements are used to set the scene for sorcery.

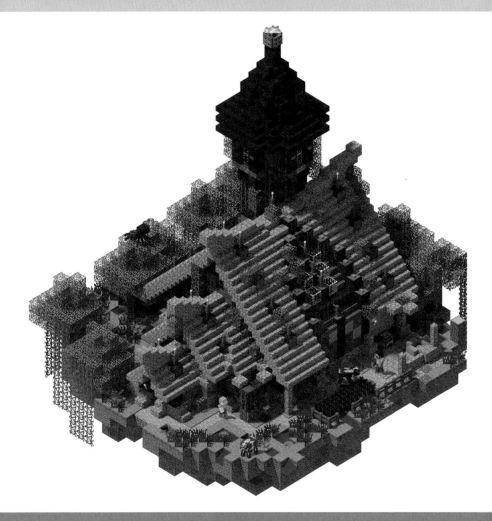

YOU WILL NEED:

SCHEMATICS

These plans show the sorcerer's house from various perspectives so you can see how it's constructed. The brewing tower emerges from the roof of the main build and the inside layout has been carefully considered to maximise the available space.

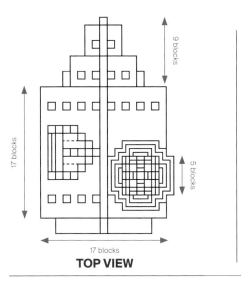

9 blocks

17 blocks

5 blocks

17 blocks

TOP VIEW

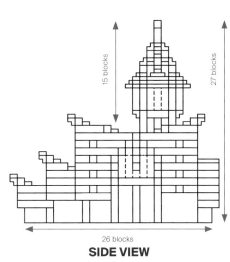

15 blocks

27 blocks

26 blocks

SIDE VIEW

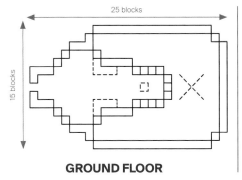

25 blocks

15 blocks

GROUND FLOOR

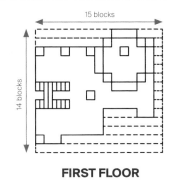

15 blocks

14 blocks

FIRST FLOOR

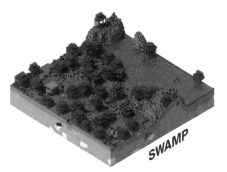

SWAMP

IDEAL LANDSCAPE

The witchy nature of the sorcerer's house makes it particularly suited to a gloomy swamp biome, which may already be inhabited by a witch. It would also sit nicely in a forest or roofed forest due to the shadows cast by the dense trees.

SORCERER'S HOUSE INTERIOR

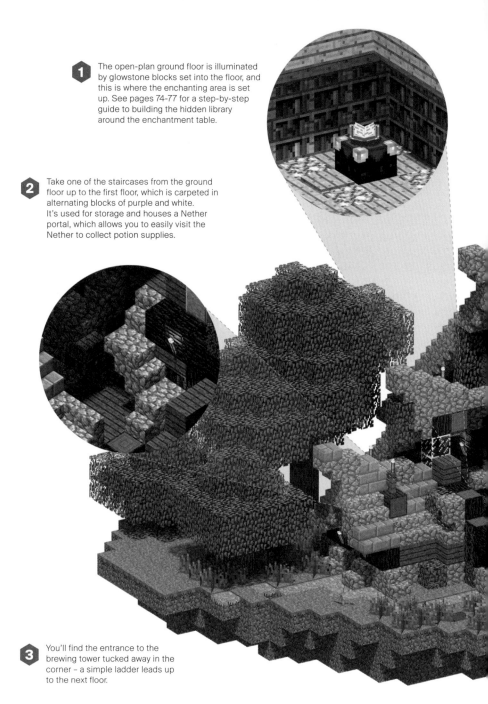

1 The open-plan ground floor is illuminated by glowstone blocks set into the floor, and this is where the enchanting area is set up. See pages 74-77 for a step-by-step guide to building the hidden library around the enchantment table.

2 Take one of the staircases from the ground floor up to the first floor, which is carpeted in alternating blocks of purple and white. It's used for storage and houses a Nether portal, which allows you to easily visit the Nether to collect potion supplies.

3 You'll find the entrance to the brewing tower tucked away in the corner – a simple ladder leads up to the next floor.

4 The brewing area sits at the top of the tower – with 6 brewing stands at your disposal you can quickly brew large quantities of potions.

5 The first floor of the brewing tower is ideal for storage. You can keep all your potion ingredients in four handily-positioned chests.

THE HIDDEN LIBRARY

This hidden library build employs clever redstone mechanics to create an impressively mystical effect. Your bookshelves will rise up from the floor, as if by magic, when you approach your enchantment table.

1 Build this shape – it's 5 blocks along the front with 2 blocks at the back. This is the first part of your base.

TIP

Make sure you have enough space in your sorcerer's house to build the hidden library – the base is approximately 8 x 9 blocks and 12 blocks high.

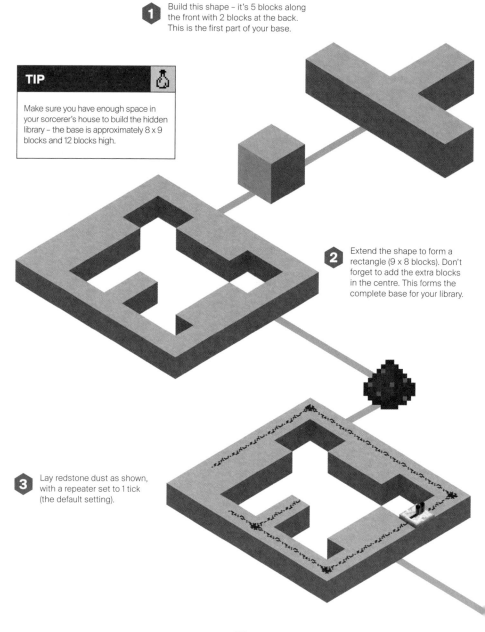

2 Extend the shape to form a rectangle (9 x 8 blocks). Don't forget to add the extra blocks in the centre. This forms the complete base for your library.

3 Lay redstone dust as shown, with a repeater set to 1 tick (the default setting).

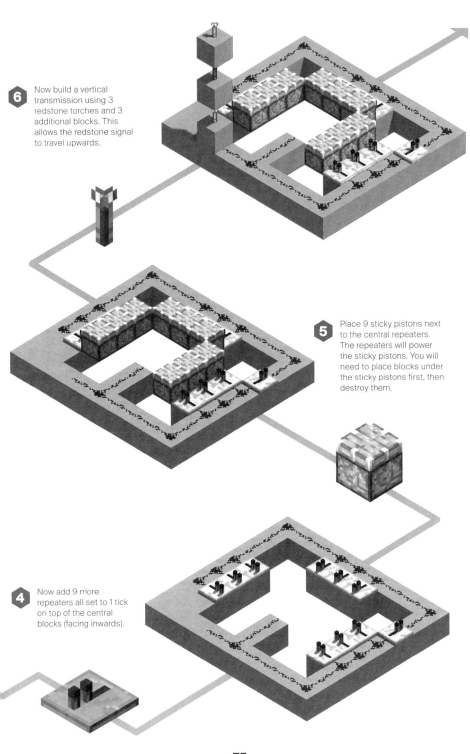

6 Now build a vertical transmission using 3 redstone torches and 3 additional blocks. This allows the redstone signal to travel upwards.

5 Place 9 sticky pistons next to the central repeaters. The repeaters will power the sticky pistons. You will need to place blocks under the sticky pistons first, then destroy them.

4 Now add 9 more repeaters all set to 1 tick on top of the central blocks (facing inwards).

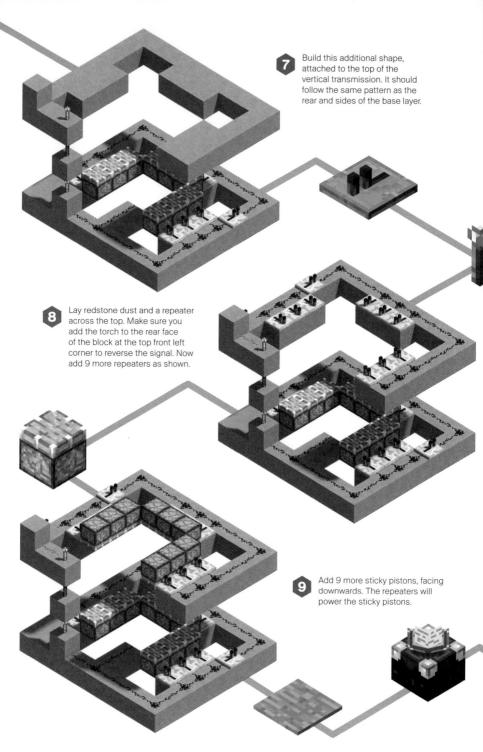

7 Build this additional shape, attached to the top of the vertical transmission. It should follow the same pattern as the rear and sides of the base layer.

8 Lay redstone dust and a repeater across the top. Make sure you add the torch to the rear face of the block at the top front left corner to reverse the signal. Now add 9 more repeaters as shown.

9 Add 9 more sticky pistons, facing downwards. The repeaters will power the sticky pistons.

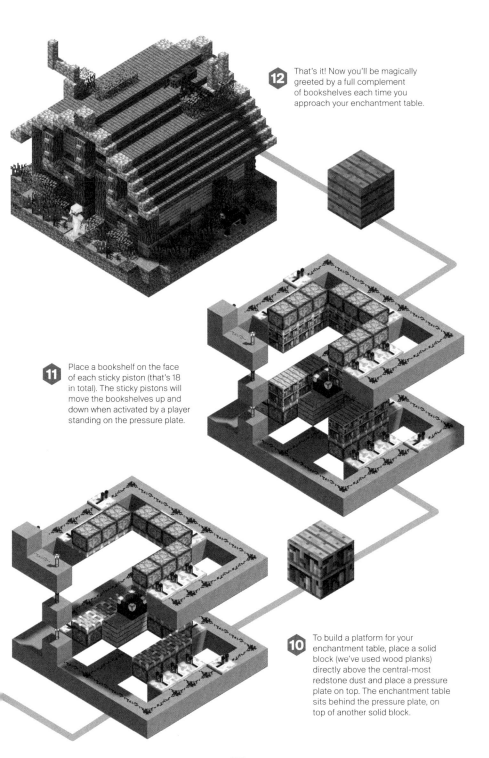

12 That's it! Now you'll be magically greeted by a full complement of bookshelves each time you approach your enchantment table.

11 Place a bookshelf on the face of each sticky piston (that's 18 in total). The sticky pistons will move the bookshelves up and down when activated by a player standing on the pressure plate.

10 To build a platform for your enchantment table, place a solid block (we've used wood planks) directly above the central-most redstone dust and place a pressure plate on top. The enchantment table sits behind the pressure plate, on top of another solid block.

FINAL WORDS

Complicated stuff, right? But whoever said that using eldritch powers to rework the fabric of the universe would be easy? And, I hope you agree, as strange, cryptic and elaborate as these magical practises may be, the benefits are rather awesome. Whether you don glimmering gear that lets you shrug off the damage from explosive blasts, enchant your armour to prickle enemies who dare get too close, or slug back a brew to help you see through the dark, you'll find enchantments and potions give you the edge in many a perilous situation. Plus, 'Sorcerer' looks pretty good on a business card, too. Bonus.

MARSH DAVIES
THE MOJANG TEAM

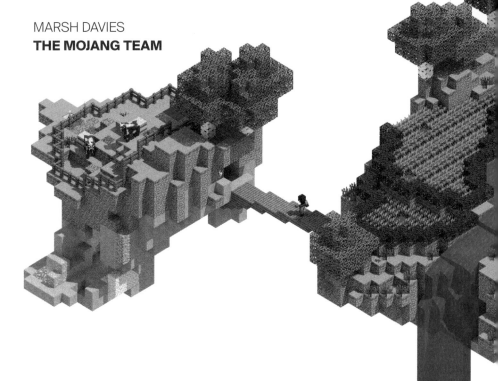